# LONDON

## Places & Pleasures

### *An Uncommon Guidebook*

*Capricorn Books*        NEW YORK

For
MARA
LISA
TANI
DEREK

# Contents

# Introduction

As guidebooks of specific, terse information concerning hotels, restaurants, and where there are gas stations increase and threaten to jostle that other publishing staple, the cookbook, off bookshop shelves, the travel book, once a popular and respected form of literature, declines. The days when a writer could enlighten the world about Sicily, northern Japan, and the secretive piazzas of Rome are almost over; their books have been supplanted by novels and short stories that are travelogues, plotless films that are travelogues, television shows that are travelogues, and now, with Telstar, one can explore the world's exotica in one, almost simultaneous, clump of time.

This book tries to straddle both categories and is incomplete in both. It is personal, directed by one set of tastes and standards and also limited to what one person can see, experience and record in a given, though generous, amount of time. A further limitation is the size of London, not only its free-form extent, but that which is hidden and must be coaxed out. London does not reveal itself with one shower of dazzle as Paris does; she is an old cat, secretive and independent, and although she enjoys purring pleasantly, being stroked once in a while, and, when she has the mind to, rubbing her back against your leg, she doesn't care *that* much to wag her tail and sit up prettily, like the excited poodle cities. Her pace is slow, and so must yours be (and that of a travel writer); she will not be rushed into showing her hiding places.

It would take pleasurable months to know all the alleys in the City alone, and although for a long time it was all of London, it is now only a brilliant deep-textured patch in an enormous tapestry. It would take weeks to know all the galleries of the British Museum and the Victoria and Albert, to become acquainted with the smaller museums. To taste and smell the flavor of dozens of neighborhoods, many of them still distinct villages, it might take years. Ideally, one would like to do it all, for the satisfaction of the total conquest of a city and because of the inherent pleasures in ceaseless prowling. But it would be impossible to enclose all the information in one book, or two or three, yet another weight to add to the tons of London documentation—hundreds of histories written at various stops in time; compendiums of the names of famous men who were, at some time or other, Londoners, immense washes of nostalgic wave in innumerable books of London reminiscenses; and the products of local pride that investigate and record—book size—the history and triumph of the neighborhood cricket club.

In all the documentation, old and new and newest, which insists on telling the astonished, controlled old cat that she is a swinger, a number of elements that mean London have become thoroughly familiar. Some of these have not been explored in this book, except as passageways to an unfamiliar context. The emphasis here is placed on the not yet too familiar: more detail for the City and somewhat less for Chelsea; more Victoria and Albert and less the mighty British Museum; the National Portrait Gallery near its more famous parent the National Gallery; the eccentric squares of Islington, rather than the pearly, plump squares of Belgravia; shopping in Mayfair, balanced by walking in Clerkenwell; a little of Hampstead and Highgate, more of Bermondsey and Southwark. In short, the attempt is to make sketchy portraits of some shyer sections of the city, worth courting and knowing. Thus encouraged by the wealth of possibilities and aided by free maps and inexpensive pamphlets, you are on your—it is to be hoped, stimulated—own, keeping in mind that London has not yet repaired all its bomb damage or yet replaced all its condemned houses; that large areas are being redesigned; that walks in old areas which still retain shadows of their medieval geography must be done in meandering, circular patterns and others must follow the shape of a tree, out to the limbs and twigs and back to the trunk of a high street to reach another branch; that rational progress in ancient tangles is impossible and, if it were possible, would make no innate sense; and that guidebooks are writ in water.

# KATE SIMON'S LONDON

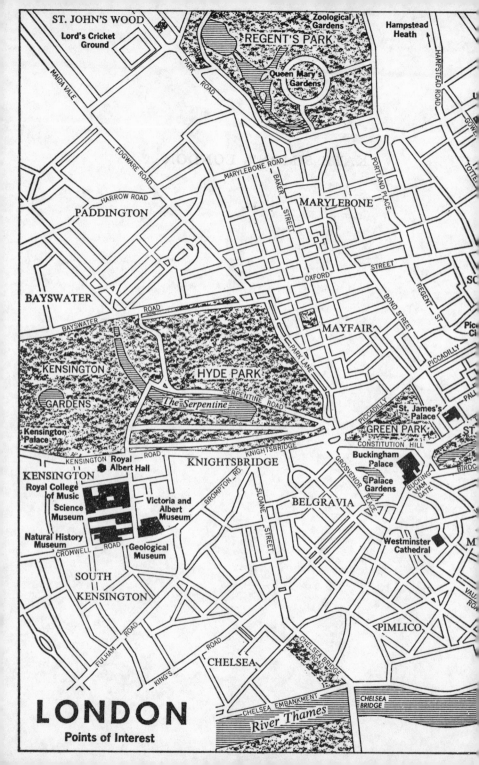

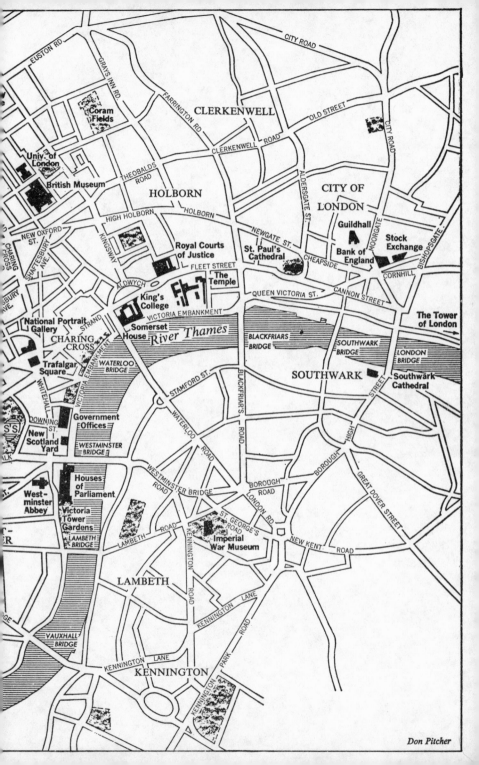

# 1　Practical Matters—Hotels

One of the ways to learn something about a London you may not see or, having seen, may not have recognized is to read the bulletin boards on corners of main streets in domesticated neighborhoods. Among the bed-sitters, with and without hot and cold water, and the self-contained flats, lessons in Italian or French, and the adverts of cleaning ladies, you may find "respectable introductions arranged for all ages and all nationalities"; "clairvoyant and psychological consultant"; "tonic massage-soothing, stimulating and relaxing—by refined, conscientious young lady masseuse, patients visited (people of education and refinement only; professional class)." "Young lady seeks interesting position" appears numerous times, occasionally adding that the young lady is French or Swedish, and who doesn't know about those Swedes and their habits and massages? You can find "toning up" treatment and have your rheumatic condition looked after. One "young lady" gives private dancing lessons but warns, underlining, "do not call or phone after 6 P.M."—too busy giving lessons obviously. "Togetherness is offered, by Ten Friends, all over sixteen," and guarantees that your party will be of matched sexes. Add them all together, and they spell a wide, relaxed taste for fun and games.

Try to be patient and gentle with the telephone; though not very old, it is tired and sickly and needs tender loving care. First, relieve it of the burden of your errors by noticing that *O* shares the last finger slot with zero and *Q*. Your dialing may produce a broad, throbbing silence or a buzzing, which is neither a connection nor a busy signal, but means you have somehow attached yourself to a number that no longer is in use. Or, repeatedly, after meticulously careful dialing, you will rouse a tired, resigned gentleman to whom you keep apologizing, who keeps assuring you it happens all the time and not to be distressed. If you are in London for some length of time and use one number especially often, a number which "crosses wires," with one or two constants—a nursing home or an antiques shop—you can make very pleasant phone pals, passing the time of day and discussing the weather, always phenomenal for whatever time of the year it happens to be, and particularly stimulating when you can explain to each other "anticyclonic gloom." If you haven't the inclination to talk, put the phone down, and while some time away by trying to remember the names of Queen Victoria's children. After that interval, dial again, and follow the ensuing deadness with all the lines you can remember out of Shakespeare's plays; after the next try, lines from the sonnets. That usually does it, and you get on to a man who is ordering wine from Harrod's. The proper form here is to mutter, "Crossed wires. Sorry," and hang up.

The bright red phone boxes on the street have become easier to use, in one sense, and more expensive, in recent years. No longer does one scurry around looking for a fourpence box or a threepence box to match the coins in the pocket. At present a call from most street boxes is sixpence, but be prepared with several sixpences to allow for temperament or exhaustion or vandalism, a revival of the eighteenth century. There is singularly little vandalism in London, as witness the unmolested miles of flowers in the parks. But phone books are torn out and coin boxes jammed and the instruction sheets guiding through each step of the way (first dial; then wait for tone; then, then, etc.) are marked up or scratched, and the GPO cannot keep up with repairs or out-of-order signs. Compensations, though, appear in the fact that the phone booths in major tube stations have phoning instructions in several foreign languages.

For what's on in London—if you don't want to be bothered with periodicals or the newspapers—phone 246 8041. For language practice dial 246 8043, whose answer will be in French plus *les prévisions météorologiques;* 246 8045 for the same information in German, along with *die Wetteransage;* 246 8047 for Spanish *y predición del tiempo.* (The exchange used to be ASK, a prettier way of doing things.)

Time has two vents: TIM or 123; for information about the earth-shaking test matches (cricket): UMP; London weather is announced with hedging and uncertainty by 2211; and if you want to be awakened in the morning, dial INF, who will phone you back a few minutes after you've made your request to check your number, avoiding the possibility of one missed plane and one startled and irate wrong number.

By dialing DIR (information), especially in the evening, when the offices are manned by serious researchers, you can, on the flimsiest clues, set an investigator working ardently, particularly if you speak to him as if he were the last hope in a desperate cause. It is enough to say, "I must reach someone very urgently, his name is Doe, and he is at this moment the dinner guest of a dentist whose name starts with a *B;* I can't remember the rest. He lives in Hampstead, maybe on Well Walk, or maybe it's Flask Walk. I'm not sure. Could you please help me?" The mantles of all the knights of chivalry descend on his shoulders. He follows and telephones every possible clue, asking for Mr. Doe, and, having found him, turns him over to you.

The banks don't bother to open until 10 A.M., and they close at 3 P.M. On Saturday morning the hours are very short, seemingly used only for the ceremonial opening and closing of doors at a stately pace. American Express closes at noon on Saturdays. Best get your weekend supply of money before 3 P.M. on Friday.

Except in large department stores, paying in travelers' checks can be a nuisance; sales clerks are not sure of the rate of exchange and have the same difficulty translating dollars to pounds and shillings as you do. Also, they say, the bank does not give them the full exchange rate. Use cash or, acceptable in a surprising number of places, the personal check of an English friend. To avoid the purchase tax, you must show your passport and have your purchase sent directly to your ship or plane or mailed home from the shop.

Do not confuse Hyde Park Corner with Hyde Park Speakers' Corner. The former is at the southeast end of Hyde Park, a tangle of underground pedestrian walks, leaving the surface an Elysian field for jaunty drivers, the Davids whose sporty frailty tests the nerve of the bus Goliaths. It is a nexus of bus stops for numerous lines, including the suburban Green Lines; and an underground stop of the Piccadilly Line. Speakers' Corner is immediately inside the northeast corner of the park. Its station for buses and tube is Marble Arch (Central Line), John Nash's obeisance to Imperial Rome, meant to mark the ceremonial entrance to Buckingham Palace but, according to popular belief, too narrow for state carriages. The probable truth of the matter was that Nash was extremely slow in planning the palace and careless when he finally did get around to working at it. The work was taken from him, and the arch moved to neighbor a path called Tyburn Road, for the almost immortal gallows that provided free amusement for generations of Londoners and to provide an opening statement to a show that might consist of rousing quarrels among Indians and among nationalists, West Indian dissidents, a slow underwater ballet of floating "flower people," a short, police-stopped march of Communist Chinese holding their little red Mao books conspicuously before them, the gentle anarchists trying to sell their word, and the religious urging theirs.

If you want the luxury of a double-decker red behemoth all to yourself, you can hire a bus for private use by applying to the London Transport Offices at 55 Broadway, between Westminster Abbey and Victoria Station.

With rare exceptions, museum admissions are free. The British Museum, the Victoria and Albert, the National Gallery, the Tate sell a remarkable collection of cards, reproductions, pamphlets, and books, in a wide range of prices, many of them inexpensive. Consider these for London souvenirs or casual gifts, as well as the talented posters issued by London Transport, 280 Marylebone Road, and a copy of the Brownings' marriage certificate, obtainable at very little cost from their church in Marylebone (p. 216). The cheapest souvenirs, no cost at all, are leaves of toilet paper marked GOVERNMENT PROPERTY in the public conveniences and museums and, for variety, the paper stamped CITY OF WESTMINSTER from the park off Paddington Street in Marylebone.

London Transport offers several city and environs tours, from as little as five shillings to about a pound; children under fourteen at less. There is a quickie of the city, another that divides the city into two tours: the west (Piccadilly, Hyde Park Corner, the Horse Guards, Westminster, etc.) and the east (St. Paul's, Old Bailey, the Tower of London, etc.) with guide service through some of the places touched on. For a long afternoon, usually about one thirty to seven thirty, there are rides and guiding through Windsor, Hampton Court, Greenwich, St. Albans and Hatfield, Knole, the Surrey Downs, and farther afield. The tours usually start at Victoria Station. For information call 222 1234; for reservations, the Private Hire and Tour Offices, 55 Broadway, Travel Information in the Piccadilly Circus Station, or the Information Center across from St. Paul's.

Reasonably honest landlords don cloaks of summer greed and ask extravagant sums for high-season summer rentals. Be prepared to pay at least fifteen guineas (thirty-eight dollars) per week for the sour smell of neglect in two cells of diseased furniture. But, it is pointed out, you will have a key to the park in the square, and furthermore, don't you think the new sunny paint on the door attractive? In some neighborhoods it might be as much as twenty guineas (again, per week) for a bed-sitter or sixteen for a room that keeps its bathroom on a landing and the kitchen, so called, in a hall closet.

Gentlemen can meet gentlemen, as ladies can meet ladies, in pubs, clubs, restaurants, and, if the police and the home-permanented lady attendants and their teakettles aren't there, in public conveniences. One of the stateliest places is the lobby of a Park Lane hotel of high repute. If it means enough to you, you'll find it.

The hotels—not those with uniformed, intimidating doormen and an army of politely inquiring porters—in which Americans are likely to congregate in immense, frantic lobbies are the fields for being searched out, stared at, and, if you consent, picked up in the heterosexual mode. Soho and its notice boards provide sex plain and fancy and so do the open, dimly lit doorways in and around Shepherd Market, off Curzon Street. Nor has Covent Garden, an old hand in the field (see Hogarth), yet given up sex, and as elsewhere, there are the railroad stations.

Some services are fairly cheap (shoe repair), others expensive (watch repair), and almost all of them slow, except in the best well-staffed hotels. The pace is oozily Latin and the final result too often slipshod.

Though it may be a struggle to check pounds, shillings, and pence on a bill, it is not insurmountably difficult (twelvepence becomes one shilling; twenty shillings makes a pound). Make sure that your waiter who may recently have been counting in francs or pesetas or lire has not suffered the same uncertainties about English money as you have.

Many churches in the City close early on Saturdays and weekdays, and some are closed Sundays, especially in August. There aren't enough residents in the City, thefts are common, and personnel to guard the churches difficult to find. Go fairly early in the day.

Most charter flights that link London and Continental cities use airports other than the international Heath Row. If you must make connections, leave ample time. Gatwick Airport, for example, is about forty-five minutes by train from Victoria Station. There may be a half hour wait for the train, and then there is the rest of the journey out of Victoria. If you should be arranging train trips, keep in mind that although London has an unusual number of railroad stations, some of them are far apart. Going from Victoria to Liverpool Street Station means traversing a large section of an immense city through heavy traffic.

Don't outstay your declared allotted time in England. It means polishing benches for hours, literally polishing because one slides from place to place as the front of the zigzag is depleted and the end filled.

After smoothing the bodies of one set, you achieve a number for starting on those in another room in the Home Office on High Holborn. A request for an extension finally presented, your reasons may be acceptable, but no one will decide that instantly. Therefore, your passport is taken, an insubstantial receipt exchanged for it, and six weeks later a stay is granted, but the wrong date was written on the slip pasted to the passport. Polishing again, this time laden with express checks, a statement of financial stability at home, and whatever other proofs you can muster against the fear that you will become a public charge of the British government. In the meantime, you have received a polite note from the Alien Registration Office with METROPOLITAN POLICE printed large, asking that you appear, which you should have done earlier had it not been for the needed correction. More benches, your worn documents again and two passport photos and five shillings as registration fee. Finally, the correctly stamped passport and a dull-voiced warning (the British tone for severity) that the next time you disregard a police notice to appear within seven days, the fine will be one hundred pounds, no excuses.

True, there has been a great deal of illegal immigration recently, dramatically described in newspaper accounts: smuggling rings; men holed up in sleazy Belgian and French coastal hotels with no registers; small craft sneaking across the Channel in the black of night and fog; passengers with scant English dumped on a dawn beach to be picked up by a member of the ring or the police. Indignant you may feel, treated as if you were an impoverished illicit migrant, but neither indignation nor cavalier disrespect of the British law will serve. Courteously, patiently, you will be tracked down.

The numbering on houses often follows the square pattern, continuous numbers around a green. It has its natural logic, which is disturbed when old squares turn into large streets where one would normally expect even numbers on one side and approximately matching odd on the other. But that does not always work; many streets, like Holborn and Bond Street, pull square numbering into a long oval, so that No. 24 may sit opposite No. 140. It is an arrangement to keep in mind when you are searching out addresses.

The best mailing bargain is the airmail letter form (no enclosures) issued by the post office, already stamped with its ninepence postage. That makes it cheaper than airmailing postcards, considering the cost of the card and the ninepence stamp. However, you have to write more than "Having a swinging time" on a form, and besides, the wealth of cards issued by the museums—Shakespeare's signature,

Persian prints, Victorian dolls, Klee and Constable, Picasso and Turner, Egyptian princesses and Italian primitives—are infinitely more rewarding shopping than a post office line. Cheapest, of course, are postcards sent by surface mail to arrive at their destinations long after your London adventures have dulled to you and your best friends.

If you are a book buyer—and it is a partial waste of London not to be—keep in mind that the international book rate for mailing is exceedingly low. (Inquire at the local post office for maximum weight and size regulations.) Parcel post shipping for personal effects you won't want—sweaters and a warm coat in summertime Rome—can also be mailed inexpensively, subject to weight and size limitations. But one should be aware of London's chronic disease—dock strikes —and allow a long, long time for arrival.

Don't put anything off for better weather; it may not feel obliged to grace your few London days.

One of the most effective ways of getting tickets for star ballet or opera performances is to arrange it long beforehand through a powerful agent, or stay at a powerful hotel or, better still, become chummy with a hairdresser in a classy salon; hairdressers know everyone worth knowing with ballet and music connections, and they, too, wield considerable power.

To sound British, if you think you can make it, say, "The United States *are*," "The public *are*," rather than the verb in the singular for collective nouns, as Americans do.

Remember, in crossing streets, to look right, then left.

That mountainous topic, tipping, is particularly difficult here where it involves percentages on nondecimal money. Areas like Southwark and Farringdon Road find a threepenny tip adequate for a two-shilling snack-bar lunch. You cannot and shouldn't do it since, obviously, you do not live on Southwark wages; sixpence ought to be your minimum. In full-menu restaurants, figure a half crown (two shillings and sixpence) or three shillings for each pound, depending on how many people serve you, how Frenchily they glide through the decor, and the prices on the menu. Sometimes a service of 12.5 per cent is added to the bill, and with that you leave a token tip.

A French waiter will tell you that you have undertipped with a growl and an angry slap at your table with his napkin as you leave. An Italian waiter will look inconsolably stricken and lonely, as if you had, with your inadequate tip, announced an inexorably downward path

to poverty and naked, starved death in the gutter. An English waiter
will never teach you, with his impassive polite face what is and isn't
enough. (But then, so many London waiters are Italian, and some
French; from their manner you will quickly learn.)

A ride in a taxi, no matter how short, is worth a minimal tip of
one shilling; after that it can rise by sixpences on a rough parallel to
restaurant tipping, and again, nothing but a polite "thank you" to
guide your future dealings, whether you have or have not undertipped.

If you have the skill and courage for left-hand driving and plan
a motor tour through the British Isles, consider the possibility of
writing for a twelve-month admission ticket to a great number of
national monuments from the Tower of London as far as Edinburgh
Castle. The cost is ten shillings for adults and five shillings for children,
and the ticket is obtainable by writing, with an enclosed remittance, to
the Ministry of Public Building and Works (Chief Information Office),
Lambeth Bridge House, London, S.E.1.

For the philatelist, the General Post Office in Edinburgh publishes
a bulletin of philatelic events, for seven shillings and six pence per
year's subscription. Write to the General Post Office, 2/4 Waterloo
Place, Edinburgh, 1. In London, some philately goes on at the London
Chief Office, King Edward Street, London, E.C.1, the section open
from 9 to 4:30, Monday through Friday.

It may be idolatry or the satisfying sound of a name, but London
commemorates and commemorates one name as a Street, Row, Road,
Garden, Crescent, Mews, Terrace, Walk—sometimes not too far from
each other, like the Sloane series; sometimes maliciously scattered,
like the many Gloucesters. Gloucester Gate and Gloucester Gate Mews
sit at the north end of Regent's Park, a considerable distance from
Gloucester Terrace, west of Paddington Station, a wholesome long
walk from any of the Gloucester Roads (you may pass a Gloucester
Walk on your way), none of them anywhere near Gloucester Street,
not far from the river, south of Victoria Station. Read your addresses
and maps carefully.

Any tube station will substitute a new bus or underground map
for the one you have folded and marked and tattered to unusability.
*What's On in London,* a weekly, and *London This Month,* as well as
other publications and the newspapers, keep one informed of events
in the theater, arts, public life, and tourist life. Banks, sometimes,
and restaurants consider it part of their responsibility to keep you
alert and informed, and there are few Londoners who won't happily
stop to give you the benefit of their information, usually fairly accurate.

During the summer months, the National Gallery is open until nine P.M. on Tuesday and Thursday evenings. A good time to go to have your favorites all to yourself and to hear a gentleman from Manchester down on holiday bellow to his wife, "Constable or no Constable, that picture's a bleeding mess." She answers, "Mmm, dear."

Not only do the tall, large London taxis afford a passenger the dignity of an almost upright entry, as opposed to the demeaning crawl in and, worse still, the contortions of crawling out of cabs in other cities, but they hum a nice, wide, fat throb as they wait for lights, like the purr of a big contented cat or a baby lying in his mother's lap. The narrow slab of window the driver shuts against you ensures privacy, a relic of carriage days, but produces other hazards. Since it is difficult to talk or pay through the slit, you must give your destination and later pay from the outside, as often as not in a fury of rain. Also, should the driver not know the way, it is necessary for you to cross the generous distance to a jump seat and holding on along the curves, communicate with him by shouting, banging on the window, in fact, putting on the undignified display that the taxi was designed to avoid.

Sometimes the communication hatch has no button and cannot be lowered, or its taciturn mechanism insists on sliding closed. Therefore, the cab must pull over, and you get out in the rain again to teach the driver how to get to your friends in Highgate.

## Hotels

For a short visit and its concomitant necessity for being centrally located, it is essential that space be reserved beforehand. During the high tourist season and times of special events, such as the Motor Show, rooms are scarce and always more expensive than you think they might be—about the equivalent of costs in Paris or New York. Out of Piccadilly, Park Lane, Mayfair, and the Knightsbridge-Belgravia-Kensington area, prices drop, and since the tube and bus systems are usually efficient and swift, living off the golden avenues, while less sybaritic, need not be inconvenient.

Currently the annexes of Olympus where the minimal rate would be about eighteen dollars a day and up and up, depending on accommodations, are:

Savoy, Strand to Victoria Embankment
Claridge's, on Brook Street
Connaught, on Carlos Place

Dorchester, Grosvenor House, Hilton, Londonderry House, all on Park Lane
Carlton Tower, Cadogan Place
Hyde Park, 66 Knightsbridge
Westbury, Conduit Street

Central, still satisfactory and a shade less expensive:
Brown's, Dover Street
Athenaeum Court, 116 Piccadilly
Royal Garden, Kensington High Street
Cumberland, Marble Arch
Mount Royal, Marble Arch
Washington, Curzon Street
Europa, Grosvenor Square
Royal Lancaster, Bayswater
Green Park Hotel, Half Moon Street
Stafford, 16 St. James's Place

And still less, from a minimum of about eight dollars:
Russell, Russell Square
Royal Court, Sloane Square
Rubens, Buckingham Palace Road
Berners, Berners Street
Bonnington, Southampton Row
Durrant's, George Street
Kensington Close, Wright's Lane
De Vere, Hyde Park Gate
Pastoria, St. Martin's Street
Gore, 189 Queen's Gate
Rembrandt, Thurloe Place
Mostyn, Portman Street
Ivanhoe, Bloomsbury Street
Cadogan, 75 Sloane Street
Colonnade, Warrington Crescent
Bailey's, Gloucester Road

There are streets that seem to be totally reserved for small hotels, some with a few private baths and most with rates starting at about five dollars.

Cromwell Road, in its endless row, includes: Buckingham (100), King Charles (247), Ashburn (111), Stanhope Court, Stanhope Gardens, Sorbonne (39), Majestic (158–60), Atlantic (143), Europe (131–137), Snow's (139–141), Vanderbilt (76).

Queen's Gate: Onslow Court, Imperial (121), Adria (88), Bute Court (28); at 5 Queen's Gate Terrace, Avery House.

Onslow Gardens: Glencourt (42), French (71), Gardens Court (65).
Evelyn Court, 50 Evelyn Gardens.

Gloucester Place, west of Baker Street, is a similar row and as a rule somewhat more expensive: Astoria (90), Georgian (87), Hart House (51), St. George's (49), Adam-Rondale (82), off Sloan Street, on Wilbraham Place, the Wilbraham Hotel.

A number of the above serve the usual meals; most content themselves with offering bed and breakfast for the prices they quote. Also in the latter category: 6 Sloane Gardens and 32 Sloane Gardens; Brompton House, 167 Old Brompton Road; Portman Court, 28 Seymour Street; Rutland Court, 23 Draycott Place; 69 Cadogan Gardens; 15 Egerton Gardens.

In areas whose existence may be unfamiliar, but not difficult or isolated: Clive Hotel, Primrose Hill Road (north of Regent's Park), modern and not too large (about ten dollars); Swiss Cottage Hotel, Adamson Road (near Swiss Cottage Station), attractive suites at about twelve dollars. Consider also the flatlets and service suites on Nottingham Place in Marylebone.

The British Museum is surrounded by hotels, large and small; the small hotels on Montague Street are garnished more neatly than those of the same size though less ambitious, and cheaper, on Bernard Street.

It is as true of London as of any other city that the railroad stations are surrounded by streetfuls of hotel, usually basic enclosures holding bed and sink, toilet and bath in the hall and to be shared. For an economy stay, settle into the hotel your friends or agent may have recommended, and then explore the possibilities of the hotels near Paddington Station, King's Cross-Euston, Victoria (*not* Liverpool Street). If you will not mind the short walk to Blackheath Station and the few minutes of riding to central London on a nineteenth-century toy train, try the Heathview, the Clarendon, or the Regency on Montpelier Road.

Students will know about hostels and YMCA housing and other accommodations recommended by the people who plan and operate student tours. The British Travel Association issues a booklet that describes size, location, current prices, whether children are acceptable and how old, how many lounges are in use, and what languages are spoken, called *Inexpensive Accommodation in Greater London,* available in London (64 St. James's Street) and BTA offices in the United States, Canada, and most foreign countries.

# 2   The Big Tall Red Bus

The London double-decker is the closest you will come to a roller-coaster ride outside amusement parks, and cheaper, particularly if you try to negotiate the winding stairs to and from the top while the bus is in fast motion, as it almost always is, except at rush hours when it has to board and deposit an unusual number of people. Otherwise, the bulk acts like a hummingbird in its constant, nervous winging. (Along with practicing looking first right and then left to cross London streets for the limited degree of safety afforded Londoners, one should practice jumping off and on moving vehicles for equal combat with the bus.)

Though mounting the stairs, arms laden with raincoat, a change of shoes, maps, and guidebooks, may be difficult while the red bull charges around squares, thrusts and turns at corners, and the descent even more difficult, the top of the bus is a delightful place to spend a day peering into offices with thousands of people keeping records in longhand, at frozen, archaic figures in clubs, down on shoppers, strollers, and purposeful striders, up at eccentricities of architecture, and, if you manage to cadge a front seat, a full wide view and genuine blasts of heat—the only ones you are likely to encounter—in the wintertime.

With time enough, a pocketful of change, and a couple of bars of sweets from the boundless imaginations of chocolate makers, it is possible to live the kaleidoscopic life of several routes, hopping on and off at salient points. The 22 bus starts among the spacious pubs and well-cut slacks and sweaters of Putney; crosses the Thames and soars into Fulham, a scene of frequent liveliness that refuses to be enlivened; follows a strip of King's Road, whose shabbiness hasn't yet been touched by psychedelia or amorphous sex, and then into the legendary kingdom, not quite as you might like it to be on a dull week-day when the peacocks are in their office pens. Sloane Street, next, gives off the high shine of money and, in an intermission of houses among the shops, makes room for the Cadogan Hotel, where Oscar Wilde addled by love and, more, the love of gesture, waited to be arrested. Linking Hyde Park and Green Park, the bus trundles up Piccadilly, and it is time for alighting to examine the palace of the Duke of Wellington (Apsley House) and on again, down the somewhat dimmed, once showy avenue whose delightful, flower-hung arcades act as reliquaries of vanished flavor. It then charges into the whirlpool of Piccadilly Circus that gathers its swirling colors from tarty Soho, from visitors shopping on Regent Street, from the theater marquees on Shaftesbury Avenue, the coagulations of decor in hasty eating houses and, as vortex, the listless, matted and tattered young, hugging their knees and their knapsacks—waiting for what?—under the buoyant feet of "Eros."

The next stop might be on High Holborn at Chancery Lane and then a short walk to the Public Record Office Museum (p. 65), after a ramble through Lincoln's Inn, communing with the ghosts of Disraeli, John Donne, Gladstone, and Sir Thomas More. Then, a visit at Sir John Soane's singular House and Museum (p. 203), and a lingering in front of the eighteenth-century houses around Lincoln's Inn Fields, especially the regal Lindsey House (no. 59–60), almost surely by Inigo Jones of a century earlier.

Run, leap, and "Ol taaht," as some of the conductresses warn, for the run over the Holborn Viaduct and a quick look at the Smithfield Market below; down Newgate where the infamous jail that at some time housed Defoe and William Penn stood behind the public execution grounds that replaced Tyburn in the eighteenth century. Immediately to your right, St. Paul's grandly beckons, and before you, the Central Criminal Court, Old Bailey, some of whose nondescript stones are said to be part of the demolished Newgate jail. Then to Cheapside, to see if you can still hear any murmur of centuries of market calls through the traffic, and into the Church of St. Mary-le-Bow of the Bow Bells whose spread of sound traditionally marked authentic Cockneyland, and on again for the cliffs of might and money—the Bank of England, the Stock Exchange, the Royal Exchange, and others—that crush Threadneedle Street (a name ascribed to a sign of the needlemaker's company that once hung here and also to an old children's game). Following Bishopsgate, which wanes from international banking to dusty pessimism as it runs northward, the bus skirts the Sunday markets (p. 108) on its run to the near north semisuburbs, which is not necessarily where you might want to be, and you might as well then arrange another route back.

The 19 bus also starts south of the river, follows the streets of the 22, and then waddles into Bloomsbury, where you might spend a profitable week or so at the British Museum. Having boarded again, ride through some plaintive streets of Islington with a pause for ticket buying at Sadler's Wells, more Islington and on to Highbury, and at the terminal, follow the conductor into one of the enormous pubs of Finsbury Park.

The 11 that comes out of Shepherd's Bush (an ebullient Friday afternoon market town) accompanies the 11 and 22 on the King's Road, but at Sloane Square veers toward Victoria and sidles along the inexhaustibly moving Abbey and the Houses of Parliament; passes the Horse Guards and the Banqueting Hall at Whitehall; blinks at Nelson in Trafalgar Square; skirts London's remaining Eleanor Cross (one of thirteen that marked the route of the funeral cortege of Queen Eleanor, wife of Edward I), standing Gothically in the frenzied movement around Charing Cross Station; and then rushes down the Strand, cutting a jaunty wave around the isolated churches St. Mary-le-Strand and St. Clement Danes, reefed on minute islands in the sea of cars. At Fleet Street it makes one of its short, nervous halts to let you off at the Temple courts, or the alley that leads to Dr. Johnson's house, or St. Bride's Church. St. Paul's arrives next, followed by the Bank, and near it the heroic, brooding Hawksmoor Church of St. Mary Woolnoth (p. 149). Northward past the Guildhall, the meeting place of the Corporation of the City of London, whose totemic griffin you may have seen obstructing traffic on Fleet Street. Back of the Guildhall, a highway called London Wall, the blank shores of a metallic river of cars, except for the persistence of one piece of medieval gateway, flanked by sustaining bits of wall, surprised and abandoned, an unreal piece of scenery dropped from the back of a truck.

As you look at the section of stage setting—maybe missed by the stagehands who are mounting *Il Trovatore* in one of the musical borough halls—let your eye travel north, your mind erase the dry emptinesses, the tall towers and leftover rows of a city that was gutted and is rebuilding, haltingly, to the raucous music of protest from unions, architects, antiquities lovers, bewildered citizens, and city planners, and try to see Moorfields as William Fitzstephen, a Londoner by birth and a monk of Canterbury, wrote it "most elegantly in Latin" in the twelfth century, as an introduction to his *Life of Becket:*

When that great marsh which washes the walls of the city on the north side is frozen over, the young men go out in crowds to divert themselves upon the ice. Some, having increased their velocity by a run, placing their feet apart, and turning their bodies sideways, slide a great way: others make a seat of large pieces of ice like mill-stones, and a great number of them running before, and holding each other by the hand, draw one of their companions who is seated on the

ice. . . . Others are more expert in their sports upon the ice; for
fitting to, and binding under their feet the shinbones of some animal,
and taking in their hands poles shod with iron, which at times they
strike against the ice, they are carried along with as great rapidity
as a bird flying or a bolt discharged from a cross-bow.

(England may not have had her Brueghels, but she had her Fitzstephens,
Stows, Mayhews, and Dickens to record affectionately the occupa-
tions and pastimes of her young.)

The edge of once playful old Moorfields is about as far as the 11
bus line will take you, but there are others, about 300 others, all red,
that stitch together the multitextured, multicolored city. The 74, shy
of public appearances, sometimes agrees to wait near the Greek restaurants, Shamrock saloons, old clothes and early de-entrailed radios,
canals and cheap butcher shops of Camden Town; then makes its way
to the zoo at the north end of Regent's Park; passes Lord Snowdon's
not quite modern enough aviary and the big courts of flats in St. John's
Wood, down to the shopping on Baker and Orchard streets. Having
picked up a load at Hyde Park Corner, it pauses for Harrod's shoppers
on Brompton Road, takes some of them on to the Victoria and Albert
and the Natural History museums, some to the bed-sitters on Cromwell Road, others to the air terminal close by, and then through Earl's
Court and Fulham, coming to rest across the river at Putney. Sometimes, with a B added to its name, it makes the journey to Hammersmith, where you can find the 71 for Chiswick (p. 206); sometimes, it
prefers to go to Roehampton, the place of some remarkable modern
housing, considered by a number of authorities among the most beautiful and intelligently planned in this century.

As must be amply evident, almost anywhere, on almost any route
in central London, something is happening. For those streets in rigor
mortis, however, one must supply a film of what once had happened.

Goswell Road, on the 4A, a despairing street of plastics, tractors,
paper factories, and ironworks, none of them powerful, and relieved
by snack bars like poor kitchens, was the principal road to the north
from Aldersgate in the time of the first Elizabeth, "replenished with
small tenements, cottages, and alleys, gardens, banqueting-houses, and
bowling-places." Now the bus plows past Ashby Street, one of the dim
rows of small houses lost between centuries and into the vast, confused, much argued, and delayed Barbican rebuilding, one finished section of housing already showing dark roots in its blonde cement Scan-
dinavian-Japanesey head while it waits for the rest to grow around it.
"Barbican" means a line of fortification topped by a watchtower,

and this was the place of the northwest barbican of the medieval city. The Little Britain Alley you pass has its name from *Le Bretoun* who owned houses and lands that surrounded the local church, St. Botolph Aldersgate. "Aldersgate" probably refers to a Saxon, Ealdred, who controlled this entrance to the ancient city. The bus slips with you into St. Martin's-le-Grand, a useful, anonymous thoroughfare where once stood a college whose charter was granted it by William the Conqueror, twelve years after its actual founding. Like medieval schools elsewhere, it claimed the power of total sanctuary. Medieval Londoners, a contentious lot who were not impressed by sanctity of church— or king, for that matter—pulled men out when it suited them, over the protests of the priests who sometimes won the struggles, sometimes not. In 1548 the college was taken over by the Crown, the church pulled down, and in its place—one can almost see Tudor malice— a large wine tavern was built to supply a number of new tenements.

The bus offers, besides shelter from the rain and superb city viewing, a smoking parlor, the right to throw candy wrappers on the floor, a thin paper ticket to keep among your souvenirs, bevies of conductresses who belong, for their warmth, their charm, their kindness, their patience—if it were a just world—in ermine-lined Rolls-Royces, except that such a cocoon would stifle their amplitude of spirit.

The conductress has, like Cleopatra, infinite variety. On a Holborn bus she is tall, rawboned, in a forbiddingly neat shirt and high-knotted tie, her hair neatly, flatly ugly. She has four teeth she tries to conceal, and the stiff mouth makes her meticulously repeated "thank you" and "please" that much more formal and guarded, the Salvation Army worker let loose in a wicked world. Later in the afternoon, she grows shorter, plumper, piles her hair in a tall, golden casque with one coquettish yellow dart pointing at her masterfully painted eye. A lovely, bouncy, beamish girl who enjoys playing Mum to her wobbling, changing world; lifts the babies up, helps the tottering down, and is genuinely sorry that you have to pay an extra fourpence—"Oh, love, you should have gotten on at the next stop, shouldn't you?"—with a beam of solicitude and the gentlest hint of rebuke because you are something of a profligate fool. At other times she is the gum-chewing schoolgirl, learning her job on weekends, laconic and careless, who will let you pay sevenpence for an eightpenny ride if neither of you has the proper change. She can be the sweetly nagging wife who keeps telling you, "Two more stops for you." "One more stop!" "This one is yours, dear." She can be a poised, cool Dravidian goddess who graces her uniform as if it were a sari or a round, shy West Indian girl who is so confused by an American accent (and you, hers) that she will not collect your fare after the first bout of incomprehensions. She can be the wit who sits down next to you on a ride through lashing rain, when the customers are few, and whiles the time away with freshets of conversation about work, husbands, styles, politicians, and food.

Her most alluring guise is that of star entertainer. On the Oxford Street bus run that picks up tired stolid shoppers and dazed children, a derelict out of the alleys of Soho, and a few visitors who are going in the wrong direction because east and west are not what they used to be back home, she wears vigorously blond hair and dangling earrings and a face full of makeup, not so much applied as splashed on. She jokes and grins at the youngsters with her straight new National Health teeth, solicitously addresses their tired mothers as "dear," listens to a destination and proclaims its price as if it were an exchange of gifts, and trills her "ta" with fresh enthusiasm each time she hands out a ticket and change. As she collects the fares, dashes back to ring the starting bell, between calls of "four on top," she sings. Loud, off tune, her Cockney ballad of love and drink and chummy violence wafts through the clammy raincoat air and decaying cigarette stubs and muddy paper tickets on the floor of the bus, pulling attention and affection out of the sagging riders, putting a shine on a sodden half hour.

Her father is Jove, thundering that you cannot get off at the light stop. Her son finds the fare-stage listing too bothersome and suggests you and he sort of estimate the price of a ride. Her brother on the 73 route is an exuberant, toothless man, buoyed on a swift monologue. Although he was born within the sound of Bow Bells, he has never been inside Bow Church or St. Paul's; he passes the Albert Hall several times a day and has never been inside, or in the Victoria and Albert, a few minutes distant. The proud working-class snobbism flows on with a wary eye for passengers, all of whom are potential searchers for trouble, most of them outright self-destroyers. "Palys Gaite ony!" he shouts at the feeble and blind who cannot read or understand the large sign at the front of the bus, informing that it does not take the full route, and for the suicides, "Moind the loights," and, "Hey, guvner, yu wantcher loife, dontcher?"

## To Remember

Keep the slips of paper marked with the sum you've paid until you leave the bus which has a bin near the exit (also the entrance) for discards; inspectors do come through.

If you are waiting at a request stop, make unmistakable, even violent gestures to stop the bus. If it is late and they are off schedule, drivers sometimes try not to see you. They must come to a full halt—or their interpretation thereof—at regular stops.

There are no transfers or transfer points. No matter which bus or how many you use, the fare is commensurate with the distance traveled, increasing by fourpence at each fare stage. A fare-stage stop is so marked, and you can avoid the increase by walking a stage ahead or, possibly, leaving the bus before your actual destination. It takes considerable intimacy with stops and fare stages and, in any case, seems a mean way to treat a city that offers so much for free or little.

There is a strong temptation to get off a bus at a red light, especially when the stop is a short distance from your specific destination. It is frequently succumbed to and frequently the cause of accidents, sending a passenger sprawling into the path of oncoming cars as the light changes and the bus lurches forward. Conductors, in their solidarity with drivers, usually call warnings, some in casual mutters, and others, inflamed, shout, "If you break your neck, it's the driver's fault, huh? Stand back. Wait for the stop," and forcibly hold you on the stairs if they suspect you of dangerous haste.

Because of one-way streets and the fancies of an old city, the return bus fare between the same points, on the same line, may be more or less than the fare of the original direction. You are not being taken—never.

The long route of a bus may at certain times of the day be curtailed. The 13, for one, whose full ride covers Golders Green to the south side of London Bridge, frequently calls a halt at Oxford Circus, where there are other lines to take over the rest of the trip; true as well of other truncated rides to central exchange points.

# 3　The Disinfected Tubes

Much of London smells of strong acrid disinfectant, the same one used in oceanic quantities in the men's and ladies' and throughout the meshwork of underground system. The odor suggesting poverty and disease goes badly with the optimism of advertising—health drinks and the security of savings combined with public information posters listing musical events, describing alluringly historical oddities you should see, the rooting progress on the new Victoria Line, the hours during which you can claim lost articles at the Baker Street office, which inexpensive pamphlet will take you on country walks, where art is exhibited.

The underground system is called the tube for obvious reasons. One has only to ride up to the Bakerloo platform in Piccadilly Station to observe the emphatic round shape and notice how a small office is shaped to the curve and cut off with a valvelike door.

Although the interconnecting systems of line are, like the Paris metros, marvels of planning and step-by-step guiding, spiculed with signs and warnings that nag and nudge you to your destination, one station defies the neat, obsessed logic. Never, never, if you can avoid it, change at Baker Street; go on to some other connecting point that requires fewer up and down stairs, fewer escalators and double platforms, with fewer informative boards and arrows that act as that many more thickets in an already diabolical maze. Baker Street is clearly only for the native who has worked it out painfully years ago and now flies it like a homing pigeon.

If the money is absolutely out and the East End shelters like leprosariums are full, it is possible to live in the underground system, provided you can summon the cost of a minimal ride and have a map (free). Get on the Circle Line which does just that, and at connecting points—Baker Street, South Kensington, Charing Cross, as well as a few others—take other lines, making sure not to approach a WAY OUT alley and its guardian ticket collector. The terrain you cover will be more varied than you think. Hammersmith and north on the Metropolitan Line brings you into the projecting brick backs of tight-rowed houses in a coldness of railroad siding, warmed only by the faces of Indian, Pakistani, Caribbean, and African tenants. You can

33

get off at South Kensington Station to admire its flower beds and at Aldgate East to examine the heraldic symbols, the flights of birds, and effigies of St. Paul's and the Houses of Parliament baked into the wall tiles.

Old Street Station's access to the Finsbury Park Line is through curves of white tile intestine, shining like animal fat, and onto a platform that breathes dank bitterness as it waits for trains that rarely come. The same shining worm lives in Essex Road Station, used, seemingly, by no one else but you at three o'clock in the afternoon. Only your footsteps sound as you keep to the center of the shining, undulating curves, afraid they might move if you touch them or might close in on you. After too long a time, hoping for the sight of an escalator or a flight of stairs, no matter how steep, the worm's mouth greets you as the black iron gates of a lift, shut. It is a singularly long moment, the worm behind you, the iron black mouth closed on you, and nowhere else to go, and when in his leisured time, the liftman descends and opens the escape hatch, the sense of escape is absurd and real.

And stand away from the walls of the escalator on Holborn Station. When lifts and stairways were replaced by escalators some years ago, an opened wall spilled hundreds of skeletons that had been lying in their plague pit for many centuries. Work stopped; discussions started. Someone decided that this was hallowed ground; maybe all the skeletons should be removed and buried decently elsewhere, not at the side of a rumbling escalator and constantly shaken by the movement of trains. Maybe, insisted another faction, we ought to shovel them back and get on with the work. A compromise was arranged: One skeleton was taken out, services said, and the whole lot pushed back and plastered over. They are protesting again and may once more emerge; the walls show ominous cracks along the handrails of the escalators.

## To Remember

Hold onto your ticket until the end of the ride, when it is collected. Otherwise, you pay again.

Some lines divide in two. A sign near the track divided into FIRST train and SECOND will bear the name of the terminal point of the division. Check with your underground map for the section you will need.

# 4    National Portrait Gallery

Here is where it started, the crowded pageant that is London and England, with the personae who stepped onto a bare stage set with sections of rough gray Norman tower. More and more came, crowding the stage with the complex dance of intrigues, the glow of silks and gold, the flash of jeweled swords. The glow dims to Cromwellian plainness and brightens again to lace, curls, and effete elegance; shades off to the dark coats and sagacious wigs of scholars, writers, and wits; blazes with military sashes and epaulets of generals and conquerors and always, nearby, a queen, a king, a consort, a regent, princesses, princes, and dukes.

The wits, the generals, and royalty move backstage for a period which gives the center stage to the romantic face and mind: Byron in dashing Middle Eastern costume; Shelley in a wild *dégagé* lily of neck linen; the startled Brontë sisters; Keats, forever young as the maidens on his Greek vase; an inept little drawing of Jane Austen; and on and on, to Empire builders and Empire relinquishers.

For viewing the parade in the logic of chronology, start at the top floor where, on a side stairway, there are sets of old effigies, probably less portraits than the popular commercial art of the time. In the glass case in the main hall there are several coins stamped with primitive portraits of King Offa, who died in 796; of Alfred; of William the Conqueror and the defeated Harold, who looks deeply troubled. Although the span is almost 300 years, the kings look alike, stiffly hieratic like Rouault's kings.

The royal portraits of medieval times are probably not from life and have the lifelessness of unfamiliarity and excessive awe—the brocades and jewels prayerfully rendered, the faces pallid repetitions of one another, except that of Richard III where some character depiction was attempted. Probably done from life, then pulled into curious distortion, is a portrait of Edward VI, the sickly boy of Jane Seymour and Henry VIII, a painter's trick of virtuosity which when viewed full on, gives the boy a long, predatory stork profile, steamy eyes, the plumes on his hat thickened to half-cooked spaghetti. Viewed through an aperture, it becomes a pleasant Flemish portrait, and the misty, bluish background of the distortion disappears. A more lyrical, easier little portrait of the boy hangs a bit farther on in the gallery, and near it a strong bust of his father, broad and indomitable, capable of sapping the lives of wives and stronger sons, if he had had them. Henry and Edward appear again in an absurd propaganda painting that shows Edward on the throne, on his left his advisers, and to the right Henry on his deathbed. In the foreground, the Pope, surrounded by streamers of "Idolatry," "Superstition," and "Feyned Holiness" is sinking, collapsing, vanquished.

Inevitably—and we realize we have been waiting for her—we come to that mighty, skinny force, Elizabeth I, standing on all England, a blaze of the sun shining for her alone; an impersonal magnificence whose pale face disappears into columns of brocaded, begemmed silks, red wig looped with pearls, clouds of ruff, the enameled chest hung with jewels. Like many of her predecessors, she may have had to sell, scrounge, pawn, and reclaim, and pawn and reclaim again, but in this effulgent image of wealth and power there is not a breath of such frailty or any other. Surrounding her are the advisers, variously friends, foes and maybe lovers—Sir Francis Walsingham; the Earl of Leicester; the Earl of Sussex; her financial genius, Sir Thomas Gresham, in a fine portrait; Sir Walter Raleigh and his earring—painted with differing qualities of skill, but each with the alertness and dash, the unique totalness that we still call Elizabethan. The inept portrait of Edward de Vere, Earl of Oxford, the "extravagant and eccentric peer," writer, and "patron of players and man of letters," a leading contender for the right to be considered Shakespeare's "onlie begetter" of the sonnets, wafts an arrogance and foppishness beyond that common in a peacock age; an unabashed, overweening confidence, amusing and felicitous.

In spite of the manifest differences, one notices a rather rigid painting style that designed or responded to an ideal of beauty which required an eggshell pallor, a long prominent nose, and a tight, little, pale pink mouth. Or could Mary, Queen of Scots, and Anne Boleyn and Elizabeth and the Earl of Southampton (he of the long hair and exquisite dress and possibly another candidate for "onlie begetter") all have looked alike?

Look at Elizabeth again, in a less Olympic portrait of a serious, intelligent, wary, and tired woman, and back once more to that great force of nature, Henry VIII, this time in a full-size drawing of the Holbein wall painting destroyed with the burning of Whitehall Palace in 1698. His feet grip the world with the familiar aggressive stance; the rich robes reveal sturdy legs and a proud codpiece, the giant roaring, "Fee, Fi, Fo, Fum, I'll have the blood of a Papishman."

Out of the pearls, satins, and sonnets to the shine of dark armor on

Oliver Cromwell and Charles I and on to a fine Rubens portrait of Thomas Howard, Earl of Arundel and Earl of Surrey; an execrable one of King Frederick V of Bohemia, whose soft throat and warm dark hair make a bearded lady of him; and a smooth, satiny, full-length portrait of Henrietta Maria (1609–69), the queen of Charles I, the daughter of Henry IV of France and Marie de Médicis and she looks every inch and silken fold of it. Near her, the George Villiers, first Duke of Buckingham, who caused her a great deal of trouble. The label on his portrait says: "His arrogant administration aggravated the ill-feeling between Charles I and Parliament. Assassinated." It looks plausible, the brocade and the gold, the disdainful beauty and towering hubris that reaches power, refuses to be moderate or cautious with it, and asks to be decapitated.

Almost lost among the royalty, a portrait of Ben Jonson as the studio of Rembrandt might have done it, and then a large gallery of the scientists and artists and philosophers in long, curly wigs or the limp turbans that were fashionable at-home gear: Pepys, Dryden, Bunyan, Hobbes, Marvell, Newton, Walton, Boyle, Purcell, Wycherley; Sir Christopher Wren in tasteful velvet and a pleased look in his eye. Nell Gwyn is here, of course, accompanied by more lords and honorables; Addison and Steele, together, among the portraits of the Kit-Cat Club, a coffee-drinking, witticism-making discussion group of cultivated gentlemen. Here, too, are Alexander Pope, very plain, and Richard Nash, the "Beau," but *beau* no longer, painted at a stage when his molten face looks like Oscar Wilde as Toulouse-Lautrec drew him; Smollett, Richardson, Hogarth, Isaac Watts, and Catherine Maria "Kitty" Fisher who died in 1767. "Courtesan" says the label and nothing else. A zesty, honest age labels a paunchy, droopy-eyed gentleman who died in 1727 as one "much addicted to racing, cocking and gaming."

Lushly romantic portraits by Sir Thomas Lawrence swim into view. Sir Graham Moore, a beauty with dark liquid eyes, a romantic lock, and a baroque mouth, and George IV as a windswept, impassioned Heathcliff. Somehow, the soft pinks of cheek, the eyes like ripe plums, storm-tossed foliage for hair, and the peachlike innocence of the expressions suggest still lifes—bouquets or bowls of fruit—rather than portraits.

By this time you may have had enough, or more than, but try to hold your patience for the several appearances of Disraeli's droll, clever face and witty body and two unusual paintings, both by George Frederic Watts. Edward Robert, first Earl of Lytton, as Watts saw him, emerges as a moody portrait by Van Gogh, and a portrait of

Cardinal Manning looks as if it might possibly have been done by Kokoschka.

In a regal, velvet-bound niche, you will find the young Queen Victoria in her coronation gown, and in an adjoining hall, members of her family set against Victorian wallpaper and the pre-Raphaelite poets and painters sitting with designs that might easily have been devised by William Morris.

Not yet gone? Stop for a moment before the satisfying portraits of John Opie and on to other monumental figures that rose out of your history books and the *Surveys of English Literature,* from Charlotte Brontë to Beatrix Potter, from the Brownings to Joyce, from Robert Burns to Bernard Shaw in an animated bust by Sir Jacob Epstein; the terrifying portrait of Aubrey Beardsley and the pustulant cartoon of Oscar Wilde, relieved by a sensitive portrait of Ralph Vaughan Williams' momentous face. A later Pantheon is a series of sculptured busts, clustered as if it were a cocktail party. G. K. Chesterton, an English version of Rodin's "Balzac," holds one group enthralled, while Shaw magnetizes another, and Vanessa Bell, Virginia Woolf's sister, disregards them all, staring out and away into a private conversation with herself. Then back, in time, to the exquisite miniatures by Nicholas Hilliard of Queen Elizabeth and of Sir Walter Raleigh, among other miniatures on a lower floor, and out to watch the sidewalk painter who works in chalks near the entrance, an appropriate personage to round out the visit.

Entrance on St. Martin's Place side of National Gallery. Open Monday to Friday 10 A.M. to 5 P.M.; Saturday 10 A.M. to 6 P.M.; Sunday 2 to 6 P.M. Free. (Since there is not room enough to show more than half the portraits catalogued, permission is given accredited specialists to view other hidden items.)

# 5    River and Docks

Down at the Tower Pier the dazed émigrés, not sure which set of planks and bridges will take them where, some of them uncertain where upriver is and what is down, and whether Hampton Court is where the Royal Observatory is, or was that Richmond? One can roughly tell the visitors from the indigenes because the latter are the families that have the largest number of boys to cope with during the school holidays. They carry the biggest food baskets and get on the boat that takes the longest trip, the Port of London Authority dock ride that runs two or three times a week during the spring and summer months.

Leaving the Pool of London (the last section of the river to which large ships may enter, ending immediately beyond the Tower Bridge, which can lift its enormous arms with amazing speed), one settles down with the sixpenny map that marks the ten-mile tour and the assuring news that come weather, hunger, or thirst, the saloon will stay open throughout the journey. The river and docks ride under a soft, gray scrim of half heat haze, half fog; a lulling, soft landscape of nodding cranes and rocking barges, of low loose buildings like large pergolas; strange structures of tormented pipes; bustling, busy-body barges and great, slow freighters; splindly-legged birds that sway on the bumpy green covers of laden barges and swans that gather for the food dropped by a huge gray Baltic vessel, dozing with its nose pressed against the bridge.

Slipping out from between the waiting excursion boats and the reds and blues and greens and yellows of tugs and barges, you enter the vast area of London docking (and at one time shipbuilding) that is and was the bread and butter of London. This immense city of docks—ninety miles of them—clasps river and land together in enormous serrated hasps, creating an extraordinary terrain, planets away from the flower-hung City banks, the dollhouse charms of Kensington, the queues in Piccadilly Circus Station, the gutter mood of Soho. There is a wide, quiet serenity here in spite of the enterprise one knows is the begetter of the landscape, a lovely monotony dotted with myriad variations.

The intelligent commentator points out the names of the docks and some pertinent facts about each: the complex of Greenland, Russia,

Norway, etc. docks bring in lumber and other goods from the north countries; Limehouse is named that because limestone was once dug from local pits; Dead Man's Dock was built over an enormous cache of skeletons, probably one of London's numerous plague pits. She points out the riverside pubs (one described by the peripatetic Dickens) and Wapping Old Stairs, where gallows stood until the mid-sixteenth century "for the hanging of pirates and sea rovers, at the low-water mark, and there to remain, till three tides had overflowed them!" She tells you that the Isle of Dogs, the great bulge of West India Docks, was the place where Charles I kept his hunting dogs, then points out the almost invisible Virginia Settlers' Memorial.

While you listen and admire her conscientious effort, and wonder mildly, again, at the capacity of English children to engulf sweets, and vaguely realize that the boys are going mad with sea fever and the girls becoming snappish and pinching out of boredom, and wonder what the twenty acres of wine vaults under the London Docks looks like, your eye wanders over a small pleasure craft that bounces around a school of barges with the upslanted, indignant faces of sharks. Among the yards of yellow planks and enormous trunks of trees, a sign that insists DOGS LOVE VIMS. Before Vims, however, you have seen the tall masts of the *Cutty Sark* lying at the Greenwich Pier and the pinnacle of the Royal Observatory that looks like the tower of a story castle beckoning to the prince from its dark woods, and soon, the unfolding of the panorama of the Royal Naval College: the creamy Wren section first; then the darker London black and white of inner buildings; in the middle distance the Queen's House. It all turns out of view at the bend of the river, to leave the stage for the riverside pubs and the castlelike Trinity almshouses in which the Mercers' Company of the City keeps, in continuance of the medieval tradition, a group of old widowers and bachelors.

The bends in the river, the deep dock slips and creeks and canal joinings make strange compositions of a church steeple standing against the stacks of a large freighter and, as background, thin forests of cranes fading off into the distance. A bucket lifts and spews, lifts and spews smoothly, slowly, in the sluggish river light and river rhythm, the brown sand of sugar to be whitened at a dockside refinery whose great plumes of smoke slip into the gray sky above a giant checker set of tanks. The stationary cranes reach out menacingly from their platforms or stand aloof as indifferent sentinels. The enormous mobile cranes alert, searching, move down the river like hungry brontosaurs in a jungle pool.

Sand piles turn into view, and a set of enormous black platforms on piles in the river shielding a long, flat coal barge preparing to slide up the river under the low arches of Thames bridges. Always the cranes, mingling with occasional trees, the beehives of neat shipping containers, the big red mouths of barges, the enmeshments of tubes, strips of park, and lengths of huge varicolored cans neatly heaped. The immense Woolwich Ferry (this one named for Ernest Bevin), a gigantic, gliding basket carrying trucks and cars, boxes and people. A motor launch goes by, and the blanket of gray-white birds lifts off the green barge cover, as if flapped in a sudden breeze, and settles again. A large German freighter trundles by gravid with lumber, obscuring for a long moment a row of sand dunes at which a covey of barges is chewing. New housing estates go by, and dredgers, granaries and soap works, drydocks and oil depots. The river widens, and it is all reduced to toys and Whistler riverscape.

Waiting for the stately exit of a dredger laden with incomprehensible twists and coils of machinery, the small excursion launch enters the King George V section of the Royal Docks and sits in the rectangle of lock, watching the water level rise. 43, marked on the side, disappears, then 44; 45 (the high water mark) is licked and threatened, then covered. At 47, lock and bridge are opened, and one floats carefully, slowly, between a narrowness of mountainous ships' walls.

The commentator tells you that the docks serve 150 shipping lines plying among 300 world ports, and the names high above you confirm it. A ship from New Plymouth is bringing wool and pelts and lamps; a vessel from Brisbane is disgorging cheese and butter into a refrigerator barge; a Greek ship is loading for a journey to New Zealand; an English ship just in from China carries tea, rubber, and timber; one is loading for the Far East, and another, having discharged its cargo from East Africa at the Tilbury Docks some distance down the river, is readying to load for the return voyage.

The romance of freighters from distant ports, memories of Conrad and Maugham, the magical drop and rise of water in locks, floating slowly in the steel canyons of ships' sides, are good enough for adults, but not for the children who are restless now, waiting for the lock to open and release the motionless launch. The mothers break out the sandwiches and promise the novelty of tea in the saloon; the mothers who forgot the sandwiches shove another sixpence into an impatient little hand, for another Kit-Kat or Aero, a bag of Toffos or Potato Crisps.

The Royal Albert Dock shows the endless beautiful same, this time enormous containers marked CUNARD waiting to be loaded; another, newer shape of dredger, a ship from Cape Town, one from Holland, another from Germany going to Central America and Mexico; a Japanese ship bringing plastics and rubber sandals, thousands of them. Freight is being taken on for the Persian Gulf by one ship, while a Jamaican freighter nestles into its special banana dock to deliver its wares; from New York, refrigerated goods, small machinery, and a yacht. The greedy grain elevators of the huge flour mills keep the peristalsis going in their distended intestines, and the crane buckets dip their hippopotamus heads, lift, drip sloppily from their hippo mouths, drink and lift, bite and drip, clumsily again and again.

In and out of more docks and then back up the river. Behind a high riser of housing peeps an enormous smokestack of a ship, a startling juxtaposition of things wrongly placed, forced by the cuts of locks and slips into the land. In Deptford a medieval castle of many round towers slowly separates into four tall blocks of housing estate. The old sugar ship is still pouring its sweet sand into the refinery, the birds still riding the bulky canvas, islands of barges sleepily rocking like fat old men, houses spiked by cranes and the smoke exploding or drifting out of a wondrous collection of smokestacks. There are tall ones and short, fat ones and skinny, some like fluted classic columns, some like obelisks, some like Art Nouveau vases, and extraordinarily attractive ones that look like prehistoric ceramics. The *Baltic Sun* moored at Tower Bridge two hours ago, is now being pulled by a tug rapidly sledding over the water toward a new Russian ship resplendent in its hammer and sickle emblem. The faint light has gathered as a pale disk of sun, the haze has grown grayer, deeper, and the many shapes begun to melt into a dim flow of shadows that pass in repetitious, soothing rhythms. Near the pier, a sudden wave of spice odor from one of the wharves and, in the distance, the thousands of City workers crossing to London Bridge Station, a restless moss that encrusts the clean line of the bridge at 6 P.M. of a weekday and soon disappears, leaving an abandoned City within the hour.

## ≈§ London Is Where ...

A decent shabbiness like unpressed pants lives around the corner from gleaming expensive toy towns embroidered with window boxes and around another corner a faceless tower with diminished people shopping at its feet, ants burrowing in the roots of a glass tree; one street away, cuddly mews; two streets off an inconsolable alley; a third corner, a dynamic schizoid street, shedding strips of decay as it catches up, pasting them frantically with thick paint, not quite fallen shreds.

Adults maintain a busy book-laden traffic to and from the many public libraries because reading is an important pleasure and no indication, as elsewhere, that a reader is a natural development from social pariah, forced back to libraries because he is elsewhere unloved.

A round lady serving at the bread counter of an exalted department store will, if you tell her you are looking for sliced bread for sandwiches to make and eat on a bench of the Chelsea Embankment, scurry around looking for a knife, leaving a line of customers because this more fires her imagination and delight in truancy. She will cut the bread for you in thick, grandmotherly slices and then wish you a very, very good day, beaming on your waywardness.

Valises, dogs, and prams are admitted to underground trains and buses, and on the latter, a conductress helps in getting them on, stowing if necessary, and getting them off.

Middle-aged ladies in slacks and sturdy seamen's jackets drive motorcycles wearing hard, spacemen helmets.

They still use "whilst" and "whence."

Worshipful Companies of Cordwainers, Ironmongers, Apothecaries, etc. maintain—sometimes on promises made in the Middle Ages— almshouses whose cottages border a small garden, in shapes and style suitable to the ruralness that once surrounded them.

Streets can be dingy, but rarely dirty. The litter of cigarette packets, empty and crumpled, of depleted candy wrappers, cigarette butts, bus tickets, and newspapers is saved for the tops of buses. Theater and cinema floors take on candy boxes and emptied ice-cream cups.

People are good-natured, possibly because they get plenty of sleep. Telly closes down fairly early as do most restaurants. Except on Friday and Saturday nights, there are no late movie shows, and those very few, except for the naked girl films in Soho, a neighborhood exempt from almost all early-closing categories. Pubs close at eleven, and most Londoners cannot afford to go on to gambling and discothéques, frequently closed to nonmembers.

You can usually walk on the grass in the parks and sunbathe on it, in any costume short of absolute nudity you care to devise, or for sixpence, hire a deck chair for more decorous lolling.

Producing commemorative plaques for some remarkably obscure people who once stopped on London soil is a prolific industry. However, there are streets in noncentral, but not too obscure, areas where there is no street sign for blocks and blocks; if you don't know where you are you shouldn't be there seems to be the principle.

A man will stop to advise you if he sees you turning a map or bewildered by the names on a bus stop and then go on to cordial conversation, but he may not say a word to you if you invade his local pub.

The telephone number chosen for the Royal Opera box office is COVent Garden 1066.

It may be the cautiousness of modern science or an echo of numerous London plagues that causes date cards in library books to be marked, "If infectious disease should break out in your house do not return this book, but inform the Librarian at once." The penalty for not doing so is five pounds.

Complaint is not at all or remarkably indirect. A scholar of Oriental painting, burdened with a rueful thought—perhaps for years—ultimately finds the place to vent it, on the label of a Japanese painting of the sixteenth century in the British Museum. The painting is of scholars who have put their books aside and are now drinking and talking and enjoying music. Following a few explanatory phrases, the label says: "The good humor associated with scholarship in the Far East has never made any headway in the West."

The international bagel, sold in East End bakeshops, from stalls in Wentworth Street (part of the Petticoat Lane Market) and sacks outside of Bloom's chopped liver and chicken soup dispensary, are thinner, more handmade, and consequently misshapen, and dry out more quickly than the New York variety.

Expense, designing talent and skillful labor have gone into making statues, columns, garlands, masks, and shields applied to buildings of Portland stone. The stone inclines to streaking and sootiness and makes neglected tombstones of white temples.

As mentioned, a library is an important entity. An impressive new branch, a tall-arched aristocrat, is immediately north of the Kensington

High Street. Another is circles of shelves around long and broad purple benches and blue, and airy spirals of stairs to reach upper sections, part of a modern community center, near the Swiss Cottage Station, that includes pools, exhibition space, grounds where outdoor sculpture shows are held, and a well-thought-out small theatre—the whole very much worth seeing, particularly if your idea of a community center means the smell of overused lockers and grubby rooms in which shawled old ladies sit on splintered benches.

In spite of occasional remissions, the winter is unspeakable, a period of being imprisoned in a cold bath no matter where one goes, indoors or out. Ordinary daylight is afraid to face the weather and shows its wan, thin face very sparsely; one goes to work in murky lamplight clouded in fog and returns home in the same dark mist. Shops look poverty-stricken because electric power is expensive, and only the queens can afford full radiance; only in the richest houses is there quite enough light for the look of warmth, if not the feeling. A sleeve-less, low-necked dinner dress becomes a badge of valor, and the absorption of substantial quantities of whiskey and wine essential.

# 6    Guildhall Museum

Having become acquainted with some of the personae, it might be worth an hour to see the props, divided between the Kensington Palace Museum and the Guildhall Museum, the former ordered, well lit, and affording an occasional glimpse of Princess Margaret's garden. The latter rests behind the Corinthian columns of the Royal Exchange, a forbidding Neoclassic building, but still a fine place for viewing a Roman floor found in Bishopsgate and the statue of a Roman warrior found in Camomile Street, very close by. It may have been the same warrior who left a beautifully sewn small girdle in a piece of Roman wall near Walbrook and who possibly left also a pair of Roman sandals. The life of ordinary Romans is reflected in knives, spoons, plates, glass, and pottery, some local and some highly glazed and sophisticated in form and ornamentation, brought from Gaul. Roman sculpture unearthed in local streets, tools for carpentry and metalwork, chains, brooches, a model of the Mithraic temple on Walbrook and a superb, attenuated bronze hand that reminds one of Marini, by an unknown Roman craftsman, were left by the early conquerors.

Of medieval times a high-backed Norman shoe that would sell well on King's Row now; brooches and rings, swords and knife sheaths, the dress and shoes worn by citizens of London in the Middle Ages, and a few pieces of church art, among them a masterly twelfth-century torso of Christ worked in walrus tusk, and, from the gateway of Bethlehem (Bedlam) Hospital, a sculpture of "Melancholy and Raving Madness," two life-size and terribly literal figures with shaved heads, one of them in chains.

Shoes manage to last somehow, and here there are several samples of several periods: skin shoes, leather sandals, a young lady's boot of stamped leather covered with varicolored tassels and several pairs of sixteenth- and seventeenth-century shoes with wide, round fronts. The shoes appear in a collection of leather objects, from hoods for hawks to a mural worked in leather cupids, flowers, birds, and leaves; a leather beer bucket and leather lantern to an immense nineteenth-century bellows, five feet wide or more, used in the shop of a wheelwright. Pottery and pipes, caps and curlers for plumes; beakers, pins, candlesticks, sedan chairs, exquisitely beribboned, embroidered and painted gloves, an old fire wagon and a model of the last state barge built in 1807, all gold and classical statuary—the minutiae and the ceremonial objects that touched London people at one time or another. Somewhere in the collection there is the treasure trove of coins found in Cannon Street in May, 1658. The sign above it is symbol and symptom of the reasonable, indirect, educational—rather than warning—tone commonly used in these matters. It explains carefully that such treasure troves normally belong to the Crown, but that the City of London was granted the rights to its own finds. You are then informed that such treasure is usually worth more in market value than hoarding it might ultimately bring or reducing it to its basic silver or gold. Also—the understated "by the way"—it is an illegal thing to keep such treasures, should you come on one.

Free, open weekdays 10 A.M. to 5 P.M. Bank or Mansion House stations. Buses 6, 9, 15.

# 7    Chelsea

One Saturday morning, resist the thousand promising, unrevealed bargains in the antiques-discards-old-clothes markets, and go instead to Chelsea, before the big parade of King's Road shapes up. Much of the world that reads and watches television has a view of Chelsea as the one road, the long room of a permanent masked ball. Not so. Behind the lightning colors and tinsel inventions lives a community that works, worries about its children's schooling, pays too much rent, tends its garden, and often dresses as simply and conservatively as it can, to sever itself from the flashy billboard road. (One rebel rides his bicycle through the heaped and tangled ribbons of bright color in a tidy black suit, bowler hat square across his brow, furled umbrella and rolled paper strapped before him, the look of "forever England" on his indomitable face.)

About 11 A.M. is a good time to go, and across King's Road from Lincoln Street a good place to stand. The sleepy and shaggy are beginning to crawl into the nearby coffee hangout for their eye-openers or to try their stomachs on a sandwich in the corner delicatessen (sort of). On the corner, backed by supplying trucks, a radiant fruit stall whose customers often present a fair cross section of the community which, like other London villages, runs the full economic and social gamut. First on the fruit line is a couple already made up for the afternoon show, hung with bells and beads and flowing purple satin; behind them, a suede suit from the Faubourg St. Honoré accompanied by a hundred-guinea suit from a traditionalist on Savile Row; behind them, a square lady in baggy tweeds that refuse to die, tweeds and lady shrieking "middle, middle of the middle, class"; and behind her, in his perky cap and many-buttoned uniform, a Chelsea pensioner from the nearby Christopher Wren's Royal Hospital, clutching a few pennies for the apple he will present to a young Irish girl who serves in the local Woolworth's and with whom he thinks he is flirting.

Almost any turning will display engaging streets of neatly kept houses, many of them of the early eighteenth century, joining at minute, irregular centers planted with a handkerchief of flowers and a tree. Try Lincoln Street, and follow it into the nest of paths in which it disappears. Or Jubilee Place and its exuberance of small gardens in which fringed and fanged Chinese dragon tulips grow in

48

April. That leads to Elystan Place and a microscopic green considered large enough to hold flaming tulips and two trees whose branches are lost in clouds and showers of blossoms.

Walk across the road toward the river, and follow the webs that surround Christchurch Street or the interlacings between Flood Street and Oakley Street, and farther west, the various Cheynes leading to Cheyne Walk and Chelsea Embankment. Near the river, your strolling should be slower, to linger at the river and to find a few specific places of particular interest. You are in Carlyle, Turner, Whistler, Rossetti, Swinburne, George Eliot country—to pick out a few of the illustrious —studded with fine old houses, and on the embankment itself, an unusual group, the break between Victorian and Art Nouveau, built by Richard Norman Shaw. Look in at Swan Walk and Paradise Walk (as recently as the beginning of the current century scabrous slums), and examine Tite Street, in its own way the most extraordinary street in Chelsea. In the eighties it became a studio street, not for the impecunious, but rather for the noblesse like Whistler whose eccentric, imposing white house still stands (No. 35) among a number of bold, individualistic houses, one of them once inhabited by Oscar Wilde and nearby another by the judge who sent him to prison.

At the end of Cheyne Walk, Chelsea Old Church, almost totally demolished in 1941 and subsequently restored and fortunately still possessed of a number of sixteenth- and seventeenth-century monuments, of which the most interesting might be, for you, that of the Gothic tomb of Sir Thomas More, who kept his house in the fishing village of Chelsea. Of an earlier time (mid-fifteenth century) there is a relic of another prominent London citizen, the powerful wool merchant Sir John Crosby. It is the hall of his palace in Bishopsgate (p. 69), a princely room with a superb wooden roof in an elaboration of arches and pendants, moved to Chelsea when the palace was demolished. Of itself an imposing place it is, in addition, as Professor Pevsner points out, "invaluable . . . evidence of how sumptuously fifteenth century merchants built in London." At the foot of Lindsey Row, nearby, Handel conducted his *Water Music*.

Try another route back, perhaps via Beaufort Street and its tangents, into the stage tropics of The Road, once Charles II's private road for reaching the house of Nell Gwyn. (To reach *her* house in Cheyne Walk, the queen had her private road built, now Royal Hospital Road.)

It should be about two thirty or three now, and King's Road is on, the stage crowded with young from everywhere in London except the area south of the river which keeps itself to itself, refusing to acknowledge any of the carryings-on to the north.

The indigenes continue the rounds of their Saturday chores in their ordinary slacks and sweaters, one arm pulled by the weight of a shopping bag full of groceries, the other dragged by sheets and towels from the laundromat. The rest is the *passeggiata* as London has known it for a long time, once in Piccadilly and, earlier, on the greens fronting the Inns of Court, to mention only two exhibition sites. It is exhibitionism in its least pejorative connotations: explosions of color to counter drab weather and drab families, to escape from one's time and its uniforms, permission to pose and appear singular. The masquerade eases the crossing of class lines, real or imagined, and supplies the proscenium for which there is, apparently, a strong London yearning. This is the field for drag—male, female, and comfortably mixed—also traditional, in a long line that runs from Shakespeare's boy Juliet and female princes in pantomimes to the young couple in an electric-guitar whirling-lights club who wear each other's clothing —she in his blue jeans and large shirt, he in her pink tights and Pucci-print blouse.

Almost above all, the Saturday afternoon display releases an indelible romanticism. It is not necessarily a romanticism that means Byronic hauteur or Shelleyan weightlessness, though these can be seen, but a romanticism that flows from wherever romanticism is or was for the present-day young: English history and literature, of course; and early films; the periodicals of the turn of the century; Art that is Nouveau and pre-Raphaelite; and the modern romanticism that hopes to be discovered as model or starlet, fantasies stimulated by photographers and agents who explore the parade.

From literature there is the cynical prettiness of Rimbaud, the manicured hand and touch of rouge of a Charlus, the tragic frailty of Keats; for the girls, the side screens of hair worn by Emily Brontë as her brother painted her, the dank tangled locks of the drowned Ophelia, and from the pre-Raphaelites, the mysterious forests of hair from which the whitened face peeps like a haunted spirit. Kyoto of 1890 provides the geisha-ghoul whose revenant look was considered highly evocative, and from Art Nouveau the snake body with the large, poison-pool eyes. From the movies, Theda Bara's hell-pit eyes over the plumed reptile boa, and the later Greta Garbo, crisply boyish as Ninotchka or reckless and doomed under the "Green Hat."

When they are not poets, the boys are Genghis Khan or Edwardian dandies or sailors in bell-bottom trousers and pea jackets, authentic or in tasteful adaptations of fine wool and exquisite cut. An aggressive masculinity expresses itself in broad, studded belts slanted low on the hips, fringed frontier jackets, and bulky Irish or Mexican sweaters.

The styles mingle and melt sexual clarities—as puffed, teased hair with curled ends and dips on the forehead, worn over the most belligerent of belts and an Eisenhower jacket of silver brocade finished in velvet collar and cuffs on one young man; or a girl with a Medusa storm of black hair, tight black trousers, black boots, black gloves, eager to be a storm trooper. The beauties carefully designed around their innate potentials: the young man with tawny hair and beard in fawn-colored corduroy with shirt, boots, and dashing Italian hat to match and the beautiful *café au lait* girl who has dyed her hair *café au lait* and manages to suggest the dark gold of women in north Italian paintings. Then there are the waifs, valiant and pale, breasting the damp cold in miniskirts and plastic flowered jackets and floppy hats to match. The waif couples holding hands—less like sexual partners than babes in the woods—can be particularly appealing, perhaps a very young and pregnant girl with a flow of yellow hair, wearing an old policeman's cape and her man, a small slender boy with almost equally long brown hair, his arm around her shoulder protectively, walking her slowly, carefully, through the crowds.

If you can't push your way through the full route, try to take and hold a position between the Kenco coffee shop and a place called Guys 'n' Dolls near Lincoln Street, a short distance beyond Sloane Square, where for some reason, the densest clottings linger. Or brave it on, for a look at the shops, the open-air Chelsea art shows indoors and out, maybe the Antiques Fair that sits in the Chelsea Town Hall for ten days in April and a similar period in the fall. Follow King's Road to see it debouch, as it turns, into respectability with a row of food and wine shops and a Woolworth's, then scratched houses slapped by the noise of buses, and beyond, an old painter's pub (once upon a time), called World's End, in a working-class London where Mum shares a glass of ale with her young child while Dad discourses inside the pub.

## Chelsea Flower Show Spring

Spring in London is when the banking stolidity of Lombard and Threadneedle streets put on flower boxes and yellow-blossomed weeds sprout in the bombed-out lots across the river from the Tate Gallery, gentling the contours of the brick and stone rubble over which the local boys scramble while their little sisters pick the yellow flowers.

It is when the cold rain lashes the petals off the trees and drives them to the streets to lie as damp pink-and-white confetti and the gray skies and the gray macs and the gray faces have been drained of color by the savage tulips like great, gaudy victory urns, the blood drunk by the fierce red and purple azaleas that threaten from every garden, the bodies strangled by the ropes of yellow pearls hanging from the laburnum trees and the million little rubies of the May tree. It is the time when announcements are published for fairs, performances, band concerts, processions, celebrations, a variety of amusements, all outdoors, once more, as every year for centuries, in the undying gallant hope that this summer it will not rain quite as much as last.

It is the time for the Chelsea Flower Show. Immense and an important one to people who measure such importance, it operates on a scale of prices (and consequently, class) that reaches its lowest entrance fee on the last day when, if one lasts it, flowers and plants are sold cheaply and sometimes given away at closing. It is the most crowded day and for a nonhorticultural visitor the best. The vast lawns of Christopher Wren's Royal Hospital in Chelsea are partially covered with a group of large tents that suggest jousting tournaments, and the extensive rest with thousands of little chairs, holding laps filled with box lunches on sturdy, tired legs in cotton stockings and sensible shoes, and snack pavilions dispensing coffee, tea, sweets, and those little flat sandwiches to interminable lines.

The flower displays are, as expert flower displays should be, myriad and unbelievably beautiful, especially to one who doesn't know that a rose can be lavender or seemingly made of rich satin shaded from cream gold to shocking pink, a heavy-lidded, arrogant *grande cocotte*. There are tropical jungles of jutting, crawling, smooth, and spiny cactus and *Midsummer Night's Dream* gardens of gossamer and silvery webs, pearly bells, and blossoms like pink butterflies. The delphiniums soar with the assurance of Florentine towers, and the spotted dahlias, strict in design and demeanor, ready to scold. At the side of one tent a treasure of strawberries, yellowish pink, wide and flattened, shaped like Dali watches and smelling of paradise.

Possibly not as beautiful, not smelling so sweetly, but certainly as varied are the human flora gaping, judging, making notes, collecting brochures, or just ambling the day away. Mainly, the ladies in their pink or baby blue sections of chimney pots set on, but in no way related to, their heads; the stout ladies with the merciless haircuts and sagging stockings and shapeless sweaters who, were they Parisian and unsmiling, would be concierges. A group of schoolboys in uniform blazers, brought by an enthusiastic teacher, show no enthusiasm for the plants or flowers but don't mind being out near where the ice

cream is. Pairs of middle-aged gentlemen with the cadences of Shoreditch discuss the merits of this tulip over that to nurture in their
patches of front yard. Contemplating the tulips, too, stands a gentleman in bowler, black skinny suit, gloves, and furled umbrella, his
face pared to a caricature of fierce nose winged with bushes of
mustache. A couple of "beats" drag their boas and India-print raja
coats slowly through the crowd, impeding the progress of the sensible
intellectuals. The intellectuals are a bit self-conscious about being here,
participating in a too basic English tradition and a passion they scorn,
but their new flat came with a terrace, so what can you do? Among
them, rooted like sturdy trees, are the elderly discussers in groups
of three and four, all in some variant of cap, long, sensible gray
raincoat, large black umbrella, and a string bag holding a sandwich
and the newspaper, and one realizes not only that the English young
are erasing superficial sexual difference, but that it is not a new
tendency; the working-class and intellectual middle-aged and elderly
have been at it for some time.

# 8   Syon House

A short bus ride (267 or 117) from Kew Gardens, going westward, brings you into the colorless community of Brentford (nothing left of the spirit it showed in 54 B.C. when it tried to keep Caesar's legions from crossing the Thames), and next to a used-car lot that sports a collection of vintage MG's, a gated entrance to large fields, golden boxes of hay, and black and white cattle lolling at the side of a path. The house you soon view, beyond two boxes of gatehouse, is a simple matter: low, broad, bordered by short towers and the teeth of crenellations, less noble than its Canaletto presentation. Over the center of the façade stands a lion with a long, alert tail that disappears as you approach the house; justly, because it is not indigenous to the house, brought here from Northumberland House in Charing Cross before it was demolished in the nineteenth century, and, in any case, it is an Italian lion, modeled after one by Michelangelo.

The Duke and Duchess of Northumberland still use sections of the house, including the rooms on public view several afternoons of the week, a knowledge which adds a certain warm expectancy that makes you think you hear the sounds of a baby crying at the top of a forbidden stairway or—until you know better—wills you into thinking that the engaging man, lavish with his time and information and enthusiasm, who is apparently in charge of the public parts and times of the house is the duke himself. (He isn't; a delightful man nevertheless.) One comes to Syon primarily to see some of the divine doodling of Robert Adam executed by inspired workmen, Italianate classicisms, Pompeian garlands and grotesques, gilded fronds and mosaic designs like jewelry and plasterwork that might be ivory carving. The exquisite jungle of decoration gathered by the most fashionable designer of his time is, however, a late show of pomp in a mighty family represented in almost every important event of British history.

You remember Hotspur, an indelibly vivid character in Shakespeare's *Richard II* and *Henry IV*. He was a Percy and a Northumberland, the family who helped destroy Richard II. The guilt that descended from Henry IV, the Bolingbroke who wrested the throne from Richard II, to his son, Falstaff's friend and later Henry V, forced the latter to build one of three expiatory monasteries a short distance from the present house.

When Henry VIII chose to have no more of his first Catherine and her church, Syon was conspicuously rife with opposition to the king; here Elizabeth Barton, a Cassandra of her time, had visions of doom and for them was executed at Tyburn, as were other members of the community. Thomas Cromwell condemned the whole establishment by sending agents to find the monastery (more strictly a nunnery, in the modern sense) a foul den of sin, pustulant with the "incontinensies" of the nuns with the friars. The house was closed and, as Crown property, peculiarly used. After Henry VIII died in 1547, his coffin rested here one night on its way to Windsor. That night the coffin burst open, and the swollen, syphilitic corpse spilled matter that was licked up by the dogs, fulfilling an earlier prophecy that "the dogs would lick his blood as they had done Ahab's," if the king destroyed the monastery.

The year of Henry VIII's death, the Duke of Somerset, the protector for the young King Edward VI, became the owner of Syon, where he built his house in mid-sixteenth-century style, and began to set out gardens of rare plants. In the plotting and counterplotting that surrounded the sickly young king and his death, the duke lost one last round and was executed in 1553, along with the girl he kept on the throne for nine days, Lady Jane Grey, the niece of Henry VIII. The house became again court property, was a nunnery briefly under Catholic Mary (1557), and then again reverted to Elizabeth, who handed it over to a Percy, Henry, the ninth Earl of Northumberland. The young earl did well with the aging Elizabeth, buying smiles from the enameled, red-wigged face with gold for ships in which to meet the Spaniards. It was this earl who founded a great library and, as a patron of learning, subsidized the writer Thomas Hariot, who recorded the adventures and findings of Sir Walter Raleigh and his party, of which Hariot was a member, in Virginia.

The Gunpowder Plot? A Percy was a Catholic friend of Guy Fawkes, and since he had been seen at Syon House with his kinsman, the earl, the latter was imprisoned for life and fined an outrageously large sum. Although Northumberland offered Syon House, now improved to considerable splendor, to the king as payment of his fine, it was still the Tower for him. In the company of the confined Sir Walter Raleigh, with learned friends as visitors and the scientific equipment and books brought from Syon House, the not too dull years were spent, spotted with convivial times when Raleigh and the earl were able to produce potables in their experiments with liquor.

On paying one-third of the fine and after fifteen years of imprisonment, the scholarly earl was released.

A Percy was a governor of Jamestown and a fighter of Indians. In Cromwell's time Syon House was the place of decision to rid England of Charles, but it was at Syon that Charles' children were sheltered during a flare-up of the plague. It was during these political upheavals that the earl, in retreat from them, appointed Inigo Jones to make changes in the house and expanded his gardens of botanical exotica.

By the mid-eighteenth century, the incumbent Earl and Countess of Northumberland, living splendidly on the estate, found the house uncomfortable and decrepit. They called in Robert Adam in 1762, and Lancelot Brown, who it is said, was called Capability because he liked the word and often used it to describe the hopeful potential of the land with which he was to work. It was they who created the dazzling interiors and the flow of lawn, the meander of waters, and the sweep of one magnificent tree perfectly placed for accent and rhythm.

From the flat, inexpressive façade one moves into the startlingly Olympic Great Hall, a blinding whiteness of statues on pedestals, columned temple doorways, an apse that suggests a section of the Pantheon, and the ceiling a wonder of plasterwork on classic motifs, echoed by the simpler pattern of the floor tiles. The cool hall gives way to the extraordinary Anteroom, a waiting room for servants, whose looks and livery would have had to be of godlike splendor for this room. It is ringed with antique marble columns found in the bed of the Tiber, topped with golden statues, and between them panels of subtle green-blue studded with large golden ornaments, and a soft-beige plasterwork ceiling that sets off the bursts of color—red, blue, yellow in high shine and restless pattern—on the floor.

The infinite variety on a strict set of themes, the lines and arcs and loops and wedges and circles and rosettes and fronds and sunbursts, the graceful mannerisms of Adam's furniture dance on from room to room and into the long Gallery. Because of the extreme and difficult proportions of such rooms, long galleries are often lengths of unplanned clutter or not dealt with at all and left as tunnels of bareness. Here the length has been stopped by gaily painted pilasters and gilt ceiling patterns that appear to expand the narrow width and lead down to large lamps and cases of objects that, again, hold and stop the long flight.

A small Print Room, which is hung with family portraits, leads to a passage of Flemish paintings and a map of the area as it seemed to look in 1635, and that could be the end, except that you might take the short tour of the house just once again, this time to examine the details of magnificent Italian mosaic tables on Adam bases, the uncannily fine metalwork and plaster sculpture, and to look at the objects and the group of Stuarts in their silks and curls and jewels and best hauteur in the Red Room. Then on to the contrasting simplicity of the tearoom, a few yards away from the house and the easy pleasure of tea and cakes and buns made on the premises, as honest as "homemade" should be, and often isn't, and as honestly priced.

Open 1 to 5 P.M. (no admissions after 4:30). Wednesday, Thursday, Friday, Saturday, from March 31 to June 30; Sundays also from July 1 to September 29; and Mondays in August. Admission: three shillings for adults; one shilling sixpence for children. May be subject to change; check with tourist information, MAY 9191 or FRE 4933.

# 9  Fleet Street

Several of Canaletto's mid-eighteenth-century paintings of the Thames (painted under Venetian skies, at times, and St. Paul's seen as San Giorgio) show the great Wren dome and, trailing off in the large riverscape, above barges and small boats and low dockhouses, a fernery of towers. A good number of these suffered demolition, by direct means and neglect, in the nineteenth century and more in the 1939–45 war. Some have been revived and refurbished, some stand only as towers, and most of those in the City, their Sunday functions diminished—since there are so few City inhabitants on the weekend —act as assembly halls for quasi-religious meetings during the week, for concerts, lectures, debates, and, occasionally, special services.

Fleet Street and its environs still show something of Canaletto's lilting rhythms of tower: the ivory spindles that lift the weight of St. Paul's dome and the scruffy, frantic mood of Fleet Street, as one faces Ludgate Circus. From the west, approaching Fleet Street, St. Mary-le-Strand and St. Clement Danes, high-masted antique barks breasting the sea of Strand traffic, and in and out of the streets and alleys, towers and steeples and ancient significances.

From Victorian novels and memoirs one learns that the Victorian easily confused himself with God—or a close relation—and to house his power, he built on the design of the most awesome of God's edifices, the Gothic cathedral. That may account for the extraordinary number—in spite of much destruction—of small and large Victorian Gothic temples. At times it reaches zaniness, like a set of Gothish houses on Eastcheap that, nevertheless, make a bright spot of rouged levity on a dusty old face. At times, they appear to be such extraordinary, stunning feats that one overlooks the esthetic in contemplation of the fact of the achievement. (St. Pancras Station, the Taj Mahal of stations, the most brilliant flourish of Victoriana—now, after its fall to contempt, newly cherished in the threat of demolition— is the prime staggering monument.) Another of its time, the Law Courts on Fleet Street (1868–82) persuades, maybe because it is *law* or possibly because the conception is nobler and less striving. The not too slavishly balanced façade leads into a quite wonderful Great Hall with enormously high rib-vaults, long arched windows obviously not meant to give light, a discretion of ornament and beautiful grillwork.

58

As you walk through, past dark arches that give on Stygian arches which should lead to hoary crypts, up to the balcony and past its doors (August is a good unbusy time when you will get in no one's way and enjoy the feeling of wandering in an abandoned abbey), you will notice that the lettering on the doors—QUEEN'S BENCH COURT, LORD CHANCELLOR OF LONDON COURT, FOR COUNSEL IN ROBES—is an attempt to harmonize with the building style. When telephones were introduced, however, they were apparently too discordant with the mood of the building, or maybe the GPO couldn't be bothered to order fancy lettering, so those indicators remain pedestrian modern, although what must also have been a disturbing innovation, the ladies' robing room, has the traditional curly sign. As you leave, have a look at the portraits of full-robed Lords Chancellors ranged in larger-than-life Olympian sternness and the easier monument to the designer, George Edward Street; once again at the fine grillwork and the oddity of a robing room outside the building proper at the side of the entrance, then at the Lord Chancellor of Victorian street clocks that emblazons the street.

The honeycomb of Temple Courts, Inner and Middle, can be reached on almost any turning off the south side of Fleet Street between Essex and Bouverie streets. Try the Middle Temple Gateway, of 1684, or to the east, the Inner Temple Gateway, a much restored, but authentically half-timbered, section of some seventy-five years earlier. Before you enter, however, look for the sign that leads to "Prince Henry's Room." No one here seems to care to specify which Henry it was, but an educated guess names him as the eldest son of James I, who seemed to have used it as a council room. After the roulades and fanfare of later houses you may have seen, this well-proportioned, comfortable room with few affectations is very satisfying. The wooden ceiling had been covered for 100 years or more, but thanks to wood borers discovered in the eighteenth century, the false ceiling was removed and the original revealed, to show the modest carving that echoes the decorations on the paneled walls. It is a room not too splendid to covet—"I could use a room like this"—until the trucks and buses on Fleet Street drive out the thought.

The room is one flight up in 17 Fleet Street and open from 1:45 to 5 P.M. on weekdays, closing at 4:30 on Saturday.

Three paces inside the gateway, and Fleet Street is gone and the snack shops and the "olde pubbyes" and the man-bearing cameras looking for Dr. Johnson, the waddling red buses and archaic, humane taxis, the Birmingham *Post* and the *Irish Independent*. Although it was much destroyed in recent bombings, and much reconstructed—not always with spirit—the large area is cocooned in a contemplative, retiring-from-the-world calm. No cars move or sit in its ramble of courts and passages, and although a number of listings in the houses seem to be those of private flats, no little girls chalk these paths with hopscotch boxes. It is still a place for the study of law, as it was in the fourteenth century when it was the property of the order of St. John (p. 197). They had it from the suppressed powerful order of Knights Templar who had moved to this land on the river from Holborn in the twelfth century. There are few *musts* here except that one must give the Temples slow, ruminative time, ambling and stopping among the buildings of a number of centuries and pseudo-centuries, some aristocrats, like the Wren buildings on King's Bench Walk, some inoffensive fillers of bombed-out space. Following the Lamb and His Cross penned over doorways of the Middle Temple (and Pegasus for the Inner) wander through the late-seventeenth-century New Court with its square blue, white, and gold clock, through the court of the fountain and trees, in and out of stands of neo-old heavy buildings and sections of the authentic, buildings marked TREASURY and LIBRARY that give off musty old-gold echoes, gentle lamps, houses named for Dr. Johnson, for Goldsmith, who died here, and for Lamb, who was born here.

Each Temple area is setting for its particular gem. About midway and west of Middle Temple Lane sits the Middle Temple Hall, originally of the mid-sixteenth century, with some later additions, a survivor of law-student feasting, masques, and plays (among them, reputedly, a performance by Shakespeare's company of his *Twelfth Night* early in 1602), of the weight of vessels and tankards on the serving table (tradition has it made of wood from the *Golden Hind*, Drake's victorious ship), but not of twentieth-century bombings which virtually destroyed the hall. Piece by piece the magnificent hammer-beam roof and the rarely beautiful carved wooden screen were put together, and again the students sit, accumulating the sittings that mark their law-learning terms. (That accounts for the fact that the hall is closed to visitors between noon and 3 P.M.)

Walking with Thackeray, Sir Walter Raleigh, Henry Fielding, William Congreve, James Boswell, Sheridan, Wycherly, and a shadowy host of others, go into the Temple Church, adjoining Inner Temple Lane. Remarkably untouched by the Great Fire of 1666, it succumbed to bombing three centuries later, when not only the fabric of the church but an irreplaceable set of medieval effigies were destroyed. Carefully restored, the church now appears as the gathering of styles and meanings through the centuries that it was before the bombings. Not only is its situation unique physically, but it is also a "liberty" of the city (free from certain civic laws), is connected with no parish, is not within the network of churches supervised by the Bishop of London, is subject only to the sovereign, who appoints the Master of the Temple.

The order of Knights Templar, having moved to their splendid New Temple on the Thames, built their Round Church on the style of the Church of the Holy Sepulcher in Jerusalem, and enlarged it in the middle of the thirteenth century. The booklet the church issues insists that the Round Church is transitional in style, Norman melding with Gothic. According to Professor Nikolaus Pevsner, it is no such thing, being Norman and Gothic side by side, but for the inexpert, it is enough to enter a Norman doorway of successively recessed columns and round bands of archway adorned with abstract and leaf designs and into the arches and vaults of Gothic, "one of the earliest Gothically conceived and executed buildings in England." The thirteenth-century chancel is a nobly proportioned hall of clustered marble shafts that fan out to delicately ribbed vaulting. Of quite another kind of elegance, the reredos designed by Wren, once discarded along with Wren pews and pulpit by the Gothic revival of the mid-nineteenth century, only the reredos brought back from a museum which fortunately offered shelter until their restoration in 1953.

Many old and much-changed churches, especially those that no longer house ardent religious fervor, have a museum atmosphere, rather than that of a church, and it is in this mood that you will probably look at the grotesques on the walls and the capitals and tombs that survive, including the famous thirteenth-century effigies, whose crossed or uncrossed legs may or may not mean that they were Crusaders (the argument goes on). One of the marble worthies in bishop's robes, his feet subduing a dragon, may have been the Bishop of Carlisle who fell from a horse in London in 1255, died, and was buried here. Whoever he was, he had been buried—as was revealed when the coffin was opened in 1810—with an infant, who may have been William Plantagenet, the son of Henry III. The discovery gave rise to interesting possibilities, the plainest one that stone coffins were expensive and that a dead infant, royal or not, was a very common object in the Middle Ages and disposed of where it decently might be, without fuss, and certainly safe at the legs of a holy man.

The Temple Church is closed on Sundays in August and September, and the hall may be closed; best to go on a weekday, in any case, when the striped-trousered gentlemen ply the Courts.

With a glance at the deplorable newness of the cloisters and old stone coffins lying at the side of the Round Church, and near the Master's House, a worn figure, beaten by rain and the droppings of pigeons, that of an eighteenth-century jurist in a splendid wig, lolling on his plinth as seductively as Mme. Récamier on her Empire couch, find your in and out way to the dignified Wren houses on King's Bench Walk and, perhaps, try one of the wines in the pub at the meeting of the Temple area with Tudor Street. Wander back into the Temple grounds to notice that stretches of lovely park leading to the Thames are closed to you and the rest of hoi polloi, reserved for the pleasure of local indigenes, leaving a bench here, a tree there, for the outlander.

The city, however, as always, provides pigeons and shrubs, a plot of flowers and ample seating on the Embankment immediately east of Temple Station.

Outside the park, nearer the river's edge, a monument of a white griffin with a fiery red tongue, the totem of the Corporation of the City of London. This guardian dragon, like the one on Fleet Street, guards the City at its western border.

Returning on Essex Street—look back at the impressive archway to the Embankment—you may, if you have voyeur's luck, stare at a couple necking fiercely at a desk marked, suitably, RECEPTION. Passion in a glass office building gives way to the calm of late-seventeenth-century houses with attractively carved doorways, one of the developments of the grasping, brilliant, cynical Dr. Barbon, or Barebone, the son of a fanatic, rabble-rousing, Praise-God Barebone (p. 202). The river site had early been the London pied-à-terre of the bishops of Exeter. It was known later as Leicester House for Robert Dudley, the Earl of Leicester, displaced by Elizabeth's Earl of Essex, Robert Devereux. A century later, Dr. Barbon had it, not without difficulties described by Sir John Summerson: "No sooner had he done so (acquired the property), however, than King Charles decided that it would make an excellent present for a faithful Earl who had done brave work in Ireland. An undignified scrabble followed: Barbon routing up the garden and pulling down the house, while the king and Privy Council pressed vainly for repurchase." Barbon was implacable, and within a year a street of brick houses, "for taverns, ale-houses, cookshops and vaulting schools" had marred forever the ancient pleasance of earls and bishops. A later Dr. Barbon may have been responsible for the stone hysteric sputtering columns and plaster turbulences that leads into Devereux Court, where Temple men take their lunches and pub refreshers between portraits of the earl and under a bust stuck high on an inner wall, battered enough and far enough from normal vision to be anyone long dead.

A minute passage east of Chancery Lane marks another section of Inns of Court, Clifford's Inn, now a sooty room of blind doors on a wall marked 1682 and 1782 and immediately east of that, St. Dunstan-in-the-West. Like many of the City churches, it has medieval beginnings and, unlike many, was not destroyed in the Great Fire when, according to the pamphlet issued by the church, the Dean of Westminster equipped forty scholars with water buckets and sent them in the middle of the night to douse the flames that were within arm's reach of the door. Inside its yards was one of the grammar schools established by Henry VI, neighbored by goldsmiths and, later, booksellers, and for centuries the church of the Worshipful Company of Cordwainers, who supervised a bequest of monies for the poor and young of the parish. Until World War II the children could earn extra money on the day of the annual distribution by running around the church, one penny for each circuit. The custom was not revived: There are few householders, much fewer children, in the parish, and for hours on end the only sound in the church is the lonely ticking of its clock over the dulled ground bass of Fleet Street traffic.

Inside the big Neo-Gothic octagon of the early nineteenth century, there are still some of the monuments of the earlier church buildings— the earliest a small bronze couple, kneeling, streamers of words, as in comic books, attached to their mouths. Other than its antiquity and the impressive names in its old vestry books—and the fact that Pepys tried to seduce a couple of girls here—the church has additional proud possessions: John Donne was a vicar in St. Dunstan-in-the-West; before the vestry door a statue of Queen Elizabeth I that bears no resemblance to any of the women in the numerous portraits; and a theatrical clock that figured frequently in London literature. Queen Elizabeth was taken from Ludgate (west of St. Paul's) where she stood until 1760, when that gate was destroyed. Now she stands in the minute yard, where you can gaze at her anonymous, placid features from a tall-backed wooden bench designed to echo her time, and examine as well two heads at the end of an arch, possibly King Lud, whose nose has disappeared, and his son, moved with the queen from Ludgate.

The upper area above the court is heavily beclocked. Imbedded in one side of the tower is an enormous diamond-shaped clock no longer in use; hanging over Fleet Street, an enormous plain black round clock, and above it, a classic temple that encases two life-size figures in Elizabethan cavemen robes, holding clubs. They strike the hours with their clubs on enormous bells, and one expects to be deafened by the thunderous noise, but a surprisingly frail sound, probably made impotent by the shrieking of brakes and crunch of tires, floats out.

Eastward on the street, stands Sir Christopher Wren's St. Bride's, rather like other Wren churches—an act of fidelity to its time, suggesting the curls and ribbons worn by its parishioners—except for its extraordinarily high steeple (the "wedding cake") and some of the interior detail. On the wall near the back, an appealing terracotta head, quite modern, of a child. It was dedicated to the first girl child born in North America, of parents who were St. Bride's parishioners. The most imposing details, however, are the numerous pews that bear memorial notices for newspapermen, editors, cartoonists, music publishers, and master printers that make the church of the Irish St. Bridget the "Journalists' Church," a reasonable designation for a church that baptized Pepys and buried Samuel Richardson. In an earlier version it buried the poet Lovelace and, much before him, the pioneer printer Wynkyn de Worde, one of the founders of Fleet Street publishing and printing.

Off Chancery Lane, or Chauncery, or Chauncerie, or Chancelar, or Chancerie, or, when the choices became foolishly numerous, New Street, there is a plaque signaling the long existence, going back to the fifteenth century, of a Sargeants' Inn, a house for the use of judges and sergeants of the numerous populace of "students, practicers or pleaders, and judges of the laws of this realm," that peopled the quarter. Near it, the Public Record Office, a long Victorian Gothic pile; two blocks away, a sign on an unimpressive corner tells that Thomas More studied there, probably before he went to Lincoln's Inn. The Inns of Chancery, which stood where you are now, had fewer students than the rest, being "as it were chiefly furnished with officers, attorneys, solicitors and clerks, that follow the courts of the King's Bench or Common Pleas. . . ."

The chapel in which the Public Record Office museum is housed has, like its neighbors, a colorful history. In 1233, the site and house which belonged to a Jew (possibly a descendant of a Jew brought from Rouen by William the Conqueror) were taken by Henry III. There the king built a house for converted Jews, and a church for them, the chapel to be used for the records of Chancery. "Since the which time, to wit, in the year 1290, all the Jews in England were banished out of the realm, whereby the number of converts in this place was decayed. . . . [Stow]" In 1377 the house was ceded to the Keeper of the Rolls of Chancery, the first of many whose names and arms appear on the stained glass of the chapel, now the museum.

In the steady accumulation of facts, literacy, and passion for the word, record offices spilled over and spread to other places for keeping. Somerset House, itself an eventful place where Edward, the Duke of Somerset, was building his palace while Shakespeare was writing his plays; where Inigo Jones, some fifty years later, was concerned with reshaping sections of the great house for Charles I's queen, Henrietta Maria, now keeps records up to fifty years, and then sends them down to the Public Record Office on Chancery Lane.

The first sonorous note of massed antique humanity is sounded in the vestibule, from the Domesday Chest in which that historic roster and other treasures were kept, first in the Palace of Westminster, then in the Chapter House of Westminster Abbey. It had three different locks, each controlled by its own key, each key held by one official, and it was only by consent of all three that the chest could be opened.

In a neat placement of cases around the walls and in the center of the chapel, arranged in roughly chronological order, ponderous documents of English history or minutiae that illuminate their times. Among the monumental, the Domesday Book (called doomsday because there was no appeal from the survey of properties), a census arranged by sworn inquest, for the purposes of taxation, by William the Conqueror. The results were readied and collated by the end of 1083 in two volumes, the larger covering more than thirty counties, including "Bockinghamscire, Oxenefordscire, Cornualge" among others, and a smaller volume that includes "Exsessa, Norfulc and Sudfulc." (If, from pride of lineage or hopes of claiming ancient lands, you need to present an item from the Domesday records, the Public Record Office will supply you with a translation.)

Soon follow the documents that moved large pieces of land from court to court, as gifts or bribes, like a casket of jewels. An illuminated charter of 1234 transfers Gascony from Alfonso X, the King of Castile, Toledo, and León, to his brother-in-law Edward, the eldest son of Henry III, in what was probably part of a marriage contract. A dourly illuminated piece of parchment with shiny ornaments and a sketch of a tight, little fortress-castle creates the principality of Aquitaine, which Edward III grants his oldest son, Edward, Prince of Wales, the "Black Prince"; the date is 1362. A curious chart of crudely drawn swans' heads shows all the beaks differently marked (this list covers 1497 to 1504) to make clear who owned what swans, royal birds not available to any but those granted special license to keep them.

Among the letters of the sometime powers of Henry VIII's time, those signed by the hands of Thomas Cranmer and Thomas Cromwell and that of the mighty Cardinal Wolsey, fallen from the king's grace, asking him for mercy and pardon after his indictment. Of the later sixteenth century, the giant shadows of Mary, Queen of Scots, John Knox, Robert Dudley, and from Elizabeth's "Golden Boy," the Earl of Essex, thrown to disgrace by his failures in Ireland (and, perhaps, the royal mercurial temperament), a graceful, ornate and groveling note: "Haste paper, to that happy presence whence only unhappy I am banished. Kiss thatt fayre correcting hand which layes new plasters to my lighter hurtes, butt to my greatest woond applyeth nothing. Say thou cummest from shaming, languishing, despayring S.X."

Catherine de Médicis is here, on paper, and Henry of Navarre and

Guy Fawkes; Richelieu congratulating Charles I on the birth of a son and heir to the throne; a letter dated 1762 from Catherine the Great of Russia advising George III that she had become ruling head of all the Russias. Somewhere near the signatures of Marie Antoinette, Frederick the Great, Gladstone, and Burke, the big, gorgeous screed of Napoleon Bonaparte; letters from Florence Nightingale and Garibaldi and the hand of Karl Marx as a stockholder in the Industrial Newspaper Company.

Records that affected the lives of anonymous millions are here: a copy of the Magna Carta and plea rolls, dating back to 1194, that evolved as the Court of Common Pleas.

The wills are signed by Purcell, by Handel, by Lady Hamilton, leaving her all to her daughter, Horatia Nelson, and by William Shakespeare or Shakspeare (he signed both ways, in the comfortable carelessness of his times). Out of the fact that he left most of his money to his daughter, Susanna, and her husband, deeding only his second-best bed to his wife, much has been made of the unhappy marital life of a man of whom one knows little. Something, though, can be fairly conjectured about Will and his wife from the position of the bed phrase. It is interlineated, as if the bequest had been entirely omitted and then, after nudging by daughter, or clerk, or wife herself, an afterthought line was scratched in between two others.

Documents referring to the Colonies are represented by a letter from George Washington to George III, most respectful and cordial; a round robin of signatures that is a promise of a company of Walloons to emigrate and live in Virginia and the Olive Branch Petition, the last plea before the Revolution, offered by a group of moderates in 1775, asking for concessions, for improved solutions of the Colonies' difficulties with the mother country. In a neighboring case, one major disappointment: The letter from David Livingstone describing his meeting with Stanley makes no mention of that famous phrase devised to stand for all English understatement, "Dr. Livingstone, I presume."

There is a graphologist's field day in the signatures of all of Henry VIII's queens, of that of Richard II, the Charleses, the Jameses, the Georges, of Queen Anne, of William and of Mary, to the signed Coronation Roll of Elizabeth II. In the center cases, the tenuous, broken threads back to some of their forebears, to the great seals and charters of early kings and a case full of large seals that represented eighty-seven barons, meant to be attached to a letter to the Pope protesting that the King of England was not to submit to Rome in the matter of the dominion of Scotland—a letter probably never sent but already indicative, centuries before Henry VIII, of resistance to papal rule. That resistance appears concrete and final in a valuation of bishoprics, monasteries, and other ecclesiastical holdings in England and Wales prepared for the Crown in 1535.

In the faded sepia of old ink, one can read—if one could read it—of the accidental death of a boy in play with another and of later times, the affidavit of a constable who apprehended one of the rescuers of a Thomas Jones, signed by the justice of the peace, Henry Fielding, shortly before his book *Tom Jones* appeared. The fog of time clears, and light falls on the oldest parliamentary writs, dated 1275; on a beautifully illuminated Statutes of Parliament scroll, 1327 to 1460; and on the file of Welsh men at arms who fought at Agincourt, 1415.

Lieutenant William Bligh reports the mutiny on the *Bounty* and his subsequent 3,600-mile journey in an open boat. Sir Francis Drake reports a victory over the Spanish Armada. Darwin accepts by letter the job of naturalist, at no pay, on the *Beagle*. Rubens wrote letters, as did Van Dyck and Inigo Jones and William Byrd, and some of them found their way here, along with those of Boswell, Addison, Steele, Shelley, De Quincey, Scott and Milton, Francis Bacon and Ben Jonson. In one case, Sir Philip Sidney's last letter, written the day before he died, in another, the writ pertaining to the death of Christopher Marlowe of a dagger blow in a tavern in Deptford (p. 185). There are old treaties and new, signed by the kings of France and Portugal and England, bearing glorious seals and no probity; echoed, without the glamour of ribbons and seals, in a signed treaty with Hitler, dated 1937.

The enormous encyclopedic spread extends over the earliest piece of English printing, an indulgence issued in 1476 to a London couple who had contributed to a late Crusade against the Turks. And, almost best for last: a piece of pale writing, dated 1378, in which G. Chaucer, controller of the Wool Quay of the Port of London, appoints a deputy to carry on until his (Chaucer's) return to London, probably authentic because the job was given Chaucer on the condition that he keep records in his own hand, the practiced hand—not common in his time—of an educated man who wrote much.

Mondays to Fridays, 1 to 4 P.M. Free. Temple or Chancery Lane stations; several buses.

# 11  Bishopsgate and Tangents
to the Tower

Spreading fanlike, east of the dusty upstairs and downstairs confusions of Liverpool Street Station, its two shillings and sixpence, no-decoration lunch neighbors and overdecorated coffeehouses, crammed clothing shops open on Sunday and its once grand, anachronistic hotels, lies a web of churches, alleys, and markets, displaying symptoms of antiquity, or simply decay, that move from charm to horror and back almost too closely and quickly to be absorbed. Much of it is held on the broad string of Bishopsgate, now a busy avenue that specializes in foreign banking—and a few other reminders of the Empire, one of them at 97 Bishopsgate, a narrow building of a tea merchant studded with enormous numerals and letters, in a blatant showy commercialism that appears more American than Dickensian (and if one knows something of Victorianism, as it acted and as it visibly shows in London, the translation of Victorian to "brash U.S. confident" can be made with remarkable ease).

At its meeting with Wormwood Street, Bishopsgate wears a golden bishop's miter to mark the medieval wall gate, repaired, rebuilt, and finally destroyed in the mid-eighteenth century, leaving only the miter and the name of St. Botolph Without (Bishopsgate) as reminders not only of the London of the Middle Ages, but of the Roman's *Londinium* whose walls were rather the same. A few steps away, at the side of the Great Eastern Hotel on Liverpool Street, you will find the plaque marking the site of the first Hospital of St. Mary of Bethlehem, "a hospital for distracted people," the famous Bedlam, which stood here from 1247 to 1676. Equipped with whatever evocative powers these two symbols of antique London can lend you, walk in among the flower beds and benches of the local St. Botolph's (there are three in the City) immediately south of Liverpool Street, having stepped over the now imaginary ditch which once bordered the churchyard wall, full of "soilage of houses, with other filthiness cast into the ditch, the same is now [late sixteenth century] forced to a narrow channel, and almost filled up with unsavoury things, to the danger of impoisoning the whole city." This noisome mess came, it was said, from houses inhabited by Frenchmen.

The interior of the present church, though built in the eighteenth century on layers and layers of church dating back to the early thirteenth, is furnished largely in Victorian style, with a strong, deeply carved Georgian pulpit and lectern and, in back of the pews, an unusual screen of leaded glass in paisley-leaf sections. At the base of the galleries run the names of the rectors of the church, starting with a John of Northampton for whom no date is given, to Henry of Colne, 1323, and on to people with surnames, of later times. There seem to be no monuments—or they are obscured—to the fact that Edward Alleyn, the founder of Dulwich College (p. 217), was baptized here in 1566, nor that Keats was, in 1795. A pleasing church, but not a particularly interesting one as it now stands. It is the outer environs that provide the interest: a small red-brick school building of 100 years ago, its doorway surrounded by brightly painted figures of a boy and girl and to one side of the building, a sign of the owners, the Fan-makers' Company, whose hall this is now and available, as a number of guild halls are, for letting to organizations for parties and dinners. On a weekday, particularly at noon, the benches are the property of local white-collar workers and the cement-spotted men here to rebuild London come to eat their sandwiches or read their postluncheon newspapers. On weekends it belongs to the sleeping men who have tottered and oozed out of Spitalfields to sleep on the benches and grass of the churchyard, giving to the neat red brick church, with its pale nursery-colored ceiling, a look of itself being derelict, particularly in the still emptiness of the weekend.

Below Camomile Street that, combined with its extension as Wormwood Street, suggests it might have been once an apothecary's row or that of spice merchants, sits St. Ethelburga's, almost obscured to invisibility by the bank buildings that press into its sides. Until the 1930's it housed small shop fronts, done away with when the street was widened, leaving a modest fourteenth-century stone archway and a vestry doorway to look for. St. Ethelburga's is minute, as all the medieval churches clustered on each other in this area probably were, and, since it was not damaged in the Great Fire of 1666, stayed its medieval self, with the necessary patchings for age and decay. The pillars are of the fourteenth century, and so are a good portion of the arches. The lovely modern screen, both frail and strong in Gothic design, the sturdy dark gallery and pews, and the solid lectern repeat the Gothic simplicity.

Back of the church, through a small door one enters a large, plain room, its refectory table holding some crockery waiting for tea, and a minute office, from which bounces a hospitable clerical gentleman who points you to the garden and warns that the two goldfish a church pamphlet has mentioned are now reduced to one. The huge goldfish, whose name is Jonah, seems not to mind his widowerhood, but pushes his belligerent goldfish face through the waters of a moss-covered fountain, built in this century to follow the Gothic style. The garden is a toy cloister garden, with a minute arcade, a stretch of flowers, the fountain that spits delicately rather than spurts, and, if you keep your eyes on Jonah, nothing to remind you of 1960's London. Eyes up, you are engulfed by newer heights, relieved, at one end, by an open view on an enormous stone vase sitting on classicky chunks over a strip of egg-and-dart design.

Having thanked the gentleman of the vestry who explains that Jonah isn't lonely because the tenches in the well keep him company and also—in one of those neat acts of symbiosis at which animals are better than humans—rub off the fungus to which Jonah is susceptible. Before you continue down Bishopsgate, look at the old iron coffer, once the alms box and damaged by thieves, then cross the street for a view of the beguiling seventeenth-century vane on the short tower.

Inside Great St. Helen's, sunk in the rubble of modern rebuilding, sits one of the most irritating churches in London, St. Helen's, Bishopsgate. It promises much, from its hidden, unexpected position, and its extraordinary double façade with soft, wavy contours. The twinship derives from the existence, from the early thirteenth century, of a nunnery church attached to a parish church. Both have magnificent timber ceilings and early arches and earlier arches, and as you stand in the doorway looking down the almost square breadth of the double church, the walls seem hung with large, elaborate treasures of funerary monuments. But you can't see them. The long lamps already lit show only enough to tease, and there is rarely anyone with the authority to turn on the rest, if that would help. One knows that there are very early tombs (of which the brilliantly painted Elizabethan suffer least, outgauding the obscurity), hanging like forbidden fruit on the wall. One knows that the church has fine bronzes, but there are always young women hiding them with their papers and sticks, the mild resentment doubled because they, and no one else, are given light. A piece of medieval masonry, the nun's "squint," is luckily visible, and a Victorian screen that stops dead in the middle, having stretched across the parish section of the church. By climbing over the legs of the rubbers, behind narrow plywood dividers that set off church offices in a slapdash way, one can find a couple of alabaster monuments carved in the hieratic medieval style, one lady's gown adorned with all-over tracery, hardly discernible under the dust.

With one last frustrated look at the teasing curves and figures, the dimly discerned convexities and concavities of sixteenth- and seventeenth-century tombs, one peers back just to make sure that that *is* a refrigerator standing where a nuns' altar might have been (it is) and out into uncomplicated Bishopsgate, wondering why the City of London doesn't ask young people from the art schools to dust the monuments occasionally, and how much really would it cost to let there be light on one of the potentially fascinating churches of the City? Maybe, by the time of publication and reading, it all will have been happily changed.

St. Helen's Place is symbolically cut off from the street by iron gates leading to a row of newish buildings, one of them the Leathersellers' Hall, styled on the Place des Vosges in Paris. In the depths of the London Marais *palais,* there is a modern turnstile for entering cars to return to Bishopsgate and a passage inside the building that leads to St. Mary Axe and the Church of St. Andrew Undershaft.

If your eye can demolish the smother of buildings around the church, cover the now empty space with merchants' houses, a great Fletchers' Guild Hall, and the principal Maypole in Cornhill, standing before the parish Church of St. Andrew (therefore called Undershaft) where the Mayings took place, when "the citizens of London of all estates, lightly in every parish, or sometimes two or three parishes joining together, had their several mayings, and did fetch in May-poles with divers warlike shows, with good archers, morris dancers, and other devices, for pastime all the day long; and toward the evening they had stage plays, and bonfires in the streets [Stow]." Garrett Mattingly describes the day it stopped in his superb biography *Catherine of Aragon:*

The Ill May Day, 1517, was long remembered as the most dangerous riot disorderly Tudor London saw. More and more English were crowding into the warren of mean streets that ran down to the Thames, and while they begged at the doors of rich men's houses they saw the Italian merchants go by in silk and velvet, and the fat Germans of the Steelyard bulging with good eating and the skilled Flemish artisans busy in their shops with leather work and jeweller's work, with armor and felt, hats and fine textiles which might have kept busy many pairs of English hands. Resentment swelled into occasional violence which, awkwardly suppressed, grew to a general tumult, the old cry of "Prentices and Clubs" was raised on a morning when every brisk London youngster was early abroad and instead of ransacking the neighboring fields and woods for May blossoms, the 'prentices, re-inforced by beggars, vagabonds and sanctuary men, ransacked the shops of the foreigners, set some houses alight, burst open the jails, and before they were overawed by men in armor and shotted cannon, gave London the look of a city in the hands of a hostile army.

The shaft, subsequently removed, was hung on hooks over the doors of a row of houses off Leadenhall, probably the present-day Shaft's Court, where it hung for more than thirty years until Sir Stephen, the half-mad curate of a nearby church, infuriated by the fact that St. Andrew's should retain the name of an "idol"—"under the shaft"—and other furies that beset him, so inflamed Shaft Alley that "after they had well dined, to make themselves strong," they took down the shaft and sawed it into pieces, each man keeping to burn as firewood the section that had hung over his house.

A church already existed here in the twelfth century, patched up and added to until, in the early sixteenth century it was entirely re-built. Like few others, it escaped both the Great Fire and later bomb-ing, so that it appears fairly near what it anciently was, except for Victorian additions and a new wooden roof with beautifully polished bosses in Tudor style, yet hardly the "fair and beautiful parish church" it was in Elizabethan times. Nevertheless, there are objects very much worth looking at in the tired, slightly unkempt church.

Immediately to the left of the entrance on St. Mary Axe, propped up as if temporarily, there is a rough stone marked in crude scratchy letters that make it enormously alive, as if you were seeing the inept hand hesitating over the right spelling and then laboriously incising the gravestone, that of a fishmonger of the parish. Moving leftward from the door, quite another kind of plaque, smoothly lettered and spaced on bronze, to commemorate "John, alias Hans Holbein, painter to His Majesty, Henry VIII sometime resident of this parish, 1491–1543." It does not mention the fact that he died of the plague; too many did, especially in Aldgate, which was particularly hard hit.

Above a few large pew seats, family size and crested, there are a number of memorials to the city's merchants: a fine domestic scene of the seventeenth century, husband praying and wife kneeling behind him; and another beguiling one, quite small, of a lady alone. Beyond, a handsome brass plaque and, next to it, a grated monument of a gentleman in Elizabethan ruff and Shakespeare-style beard, stone books jutting at him from each side of his niche. This is John Stow, tailor, collector of old documents, invaluable historian, and obsessed docu-menter of his sixteenth-century London, much richer in marble death than at the penniless end of his life. The quill in his hand, you will notice, is quite new, replaced the most recent April by the Lord Mayor of London who comes each year to mark the anniversary of the death of a member of the parish who once lived where Leadenhall and Fenchurch streets meet.

Short turnings in the immediate neighborhood will confront you with the ubiquitous might of London shipping on Leadenhall and lead into the many-petaled iron flower of Leadenhall Market, to the swell of huge bay windows on the Billiter Street side of Lloyd's (what can happen to a coffeehouse if it really tries). On Leadenhall, there is actually a Dombey and Son, "Ladies and Gents Cash Tailors," a run of dead black wall—almost a London signature—out of Fenchurch Street Station, and via a short detour, a brilliantly dressed-up bank with the questionable symbol of Icarus, that dreamer and failure, imbedded large in its side.

A short distance east and south, a splendor of new ironwork inside a court off Mark Lane, once probably "Mart" Lane, and the nearby churchless tower of All Hallows Staining, a reference to a medieval alley of painters and stainers. Resisting the Lorelei call of a pub bedizened with fruits and life-size dolphins, find your way, on Hart Street, to Samuel Pepys' church, St. Olave's. It was dedicated to a martyred king of Norway and, after reconstruction following World War II, rededicated by King Haakon VII. Much of the marble and stone is medieval, the door to the vestry is fifteenth century, and there are wooden elements of the seventeenth-century (some from other demolished churches, as was the reasonable common practice, and still is). Among a number of ornate memorials of the nineteenth century, a flat, dull Victorian portrait of the bewigged Pepys, who had worked in the Navy Office on Seething Lane. A much more successful monument is that of Elizabeth Pepys, erected by her affectionate and errant husband, a lovely lively head that bursts eagerly out of its stone frame, in the act of charming.

A sign near the entrance to St. Olave's informs that you may take photographs, but brass rubbing is not allowed. And to make absolutely sure, the brasses are covered with sections of carpet. If there is a church authority around, you will be shown them on a polite request: if there isn't, you might carefully lift corners for a quick look. One reward may be a glimpse of a kneeling lady, large, and smaller figures adjoining her. Weaving the group together, graceful bands of admonition or conversation or Gospel. Find the weather-beaten churchyard, truly funerary despite its flowers, on the Seething

Lane side for the seventeenth-century gateway described by Dickens as that of "St. Ghastly Grim," whose yard is one of those "Churchyards . . . so small, so rank, so silent, so forgotten except by the few people who ever look down into them from their smokey windows. It is a small, small churchyard with a ferocious strong spiked iron gate, like a jail. This gate is ornamented with skulls and crossbones, larger than the life, wrought in stone, and thrust through and through with iron spears."

Escaping the spears and threatening grin of the skulls, especially of one wearing a triumphal wreath, sit for a while in one of the flowery oases the City provides, plus a plaque for Pepys' Navy Office, burned down in 1673 (only a few years after he had witnessed the Great Fire from All Hallows Barking nearby), and look up at the less showy side of the Port of London Authority Building, here contented with fat, fluted Corinthian columns, studs, seals, wreaths and fasces and cornucopias, all cleanly and sharply defined.

It could be time to mingle with the immense summer tourist crowd on Tower Hill, the swingingest part of London, as busy as Coney Island in an August heat wave. Tired people dragging exhausted children, brisk lines running in and out of the fresh new conveniences, tea and sandwich stalls, soft-drinks wagons, ice-cream trucks, a babel of languages, and their owners studying booklets on *Londra, Londres, und London*. Before you embark for one of the Thames River tours or wait with the crowds, possibly for hours, to view the jewels, see what is going on just outside the park at the back of All Hallows Church. On good days you can almost always find something to argue about with someone, particularly if it's politics, economics or religion.

The best time is between noon and two thirty, when the office workers are out and the tourists not yet too weary to listen and respond. Church adherents, missionaries of orthodox and offshoot sects, are in fair supply, and so are listeners and vehement arguers surrounding an old-line Socialist. A single taxer doesn't do too well because most of his audience is diverted by an entertainer—sometimes a shaggy old bum who attempts to dance and sing, sometimes a more skilled, dynamic performer. One star is a very thin, almost toothless man who likes to work naked to the waist with his ribs pointing accusingly at the pale sunlight. He has the face of a heavy drinker, both drawn and puffy, with broad, flaccid folds under his eyes and a bright, hectic spot on each cheekbone that makes him look masked. Turning, talking, gesturing widely with his tattooed arms, he points to a body, breathing and moving occasionally, wrapped in a shroud of sailcloth and bound in chains. The performer wields, bends, and slashes with two swords, the patter flowing, and then inserts the swords under the chains that bind the body. Never halting the words that splatter and spurt from his gapped mouth, he announces with a magician's portentous gesture that his companion will free himself in three and one-half—not four, or even three and three-quarters—minutes! But for all the effort and the entertainment that will follow, a few pieces of silver are needed, and this must come—flourishing a white cotton sack—from the adults only—that is, the people over sixteen. He begins the money round, then stops. "Ladies and gentlemen, please do not give your children money; I cannot and will not take money from the kiddies, anybody who has no money, all he has to do is this [slapping his pockets], and I'll be glad to offer him our entertainment for nothing!" The noblesse forces the coppers out of the children's hands, to be changed for sixpence in Papa's.

## ✍ *London Is Where . . .*

The citizenry is not imprisoned in gluey lift music or assaulted by triumphant fanfares of soap commercials in taxis.

People are "mature," if any people have achieved that theoretical ideal of the patient, controlled, judicious, kindly, tolerant man. And if one stays long enough—long enough, for instance, to find that Victorian bawds of buildings are beginning to show endearing old charms—there comes the time of a sudden, strong need for abrasion, the rudeness of Paris, the rough speed of New York.

Felons, traitors, murderers, horse thieves, conducted out of the medieval hospital-prison in Holborn to be hung in Tyburn, were given an immense bowl of ale, not only to befuddle them, but to carry to death the taste of life's choicest pleasure, an estimation that persists, most recently reflected in the agonies of fury and counterplotting to circumvent roadside breathalyzer tests.

An old lady sleeps soundly in a deep chair of a collection of frail antique French furniture in the Victoria and Albert Museum, confident that no one will disturb her.

The lounges of small, exclusive "county" family hotels are hosts to men who stammer, hawk, and *uh-uh* in desperate bursts through choked voices and women who whoop in the accents of elderly "hockey stick" girls, speaking of their horses as if they were good, clever children and their children as if they were horses. For each other, shouts of "Splendid!" and "Well done!" as if each in turn were jumper and spectator.

Charles Lamb said, "All the streets and pavements are pure gold, I warrant you. At least I know an alchemy that turns her mud to metal —a mind that loves to be at home in crowds."

No one wears rubbers, and only the girls who cannot afford leather, not rainproof, will wear tall plastic boots.

Minute alleys that no one would care to find and the people already in know too well have the largest street signs—and the most historically explicit. Near Villiers Street a path is marked *York Place, formerly Of Alley.* In Southwark a slit of street is dignified with *Three Tuns Court, Late Three Tuns Passage* stamped large and the major attraction of an alley that leads to litter, one print shop, and a gas streetlamp.

Shelley thought hell was.

There is such a multiplicity of grotesque buildings that once the eye sits back in its socket and the mind relaxes, having given up trying to understand them, one becomes accustomed to them, and soon indifferent. But in time they become potent images for nostalgia to feed on.

There is, they say, a witch society.

Love on the top of the bus is like this: He is wearing fawn-colored corduroy trousers and a bright India-print jacket. His hair is coiffed in the fashion of that week, smoothed down in soft waves in back and a suave fringe to his eyebrows, springing fuzzy and alert as a cockatoo's at the top and bristling along his cheeks in a broad sweep curving to the chin. She is wearing blue jeans and a big blue sweater, her hair very straight and blond, the jagged lengths trailing over her sweater as wisps of yellow cloud. He takes out a comb and very carefully, section by section, neatens each area of his sculptured hair, then hands her the comb, which she pulls through her hair. In the meantime, he shoves bits of chocolate into her mouth, then lights two cigarettes, puts one in her mouth, hands her a newspaper, and lightly kisses her cheek as she reads.

The girls look like newborn foals or goats—leggy, startle-eyed, moist, and vulnerable. You will have seen them almost everywhere, at their least self-conscious when they are at work—in a kinky boutique, for instance, or a fashionable hairdressing salon, where a variety of physical types, all in similar uniforms, make an interesting array. The bright-colored minidress makes one with low buttocks look like a duck with abnormally long legs from a back view. A plump girl looks like an enormous magazine-cover baby if she's pretty and, if not, like the dreadful glandular anomalies of full sexual development at three or four years of age. The very skinny girls look frighteningly fragile, but the muscular girls have it the worst; with their full, hard calves and broad backs, meager breasts, and Mother Courage faces, they look like junior transvestites, poor things, for all the fall of hair and baby-doll eyes.

There is an always close and easily tapped fund of righteous indignation that rises to march on Trafalgar Square to protest the government's stand on Vietnam and the use of nuclear power in warfare. It always writes letters to the *Times* and finds vents in opinion programs aired on the radio. One lady wrote a letter, broadcast straight, without comment, protesting that all the Regent Street shops and those on Wigmore Street and Oxford Street permitted their wax mannequins to be stripped and dressed in full view of the passing public. This never seemed to happen to male models. Why not afford female mannequins the same privacy? Is this not discrimination against women?

A tube station has a handsome grillwork gate marked *Private*. It serves the subterranean pathway that leads to the Houses of Parliament.

There is a carefully wrought mosaic sign to mark the site of Peele's Hotel, established in 1518 (Fleet Street at Fetter Lane). In its coffeehouse days later it played host to Dickens, the Duke of Wellington, and Macaulay.

A gentleman in striped trousers and black coat will approach two American ladies in the Temple Church and lead them from medieval images to symptoms of recent bomb damage, charming all the way and embarrassing the ladies. They do not know whether he has come out of an office for a breather, has just left a wedding, or maybe professional guides in such a historic site are required to wear this— to them—most formal costume. Should they tell him they don't want a guide? Must they tip him? Should they thank him and leave it at that? They abandon the problem by saying a sudden good-bye, leaving him and the church in mid-legend.

Women appear to be more nervous than they really are, particularly in the wintertime, when they keep picking invisible things off their lips and eyelashes, the detritus of hairy sweaters and shaggy hats.

Theater bars and buffets are often divided, like transatlantic steamers, into classes. If you hold a balcony ticket in the Royal Opera House at Covent Garden, for an example, it is almost impossible to meet a friend more favored by the gods in the stalls crush bar. The open modern spaces of the Royal Festival Hall permit a mingling of the classes if one can negotiate the stairs, and the intervening terrain, and time for a drink, in the fifteen-minute interval.

Private parks still exist, closed to all except local householders who have keys. Some of them are doubly safe from invaders because they sit in uncontrolled traffic which must be braved before approaching the forbidden wood. If you fail to reach the wood, there will still be the distinction of having been flattened by a silver-gray Bentley. (And that brings to mind a Mexican song: "God, if I must be killed, let it be by a Cadillac and not a cow.")

A protester—for or against anything—is not necessarily a nut.

Fruits and vegetables are arranged on stalls like beautifully designed carpets—unmatched for composition and color sense except by Mexican market vendors.

Bus and tube stops are named for forgotten coaching stops: the Angel, Swiss Cottage, Baker's Arms, Burnt Oak, the Green Man, Elephant and Castle (for the Infanta of Castile), for a few.

A shop advertises that it is a "family business" and shows a large photo of the whole tribe to prove it.

Americans are considered materialistic and antiintellectual because they discuss things and their cost, house improvements, the car they are going to buy, the football games, and what was on the television last night, just like Londoners.

The Puritan shadow of John Knox and Oliver Cromwell still darkens pleasures. After two days of sunshine, dour mutterings of "We're going to pay for this" and, if it should go on for four days, the dire sound of "drought."

Birds and doves sing in the backyards, in commons, in squares, in three-treed squarelets, and in parks. The most valuable and central real estate is wasted on parks. One practical royal lady once asked how much it would cost to convert the public parks to royal use and was told by her Prime Minister, "Two crowns, madam," and he may not have been exaggerating greatly. Londoners have held and fought for their greens tenaciously and, when necessary, violently. A Londoner will bear much, accede to much, tolerate a good deal more, but do not touch a blade of his grass.

Gypsies, often in long skirts and loose, oily hair, as often dressed in ageless, shapeless cloche hats and threadbare coats, go from door to door in mews paths, offering fortunes or lucky black cats out of cavernous reticles. In the market the opening ploy is a sprig of heather for luck.

A red-eyed, drooping, lumpish bulldog will be addressed by a woman, "Isn't he sweet? Come here, darling. Want some sugar? Sure he wants shuggie. Oh, he's shy, poor darling. Don't be afraid, love, come, come." She will not permit herself to talk that way to a child.

The BBC keeps a carefully balanced schedule of news, pop records, comics, meticulous, microscopic examinations of who now, on records, sings Brahms' *Alto Rhapsody* better than did Kathleen Ferrier (no one), tentative weather reports, lessons in Chinese, shorthand practice, and soap operas that obey the times with homely discussions about the hazards to children of working mothers, quoting experts, and psychological insights according to Freud in hemming and hawing elderly voices with Midlands accents. At off times, one can pick up German opera, French rasping monotone passion, and songs of the Scandinavians. But it all stops, obliterated for as long as the weather holds and the match goes on—and that can be many hours—during important cricket contests.

The swan, that angry royal bird, which cadges food from the passengers on Thames launches and forms long white daisy chains to bind the fierce black lilies of smokestacks, the white stocks of church steeples, and the angular dry marsh weeds of derricks are still taken up in the middle of July as they have been for centuries, for marking, probably the same markings one sees in the Public Record Office (p. 65.) The event is listed in the "Engagements" section of the *Times* as "swan-upping" and can be observed from the Temple stairs near Blackfriars Bridge at about nine thirty in the morning.

Most ice-cream wagons announce themselves on their afternoon rounds in a series of gentle, churchly chimes, while one that plies the streets bordering Blackheath, prefers the traditional, secular "Green-sleeves."

There are still Druids in England, in fact enough to form one ortho-dox group and one dissident splinter group. They hold their harvest festival, at the time of the autumnal equinox, on Primrose Hill, north of the Regent's Park zoo, dressed in long cloaks and garlands, car-rying banners and sacred vessels through their set of mysteries.

Gambling is fascinating, and so are horses, more so than girls or children; but dogs are the cosseted glamor kids here. The society keenly alert to cruelty to animals receives a startlingly larger fund out of public support than does the equivalent body that looks to children. The story is told, absolutely authentic, about a lady who took her two dogs of interesting bastardy to a garden party. As it began to rain on her new white linen dress, the dogs scented an alluring bitch across the lawn and dragged the lady in white to a fall in a muddy path. A gentleman ran to her, she extended her arm for his gallant help, but he disregarded it and, instead, looking down at her interestedly, asked, "Of just what breed are your handsome dogs?" She told him what she knew of their heritage. He thanked her and left her in the mud.

# 12    Whitehall—Banqueting Hall

"My Lord has gone to consecrate King Henry at Whitehall" is a line from a Kentucky mountain ballad brought from England centuries ago and still sung as "Mattie Groves." Which Henry is not clear, and if the lines refer to the stubbornly libidinous Henry VIII, it would be not to his consecration, but rather his marriage to Anne Boleyn, which, it is agreed, probably took place on this site, long before the present banqueting hall was built.

As it stands now, a creamy classic box, recently refurbished and polished to glow calmly among the streaked blackness of the rest of the Whitehall buildings, opposite the engaging eccentricities of the Horse Guards Building across the street, it is a silent place, its only noise the rambunctious, swirling apostrophes of the Rubens ceiling and the echoes of its own multicolored history.

It must have given Henry VIII particular satisfaction to take this busy hamlet, its splendid apartments and grounds, away from Cardinal Wolsey, who, like Richelieu in France, lived as luxuriously as his king. In addition to the "pleasure buildings" that Henry added to Whitehall, he built a banqueting hall. Finding it somewhat lacking, Queen Elizabeth built, in 1581, a large wooden hall nearer her private quarters. That was replaced with a sturdier building of stone and brick, burned down in 1619. Rebuilt, it still wasn't adequate for a variety of festivities and entertainments, and the present hall was built to become, in its early history, the theater for masques. Lumpish in the time of Henry VIII, they became more artful in Elizabeth's day. (Those who have seen Benjamin Britten's *Gloriana* will remember as one of its charms an Elizabethan masque.) In the new hall, designed by Inigo Jones and opened with a masque by Ben Jonson in 1622, the entertainments grew spectacularly effulgent. The inventive Inigo Jones produced varieties of scenery and magical effects, while writers who followed Jonson (out of favor with Jones, with whom he had had crossings of the ego, it is said) poured on the rich, round prose for royal guests to speak, sometimes by Fletcher and later by Milton, to music by the leading composers of the day.

The Inigo Jones Banqueting Hall, built at the behest of the Stuart James I, brightened with Rubens' paintings by order of the Stuart Charles I, dimmed when the Stuarts' light went out. The innumer-

82

able candles and torches used in lighting the masques imperiled with their smoke the glorious ceilings dedicated to the godlike deeds of James I, and in any case masques soon fell out of fashion, examples of waste and extravagance to the Puritans who came to power after the beheading of Charles I, the most vivid incident in the hall's dramatic life. Immediately outside the hall, in 1649, a scaffold was erected to execute Charles I. He said calm good-byes to two of his children in St. James's Palace, gave them some jewels and the next day, on a late January morning, walked back through St. James's Park to Whitehall. The warrant for the execution received its final reluctant signatures (Cromwellian hanky-panky is sometimes suggested), Charles was summoned early in the afternoon, paced through the Banqueting Hall, and stepped through a window onto the scaffold. Both executioner and his assistant were masked. The king put on a white cap, took off his outer cloak, and laid his head on the block.

During the time of Cromwell the hall stayed with serious court functions, but returned to gaiety with the Restoration, when Charles II brought in splendors of music, brilliant candlelight, and the rustling silks and gleaming shoulders of his harem, and the walls reverberated with great banquets. During quieter hours the king practiced here, as his forebears had, the magic of the king's touch, curing by the laying on of the royal hands. He gave coins to the poor on Maundy Thursday and washed their feet, or possibly one symbolic, not too dirty, pair.

James II continued the washing of feet, the laying on of hands, and the doling out of coins until he was forced into exile in 1688. The Protestant William of Orange would have nothing to do with the Papish symbols or much with the hall after his welcome there and the ceremonial proffering of the crown to him and his queen, Mary. Foreign dignitaries were still entertained at Whitehall, but the royal family moved to the palace in Kensington to avoid the cold shrouds of river mist. Ten years after the last Stuart King left it, the whole of Whitehall went up in flames, leaving only sections of gate and the Banqueting Hall intact. The profane beauty was then to have a holier purpose: to replace burned chapels in the enclave, the new one an adaptation by Sir Christopher Wren. Several later hands made improvements in the chapel, the most notable those of Sir John Soane, who covered the exterior with London's favorite Portland stone, losing some of the variety Jones had designed but keeping the interior shape fairly close to Jones' specifications. A chapel until late in the nineteenth century, it was later used as a royal military museum, which moved elsewhere a few years ago.

The hall was repainted, the Rubens cleaned, and the glorious old hall is now fresh, regal and inviting (a particular Inigo Jones combination) and waiting. For what? Who in present-day London can fill it? The royal family blazing in the Crown jewels, and officers of the City companies in full regalia, and the Lord Mayor, on his ceremonial days. But who else will help fill the hall with the susurrus of silks and the gleam of curls? The little girls in painted-on lashes, slick in vinyls, like plastic dolls? The dandy in vulgar shoddy, flippantly cut and soon to come apart at the seams? Possibly it might become a museum for the most exquisite of court costumes, gathered from other museums—not too many of them—each to shine in its own noble space. Or a chamber music hall, nothing later than Mozart and nothing heavier than an octet. Or a gallery of small portraits—Flemish, French and English, and miniatures—none later than 1750. Otherwise, what is to become in this inappropriately egalitarian age of the beautiful, useless hall?

Open 10 to 5 P.M., Sundays 2 to 5 P.M. Admission 1 shilling for adults; sixpence for children. Strand, Trafalgar Square, Westminster stations. Any of the numerous buses that serve these points.

# 13 Covent Garden, Magistrate's Court—Bow Street

The market where, Ruskin suggests, Turner may have developed his sense of color, wandering through it frequently as a boy when he lived on Maiden Lane, where Dickens found much material, has always been part of the theater (and gaming and vice) area. One may approach it then from one of its tangents, a theater street, St. Martin's Lane.

Diagonally across from the Salisbury pub, on St. Martin's Lane (No. 50–56), a long sign declares its houses to be those of a merchandising board. If you look close, there is a man's-width-size crack in the façade, and closer still, you will find a street name imbedded in the wall: Goodwin's Court, a narrow row of the eighteenth-century, mainly used by architectural and theatrical offices now and a restaurant, all enviably functioning behind beguilingly rounded windows and mahogany doors (a local fable has it that the indestructibility of that wood, brought from hot, distant countries by merchant ships, was discovered here). The line of contented, glossy, delicately rounded houses under their blue-flamed old lights, ends at Bedfordbury, a dark frame for the pretty light, one of the black streets with prison-like houses that Dickens described, and around the corner, New Row, a village high street, in spite of its proximity to the broad anonymities of theater streets, the Strand and Trafalgar Square. It contents itself with the usual, one sweets shop, one hardware store, a tea and coffee shop, a stationer's, then nods to the theater by sporting the Theatre Zoo, a gathering of masks, animal costumes, wigs—Chinese, golliwogs, courtly, benevolent and frightening—and mounds of junk jewelry, probably meant for theatrical wear since London ordinarily wears little, although it should to sparkle through the gray days.

Look up along the roof edges on St. Martin's Lane, and search for a stray frond of greenery or flowered vine. Above an uncommunicative façade that walls up a good collection of glass and furniture—the London habit of hiding shows of possession—there sits an army of tubs, and from them, a lush efflorescence of big gaudy English blooms in tropical density, never to be suspected (no more than would Goodwin's Court) from the dusty, laconic street.

Like Les Halles in Paris, Covent Garden has been threatened with expulsion and relocation for a time. It will happen ultimately, but the chances are that for some time still you will be able to leave the Royal Opera House and immediately find yourself in a shapeless quiet of resting trucks and a few dimly lit pubs and cafés, a rudimentary coffee stall hung with a few regulars waiting for the market to stir, all guarded by the gray Anglo-Tuscan ghost of Inigo Jones' St. Paul's Church, Covent Garden.

Later in the night, more trucks will roar in to heap sidewalks and the backs of men and barrows with sacks of potatoes and crates of cabbages and the airy weight of boxes of gladiolus. The café windows become smoky with the cigarette fumes and the sweatered warmth of the drivers and porters. The good-natured altercations of truck drivers competing for easier positions begin to fill the narrow streets, and the greetings of men gathering for the night's work. The clatter of barrows and the gasp of brakes, the thud of crates and, in time, the voices of purchasers and vendors, climb the walls and swell into the doorways of the blind old brick houses. The inner halls of the market are, in the early morning hours, singularly quiet, an appropriate garden gentleness for the vegetables and flowers; the robust calls and vigorous movement stay outside.

Although there is something chic and almost daring (and British, because it is likely to be cold and damp and good exercise for that stiff upper lip) about going to famous old markets at four in the morning, it is just as well to go to Covent Garden at about eight or nine (after slithering through the icy, scaly damp of Billingsgate). Eight o'clock is when the Eliza Doolittles who hadn't the advantages of life with Henry Higgins come to buy their "rowses," arguing prices with a lustiness that shakes the lumps and swoops of their battered hats. The plain, hardworking flower carts turn savage with the shocking brilliance of anemones and the phallic spears of large, unopened buds. One owner of a flower cart finds no contradiction in heaping the pagan colors and licentious shapes on a cart painted with dire evangelistic messages spiraling to YOU HAVE BEEN WARNED.

The full daylight hours give you also a fuller meeting with the church and the market square, the Bow Street Court and the Opera House, an incongruous grouping now, although there may have been times when it made sense.

One possible reason for the market's slowness to move elsewhere is the fact that it is deeply and anciently rooted in its place. It was the vegetable gardens for Westminster Abbey (that gives you the right to call it "Convent" Garden, as many visitors do) in medieval times and into the Renaissance, when it was expropriated to become private property. Of the hundreds of London squares, it was the first and, to judge from early engravings, an exceedingly distinguished square. It was designed by Inigo Jones on the scheme of the Italian piazza— and actually called the Piazza—in 1630, commissioned by the Duke of Bedford. Later owners, not contented with the revenue from the blocks of houses, decided to revive the market, of which there was always a patch to the south of the unfinished square. In time the market overwhelmed the houses, all of them now gone, leaving only a scrap of arcade and a door that may be Jones' and his church.

The church is a most moving place, not quite alive or yet dead— an imposing entity, almost abandoned. It is moving for its monumental simplicity (maintained in the nineteenth-century rebuilding), its memories of the deaths of luminaries in the English theater, and its modest entrance walk on the side opposite the famous façade, where old men sit on the benches of the green path, surrounded by the backs of narrow-windowed tenements. The church might have been altogether theirs, as Spitalfields Christ Church (p. 104) was taken over by its broken men, if it weren't for a few experts and the fact that Shaw chose its pillars for the opening scene of *Pygmalion*.

# Magistrate's Court—Bow Street

Across the street, last night, on the stage of the Royal Opera House, Mimi died and Rodolfo shrieked his guilty lament. After a sleepy interval, drama in a coarse peasant smock returns to the neighborhoods as the growl of barrow wheels and the beefy exchanges of porters, rests again during the breakfast and going-to-work hours and returns at 10 P.M. in a Jacob's coat of gray patches and black and patches the color of blood.

Court I is a small room with a number of restless doors through which policemen and prisoners, personnel of the court, witnesses, and spectators appear and disappear with wraithlike speed and quiet. Above the magistrate dressed in his business suit and stern benevolence, the familiar British lion and its legend *Dieu et mon droit*. Below the judge, a maze of small areas for the press, for witnesses, for court recorder and social workers; opposite him a railed platform, like a bridge, sometimes casually guarded at both ends by lounging, alert policemen, where the prisoner sits through witnessing or stands to be questioned and sentenced. Behind him the pews for spectators, most frequently shabby old men, friends of the defendants or émigrés from the benches leading into the market church, sitting out a day of entertainment and warmth.

It is extraordinarily low-keyed and quiet, almost like a neatly run hiring hall. The defendant, guided by the arm of a policeman, glides out of the side door and up to the bridge. The first few cases are simple and monotonous, mainly traffic violations, the accusations read out in a mumble, the guilty or not guilty pleas established, a fine of twenty shillings or forty shillings imposed. The lulling, trance-like smoothness, an underwater soundlessness, deepens as cases held over, postponed, are muttered through in an incomprehensible mute play and ushered out, leaving questions never to be resolved for the visitor. The four colored boys who shamble in and out are asked if they have anything to say this time; they haven't and shuffle out again, no sentence imposed. Why? What was the offense—cutting tires or murder—and where do they go from here and for how long?

The next man is middle-aged, in a charity coat, too long and wide for him. He has a predator's face. One would call it hawklike if he were successful, but smoky with sunlessness and casual bathing, the patches of skull between unwashed twists of hair, the sulking, trapped droop of the head are those of a crippled vulture. His recent history is read. He was picked up last night at a little after eleven in Soho for spitting at an old woman and, after she protested, threatening to beat her. He has had several convictions for indecent exposure, was fined and did time for the offense, and here he is again. Had he anything to say for himself? And what did he mean by shouting at the arresting officer, "I want to go in for three months. This ought to put me on the inside, where I ought to be." He says that he hadn't spat at the woman, but toward the ground, and she got in the way, but anyhow, he wanted the police to protect him from himself; he had tried for admission to a hospital, but there was no room. Admonished to watch out and fined forty shillings, he drags himself out, rotting with the self-horror of which no one wants to relieve him.

A street fight; a young Irishman repeatedly deported and now picked up with a long knife in his possession which, he told the court, he carried in self-defense only after being cut up in Camden Town; he is turned over to the immigration authorities once again. A jaunty young man with a face of stupid cunning appears wearing a black mourning band on the sleeve of his tan jacket. Yesterday in Victoria Station he approached a luggage-bearing woman, volunteered to buy for her francs at a superior rate of exchange, and never returned with her eight pounds. Sometime later he offered to buy a ticket for another woman, also laden with vacation luggage, and she, too, was convinced that anyone wearing a mourning band, in the shadow of recent death, must be kind and gentle and honest. Neither money nor tickets nor man reappeared. But the pickings were good and the cupidity intense; he lurked in the station, still in tan jacket and black armband, and was picked up some hours later. Given his choice of a fine or a month in jail, he tries again the magic of his black amulet. Shambling out after the sentence, he points to the band and mutters something about his stepmother just dead—reminding one of a case reported in yesterday's papers of a man who had killed two wives and asked for a mitigation of his sentence by promising never to marry again. The judge remains unmoved.

The ritual droning slides in and out of the doors and along the wooden paneling, the dull voices like a late, sleepy TV show to which one pays half attention. A girl is brought in, her name spoken, her age nineteen. Her hair is cropped short, a functional haircut around a broad peasant face. She wears a simple cotton dress, pulled taut over advanced pregnancy. She must be in for lifting a compact from a Woolworth's counter or a hair-pulling match with a neighbor over space on a laundry line. She is asked, politely, if she pleads guilty or not guilty to a charge of soliciting. She whispers, "Guilty." One refuses to believe it; this plain chubby girl who belongs on a bench in a prenatal clinic of Lambeth cannot be a prostitute, and who are the men that would, in a town where sex is as easy as reading public notices in Bayswater or milling around St. Anne's Court and New-port Place and almost any other street in Soho, choose a woman who is less than two months from term? The whole thing is a grotesque mistake, a scene viewed in distorting mirrors. A tall, softly spoken probation officer enters the witness stand and, reading from a sheaf of papers, unwinds her story, grotesque because it is so per-fect a cliché and classic. She was brought up in orphan asylums and foster homes. At fifteen, she was picked up by the police several times for entering and driving off in strangers' cars, then sent to a correction home for three months. From the age of sixteen on, she was picked up in Leeds, in Manchester, in Birmingham on charges of prostitution and in London shacked up with a Turkish Cypriot who, she says, is the father of the baby. He is gone now. The judge asks her to stand and questions her about arrangements she may have made for the delivery and what she thought she might do with the baby later. She has made no plans or arrangements. The judge addresses her urgently, without anger: "Do you realize what might happen to your baby if you keep this up? What a dangerous thing you are doing, besides the fact that it is illegal? Don't you care —you must—what you might be doing to an innocent child?" The answer is, "Mmmm," and a shamefaced nod. The judge calls for a woman probation officer, who leaves with the girl and returns about fifteen minutes later to report that hospital arrangements have been made; no fine or imprisonment is imposed; she will be under probation for a time and then probably continue drifting.

The back at which one stares some minutes later is broad and fleshy, a back out of Indian sculpture, topped with disheveled silky Indian hair and, to judge from the profile, a face of baroque Indian curves. The complainant is conducted to a side witness box, the antithesis of the prisoner: very few hairs draped over his bony skull, a small, thin frame, and a precise, spare face. The prisoner is asked whether he understands that the case may continue on in criminal court and that whatever he has to say may not necessarily be held against him but will be recorded. He growls some sort of assent. The complainant states his name, position, and address. The prisoner is a neighbor whose habit it is to linger in a joint alleyway in pajamas not always carefully arranged. "I said to him, after several times, you are not in India, you are now in England. He shouted at me, 'I am not an Indian, I am a German, and I'll do what I like.' Last Sunday I was playing with my baby and my wife [here a few hands rise to hide smiles and the threat of a snicker], and I saw this man again improperly dressed. I called to him to go inside, and he said he would kill me. I went outside and continued to talk to him and he came at me with a knife. I put my hand up to protect my head and he stabbed me in the hand." The hand is held up to show the cut. "Then my wife pulled me inside and called the police. A police officer took me to St. George's Hospital, where eight stitches were put in my hand."

The carefully spoken testimony in a slightly foreign accent has been taken down, to judge from the stops and requests to speak slowly, in longhand. The report is read aloud and signed as accurate by the complainant. A police officer, who looks like the burly, young, innocent police sergeant of an English thriller, gives his testimony as does the doctor of St. George's. Again, the written statements are read aloud and signed. The prisoner is asked if he has anything to say about the veracity of the statements or if he wants to add anything. A surly, impatient thrust of the large, round body and, "No, I just want to kill him." A glance from the judge, and a policeman moves smoothly to block the gap, lounging and nonchalant, between accused and accuser.

The case is to be heard in criminal court in a few days; some droning instructions, gatherings and exchanges of papers, and luncheon recess is called, the close of an ordinary morning.

# 14  The Royal Mews

Mews were the shelters for falcons at their time of mewing, of shedding plumage and growing new. The mewing falcons had been kept, through royal generations, in the area where the National Gallery now stands until they were moved to make room for the horses rescued from a fire in the royal stables in Bloomsbury.

George III's purchase of the palace of the Duke of Buckingham added to the royal stable and coach space, redesigned and expanded by the popular and busy John Nash immediately after George IV's accession to the throne.

It is understandably a large area and, in its public hours, full of neat, knowledgeable London children, those who know a great deal about horses through the osmoses of birth and atmosphere. The royal stable is of soft, rounded designs, a flow of ellipses and lunettes and arches melting into each other. The tiled walls curve gently as if to deal tenderly with the horses, which stand in golden straw, their tails neatly tied, their fine, patient backs blanketed with handsome cloths bearing embroidered crowns and E II R. The men at the turnstiles, in the stables, wandering on their varied duties through the yard (with a sharp eye open for the kids) are suitably dressed, too, in black bowlers and brown country jackets; tawny, many-buttoned, long coaching coats; and hard-topped hats with black cockades over long, horsy faces in rawhide skins.

The show, however, is not so much the horses, as the physical appurtenances of the dream of "happily ever after" that invades the lives of the pragmatic, romantic, matter-of-fact, sentimental, skeptical English, for whom the royal family is the fairy tale of riches, elegance and fame, sterling virtue and indulgence in refined high jinks to be examined and enhanced at kitchen tables over teacups. From light pony phaetons and curly sleds to stately Rolls-Royces and a French charabanc given to Queen Victoria (a regal bus-station wagon of padded brocade, carved woods and polished metals, used for outings in the country), one examines the gamut of carriages once and still used by royalty. The range includes the light graceful landaus which lead the procession at Ascot and the state landau used to convey foreign royalty; the very beautiful state coach in which the Queen rode in Princess Margaret's wedding procession and

91

which, in recent years, has carried the imperial state crown to the House of Lords when Parliament opens. The Queen rides to open Parliament in the Irish state coach, a rebuilt version of the coach bought in Dublin by Queen Victoria, nobler than most of the others, with a gilded rail of ornaments along the top and surmounted by a crown. The most elaborate, a staggering compilation of the gilded, carved, painted ornateness that made gay and playful or ponderous and vulgar (depending on who hired which architect-designer) a good number of London houses in the latter half of the eighteenth century, is the gold state coach, Cinderella's carriage, in which Queen Elizabeth rode to her coronation. Nothing lacks in its neoclassic goldenness. Beside the royal crown: lion's heads, conches, cupids, roaring tritons, shields, plumed helmets, dolphins, wreaths, and inescapably, allegorical panels painted by a fashionable Florentine, clearly the "very superb" coach that George III wanted and got.

There are collections and collections of wonderfully made harness and whips, portraits of English monarchs, and remarkably luxurious, horsy gifts received from other monarchs: a bridle and saddlecloth sent by a sultan of Turkey; a Mexican saddle encrusted with silver; an Arab saddle from Libya; a remarkably worked saddle given to Prince Philip by the Maharajah of Jaipur; and Russian saddles and bridles presented to Queen Elizabeth by Nikita Khrushchev.

Take a youngster, don't take photographs, and don't smoke.

The Royal Mews are open every Wednesday afternoon from 2 to 4 P.M. and the same hours on Thursdays from May to September, as well. Admission is one shilling for children, and two shillings and sixpence for adults. Victoria Tube Station. Buses 11, 39, 46.

# 15   Westminster Abbey

The pictorial symbols of a city—the Eiffel Tower, the New York skyline, the Colosseum—are necessarily quick views that light the name for one particular period of a city's life. Both Trafalgar Square, commemorating Nelson and the victory that expanded British sea and mercantile power, and Big Ben on the Houses of Parliament, of a later time in the nineteenth century, speak of a time when London as banker, shipper, and merchant for much of the world vibrated with activity. The enormous mercantile wealth was reflected in large, heavy, ornate public buildings, palaces on the edges of the parks, the silks of China and the jewels of India dazzling out of shop fronts, immense eating and drinking, and a guilt that responded to the demands of an antique liberalism, a nagging taste for social justice. The great profits began to build workers' housing to replace the dank warrens of slums, established shelters for the aged and indigent, schools, and libraries. The Victorians were frightened and spurred on by the reformers and churchmen who spoke of Socialism. Whatever the reasons, there was enough pride, ambition, money and dedication to public welfare to change the face of London, between the years of the two monuments.

It was a vivid, fleshy time (truly "swinging") that brought London to a size and commercial activity that outdistanced any other city of the world. But that was one brilliant spot in a large, many-centuried tapestry, and for its chiaroscuro, its dun-colored patches, and its stained-glass reds and purples, the better symbol would be Westminster Abbey. The fact that it cannot be a straightforward, one-meaning symbol makes it paradoxically a better symbol of London than the other cliché images. Like the city, the abbey cannot be seen or encompassed easily. It is a confusion of oddities and beauties, a too-muchness of periods, uses, and styles; an amalgam of antiquity, accretions, destructions, and revisions; and above all, probably the most imposing single witness of English history.

1966 marked the nine hundredth birthday dating from the coronation of William the Conqueror, although the building was created by Edward the Confessor on the site of a predecessor of early Christian times that, like so many early churches, cloaked itself in a miracle to achieve the dignity and traffic of a shrine. The birthday

93

was celebrated by a number of special exhibitions and events, one of them Beethoven's *Missa Solemnis* performed—or the word may be "used"—as part of a service in the abbey. The soloists and the choir and the London Philharmonic were the best that a musically sophisticated city could produce, and their music making, unseen from the Poets' Corner, rose from invisible depths up into the vaults, floated along the delicate ribs, and settled as great ropes of sound banding the clusters of ivory pillars. The nineteenth-century music, performed by an apogee of English performers, halted to make way for the ancient rites of prayer and communion in the vast, rich solemnity, was a heady experience in the meanings and mixtures of London-Westminster Abbey.

A headier mixture of significances was the service of thanksgiving for the harvest a few weeks later. It was a blustery afternoon, damp winds whipping the clouds above the river and around the space that sets the abbey, pulling at the scarves and purpling the knees of the several hundred children brought by their parents to see Princess Margaret, who attended the service. The crowd was smaller than it might have been, not because of the weather, but because of a horrifying error in tact. It was the week of the disaster in the Welsh village of Aberfan, where a mountain of slag fell on a schoolhouse and killed most of the children of the village. Princess Margaret visited and then broadcast an appeal to the good, kind people of England to send toys, and they did, inundating the village with a wealth of *memento mori*. There were Londoners who found it hard to forget this ill-advised gesture.

There were several matters to ruminate on before one entered the abbey: the imponderable antiquity of a harvest thanksgiving which, in one form or another, must be as old as the first crop; a service in a church—for a time a cathedral—more than 900 years old, built on ground hallowed long before that; the cold, damp wind penetrating the layers of sweater and woolen socks of the crowd waiting patiently for hours, before the service and through it, to catch a glimpse of a member of the royal family supported (though it is a rich family in its own right) by a Labor state, to satisfy the Englishman's devotion to his antiquity and traditions.

On a sheltered lawn angled in by the abbey bookshop and the western wall, modern harvesters, bright red tractors, new mechanized plows brought to London by manufacturers and members of the appropriate unions. Inside the entrance, a large table bearing immense cabbages, carrots, gourds, fruits, a nut-brown country ham, a huge wheel of bread, and, under the table, a pristine row of quart milk bottles, echoed by a row of pint bottles of cream. The old abbey had dressed itself in magnificent arrangements of fruits and flowers, bold and rich. The sheen of the ancient columns was set off by a burst of deep-red flowers, the explosion of a great spray of golden marsh grasses, a baroque enlacement of purple and green grapes, the strong shapes and colors of peonies, the singing colors of massed chrysanthemums, and, on a table, a carefully designed fortress of thousands of apples, carefully placed, all pure young green except for one red apple here, a yellow there. In this splendor, there was a thanksgiving procession of food offerings carried by members of agricultural unions. The president of the National Farmers' Union read a lesson, a representative of the YMCA Farm Training Scheme led one of the prayers, and all the congregants sang lustily antiquated hymns, interspersed with the ringing of handbells and the pealing of Westminster's bells. A liberal churchman then offered his interpretation of Jesus Christ as a worker and enjoyer of the fruits of the earth. Warmed up by the hymns, the earthy service, and the blaze of harvest colors, the enormous congregation gave itself to singing "God Save the Queen" in all its verses, then went back to tea and telly, which alternately fought and apologized for the twentieth-century phenomenon of a wage freeze, showed the training of girl soldiers in China, and tried to explain how an antimissile differs from an antiantimissile.

At noon on Tuesday, June 20, 1967, the memorial service for John Masefield, the poet laureate, began after the last wisp of organ chorale faded into a curve of a vault. The congregation was small: members of the family, friends, writers, representatives of the Arts Council, literary societies, and publishing houses, the Master of the Honourable Company of Master Mariners, the Lord Mayor of Westminster, and, to represent the Queen, the Earl of Westmoreland, gathered on both sides of the aisle near the Poets' Corner.

A few of the luminaries sat framed, like saints in Sienese paintings, in the carved depths of the choir stalls.

The procession in its long, richly embroidered medieval cloaks, moved slowly up the aisles while the service was spoken, followed by chanting and choir responses in modern tunes to old modes, and the lesson. The anthem was of John Donne, a prayer that we dwell after death in a heaven "where there shall be no darkness nor dazzling, but one equal light; no noise nor silence, but one equal music; no fears nor hopes, but one equal possession; no ends nor beginnings, but one equal eternity. . . ." C. Day Lewis read from a few poems by Masefield, and after a hymn written by John Bunyan,

Robert Graves spoke about Masefield from the pulpit. He had not studied the spongelike acoustics of the abbey and its speaker system. Shakespeare and Goldsmith, and their companions in the Poets' Corner heard a curious ebb and flow of three words opening a sentence, then melting into a shapeless wash of sound. It was an impressive sight, however, the strong features in the tight cap of white hair high in the pulpit, a candidate for the laureateship forging another link in the endless continuity of English poetry.

The service continued with prayer and a hymn by Masefield and then the committal of the ashes, the appropriate words spoken by the Archdeacon of Westminster while two newspaper flashbulbs illumined the abbey floor. After the return of the procession, a prayer to "illuminate and inspire . . . all poets, writers, artists and craftsmen. . . ," followed by the reading by C. Day Lewis of Masefield's "Consecration," and the service was over, to give way to cleanly overalled and respectful stonemasons, who removed the purple cloth over the floor gap and readied to set the commemorative stone, near T. S. Eliot and Thomas Hardy, while the abbey bells tolled.

The ecclesiastical forest of beauties and eccentricities, densely populated with the illustrious dead and the clots of tourists like alarmed birds, one eye fixed on the guide, the other roving and straining for a tombstone underfoot or on a wall, is a demanding place, and as in the British Museum, you must make a selection that will be meaningful to you. The Poets' Corner, possibly, and its thunderous roll call; and in the dazzle of the shining names; the Chapel of St. Faith, an oddly shaped modest thirteenth-century structure arched with lovely rib-vaulting, the floor covered with some fine tiling of the same time.

Nor should you miss, among the overwhelming number of monuments, the early hieratic ones in the royal chapels: the colored marbles and mosaic Cosmati tomb of Henry III (who died in 1272); the tomb of Edward III with a graceful bronze hand holding a scepter and, at the side of the sarcophagus, a small figure of the Black Prince surrounded by personages; the skilled enamelwork on the belt, cushion, and shield of the Earl of Pembroke, half brother to Henry III. Set apart is what is left of a once magnificent shrine of Edward the Confessor, still possessed of the original Italian twisted columns studded with bits of mosaic, and nearby the oaken steep-backed Coronation Chair of 1300. Below the seat, the rough Stone of Scone, brought by Edward I from Scotland, repeatedly the victim of threatened theft by Scotsmen. The tombs go on in their unbelievable number, making this aspect of the abbey the last chapter in the National Portrait Gallery stories (p. 35), as well as a survey of monument art, from the long, cool, detached effigies of medieval times (look at Queen Eleanor, who died late in the thirteenth century), and—stopping at Giotto-esque, semiobliterated paintings nearby—on to the lacy Gothic tombs of a slightly later time, bursting into the rich elaborations of Elizabethan tombs, silvered, gilded, and as sharply colored as inexpensive toys. Sometimes they are as gaudy and bright as the monument to Anne, Duchess of Somerset; sometimes subdued, as in the beautifully carved and incised marble that decorates the sepulcher of Frances Grey, Duchess of Suffolk and mother of Lady Jane Grey, the nine-day queen.

Walk through the Chapel of Elizabeth I, under the intricacies of ceiling in the Lady Margaret Chapel, and past the banners, the carved stalls, the monuments, to Henry VII's Chapel, a thing of wonder, its breathtaking ceiling, called by Professor Nikolaus Pevsner "a superbly ingenious fantasy on the theme of fan-vaulting" and "technically . . . a spectacular tour de force." It is not—no matter how much the weight of centuries and confusions of periods and thickets of famous tombs seem to close in on you—to be missed.

The abbey treasury is constant, unbelieving confrontation with the physical fabric of history old enough to be legend; here the seal and royal charter of Richard Coeur de Lion; there the charter of Offa, King of the Mercians in 785 granting the monastery lands in "the terrible place," the Isle of Thorns, now Westminster. One of the five extant genuine impressions of the seal of William the Conqueror marks a grant of land in Surrey to Westminster. Geoffrey Chaucer is represented by a lease for a tenement in the garden of a chapel where Henry VII's Chapel now stands (the rent was fifty-three shillings and fourpence per year), and William Caxton, the printer, by a record of rent paid for local premises. The illuminated manuscript made in 1382 for Anne of Bohemia, the wife of King Richard II, spells out the coronation service that was used through the coronation of Elizabeth I and its matter still the core of present services.

You can find out how much the costs were for building the nave of the church in 1401 to 1402 and see a strong, beautifully worked head of an abbot of Westminster of the early sixteenth century, lost when it was used as filler in a buttress during eighteenth-century restorations, to be discovered again in nineteenth-century restoration. The romantic Essex Ring, supposedly given by Elizabeth I to the Earl of Essex and to be sent to her when he encountered difficulties (to no avail), is part of a collection of royal rings and crowns and bracelets, scepters, swords, and in the variety, a thirteenth-century spoon used for anointing. There are funeral lances and hollowed tree trunks used as water pipes and effigies in wood and wax of royalty and near royalty. Lord Nelson stands relaxed and slightly pensive, while Charles II, as a wax figure made in his lifetime, poses beruffled and becurled, hung with ribbons and lace, hands and head about to move into a basic ballet position. William and Mary appear in their ermined robes and jewels, holding orb and scepter, and Charles II makes a second showing in a plumed hat and the robes of a Knight of the Garter.

Having left the colored effigies and slipped on shoe covers to protect the ancient tiles in the Chapter House, one passes two curious monuments, a head of James Russell Lowell, who was ambassador to the court from 1880 to 1885, and a Roman coffin found nearby, probably the earliest memento of abbey dead.

The effect as one enters the octagonal room beyond the thirteenth-century pillar that supports the entrance arches is that of standing in the shade of an immense stone tree, the trunk a central pillar supporting a proliferating set of shafts curving down, like the great palm trees that may have been a remembrance of the Crusades which crept into European architecture. Around the inner section of the walls, some of the most famous of English medieval painting; rows of tight boxes, explicit, exhaustively instructive, one series dealing meticulously with the Apocalypse—hideous beasts, false prophets, dragons, evil spirits, and cups of abomination—and the consequent triumph in heaven, a Last Judgment rather more skillfully painted. Not all of this is clearly visible or remarkable painting, particularly when one considers that the murals here were probably painted between 1400 and 1525, later than Giotto's "Life of Mary" murals. But there is neither justice nor profit in comparing Italian with English painting; these have their own distinct dour appeal. The loveliest things, however, other than the bower of ceiling, are the antique tiles over which you are sliding, helping restore the brightness and vigor they must have lost during the centuries when they were covered with wood or linoleum.

Under the great umbrella of stone, among the bits and pieces of medieval centuries pasted together by the nineteenth, you are standing in the womb of British government. Primarily the meetinghouse for the monks of the Monastery of Westminster, it was used by its royal builder, Henry III, as assembly hall to meet with the feudal barons in matters of government. The Great Council meeting in the spring of 1257 is generally considered the rudimentary first sitting of Parliament. A century later it became the meeting place for the Commons, the mercantile powers who had pushed their growing guilds and insistent voices into notice. Under their feet, in the basement, the coffers holding the royal treasury and around them the ecclesiastical might of the abbey. Seemingly a thing of forever, the abbey was ultimately dissolved, and the Chapter House became a record office, filled with tier on tier—along its walls and the gallery which then existed—of the details of deeds and births and deaths, property exchanges, proclamations, correspondence, costs of stone masonry and cloth, the labor hired for the digging and filling of ditches. The vast accumulation was transferred in 1866 to the Public Record Office, and a few of the most remarkable put on view at the Public Record Office Museum (p. 65). The Chapter House was then restored to the empty, noble relic you see now with no practical purpose but its own fine excuse for being.

Out of the abbey, sit with twentieth-century London for a while, and study reminders of the nineteenth, on the low wall that surrounds Abraham Lincoln. In front of you is a garden burdened with heroic statuary, in the usual aggressive public-monument style, and to the right, the abbey whose darkened stone, etched and defined with skeletal white which makes of it a negative, flat and unreal in the thin sunlight, a dusty, ancient echo to Parliament's stalwart voice. Behind you, the Middlesex Guildhall, a convincing piece of Victorian Gothic whose façade is peopled with stone warriors and ecclesiasts, ladies and burghers, and, over the center, a flourish of shield and a plumed helmet.

And as you walk toward the corner of Great College Street for a remarkable profile view of the Parliament Buildings, you are surrounded by Lilliputians dragging flight bags (the current fashion in the primary grades, and available at most markets) full of food and an extra cardigan for the day of London sights, propelled by a hardworking teacher and a dedicated mother. Behind them, a covey of tourists in necklaces of camera and light meter, already glazed with the day's sight-seeing and the threat of more. A priest moves like a black and white sheepdog, forcing a line of knifelike boys with Mersey accents, laden with straggles of bags and lumpy boxes, into a coherent group, halting one group, releasing another into the brisk irregular lines of heavy traffic. You can easily escape the traffic, if you go back west of the abbey, into Dean's Yard and the sedate, scholarly squares that yield to the retiring, uncommunicative blocks of flats, on Marsham and Tufton streets, for instance, that lead to the Tate Gallery.

Before the Tate, though, it might be feasible to see what little one is permitted to of Lambeth Palace, diagonally across the river, and in some ways a companion and parallel to Westminster Abbey.

Built at the turn of the twelfth century into the thirteenth along greens that then ran to the river, Lambeth Palace was meant for the archbishops of Canterbury and remains their palace. In its long eventful time it was attacked by Wat Tyler's rebels, who forced the incumbent to shelter in the Tower, it received royal guests, and it had at least one ecclesiastical tenant of haughty ungovernable temperament, attributed to the fact that he was Provençal. On a visit to the Priory of St. Bartholomew's he was given the honor of a solemn procession and then told, flatly, that he wasn't welcome. John Stow reports the encounter, out of older annals, and continues:

He [the archbishop] forthwith fell on the subprior, and smote him on the face, saying, "Indeed, indeed, doth it become you English traitors so to answer me." Thus raging, with oaths not to be recited, he rent in pieces the rich cope of the subprior and trod it under his feet, and thrust him against a pillar of the chancel with such violence, that he had almost killed him; but the canons seeing their subprior thus almost slain, came and plucked off the archbishop with such force that they overthrew him backwards, whereby they might see that he was armed and prepared to fight.

The Frenchmen of Lambeth attacked the canons, who ran "bloody and miry, rent and torn" to complain to the Bishop of London who sent them for help to the king at Westminster. The king would have nothing to do with them. The citizenry now aroused and ready to "have hewn the archbishop into small pieces, who was secretly crept to Lambhith," invaded the palace, fighting and shouting, "Where is this ruffian? that cruel smiter! he is no winner of souls, but an exactor of money, whom neither God, nor any lawful or free election did bring to this promotion. . . ." The archbishop emerged and complained to the king, in time, of his maltreatment by the canons of St. Bartholomew. There Stow leaves us with nostalgia for a lusty medieval time when powerful princes of the church and their cohorts fought like Saturday night in Camden Town.

Lambeth Palace, still medieval despite many changes, is extremely quiet now, and much of its interior private from the public eye, except on special occasions. One of the entrances, next to a nine-teenth-century church with a tower 400 years older, is a distinguished

Tudor gateway, and on the river side of the building, an earlier tower, named for the Lollards. They were followers of John Wycliffe, the Oxford scholar who translated the Bible into the Vulgate and, expelled from Oxford, became the leader of a church reform movement that may have been one of the earliest stirrings of the Reformation. It was in this tower that Lollards were believed to have been imprisoned, and through its gate one may enter for a quick look into a portion of the famous library, primarily devoted to church matters, in the Great Hall. It is a treasure trove that reveals, now and then, fascinating items such as the recent exhibition of books on Elizabethan Puritanism, and in a side case, the suede gloves, embroidered in silver, which Charles I handed to Bishop Juxon (the Archbishop Juxon whose arms can be seen in the hall) just before his execution at Whitehall.

Out of the violence and learning, the spirituality and blood of the Middle Ages, one can leap through time, across the river, to the Tate Gallery for the incandescent late Turners, the strong, silent world of Henry Moore, perhaps a superbly shown collection of Picasso sculpture and drawings or a groovy "with it" collection of bright slats and pipes, plastic drains and apoplectic newspaper photography enlargements, colorful loops and bumps, cloacal basins and vinyl turrets happily turned out by large children shouting, "Look, Ma. No mind."

However, there were other art times and schools no more satisfying than yours. For that sort of consolation, look for earlier paintings at the Tate, beginning with the Cholmondeley twins, born, married, and brought to bed on the same day, circa 1600. Together in bed, fully dressed, belaced and jeweled, with their shieldlike bodies flattened against the dirty-white pillows, they hold their respective babies, who also look like twins, in stiffly parallel bundles. By the time the artist reached the bedcover, he had exhausted his skill and patience, and he left it a murky red-brown with chalky spots that might be cloth, earth, or mud puddle.

Portraiture improves in the paintings by Marc Gheeraedts of Anne Pope and Lady Elizabeth Pope, shown as Flemish beauties with round foreheads and the familiar look of being shaved and skinned. Then, the same painter's "Earl of Shrewsbury," hieratic and still, but expressively large and bold at the same time. The mood changes to effulgent candy box in the paintings of lovely ladies by Peter Lely, smooth, sweet and rich as good chocolate. The sweet and rich continues on, with welcome interspersals of solid bread, in the ice-cream families of England's golden age of painting. Among the infinitely tall ladies with dark pearl faces, one finds Gainsborough landscapes, trying for Constable effects; Hogarth portraits, some conventionally characterless and a number of them robust, sure statements; Thomas Lawrence's lyrical, fleeting touch is here, particularly deft with a portrait of a Princess Lieven, a light and lovely thing—somewhat Ingres, somewhat Renoir. The Constable paintings carry the shock of prophecy in enchanting landscapes of about 1820, magical small cloud studies, dramatic views of Hampstead Heath and the amazingly modern "Dell in Helmingham Park," a heavy, passionate laying on of colors that one associates with much later paintings.

What is there to say about Turner? There are people who find him overrated. There are people who stand bewildered, mesmerized before the sharp, Rembrandt-esque self-portrait of 1798; the advanced Impressionism of paintings—"Eton," "Windsor," among others—done as early as 1805–10; the red-browns melding into orange that look as if they might have been done by Redon who wasn't yet born; the courage in his time to paint the mysteries of shimmering, undefined space and atmosphere, discarding the safety of specific shapes and dimension, to let them disappear in the blazes of color. Where these splendors of sunsets and burning ships came from remains in the mysteries of genius, but one can see the simple tools that shaped them in the last Turner gallery that holds his ship models, the jars of ground paint, a box of little round flasks of water colors, and his palette tempestuously smeared.

In a gallery below, the disturbing Blakes and the calming, no-impact murals on the walls of the cafeteria, for which you might be eminently ready.

Open weekdays 10 A.M. to 6 P.M.; Sundays and bank holidays 2 to 6 P.M. Free. Westminster Station, then buses 77, 88.

# 16 Spitalfields, Whitechapel, Shoreditch, Bethnal Green—Geffrye Museum and Bethnal Green Museum

Once again at Liverpool Street Station: Southwest, there are the fortresses of the Bank of England and the exchanges, plebe and royal, worlds of banking and shipping in Victorian buildings and neo-Georgian buildings, tall modern, and horizontal modern, and decorations of Jovian might, like the enormous golden doors crested with eagles and crowns of Barclay's Bank on Lombard Street. The more pedestrian might of heavy ship's chain decorates a new building of the Baltic Exchange on St. Mary Axe, while a mixture of local charms reveals itself on Clement's Lane: a sign noting that in 1784 Dositey Obradovich, the first minister of education in Serbia, lived here; a burst of copper steeple and four Gothic pinnacles on Cornhill; near the end of the lane the dragon of an ironwork sign and, at the corner, the handsome friezes of the new Clydesdale Bank. To the east and northeast, the Sunday markets area (p. 108) and directly west, the Guildhall, sections of ancient wall, new housing, and slow, very slow, reconstruction.

Try it directly east, for the sort of corner all big cities hide. Almost directly across from the station turn into Artillery Lane, where centuries ago the gunners of the Tower practiced weekly against an abutment of earth in a closed yard. It separates into two grimy alleys, brightened by one moribund beauty, an eighteenth-century storefront, once proudly ornamented, now splintered and scratched. The sounds you are likely to hear, particularly on a Saturday afternoon, come from the local pub where the singers are no longer capable of standing too well, but leaning and bending, weaving and tottering, they give out lusty, if uncertain, music, and from Artillery Passage, a lively warren of Indian and Near Eastern names, where women call out of windows to disappearing boys. Two odd smells weave through the usual combined odors of damp poverty: the odor of smoked fish

103

from an establishment on Frying Pan Alley, around the corner, whose
resting trucks carry, as if they were girls in a beauty pageant, large
gaily painted mermaids with bright smiles; and that of a strong disinfectant which blasts out of a shelter on Crispin Street, one side for
women, the other for men. One inert figure lying near the doorway
has not quite made either.

Dead or not quite alive, he may be one of the slow suicides you have
begun to see in the weekend yard of St. Botolph Bishopsgate (p. 69),
or standing blankly, or lying at the side of Spitalfields Market, to
which Crispin Street opens. The large wholesale produce and flower
market stands on what was once a Roman burial site, and possibly
also used by later Saxons, discovered late in the sixteenth century,
when the ground was cut for clay to make bricks. It gave up not
only funerary urns, but oil jugs, coins, sarcophagi, and a quantity of
long, large nails, which the Elizabethans with their taste for dark plots
and bloody deeds liked to think were driven into the skulls of the
dead Romans in wholesale murder.

Brushfield Street, the south side of the market, presents the façade
of one of the noblest, now derelict, churches of London, Christ
Church, Spitalfields (1723). The brooding Hecuba of a church was
the work of Nicholas Hawksmoor, a pupil of Wren, a member of
his staff, and a revolutionary of style who took the church out of
the foamy, secular charms of the master and clothed it in monumental dignity and religiosity.

It is not an "attractive" church in any light sense of the word
and is now unused, gathering dirt and damp rot from the rain that
comes through the broken windows, a dead pigeon on the floor, and
not too much hope of revival from the monies collected in an indifferent, poor parish. Its ponderous deep shadow stands with terrible
appropriateness over the bodies that inhabit its green, described as
recently as 1956 as a "pleasant, peaceful patch" in a run-down
neighborhood, once the center of silk weaving in the city. Now the
green is a meeting place for the drinkers of methyl alcohol, cheap and
purchasable at hardware stores, which have more relaxed hours than
pubs. Sometimes the money is earned by a few hours of early-morning
marketing carting and the alcohol shared—or fought over—with companions whose eyes and legs have been too deeply affected to work at
all. On the steps of the church a man sits, just sits, in dirty limp
clothing, clutching a bundle wrapped in old newspapers, staring dully
into the street. A woman with a wilderness of gray hair and dirt
streaks on her broken, uncomprehending face leans against a railing
of the churchyard, motionless, her back to the broken-voiced con-

viviality on the church green. There a semicircle of meths drinkers urge on the one woman among them to rouse a man prone on the grass, her man apparently, because she crawls the few yards of lawn to his side and, tenderly, lovingly, with clumsy, wavering motions, pats his cheeks, gently lifts his head, tries to cajole and tease him into responding. He stays inert.

Off Commercial Street there is a small street, named for Walter Brune and his wife, Rosia, who late in the twelfth century founded a priory and "hospital of great relief" that held 180 beds, "well furnished, for receipt of the poor." St. Mary Spital lasted as hospital and church property until its absorption by Henry VIII, but there remained an old churchyard pulpit, and a building from which the local worthies and the children of the hospital could hear the sermons. The population of the community remained fairly stable until the Great Fire forced people out of the City into this and other areas. Shortly after came the Huguenot refugees from France. Many of them were skilled silk weavers, and their advent expanded the silk-weaving industry greatly, extending the craft area from Southwark, where there had already been weavers in Queen Elizabeth's day, through Whitechapel and Mile End, to Shoreditch and Bethnal Green, the concentration of merchants and controllers remaining in Spitalfields itself.

It was an area of abject poverty; merciless exploitation of child labor; riots; particularly against Irish immigrants who consented to work for lower wages; and great wealth. The whole complex structure collapsed with the Industrial Revolution, after which Spitalfields fell into desuetude, picked up a bit by the building of the large market. Since there was no need to rebuild, except for breaking through a few thoroughfares, Spitalfields still has a considerable number of its eighteenth-century houses, little tenements over small shops now, but of their indigenous shape. Walk some of the streets north of the market, or confine yourself to the eastern streets, near the church. Fournier Street, for instance, a dingy set for the imposing, sooty, and serenely balanced back of the church, is crowded with manufacturers of clothing in a small way, but the doorways—pilastered or columned, with carved supports for elaborate hoods—speak of older, richer trade. At the meeting with Brick Lane stands the Great Synagogue of Spitalfields, almost as unused as the church. Jews still in the area will tell you that thirty years ago the synagogue was packed for all services and had to turn people away on the High Holidays. Now on bits of tacked-on paper and in chalk, one of the few left (not enough to make the minimal congregation of ten, in many instances) advises an indifferent world that prayers can be chanted at 7:15 A.M. and at 6:10 P.M. The pattern of mid-eighteenth-century houses lines Princelet Street, and Wilkes, marking a corner with a large blue house, a red door, and a rusticated keystone, and continues on past unused warehouses, unaspiring windows of furriers, and a savage little alley called Puma Court.

Continuing down Commercial Street—trying to imagine behind its truck-ridden face the shadow of the splendid house of Elizabeth's good friend, the Earl of Essex, that stood here—walk into Fashion Street, whose corner is a meeting place for those Spitalfields drinkers who can still converse, except one woman who stands, clutching the indispensable bundle of rags, on the corner, immobile, as if forever. This is Jack the Ripper territory and still looks it: bottles, empty and broken in doorway; garbage and stench; a small Greek grocery; and on one side of the street, a Moresque fancy, long used as a warehouse, losing its Scheherazade curves in dust. Thrawl Street and Flower and Dean Street present the century-old housing—great advances in its time—that spread through vast areas of the East End, much of it being replaced, some of it standing tight, dark-eyed, sturdy and dour, belted by heavy iron grating to protect its basement windows; square holes into the gray yards and stairways open to the weather.

Brick Lane may or may not have had anything to do with the Elizabethan brickworks, although proximity and name urge the notion. The same authority who speaks of Spitalfields' Christ Church yard as a pleasant, public garden (Harold P. Clunn) describes the Brick Lane of a generation ago as the "nadir of East End poverty" and adds that improvements since have made it an "East End Bond Street" whose "shopfronts and window displays would do credit to a West End thoroughfare." Brick Lane is slipping again, not yet a "nadir," but the shop fronts of shoes and yard goods are faded; the whines of small lumberyards have replaced the millinery; a broken, burned Victorian splendor sags threateningly over the street. The once talkative Jewish boardinghouses for men are tenements for quiet Indian children. Small shops devoted to buttonhole making, zipper supplies, and pleating are still, as always and elsewhere, Jewish, but they are surrounded by a Pakistani Social Club, a New Bombay restaurant, while Hot Beigels (the spelling connotes the Polish pronunciation and provenance of the Jews here) competes with an Arab Club. Derelicts wander on the street, and the usual swift-moving, hortatory madwoman. The rest are customers for the local movie, which shows Indian films, and the "Continental" groceries that carry stocks of curry powder and sacks of couscous. Two Madrasi gentlemen discuss the day's news inside the corner on Heneage Street, against a background of Hebrew lettering proclaiming a synagogue, from the look of it not much, if at all, used. The eye is caught by an old-time chicken market, but it lacks the letters that say kosher inside a Star of David. Jewish New Year's cards are still printed on Brick Lane, and kosher Hungarian food is still cooked and served, at No. 19. Eggs are still sorted and candled in the old, careful style, but the street smells of curry and the people who buy fish-and-chips in newspaper wrappers from Alf's Fish Bar (at the corner of Hopetown) are West Indian, East Indian, North African, South African. Although Alf is Jewish, born in the neighborhood, brought up in the neighborhood, and an affable, informed historian of local matters, he has no Jewish customers. Not only do they distrust the oil and the dishes, but there aren't that many of them left. (Go in to Alf's if only for a paperful of chips and a polite word from Alf and a look at the tall protective fence around his frying vats, the old tiling and pressed tin on the wall, the blackboard that tells you plaice, haddock, and cod are offered, the sign that gives the glad news WE ARE NOW FRYING NEW POTATOES, the red door, and the indispensable large salt and vinegar dispensers on the red tables.)

According to Alf, the breweries near the north end of the lane are "maybe three hundred years old." Local pride causes exaggeration; they are not anywhere near that old, but interesting buildings to see and well designed—complex, busy, surmounted by an enormous tower and incorporating as offices what seems to have been a serene church once upon a time.

Brick Lane is undergoing the changes, as is much of once Jewish Whitechapel and Bethnal Green, that have in recent years affected the Lower East Side of New York, with an infusion of newer peoples, which replace one dominant color with a twisted strand of many. The strand takes on ugly hues on Old Montague Street, where, in the summer of 1967, arrests were made for drug possession and sales. One look down this alley convinces that all vices practiced in black, dirt-crusted corners, might live here, in a newer version of Doré's London and Dickens' and Mayhew's. It was once a respectable little hollow of Jewish shops where old ladies plucked fresh chickens and the groceries sold garlic pickles and oily herrings, and a neighbor could pick up a Hebrew prayer book for not too many shillings. One old lady still sells a few eggs and cans of soup; one grocer in a neat, small shop keeps a tray of herrings; two old bookshops seem to exist solely on the holy miracles in their tomes. The rest is an Indian restaurant; a Pak-India sweets shop; unused, bomb-damaged houses closed with corrugated tin and wooden slats bound by rusted iron; and a few houses with dirty, swollen bellies, broken windows, fallen stairs and bricks. The perilous stoops are used by the whores who gather to serve the Indian and African men who saunter, and wait, talk a bit, saunter again, have a drink in a boxlike café, and a look out again, to see what girls have gathered on the crumbling stairs or may be emerging from Black Lion Yard, the narrow street that leads to Whitechapel, the buses and the tube stations.

From Whitechapel, one can see a sign over the Yard that designates it the Jewelry Centre, which it was for many years. Whitechapel couples once examined the windows of the full row of jewelry houses to look for engagement and wedding rings. The boys' bar mitzvah watches were bought here and the brooch for Mama on her fiftieth birthday. Examining, bargaining—"Harry offered me the same ring for two pounds less"; "I swear by my dead mother, may she rest in peace, it costs me more"—going away, being pulled back in the ancient market minuet, were an important part of the festivities. There are only three or four jewelers left now, and Dave, the sweets and tobacco supplier for the jewelers, a polite, patient man, saddened and exiled in the island of Indian sweets shops, a Pak butcher, a Halal (Arab) meat shop, and the stream of people running through the alley: African men, Indian children, dead white faces with black-ringed eyes under coarse hayricks of hair, the many stages of insobriety, the old ladies in the Orthodox wigs stooped and creeping up the hill, too tightly enclosed in years and dim vision to notice the changed voices and faces around them.

Out of Black Lion Yard and across Whitechapel Road, an astonishment in the shape of the Church Bell Foundry, a pair of Georgian houses with a set of fine doors. Behind those doors, it is said, was shaped the Liberty Bell of Philadelphia.

If it is Sunday, and you haven't yet gone, there might still be time for the Petticoat Lane (Middlesex Street) Market immediately eastward with a stop at the Whitechapel Art Gallery, a large, well-lit, and unaffected room to see what may be showing. Or if it is a weekday, look in at the gallery (free, and a sign makes a point of telling you that you may smoke) in any case, and then turn into Goulston Street, and watch the local boys disappearing into the Whitechapel Baths and listen to the broad, echoing sounds that are dozens of young voices bouncing against swimming pool walls. Of the Sunday market only one jellied eels, winkles, and prawns stand holds the fort.

The weekend spaces of pushcarts, hucksters, frying onions, swathed long African skirts, and cheap kitchenware are gone. Entertainers and overripe fruit have given way to parked cars and the Sunday barrows and wooden supports piled mountain high in a yard between Middlesex and Goulston streets, creating a pattern of dark threads against the blue stairwells and poles and the spirals of descending and ascending figures on the housing estate stairs beyond.

Here, too, the changing colors of the neighborhood are nicely juxtaposed on New Goulston Street. A saried mother and her doe-eyed daughter shop at the Taj Mahal Grocery, while the older son stares at the imitations of Carnaby Street in the windows of Litman's Men's Clothing, bannered by a street rack of suits. Goulston begins to sprout woolens shops, a strewing of trunks and suitcases at one corner, a delicatessen that calls itself Israeli, and Taj Trading, the supplier of local sari silks, some of it dreadfully sequined for the current local style. The heart of all this eating and selling and gossiping is Wentworth Street, the daily market that remains when Petticoat Lane contents itself with its busy weekday shop life and salamis, denuded of stalls.

A woman buying fish wears a tall headdress in the sunburnt colors of African cotton; an elderly gentleman sampling a grape wears a cap like Nehru's; several bent shoppers drape babushkas over their wigless heads. Above them soars a white Sikh turban, and one old man, wrapped in the mists of Cabala, wanders through in a deep, black, round hat of the Hassidic Jew. No trace now of royal grants or church, not even the chromos and cheap mother-of-pearl rosaries and plaster saints, in cheerful colors and inconsolable expressions, one usually finds in markets.

Assured by the presence of delis and bakeries—one permits you to taste its sturdy wares along with tea or coffee at a table—and a joyous blue set of "Gentlemen" and "Ladies," wander among fish and gay banners of cotton remnants, herrings and flowers, rye bread and weeds, fake furs, records, nuts, cheesecake like sweetened clay, cheesecake that is a bit lighter (though not too much; airiness in texture or taste is not for Wentworth Street), fish and shoes, grapes and ruffled nylon nightgowns like rococo clouds. When the market shows signs of closing (more or less at two o'clock, depending on the weather), cross Commercial Street to an extraordinary set of buildings, Victorian adorations of the Gothic. Out of the dark brick banded with glazed brown and yellow, perpendicular arches and bosses of stone, a round turret and solid iron balconies, peer the trembling white heads of the old, for whom this is now a hospice. Around the corner, on Com-

mercial Street, sharing a rectangle of park used by the old blinkers in
the sun, and some of the earthbound architecture, there is the famous
Toynbee Hall, founded by Oxford graduates—among them Arnold
Toynbee—as a settlement house for advisory and educational work
in the area. On the walls of a modern arcade and in a red-brick
close with a suggestion of round tower and a Quaker meeting hall that
looks like a village church, the range of activities shows in signs and
bulletins: day and evening classes; clubs and groups of educationally
handicapped children for which volunteers are wanted; an eating
place; a theater; a cinema; bulletins of local art shows and museum
exhibitions; aid for invalid children and old people; an osteopathy
service; a Campaign Against Discrimination section and a Citizens'
Advice Bureau. It is an impressive array grown out of Victorian guilt
and enlightenment, maintained by the London taste for education,
further and enchantingly exemplified in the Bethnal Green Museum
and the Geffrye (pp. 110–112), not too far off.

## Geffrye Museum and Bethnal Green Museum

The Geffrye Museum is a fine example of the English talent for making
the search for information appealing, easy, and at the same time
thorough. It began life early in the eighteenth century as a set of almshouses established by the will and money of Sir Robert Geffrye, a
Master of the Ironmongers' Company and one time Lord Mayor of
London. As the city grew to and around the pretty Georgian buildings, the Ironmongers' Company built new almshouses in the country,
and after a considerable time of legal disputes Sir Geffrye's sanctu-
aries were sold to the London County Council, which refashioned the
interior (the outer shape embracing the gated garden is as it was
250 years ago) as a furniture museum suitable to a neighborhood that
still houses a number of cabinetmakers.

The phrase "furniture museum" strikes a stodgy, misleading note;
the Geffrye is an alert and lively place, a set of rooms exemplifying
artifacts and furnishings of various periods. One section deals with
shop fronts of the eighteenth century taken intact from old streets,
another with tools and materials of an eighteenth-century woodworkers'
shop. The authentically furnished rooms start with the sober, carved
oak in furniture and wall panels of the time of Elizabeth I. The Stuart
room, still fairly simple but for its plasterwork ceiling, stems from

the busy time of rebuilding and refurbishing immediately after the
Great Fire of 1666. Then follow successively the designs of the great
eighteenth-century furniture makers into the Regency, on to the clut-
tered eclecticisms of Victorian times, the calmer but not as engaging
Edwardian, up to modern times, calmer still, with the reasonable,
worthy stamp of the Scandinavian.

The rooms are hardly dead shop groupings: Ornaments, china, clocks,
and portraits are placed among the appropriate architectural details;
windows are backed by contemporary street vistas; and costumed
figures re-create the styles of dress for each period. Every room has
an informative panel offering additional matter of social history, the
movement back and forth of international influences in design, famous
names to help spot each period in history. The spirit of the place, soaring through its antique history and possessions, is youth. The first
building in the left wing is a children's workshop hung with riotously
colored and boldly designed fancies of young splashers and announcements of art shows and films. At almost any time a group of schoolboys is being taught, by an inspired teacher who is a member of the
museum staff, what it meant to read, to write, to eat, to sit in a room
of the Restoration. Out of the wealth of costumes which abound in
London, she has dressed one boy in a properly sized costume of the
dour time of Cromwell and another in the silks, floss, and plumes of a
gentleman of the time of Charles II, thus immediately establishing the
released swing of mood after the Commonwealth. As they stand,
modeling, at first abashed and then easier, the Charles II boy begins to
strut a bit in his small space and fingers the plumes on his cavalier's
hat, while young Cromwell straightens and scowls for his role. (There
is an actor in every Englishman.) As they grow into their parts, the
lady asks, "If you had to choose between these two tables, which
would you pick?" The answers come quickly, and from them recog-
nition of uses, ingenuities, and design principles emerge. "If you were
a designer (and remember the tools to which cabinetmakers were
limited) how would you improve this cabinet?" rouses a show of
hands and eager, informed discussion.

In the halls students of design and decorating are making notes from
charts and displays. Their friends wait for them in the small coffee
bar, hung with a photomural made from an eighteenth-century engraving of London south of the Thames and a delightful checkerboard panel of ewers, dishes, silver, and china of mixed periods. A
speaker pipes in impeccable Swingle Singers' Bach, a neat quintessence of the learned, amiable, intelligent, looking back, looking forward, ambience.

The Bethnal Green Museum is a companion piece not only by proximity but in the fact that it, too, commemorates the local furniture makers, though its major displays are devoted to the Spitalfields craft of silk weaving. Physically, it is absolutely nothing like the Geffrye. In contrast with the intimacy of the latter, it is a glass and iron hall, one of the temporary buildings set up in 1856 to serve as the South Kensington Museum, the forerunner of the Victoria and Albert. When that ponderous, great museum was erected, this interim building was moved to its present site and served not only as one of the remaining examples of its type of mid-nineteenth-century structure, but also as host to a variety of exhibitions, from treasures now in the Wallace Collection and the Tate and Dulwich to examples of animal products and foods. During the war it became a Meals Service kitchen, then took on its function as an adjunct of the Victoria and Albert in 1950.

Considerable space is devoted to historical prints of the neighborhood and nineteenth-century English painting, as well as masterful craftsmanship in English silver, porcelain, glassware, and pottery. One gallery is devoted to furniture and the evolution of that craft, and much of the rest is reserved for the beautiful textiles and embroideries, the varied and charming boxes from which the gifted needlework emerged, and, most important, the enchanting costumes they made, for a diversity of ladies going back to the early eighteenth century, for brides of the nineteenth and twentieth centuries, and to dress a large collection of costume dolls.

To go with the dolls and as an adjunct to the history of furniture making and interior designs, there is a beguiling (and as V and A collections usually are), impressively large gathering of toys, more dolls and dollhouses.

Admission is free in both museums. The Geffrye is open Tuesday to Saturday 10 A.M. to 5 P.M.; Sunday 2:30 to 6 P.M. The Bethnal Green is open Mondays to Saturdays 10 A.M. to 6 P.M.; Sundays 2:30 to 6 P.M. Both are closed on Christmas Day, and the Bethnal Green on Good Friday as well. For the Geffrye take the 22 bus which stops in front of the museum. Then, if you like, go back on the 22 to Hackney Road and change for the 6, 6A, or 253 to Cambridge Heath Road, a few minutes' walk from the Bethnal Green Museum.

South of Bethnal Green Road the vendors of puppies of several breeds, familiar and unrecognizable, gather on Sundays (before one o'clock) on Sclater Street to display their caged wares that yip or sleep or flirt with one or another transported child. Toward Brick Lane, the custom becomes birds and the accouterments they need and, suspended against a wall, plastic sacks, each holding one goldfish and its allotment of water. Around the corner, on Redchurch Street and the happily named Chance Street, a three-card gambling game, a now-you-see-it, now-you-don't London variant of the shell game, eats up a shocking number of pounds less nervously than it does on Petticoat Lane, where there are more policemen in attendance. When the monotony of losses is enough, walk down Redchurch to look at the highly enameled shoddy furniture made and sold in local shops whose ancestors made the splendid bookcases, tables, and chairs that sell for awesome sums on Mount Street, South Audley Street, Bond Street, and their tangents.

The puppies, birds, seeds, cages, dart sets, and children are left behind as the street swells to a large omnivorous area of market everything: jellied eels and tea, records, fruit, hot dogs, a muddy ramble of discards on a rainy day. Near the center, on a high platform, stands a sturdy man in a white undershirt dampened with the sweat that rolls off his cheeks and on his chest a large Star of David. He wraps a colorful blanket around himself and in a coarse, vital voice shouts: "I've got a present for somebody." Loosening his Indian robe, he takes up a plastic-wrapped bedspread. "Who's got a double bed? Come now, somebody here likes to sleep near 'is wife? What are you, a bunch of poofs? . . . No, you don't sleep in no bed," to a feeble bum someone has pushed forward. "All right. I'll make you a gift of it," and the hypnotic money patter begins. "I don't want ten quid, I don't want nine quid, and I don't want eight quid or seven quid. I'll give it away—today is prizes day—I said I'll give away the bleeding imported twelve-by-eight spread for a bleeding five quid." No takers. He throws the bundle to his assistant, who repeats, self-effacingly, "Five pounds. Five pounds, anyone?" waits a moment and returns the cover to the platform. The boss man takes up a comforter. "Here I am holding a double blanket of the finest wool. The freeze is coming; the weather reports say zero next week and blizzards. Who'll give me three bloody quid for it? Here," to the assistant, "give me back that cover." He lifts both blanket and cover in their neat plastic cases, balances them high on one steady hand—the circus strong man now—and begins the chant again: "I don't want eight quid or seven quid or six quid. Give me five bloody pounds, not guineas, pounds, for the lot. It's present day; I'm giving everything away." Seeing a camera trained on him, he calls, "Hey," and after a moment, "Okay. I'll smile for you. I've been on American television," turning to his audience, "Imagine, American telly!" Back to the camera, "Say, where are you from? If you're German, you can't have no picture, nor Arab neither, we don't want 'em around. American? Okay. You can have a picture." He stretches his mouth to a big caricature smile, still juggling the plastic bags, then throws them to his assistant, and again picks up the "Indian" blanket. He spreads it full and resumes the liturgy: "I don't want four pounds for this beautiful, artistic, all-wool blanket, I don't want no three pounds, ten shillings, I don't want . . ." and the incantation fades, as one leaves, into the voices of radios and the bawling that follow the stings of love, from the records stalls.

Outward and north of the Indian blankets, the yip of puppies, and the silent flights of goldfish sits the still, mighty eighteenth-century Church of St. Leonard's, Shoreditch, in the momentous style of Hawksmoor, learned by his follower, the elder George Dance, and behind the church that rides like the crest of the wave made by the joining of Hackney Road and Shoreditch High Street, the gentle Sunday flower market, of small plants and cut flowers—lovely, unremarkable, common flowers—that sell for very little and for less as the morning wears on to one o'clock, time to empty the water buckets, pick up the roses that fall to the street, put the unsold chrysanthemum plants—"three [blooms] for five bob"—away, and call it another Sunday.

Covent Garden has infinitely more varied and fresher flowers, but nothing of the impromptu mood—vendors like large, robust children selling flowers on a roadway for a lark—or the shapes and faces of eighty years of public housing that this neighborhood presents, still working-class but not the mean warrens and dens that these streets were for centuries. On Columbia Road, there are one or two large pubs that tinkle piano music and are as safe and private to the locals as Mayfair clubs to their gentlemen, shops that sell jellied eels and live eels, a few derelict storefronts of the nineteenth century that shield unprepossessing fur enterprises, streets with French names—Tuilerie, Gascoigne, Chambord—probably echoes of the French spoken by Huguenot weavers. A complex of new housing near Edwardian housing, made plump and jolly with green grillwork and balconies and rows of stone lozenges. At the end of the flower stalls, dark, narrow-backed housing of the nineties and around the corner from that, the back of a Peabody (an American philanthropist) Trust House, in light brick with a pleasant flow of balcony. On the corner, an animated pub, garnished with colored lights and wax flowers and songs, making the weekly Christmasy gaiety lacking at home. Have a drink with the men around the piano in the public room or the ladies—spare or fat, rarely in between—in the saloon section, and go down the narrow street toward the big docile bulldog that sits solidly and quietly as a cement garden animal; past a handsome colored youth at a door painted bright blue, to contrast with his neighbor's yellow door. Man, dog, colored doors, and the narrow angle of street have the insubstantial charm and color of a stage drop.

Around back to the market, to get the dozen roses for four shillings now or an armful of geraniums at six, saunter among the good-natured calls of Cockney ease and intimacy and the ring of genuine politeness in the "much obliged to you" as you get your change. Down the middle of the street, walk a few of the neighborhood children, some of them too thin, too pale and old, and behind them, their big sisters, delightful gaudy girls in stiff, not quite chic minis, accompanied by the blackest of eye makeup and the yellowest of hair, aiming for King's Road similitude, not quite reaching it—a little too emphatic—and somehow more appealing.

By way of Brick Lane, and what the locals call its cosmopolitan population (Euphues still lives in England), plus a few wavering gentlemen who carry tenderly three or four bottles whose return may buy them another drink, into its southern extension, called Osborn Street—once known for its anarchist cafés—across Commercial Road, and into *The Market,* Petticoat Lane, if you haven't yet been there. If you have, try another, less familiar one, to the east and north.

Where Shoreditch High Street, Hackney Road and Kingsland Road meet, between the Shoreditch Station and the Town Hall, Old Street narrows to an end. One block to the west brings you to Hoxton Street, where once upon a time there were popular music halls, and now lively market stalls, fish-and-chips shops, unselfconscious pubs that ring on Saturday nights and Sunday afternoons and sweets shops that remind the public as Mother's Day approaches, "Don't forget Mum." Hoxton curves into Pitfield Street and a lively spread of pre-World War II tenement housing in fresher colors, but not too different in design from the usual Victorian structures.

Out of the housing playground noises, one enters a silence of working-class respectability shut in rows of small houses, some well kept, some dull and ashen, and—it may still exist—a large field of low white boxes, papery temporary housing backed by tight lengths of older tenements. The mood lightens at the corner of Southgate Road and De Beauvoir Crescent with two substantial pubs, the Rosemary Branch and the Southgate Arms, and sinks again along De

Beauvoir Crescent and Whitmore Road, in bits of murky canal and stretches of demolition.

De Beauvoir Square is the relief and surprise, dedicated to green and benches and a small playground and flanked on two sides by gray-brick houses with curly Dutch roofs over bay windows and a agile rhythm of roof achieved by alterations of design elements.

Leaving by St. Peter's Way, and if it is Saturday afternoon, carried on a faint wave of murmur to the burst of noise and color of the Kingsland Road's market, flea and nonflea cheek by jowl. Outside the row of nonglamor shops of overenameled furniture and hard wool coats with imitation fur collars, prams bubbling over with the highest-heeled and gaudiest shoes in London, cradling stiff pink and yellow and white hats, all starch and nylon straw. The young are smearing their cheeks and trying their teeth on the obdurate surfaces of jelly apples, while their parents crowd the winkles and mussels and jellied eel stalls, skillfully juggling cups of winkles, spoons, and chunks of bread, splashing the vinegar, standing and talking and chewing— London's working-class cocktail and garden party. The next eating stop is at a stand of frying things, puffy and doughy or sausagey and on to the soft drinks while Daddy hides from the market brouhaha and the family in the soft, boozy womb of a local. The family goes on exploring—the older boy examining watchbands and dissociated watch faces; the younger, a brand-new bike shining out of bins of old tools and clock keys which have lost their parents. Mum examines the lengths of cloth, old and new, and what with the utmost courtesy is called fur and remnants of lino, judging just how much of her kitchen floor she can cover with a sparse piece. Then she stands in admiration before the mirrors blazing with shiny, gilded flowers and vases bristling with ornaments. Farther on, old dishes and new dishes, covered with roses and gilt curlicues, and beads and baubles and sewing thread and mountains of nails from upholstery tacks to the spikes of skyscraper welding. No antiques, no finds, no bargains worth dragging back across the ocean, but a cheery, vivid, indigenous market.

# 17  Flower Weekends

Having done Portobello Road, or Carnaby Street and later King's Road, the restless—lazily, slowly restless—young prepare for their evening. It may lead them to an anonymous road, in slowly awakening Chalk Farm (north of Regent's Park and south of Hampstead Heath). Over railroad sidings and back of a stone watering trough for cattle there is a Victorian Round House, which also served, for a while, as the storage vaults of a large liquor company. On the wall of the circular building appears the symbol of Centre 42, whose artistic committee, headed by the playwright Arnold Wesker, proposes to use the Round House, after refurbishing, as an arts center which will encompass theater, ballet, painting and sculpture, poetry readings, and music. While the plans cook, the Round House is used on occasional weekend evenings for "happenings," such as miniskirted and high-booted girls wading around in small seas of Jell-O and varieties of psychedelia. Too often, with imitators imitating imitators, the results are disappointingly unswinging, leaning to the catatonic.

Though some of the young may gather earlier, it is time enough to go after the pubs close at eleven. Outside, two bobbies do not exactly guard the entrance but, in the indirect English style, breathe awareness of it. Inside, at the head of the stairs, a sign advises that anyone selling, using, passing drugs will be handed over to the police. Then you dive into *it*, whatever it might be called. A steady turning of lights plays a dazzling flood of colored spots along the floor and breaks as shafts over the spectators. On a left wall, a Mexican bullfight film, soundless, broken off and blanked intermittently. In front, two huge screens, one lingering on horizontal bands of color that change fitfully and then hold. The other shows frenzied dashes and flows of colored liquids breaking into droplets and bubbles, sucked back and spat out again in a pounding rhythm as of heart and lung action. To match the visual pounding, ear-breaking sounds forced out of drums, guitars, and organ electrified to the maximum, bounding off the round walls and into the high ceiling. As the musicians blast and rock and shake like ineptly handled puppets, two girls dressed in minislips shake and bump and grind indefatigably at either edge of the stage. One of them is too skinny to have really shakable parts and either too inept

**117**

or too shy to try; the other is a girl who does so well and enthusiastically that one begins to wonder about the dope sign.

On the floor, stand the hundreds of young, mesmerized by the
flashing color, paralyzed by the noise and the thumping ebbs and
flows on the screens. A few of them, fortified by the pubs, dance awhile,
then hide under a sweater draped like a photographer's hood to kiss
as they rub against each other. Several couples shake and bounce and
jerk more decorously, never touching or even looking at each other
or even sharing a style. One splendid young man hidden behind a
raven's wing of black hair snaps his fingers high above his head and
then thrusts out a graceful long arm in his dream of himself as
Belmonte-Artemis; his girl shakes lazily in her dream of unmitigated
sex in the hot tropics. The frightening ones are those who dance all
alone. A boy in a bandsman's suit with bronze buttons, wearing
glasses and the hairlessness of fifteen, turns and sways and prances,
eyes closed, totally inside himself. And around him are the prowlers
with the bottles of wine, the eager necks and the alert, pickup eyes,
not quite as young as the girl in a bright-pink safari suit, just short
enough and tight enough to display her peachlike buttocks, or the
spectacularly beautiful boys of sixteen and seventeen, simply waiting,
or the young man with black hair to his shoulders and a sweeping
mustache, long lace cuffs, and a lace stock for his cavalier's coat.

They stand, the *au pair* girls, the shopgirls, the showy boys, and
the timid boys, made comatose by the assaults of sight and sound
while waiting to be quickened. Except those few who stay sharp
enough to become interested in the screen bullfight and the nude that
jumps from screen to screen to be blistered by the pulsating blood or
striped in green and purple bands or—and very few of the hundreds
laugh—sent bouncing off the back of the charging bull.

You may be one of those who is tired of the doomful sounds made
every time the young are mentioned, doubt the artifices of togetherness,
and feel that humanity has been much of its time a "lonely crowd,"
but here there is a quintessence of loneliness: No one talks; it is impossible; few dance; there is no young horseplay or laughter, little
movement; only the standing alone among the other lonely saplings.

Back of the boys asleep on a bench near the exit, there is a table
laden with the *International Times,* a not quite printed set of sheets
dedicated to snarling at fuzz (police), the Establishment (all entities,
moods, and statements non-"beat"), revealing and extolling whatever
is psychedelic in all possible meanings of a most elastic word. Necessarily, there is an article about sex explaining the not very mysterious
messages of billboard cards and going on to describe a few historic

whipping sessions. Defiance of the authorities and literary freedoms appear in a photo of three girls wearing placards on Portobello Road: one placard is a large *F*, the second a large *U*, the third a large *C*. The fourth letter was obscured. The police had stepped in but—the English skill at compromise and providing safety valves that prevent serious explosions—permitted other combinations, *FCKU*, *UFKC*, *KUFC*, etc. The sheet gives instructions for smoking banana-skin fibers—an overelaborate process for a questionable kick—and a recipe for extracting pure canabis resin, "superpot." Politics is dealt with in an article that identifies Kosygin with capitalism and links Mao Tse-tung with Jesus Christ in his gentleness. The cover is of a nude whose body and face are painted with floral arabesques and, under the title, the redundant defiance: "BUST OR NO BUST WE HAVE GROOVY GIRL AND WE ARE PUTTING HER ON FRONT PAGE TO SAY THAT FREE SPEECH FREE IMAGE LIVES ON IN GREAT (?) BRITAIN A PRETTY GIRL IS LIKE A MANIFESTO MORE WILL BE SAID AT FREE SPEECH HUMAN BE IN BANANA WEEKEND TURN ON AT ALEXANDRA PALACE." More details about the coming turned-on weekend, listing pop and folk groups with fanciful names who would appear, and the extortion to "come holy sexy unholy stoned straight come and be free speech free body paint know yourself as fleshsoul." In straighter Establishment type, the information that admission would cost one pound, the profits to go toward the defense fund of the magazine which had been stopped as an obscene publication.

Alexandra Park is a vast green to the north of London, on a rise, with high-vaulted and glass-domed exhibition halls that dominate gardens, reservoir, lawn, and waters. The fourteen-hour Technicolor dream unfolded in one of the largest of the halls, the Alexandra Palace, at whose door there was—contradiction to the free-form, dreamlike permissiveness promised—a squadron of sturdy young men who made sure that no gate-crashers slipped by. Once in, a vastness of nothing. A place blinded by enormous searchlights and deafened by the assault of a dozen groups of electrified guitars and bellowing microphones. In time the ears began to accept the throbbing and pounding of noise. The monstrous, glaring eyes were hooded, and through the fog of smoke from cigarettes, from slender candles carried in some illusion of holiness, from sticks of incense meant to hide the smell of marijuana, one began to see the slow molecular oozing of thousands of figures around the big impromptu control tower in the center of the hall and sleeping around the tall, slender pillars. Toward the back, an immense organ grated with thin-planked scaffolding, and near the entrance, a bright spiral for sliding down, seated on a doormat; sixpence per ride and popular with the non-somnabulist nonoozers. On the upper walls, the same movies, not as ardently propelled, or as incessantly, as there were in the Round House last week. From the dimness of almost still bodies floats a blond girl with a broad, placid face and lank, unbridled hair, wearing a loose North African cloak and carrying, as if it were a rosary, a Woolworth necklace. She appears and disappears throughout the night, always alone, always with the same inward smile on her face, fingering her beads, very privately a nun—or a travesty of a nun. Another unaccompanied wanderer expresses beatitudes with two wands of daffodils in her *sevillana* hat and three wilting in her hands. The believers in the good peasant life wear primitive jackets or rough sheepskin tied around their shoulders, recorders in their hands, while others, who know the good life is anywhere but here and now, sport caps from Afghanistan, milkmaid dresses, Oriental embroidered coats, and old policemen's capes (the relics of dead fuzz are acceptable). On the headband of one young man: INNER SPACE; a heart or a voodoolike design, is drawn on the faces of several others.

The fantasists among the girls, betraying the deep conservatism of nest builders, are rarely as exuberantly gorgeous or imaginative as the men, whose faces are painted gold and red and white, the designs picked out with sequins; who wear long, red, crushed velvet robes that, under a thatch of hectic black hair, might be the robe of a provincial Boris or old man Karamazov. The girls settle for mini-skirts or blue jeans or the tiny dresses like damp undershirts, when they are not sniffing flowers or telling beads. By far the biggest, bushiest, longest expanses of hair belong to the men, and it doesn't take too much imagination to picture the millions of lice contentedly nesting in this paradise of unwashed crowns and beards.

There is no letup, ever, of the noise; but occasionally a new beat is felt, and following it, one comes to a group of Afro-West Indian drummers in attractive caps and loose cloaks of strongly colored African cottons. The drumming is superb, a matching and countering, a coming together and an opposition of rhythms—ceaseless, frantic, and controlled, accompanied by sporadic shouts of encouragement and enthusiasm. The brain is lulled, the ear seduced, the eye mesmerized by the swift, fluttering fingers and thumping palms. The crowd grows larger and denser, shaking, tapping a bit, concentrated on receiving the rhythms. Two figures close to the platform expand their gestures from consent to ecstasy. One is a girl in an ordinary dress with hair demurely tied in two childlike clumps. Her eyes closed, she stamps and turns and shivers and extends her arms in darting, angular gestures. Near her a blond young man in a shirt made of a red plastic sack shakes and trembles and stamps, faster and faster and more violently, his eyes shut, too. As if to crawl into the gullet of the rhythm, they both mount the platform, she bound in a frantic monotony of gesture, he spreading his arms and fingers in figures of Indian dancing, pulling them back to meet under his chin as he moves his head from side to side, a smile borrowed from a dancing Siva on his sweating face, his feet trampling the world like Siva. The girl ultimately drops off with exhaustion, but he is indefatigable with the tirelessness of drugs or madness.

The mountain of noise presses down on the highwaymen's hats and the feather boas. The tower's giant eye burns through the mist and pours its hot, dry light over the organ, where dozens of insect figures are climbing over the shaky scaffolding, a few of the brave stamping a triumphant dance on the frail top plank. A strong tutelary voice cuts through the noise in the crazy kindergarten: "Get off! Get off! It's dangerous!" and the large, lithe children clamber down in the dark of the closed Cyclops eye.

The energetic among the slow, swamp creatures continue to whirl down the red sixpenny slide and, bored with that or the sixpences gone, place their girls on their shoulders and charge them at each other like jousting knights. A few yards from the bumping, squealing girls, one girl lies in a nest of sweets wrappers, banana skins and the glint and stains of a broken wine bottle. Although one of the commodities offered free—along with the candy floss that leaves pink tufts on black beards—is love, few of the aimless walkers stop to worry about her. Ultimately, someone lifts and drags her off the floor under the flat saurian gaze of a silent group sitting alone and together nearby, equally oblivious to the couple (of the forbidden years, over thirty) writhing in the same bed dance they performed on the floor of the Round House last week. One begins to find other Round House acquaintances: the frenetic young cooch dancer; the chic Italian couples who have come to swing with swinging London and by now clearly hating it and each other. The sleek, coutured-by-Cardin gentlemen who have left their tables at Deux Magots to try another weekend across the Channel; and, most memorable, the cavalier of the shining black hair, the dashing mustache, long black stick, and the cascades of white lace at wrists and neck.

The night grows older and more tired. The small snack bars are crowded with drinkers of coffee and eaters of pasty cake conversing meagerly. In the center of the hall someone empties still another bag of chicken feathers to drift onto shaggy heads and down to the floor to lie with the cans and bottles and orange skins. The punk sticks have been used up, and the slender candles, the daffodils wilted and drooping, the balloons fewer and leaner, the soap bubbles wafted more slowly out of the plastic rings. Beyond the arches at the side of the hall they sit or lie, still expectant, strangely reminiscent of a crowd gathered along the wall of a Mexican shrine, pilgrims who have walked all day and now ease down among their poor bundles for the devoted waiting that may bring them a miracle. What is the miracle these young—many from the provinces, some from other countries—wait for, as they lie like lees in a bottle? Some alone, curled protectively on themselves or stretched out flat and open, others in symbiotic designs, lie crumpled together like the debris around them or folded on each other like neglected puppies. In the universal waiting one couple necks violently for the cameramen who will pluck this incident out to show how wild and sexy this vegetable event was. Another couple, responding to a national atavism, plays picnic: She takes neatly wrapped, thin sandwiches out of a rucksack and puts them carefully on a blanket, while he uncorks a bottle of rough Portuguese wine. The food eaten, they settle down to the sensibly bucolic; both lean against their pillar, he tootling on his recorder while she reads the newspapers. Toward the back of the hall, near the exit, someone has placed a plastic igloo bordered with bunches of bananas—*the* symbol—and inside it a half dozen girls and boys are seriously working at blowing up balloons.

The next morning, just before noon, Alexandra Palace has put on its usual Sunday guise. The big pub and restaurant with a view, closed the night before, is serving the people who have come to examine exhibits of camping equipment. The playground is full of children, and distant lawns sprout picnicking families. Down the hill comes the cavalier, the back of his pants dusty, silken hair, black stick, white cuffs still impeccable, accompanied by an Isadora Duncan in a flowing robe and a girl in blue jeans and leather jacket. At the entrance, sitting propped against the wall, five or six tired left-overs, the boys British, the girls American. Still hoping to find out that *something* had happened, one asks. Oh, yes, a young musician had got up into the organ and played some Bach. Appropriate for a Sunday morning, one suggests, waiting for a snarl. Yes, isn't it?, sweetly. One girl, asked what she thought of it, spat out, "It was a nothing, just a plain nothing; you should see a happening in San Francisco." The other girls nod agreement, but the boys, trying to defend the regional product, can go only as far as, "Oh, it was all right." One girl, hearing an American accent, says, "Where are you from in the States? From New York? Where? Oh, my family lived in Yonkers, but I lived in New York," the plump face suffused with pleasure and homesickness. Clearly, they are broke and undoubtedly hungry, but one cannot offer them money, the ugliest characteristic of the ugly American. Cigarettes are passed around, and out of one pretty, sullen mouth, "My God. A real American cigarette." And this cry of pleasure and the homesickness click a number of the night's pieces into place. It was a Halloween party for which no one had an address; they were looking, waiting, but no one came to get them. These were, the thousands of them, young children, two-year-old sayers of no to everything, whether they like it or not. They need the simple, easy tunes of the recorder, the candy floss, and ice on a stick, the accomplishments of blowing up balloons and wafting iridescent bubbles, the triumph of soaring feathers in pillow fights and dressing up in grown-up rags. (Whatever else it means, the banana is one of the earliest solid foods given infants, mashed for sucking infant mouths.)

It is a telly generation, conditioned to have things happening before it, while *it* happens to nothing. The maniacally incessant screen images, the unbearable, paralyzing noise are a thousand television sets gathered as one braying monster—and a necessity. The only other place to be is the quiet igloo-womb, where one may eat lollipops and cuddle in the plastic amnion, and perhaps the world and its wars, birthing and rearing children, the woeful droop of buttocks, and the hardened eardrum will never reach them.

Immediately after this event there was a television show based on some aspects of the long night and, after that, a discussion of the show with two television interviewers, a local journalist, and two supreme "flower" leaders, both from Canada or the United States, to judge from their accents.

It was a Mad Hatter party, the British gentlemen kind, eagerly asking questions. Waves of sincerity misted the screen as they tried to find out the meaning of "psychedelic" (the "beautiful people" rejected the word as meaningless). But why make a strong point of "communication, love, tenderness" if words, surely an essential vehicle of communication, are rejected? Suzie Creamcheese, one of the invited "beautifuls" in veils of hair and witch eyes, laughed and laughed and threw another handful of confetti over herself and her partner and, in the approved floating halts and starts and monosyllables, said that words get in the way of real communication and that the beautiful things happening at the Alexandra Palace were ineffably happy and loving, beyond words and all that logic jazz. One kindly elder, settling back in the warm cushions of BBC liberalism, says, "I approve of . . . well . . . this . . . what you're doing, concentrating on love and understanding and gentleness, infinitely better than the violence of the young Red Guards of China." "Oh, no," says Suzie, laughing under her shower of confetti and stroking the arm of her bearded, brocaded friend. "The young Chinese are communicating and loving in a new kind of nationalism, not the old kind that makes imperialism and wars." The paternalistic, interested face closes, appalled at the violence under the beatitudes. The compere carries on with a question to the young man, the editor of the forbidden paper, and asks him whether the television show was just. He thinks it was, more or less, but he objects to the fact that the paper wasn't mentioned often enough and that not enough stress was put on the fact that 10,000 people were willing to pay a pound each in support of the paper. From the beard and well-coiffed long bob and the dazzle of metallic shirt and tie comes no stumbling among words but articulate iterations that keep imposing the name of the paper, like a TV showman advertising his forthcoming night-club act.

The final question: "How long do you think this will last?" Suzie, the antiworder, leaps forward with her bubble of laughter and a wave of the arm and hair. "It's over now, the moment it happens. But at the same time, it's transforming the arts, and what is in me now will go on in my children, and they'll pass it on." The "with it" journalist nods enthusiastically; to him, this—whatever it is—is a true, valid, burgeoning force or maybe a way of proving to himself that he isn't really middle-aged. The anti-Red Guard man remains handsomely, Britishly aloof, and the compere soon closes the program, leaving one with the conviction that the young man will make a place for himself, in time, as a well-tailored, successful journalist or highly placed huckster, and Suzie with her screen of soft hair, her plunging neckline, her studied incoherence, her gleeful exhibitionism—like a baby splashing in a tub—could go far, and very likely will, in the Establishment world.

The wanderers take their desert boots and dusty peplums southward to the city, many of them walking. They might stop in Highgate's woods to lie among the trees in the light, smooth, dappled green like watered silk or picnic on the remaining bread in their sacks on the lawns, watching for one disdainful moment the white cricketers.

Then they might wander down to see what Hyde Park has to offer. The first encounter is disappointing, a group of mothers gathering signatures for a petition to keep the threatened maternity ward of a hospital open. Mothers, especially do-good, agitated mothers, are in the hierarchy of the enemy. On to the next, more amusing and un-shadowed by Mum: a group of men, beery types, one in a cap and vigorous on the castanets, the others lustily singing robust hymns and everyone jigging easily in simple, impromptu steps. Opposite them, an attractive, shouting argument around an Indian speaker. His crowd of volatile Pakistanis and Kashmiris, Communists from Kerala, and conservatives from Bombay keep shouting to each other, "But what about—" Between questions driving through each other and the in-comprehensible accents, the show palls and the rucksacks move on to stare blankly at one shy, embarrassed missionary lady alone on a frail box, about to get off, but in the presence of her new audience, she suggests—too timid to exhort or urge—a ladylike return to Jesus.

A dealer in the occult stands over a sign that invites you to his offices in Stepney, where a rich inner life will be revealed to you, "the blue-white diamond you have in you" there opened for your con-templation and profit. His rich inner life is apparently a goad and sting. He shrieks, "You are filth, living in filth, like animals," the fury squeezing and crumpling his face, his too small set of new pearly teeth slipping in the force of the vehemence. Near him, a splinter-faction Communist has a fine time shooting at the world's favorite target, the United States, rarely neglected by any political Hyde Park speaker.

One of the regulars (recently arrested; it *does* happen in Hyde Park), stands before a banner marked COLORED WORKERS. He is a dapper Indian, quick, intelligent, flashy, illogical, contemptuous, and salacious. The problems of colored workers lie in a covered corner while he explores the sex life of the Englishman, a pitiful thing. On holidays, he says, the Englishman goes mountain climbing while the English woman saves up all year round for two weeks in Italy where "the spaghetti is longer." (Great roar from the crowd and the speaker who enjoys his own wit.) He attacks the myth of the virility of colored men, a fiction to make him appear more animalistic and an expression of the white man's impotence, and then describes the timid, lackluster way of an Englishman with a maid and the direct, hot vigor of the colored man. No one questions his logic or what this has to do with workers, but hopes he'll go on and maybe become more explicitly graphic.

Weaving among the vendors of Christ, occult fury, titillation, wit, anarchism, hospital wards, anticolonialism, anti-Americanism, is a small, plump woman in her fifties, her pouter pigeon shape decently contained in a silk Sunday suit, complete with white gloves, shoes, daisy pot hat, and neat glasses, who goes from one group to another shouting, "Another unqualified liar. Shut up. Liar. You don't know what you're talking about," and, after singing out sturdily a few lines of an old music hall song, moves on to repeat her performance elsewhere.

The wanderers soon grow bored; the turns are the same as last week; the only novelty is the unspeakable mothers. Next stop, Trafalgar Square. A few (a very few because not many of this group believe in any political action or, it seems, any action at all) will go down to Whitehall to join the March of Shame for Britain's complicity with the United States in the Vietnam war. They help carry coffin-shaped black boxes marked THOUSANDS OF VIETNAMESE CHILDREN, banners that say, WE ARE ASHAMED OF BRITAIN, and American flags with swastikas for stars and stripes of bombs. They mingle with young anarchist and Socialist groups and listen, unresponsive to the wit or lack of it in speeches made by a bogus Harold Wilson, George Brown, and Queen "Kathleen." (It is a much more serious offense to impersonate the Queen than the Prime Minister, explained by the fact that the Queen cannot answer back.) Then, wherever they are —the girl in the bare blue feet and the man with the yellow jungle head and the boy with home-dyed hair of grassy green—they sit down, to wait, again to wait.

In the meantime the "weed people" are sailing small red and white boats on the Serpentine in Hyde Park and propelling family-sized rowboats. The ducks contend with dogs for the profitable edges of the water. The children make tracks to the sweets stall, a steady row of ants to and from a store of treasure. The immense lawns are littered with inert bodies willing the sun to come out and stay. On the sixpence canvas chairs, two nuns converse, and an old lady dressed in black reads her *Corriere Milanese*. A few intrepid swimmers try the southern waters of the lake, while the cowards drink and eat in the restaurants shaped like a modernized cluster of African huts. On the bridge the lazy and sated look down on the fishermen, the gliding lines of boats and ducks, the whirling of leaves in the water, the pink flesh over the reds and blues and yellows on bathers and then across the many tones of green to Victorian turrets reaching out from the tops of trees and one crane on a new building site, hanging high and fragile in the waning afternoon light.

# 18    Hampton Court Palace

Possibly the liveliest, most brilliant ghosts in all of England live in Hampton Court. (We shall come later to a more orthodox pallid, mournful female ghost who supposedly still walks the halls.)

While Henry VIII was making do with minor palaces, Thomas Wolsey, Archbishop of York, a Renaissance prince-prelate, leased country land on the Thames from a churchly order and built himself a palace. It encompassed, beside the cardinal's tapestry-hung chambers and halls, apartments and offices for the varied personnel of his staff in his capacity as Lord Chancellor and head of the church. As a power in European politics, he was host to representatives of other powers with large retinues; for these, not quite 300 chambers were kept in readiness. Guests were fed from immense kitchens, which employed dozens of cooks, waiters, and chars, and were seen to by people who took care of the laundry, the fireplaces, the grounds, and the large stables. The total number of servants, clerks, secretaries, grooms, and footmen ran into the hundreds, and the cardinal's revenues were enough to support it all.

Henry received Hampton Court from Wolsey as a gift or bribe when the cardinal, who had not succeeded in wresting an annulment of the marriage of the king and Catherine of Aragon from the Pope, became frightened of the anticlerical winds howling about him and through the storm, the sound of the headsman's ax on the chopping block. The gift was a fruitless gesture. Soon after, Cardinal Wolsey was divested of all his lands and wealth, which became the property of the king. Having been stripped of all possessions, the cardinal was pardoned but had hardly settled into obscurity in his native York when he was arrested and only avoided execution by dying on his way to London.

Henry VIII expanded Hampton Court, added newly acquired treasures to the cardinal's fine silver and furnishings, and acted out his noisy life in the palace halls, dragging all his wives, willing and unwilling, long-term and short-term with him. When he took the palace over, he was still in marriage one, to Catherine of Aragon, the widow of his brother, Arthur. Anne Boleyn was in the palace at the same time and took part in court entertainments, but the queen had seen other royal mistresses, including Mary Boleyn, Anne's sister, among the court ladies before. Not too long after Anne Boleyn was delivered of the child scheduled to be the son and heir whom Catherine could not produce and who turned out to be, instead, Elizabeth I, the king's lustful eye fell on Jane Seymour. Anne's long, slender neck was severed, and Jane became queen and stayed queen long enough to produce the male heir, Edward VI, and to die of fever following childbirth. Anne of Cleves, whom Henry referred to gallantly as various kinds of Flemish farm animal, came to Hampton Court and was soon put aside, neck intact, to be replaced by the much prettier Catherine Howard, who didn't have the sense to rid herself of former lovers and with them, at age twenty-one, was beheaded. Catherine Parr married the king in Hampton Court, took care of him in his sick rages, supervised the lives of his children, and, with the combination of luck, patience, intelligence, and Henry's fatal illnesses, earned herself the title of survivor.

Elizabeth I used Hampton Court as a pleasure palace for riding and hunting, the amusements of masques and balls, and always some business, political or financial, from which she rarely altogether took her attention. The Stuart who succeeded her, James I, sported and held serious conclaves here but left a less vivid specter than his son, Charles I, who was imprisoned at Hampton Court for a while before his execution. The royal possessions were then sold off by Parliament, the palace kept for the use of Cromwell, and the art treasures from the incomparable collection of Charles I dispersed throughout the world, enriching ultimately the Louvre, the Prado, and a number of private collections, some of them later bought back by English museums.

After the weediness of Puritanism, Hampton Court blossomed again with Charles II, who brought his numerous shiny ladies to court levees, an awkward but necessarily acceptable fact to his queen. When William and Mary came to rule, late in the seventeenth century, they found much of the Tudor house too old, and they called in the accomplished Sir Christopher Wren to build them an entirely new palace. Only one section had been rebuilt, however, by the time Queen Mary died, and the interior of that was furnished and decorated by later monarchs, while the older buildings were left more or less intact. The royal commuting between Whitehall and Greenwich and Westminster and Hampton Court in magnificent barges or carriages stopped with the death of George II in 1760. A century later the palace became a crowning gem of the stately homes opened for public viewing by Queen Victoria.

In spite of redesigning and rebuilding, the loss of Tudor luxury, the changes wrought by Reformation and Restoration, by Stuarts and Dutch royal families and Germans on the English throne, Hampton Court belongs to Henry VIII. Whether they bear the symbols of Wolsey or improvements by George II or the careful patching of arts councils, the sturdy red-brick courts leading into one another by strong archways, earthbound, energetic, and practical, flanked by towers, embroidered with the sober stone lace of their time, they are his. The second gate tower, named Anne Boleyn's Gateway because it was built in her brief time by Henry, leads into a court that holds an astonishing clock, built for Henry in 1540, that tells all one would possibly want to know about time from minutes and hours to phases of the moon, the signs of the zodiac, and high tide in the Thames. Not quite as precise, but possibly more satisfying as humbler craftsmanship are the Tudor chimneys (almost all faithfully remade) that rise from the low rectangles singly and in clusters, like field flowers in a peasant's hand. Nothing to work with but red brick and their own ingenuity, the sixteenth-century artisans produced an amazing set of variations on the small-turret-made-of-brick theme, swirled the pattern, or arranged it in zigzags or diamonds or as bands or spirals piercing the attractive crowns.

The mood changes entirely in the Fountain Court wing designed by Christopher Wren, less "English," more of the Continent, buoyed by the play of white continuous arches, balustrades and classic vases, and the dazzle of many latticed windows set in a manicured "French" garden. Because of the warm color of the brick and the touch of fancy and excess in the windows, the house is mellow and amiable, quite unlike the austere beauties on which it is patterned.

In spite of the loss of splendid objects removed a long time ago, there are still artifacts for almost every taste. For the fancier of Tudor workmanship, the linen-fold wooden panels; a reminder of English Gothic in the Chapel Royal and its complexly vaulted ceiling, and the Great Hall, with its wooden hammer-beam roof a succession of broad arches, elaborately carved and hung with ornate pendants. (Somewhere among the restless griffins and lions and rosettes you may make out the initials of Anne Boleyn, whose pregnant presence seemed to inspire Henry to enthusiastic nest adorning.) For the practical, a view of the enormous fireplaces and ovens and implements used at sundry times, the serving hatches, the wine and beer cellars. The amateur of painting can while away some time comparing Mantegna's cartoons for "The Triumph of Caesar" which Charles I bought from the Duke of Mantua, to the ice-cream figures in whipped-cream clouds that float across a number of ceilings. Elsewhere, Italian paintings of several periods and the lovely wooden fruits and birds and flowers of Grinling Gibbons; the inescapable portraits of worthies ennobled by a painter's tact; and that famous gallery of ladies, "The Windsor Beauties," of the Court of Charles II, all rather sullen, as painted by Sir Peter Lely, very highly thought of in his time. The extrasensory *aficionado* might walk the Haunted Gallery, listening for the shrieks of Catherine Howard, doomed by her stupidity or lasciviousness, or the tap of the treadle on an old spinning wheel, no longer visible. The gardener can stay with the greens and the flowers, rigidly contained in the French style. For interiors enthusiasts, the cut velvet furniture of Queen Anne and the furnishings of state bedrooms, drawing rooms, and galleries and the large orderly views from some of the windows.

Lastly, the famous maze, which can be amusing when you are in the safety of a gaggle of schoolchildren who run and twitter through it confidently on a light summer's day. In a late winter afternoon, when the thick shrubbery becomes a black wall and you've lost your one companion around a bewitched curve, and nowhere seems to lead any-where, and the maze grows infinitely convoluted, and each minute holds its breath and stands terrified, and suddenly you are very tired, it is quite another experience.

By train from Waterloo Station or Green Line Bus 716, 716A, 718. Times vary according to season, but 9:30 A.M. to 4 P.M. weekdays and 2 to 4 P.M. on Sundays are safe. Admission two shillings for adults; one shilling for children.

# 19   Islington

Islington is to London what the Marais is to Paris—a parallel not to be examined too closely, however. The best Islington can show to compare to the Place des Vosges is Canonbury Square, a neat rectangle of early-nineteenth-century houses set around a geranium-filled park, its remnants of antiquity a section of sixteenth-century tower imbedded in later angles of stucco and, according to authorities, two Elizabethan summer houses, sheltering behind the walls that close off some of the local gardens and houses. Like the Marais, the light of Islington seems to be available only by passage through brooding areas where the weather always seems gray and damp. Like the Marais, Islington has its haters and lovers among the hordes of the indifferent Londoners who know it only as a peculiar, inconvenient place for the Sadler's Wells Opera to choose; to tourists it is terra incognita, the matrix for the antiques, baubles, and Victoriana of Camden Passage.

Islington is not for lingering and savoring as is, for instance, the City on Saturday morning. No bashful little medieval church will peer out of a gorge between two office buildings, nor will a turn in an alley blossom into the chic iron and glass of a Leadenhall Market. Islington is an area for two hours or so of walking in a revealing set of London urban moods: the decay of neighborhoods and their revival; who lives in the decay, who motivates the revival; lumpish classic and its graceful versions, the dour presence of Victoria and Edward as heavy grim housing; eccentricities and monotonies, fostered by land and building speculation that grew with the great spurts of expansion in the eighteenth and nineteenth centuries; and examples of almost every kind of square in the large London repertory.

Islington was at least a place-name and probably a minute village early in the history of London, one of the end destinations of walkers out of the city on causeways built in the early fifteenth century over the marshes of Moorfields. By the time of Henry VIII "Iseldon" had enough inhabitants to enclose the common fields with "hedges and ditches, that neither the young men of the city might shoot, nor the ancient persons walk for their pleasures in those fields, but that either their bows and arrows were taken away or broken, or the honest persons arrested or indicted. . . ." Always, and still, passionate of their greens and rights, and one morning spurred on by a leader who ran

131

through the city calling, "Shovels and spades! Shovels and spades!" a great number of Londoners marched on Islington, tore down the hedges, and filled in the ditches. In spite of complaints and the threats of legal action, the fields stayed open until, in Elizabethan times, they were built on with summer houses sitting in gardens, "some of them like Midsummer pageants, with towers, turrets, and chimney-tops, not so much for use of profit as for show and pleasure, betraying the vanity of men's minds [Stow]. . . ."

Islington continued as a place for midsummer pageant houses and sorties out of the city to wander among its bucolic charms and take the famous waters of the wells in elegant garden settings (one elaborated and exploited by a Mr. Sadler), frequently visited by royalty, and patronized for more than 100 years by believers in curative waters taken in the teahouses of pleasure gardens.

It is gone, all gone, leaving an evocative hodgepodge, eccentric squares and the blank unused, waiting for demolition or rescue.

Out of the Black Hole of Calcutta tube station named the Angel for a coaching inn that stood there for more than two centuries, going toward Camden Passage, you will quickly have the measure of the neighborhood: the hoardings on shops and houses, the clothing on the shoppers on the High Street, many of them colored people who, like colored New Yorkers, don't inhabit en masse the houses on stately rows. Having bought your treasures, squeeze your way into Chapel Market (off Liverpool Road), not too large and a bubbling minestrone of working-class buying and selling. Among the fruits and hideous rugs, the china, the toys, the fish and meats, the presence of other market basics: one Woolworth's, one Sainsbury's, one Marks and Spencer's, several small, cheap snack and coffeehouses, and, near the Penton Street end of the market, a large red-tiled pub, called the Salmon and Compasses; outside it a boy finishing his father's pint of almost black brew. In the middle of the market the ladies can take an hour or two at bingo or pressing sixpence pieces into the machines that rotate lucky or unlucky fruit combinations. The younger ladies, wheeling prams, concentrate on the local version of a Kensington emporium, repeating the clichés of vibrant color, signs that say FREAK OUT, and racks of cheap, bitty dresses like clots of confetti. Around the corner, on Penton Road, a market appurtenance, secondhand men's clothing, and one definition of the neighborhood at the end of White Lion Street, an English and Continental imports store, which means fringes of Italian salamis, vats of olive oil, and Italian sesame-seed biscuits.

Back on the market street, watch the children, many of them in their year-round armor of drooping sweater. When school is out and the streets become vacation grounds, dozens of children hang around the markets, looking, listening, crowding the ice-cream and sweets-shops counters, dashing on mysterious errands around the stalls and through the bulges of shopping bags. Their older brothers gyrate, hum, snap their fingers as living, free advertisements for the record shop they decorate. An itinerant key maker trundles his wheeled stall through the discarded cabbage leaves and the blaring of the phonograph, through the shouts of "Peaches, beautiful, ripe peaches, three for two shillings," "Go'geous [sometimes Cockney has a Southern accent] cowliflaar, a shillin' a 'ead, tike 'em awhy," and comes to rest near a masterfully designed stall, a careful composition of the pale green and lacy white of cut cabbage, the gold silk of large onions, the beiges and browns of small and large potatoes held in a fence of immense dark-green gourds.

Out of the market, in Bromfield Street, as it meets Parkfield Street, notice a gorgeous strip of ironwork that spells out SALOON, and in Park-field Street, the fierce, happy shouting of boys who are helping demolish a row of houses still adorned with carved wooden supports for their decayed overhangs, rather like those in Spitalfields (p. 104). The boys hammer and chip and bang in the ruins, occasionally shrieking as if they had seen a rat, and they easily might. Berners Road leads out to the façade of the Royal Agricultural Hall, a century-old splendor whose vast interior was used for many kinds of exhibition, but no longer. Across Upper Street and the lower end of Islington Green, the most serious, fancy funeral parlor of them all, in a splendid collection, the noble house of H. M. Repuke, the name in huge, golden letters, repeated and repeated again in white on the black face of the cur-vaceous clock. A large chaste candelabrum sits in each window, and on the sides, ornaments and golden stallions, a credit to a busy trade of Islington.

From the corner of Mantell Street and Liverpool Road, the narrow, irritable backs of late-nineteenth-century row housing and their militant chimney pots marching in phalanxes of tight threes. The terraces of Liverpool Road flow on, some raised and set back from little street gardens in sundry stages of neglect or abundance, their 1830 to 1870 shapes sometimes dissolving, sometimes well corseted in fresh plaster and paint—all of them shaping a long, quiet, rural street if it weren't for the shrieking band of trucks that tears through the somno-lence.

Turn into Cloudesley Square, absolutely quiet in a peculiarly dis-turbing Islington silence, for a look at the common local—and London

—rhythms of houses falling and houses rising. In place of the expected patch of inner green, this square hugs an overlarge gray "Gothic" church and thus converts itself into a Victorian ideal, the medieval village. Its exit to the south, Cloudesley Street, designed about 1825, tries for variety—and achieves it—with showy windows alternating with recessed windows, doors with pillars and doors without, sections of roof pitched back, some not. It is no architectural wonder, but an engaging oddity, enhanced by its flagstone sidewalks and its piazza shape enclosing a mob of vigorous, glittering, dirty children.

Gibson Square, across the road, breaks its uniformity in a more restrained manner, placing long, contrasting double pilasters joined by the usual Greek triangle on the end houses. What is left of its park is exceedingly pretty, all of it to become imminently a "good" square to rival the supremacy of Canonbury.

North, immediately, of this settlement of local pride and Adamish strivings, there sits a glowering, insane contemporary (about 1840), Milner Square, a compendium of blackened prison or warehouse elements impossible to connect with normal free human beings except for the saving presence of a playground enjoying brisk patronage, in the center of the square. It needs the sounds of children's voices, the spinning and swooping lines of play equipment, and the peachiness of fat blond babies in prams. All that is potentially threatening in long strips of dark wall pressing in on narrow, overlong windows, in square stuccoed entrances guarded by two hard slabs of wall, and a solid run of iron fence sharpened to spears is gathered here. As Sir John Summerson says of it, in his *Georgian London,* "It is possible to visit Milner Square many times and still not be absolutely certain that you have seen it anywhere but in an unhappy dream." Altogether suitably, the exit from this early Victorian hell is through a tunnel that leads into the flakes and scrapes of Almeida Street, laced with long, curly iron flowerpot protectors (another trademark of Islington), past Battishill Street, which has gone crazy with paint pots, like a nursery in a rainy week and confinement too long. On Upper Street a restless compendium of garlands and deep-set windows, swellings and concavities, stone urns and chess pieces pressed down by an openwork cupola above apoplectic Edwardian faces, and immediately below, companions to the architectural mélange, the Islington Chapel of 1888, next to the columned Parish Church and across the street, the Northern District PO, which needs the support of four carefully draped caryatids.

One writer has referred to Cross Street as a reminiscence of Bath. If it once was, it now isn't. Following the essential gathering of pub, fish-and-chips, stationer's and sweets, and a hopeful antiques and "things" shop, a row of houses on a raised terrace that curves nicely with its burden of pillared, pedimented, embittered houses, sheltering some of Islington's many Negro families and the old men in baggy pants and caps who stand quite alone on the streets or—always alone —sit on the benches of the squares, not reading, not looking at passersby or other bench sitters, peering weak-eyed into a void.

A glorious gold and black and glass SUPERIOR FUNERALS shines out of Essex Road, easily the most attractive and shiningly kept store-front in a line of the dowdy and less meticulous, surrounding death with the glamor that neither fried plaice nor gammon nor veal and kidney pie can ever have. Both north and south, Essex Road has its architectural wonders to reveal: South leads to the Islington Public Library, a World War I confection that searches out several styles of stateliness gathered around a large broken pediment with thick, coiled ends, like rolls of white paper around cabbage leaves, pressed against the inevitable shield. North offers you Sidney Smith's attractive shop in terra-cotta wood, gold lettering, panes of elderly glass, through which glow gold, silver, cutlery, clocks, and ornaments, lingeringly examined by the old ladies in their frizzed hair and bedroom slippers, who travel and explore in devoted, jabbering couples. Almost across the street, mercurial Islington tries its hand at still another form of architecture, early-twentieth-century Egyptian, expressed as a movie house with gaily colored papyrus leaf borders on its outer and inner tomb en-trances, surmounted by dynastic pillars.

The surrounding streets of pathetically clean and dreary houses sit in their strange, shocked silence (a quiet possibly, still, of the pause between bombs) that muffles even the roar of the herds of trucks on New North Road. A young woman, stylish and spritely, passes with two little boys and a baby in a pram, a man goes into the store-post office that advertises cigarettes and post office savings simultaneously, a woman pokes her head out of the window; but the effect is of a dead city, a wasteland cemetery that stretches toward the stelae of sky-scrapers in the distance.

The contrast lies north of Essex Road Tube Station, a peculiar old thing (p. 34). Walking toward a stand of greenery, you are soon sur-rounded by the vaunted charms of Canonbury which keeps itself to itself, fiercely secluded behind its trees and walls and fiercely scrubbed. Not all of it is by any means alike, though the tone—that pervasive, brooding quiet—blankets this area, too. Canonbury Park South and North and Grange Grove are burnished, respectable suburban streets of fresh, simple houses with vines and trellises trying to surround their new doorways, and the Islington window ornament which must at some time have made one Edwardian ironmonger very rich, and on Grange Grove, a housing estate that attempts the low, pleasant cotter's house look. Along the way you will have found Canonbury Square (early nineteenth century) with its good, lustrous door knockers and cultivated parklet. At the northeast corner of the square, where Alwyne Villas comes to an end, stands Canonbury's red-brick Elizabethan tower, now surrounded by the prepossessing eighteenth-century Canonbury House, and, of a somewhat later time in the eighteenth century, a gleaming row with heavy doorways over curves of steps. The tower also looks down on a telling mixture of modern London—a borough of Islington day nursery, an enterprising theater group, and the Francis Bacon Society, maybe still plotting to tear the laurels from the usurper, Shakespeare, and place them on the brow of their more learned man. Alwyne Villas, leafy and semirural, probably not too much changed from the time, 1821, marked on one of its houses, leads into the more wayward Alwyne Place, whose villas must have been a dream of suburban living once: heavy stone eyebrows over doubled entrances, bouquets of stone flowers, contortions of metal railing and etched glass, solidly ranked behind a strip of grass.

Following Willow Bridge Road brings one to a phenomenon that enhances and haunts Islington, the New River, channeled early in the seventeenth century to bring water to the city from Hertfordshire. You'll find it, quite tired and almost ready to give up, where Douglas Road and Alwyne Road almost meet at Willow Bridge Road. Sometimes it flows, a little, but much of the time it oozes or rests muddily, cosseted and landscaped into its lyrical burial ground. Here and southward, between Duncan Terrace and Colebrooke Row, the not so New River is interred in long, narrow parks with serpentine walks, and funerary falls of willow whose leaves cover the snail-slime track. At the side of swaying fences, bursts of indecently candid roses; on the strip of bank across the river, brown bundles of duck as sleepy as the river. A tall clump of trees opens suddenly to a line of wash and the pangs of love suffered by the Rolling Stones. The only other sounds are the distant voices of children, a gardener's scythe clanging against a rock, the hushed voices of two women sitting on a bench, their voices swallowed by the heavy, airless local quiet that breathes from the old people on the benches near St. Paul's Road, from the empty, square villas.

You might not yet be ready to leave Islington or, tantalized by its evasive flavor, decide to return, coming on it from the confusions of Sir Giles Gilbert Scott's cathedral station, St. Pancras, and big, plain King's Cross, soon to become a city planner's dream and, according to critics, a citizens' nightmare. After a look at the boisterous garden of the police station on King's Cross Road, near Acton Street, cross into Caledonian Road, a shopping street that gathers vigor and humor north of Richmond Avenue. On the bridge over the canal, boys are shouting derision and envy at boys fishing below (you'll find that Islington fishes its local waters as lovingly, and as unrewarded, as the fishers of the Seine), then into new housing, and near Copenhagen Street notice a common habit of old shopping streets, storefronts obliterating and bulging out of the lower façades of older houses.

Among the newer shops you will find the red guardhouse of a telephone and realize that you have seen none so far. Maybe the destruction of books and apparatus is too great in these neighborhoods, or possibly the neighborhood hasn't yet demanded more since it leads a self-contained life, friends and relatives immediately reachable around the corner or to be found minding the kids in the playground of a local square.

Beyond fenced, unfilled bomb sites gazed on by new housing and semidetacheds with scrawny gardens, one comes on a red-brick edifice, St. Mary's Public Baths and Wash Houses, which absorbs young men carrying tight rolls of towels around fresh underwear and—especially on Saturday before noon—issues forth young mothers and their scrubbed, slick-haired children. Gazing at them with some awe and considerable pleasure, as she waits for her mother to appear, stands a Topsy whose hair has been tightly twisted over twenty minute braids, pointing straight out like alerted antennae. Wander into Woolworth's, and if you can push your way in, buy a packet of biscuits at Sainsbury's, look at the cuts of meat, the kinds and prices of vegetables on the stalls, the prints on cotton aprons, the price tags on work pants, and above all, the miraculous variety that two eyes, a nose, a mouth, hair, and skin color can shape and reshape infinitely.

Adorned by a timidly florid library, sits Thornhill Square, off Lofting Road, swelled by its Crescent, displaying the complete community mixture, something for everybody: the gray stone church and flowered yard for contemplation and, across the street, the square green which is one-third bosky dell with a shady path or two; one-third benches, lawns, and roses for the parents of the children who occupy the last third, a playground. A new wave of child care and protection exaggerates itself in a toilet for girls, another for boys and a sign, ADULTS NOT ADMITTED. (At least one adult should be admitted to report that they badly need cleaning and painting, an astonishing contrast with most insanely clean London toilets.)

More nineteenth-century housing streams in all directions, surprised

by a lone high riser in the distance: some of it burbling gaily with
orange windowframes, next to purple doors, red windowframes and
blue ones, and one blank window—possibly to save on an early window
tax—adorned with a stone wreath; some of it bulging villas studded
with stone florescences and pocked with age; some of it trying to form
a middle-class "good" neighborhood; others sinking along with their
rotting plaster wreathes into numbness, a dry metallic odor of monotony, an expectation of misery or violence.

Barnsbury Square, however, shows off a few large shining houses at
its opening to Mountford Square, and Barnsbury Street is one of the
striving streets, beginning with the advantage of sparkle from a generous spread of window, of an antiques and country furniture shop (the
first harbinger of new-money improvements in a neighborhood), the
nice, big, Draper's Arms pub, whose chatty old ladies in the wrinkled
stockings and high-shouldered coats never, never looked at its "classic"
façade or into still another oddity of Islington squares, this one called
Lonsdale. Around a pretty French formality of restrained flower beds
which, in turn, try to contain an impassioned burst of pink-yellow
English super-roses, a tight, tight row that to us, 125 years away from
its creation, looks like familiar Ivy League college-Gothic. Without a
hairsbreadth gap between them, they press on each other their sharp
gables wearing hard white hats on their alternations of broad and
narrow windows. It is strange and strangely pleasant, the proportions
good, the style unexpected, the houses exceedingly well kept, the young
people who emerge not too far in age from the students one expects
to see. The pretty brown children trying to pay court to a fat, fierce-
eyed tortoiseshell cat—the brown and black animal with emerald eyes
that battens and grows huge in Islington—might be the family of a
young don in African studies.

Cross Upper Street, via the alley between the Infirmary and the
church, a narrow passage compensated by two names, St. Mary's Path
and Church Lane, and into St. Peter's Street, some of which has practically no sidewalk in the Italian style, and wander around through
the village streets, around the gray churches that gather them together
in an attempt at rural homogeneity. Danbury Street is a toy village, its
shop fronts lavender, peach pink, Della Robbia blue. One white house-
front smothers itself in flowers; the stationer's shop-post office is fire-
engine red; and a greengrocer decides that the color of oranges is the
suitable hue for his wood.

At their northern ends, Duncan Terrace and Colebrook Row are
one, a strip of street that curves in from Essex Road, picks its way
through dump heaps, one of them third- and fourth-hand furniture

that rests at night in a brick cave at the side of a truck parking lot. The adjoining garage holds up a pale woebegone house ornamented with a disk that tells you this was the house of Charles Lamb, not, apparently much loved here. The street ambles on and then divides, leaving Colebrook Row some new housing and a few remnants of the early eighteenth century, one driving school, one buttons and zippers shop, and, folded into a space under fenced-in trees, a stall of *objets* and art (weekends, usually), supervised by the same attractive, over-confident young that eagerly show their skills on the high streets of Hampstead, Chelsea, Greenwich Village, Provincetown, and Taos—in fact, in too many places all over the world. In spite of its ugly church, Duncan Terrace does better with cozy rounded doors and grillwork balconies, the grace note of Charlton Place and many young couples with fresh, newly hatched babies. The careful coddling of the New River appears here again, suggesting large wilderness and nobility with carefully arranged rock formations and stocky pines, Japanese to about the same degree as are Whistler's ladies.

Closer to City Road, the thread of water disappears and is replaced by flowers in *fauve*, tropical combinations—the Londoners' substitute for sun and warmth and the ebbing of passions—bordered by a group of houses with lovely lanterns sunken into the fans over the doors of once fine houses, now small clothing factories that give out the sounds of Indian music over the whine of sewing machines.

The fenced-in thickness of trees on Colebrook Row turns out to be the private fisheries of an association of London anglers. Walking down Vincent Terrace, peering into openings between the trees, you would expect to see a gathering of some London anglers, but perhaps that is a sometimes thing, or was. The local fishermen are a few little boys, one of whom, obviously not to be trusted, wears a life preserver that threatens to slide down over his nonhips. As background for the boys, the backs of houses, handkerchiefs of garden studded by prams and toys, a hopeful sunbather and on the balconies, a bright red rug, a pair of yellow slacks, a pink baby's blanket, rather like the hangings out of Renaissance windows for a great *festa*. The fronts of the houses, on Noel Road, following a curve of brick and a view of elderly, indus-trial brick, are no worse or much better than the local others, interesting only for the color of their waterfront yards and the fact that one of its bed-sitters was a nest of madness that whipped itself into murder and suicide. The young playwright, Joe Orton, lived here with his lover, a less successful writer. They both had served prison terms for defacing library books, mainly by substituting obscenities, verbal and photographic, for the innocent original matter in them—an act of protest against censorship, the Establishment, and the usual et ceteras. After their release from prison, the taste for juicy pictures expressed itself as wall decorations, which, according to the newspapers, were numerous enough to be wallpaper. Orton earned a great deal of money in a fairly short time and was in the process of earning considerably more; there was an impressive sum of money in the bank; things seemed to be going dazzlingly well. But they continued to live in the bed-sitter jungle of dirty pictures. One day, in the summer of 1967, Joe Orton was found hammered to death and his "room-mate," as the journalists put it, a suicide. (P.S. The comment occasionally heard soon after: "It *would* happen in Islington" or "Islington is the place for it." They are not sure why they say this, murmur something about its isolation, its populace of unused people, its troubled mood.)

Elia Street, another nod to Lamb, is a bumpy little row of two-story houses sloping down a broad street that opens on a wide sky for its brisk march of chimney pots, and then you are out on City Road, immediately below the Angel Station, at the side of a triangle worth lingering and turning on for a minute or two as a compendium of peculiarities. It has a lampless lampstand and a big Esso sign to introduce a gas station and, as backdrop, a large, bowed building exploding with design and harsh color. In a borough of startling buildings (in a city that makes a specialty of them), this is not the prize; that might go to the bulbous old Lyons Corner House whose color is that of old cleaning rags, to the north of the triangle. Above the omnipresent LADIES a clock with a cushion top lists the works of a dealer in metal objects, and on the avenue a group of nineteenth-century shops of listless displays. The busy triangle offers the welcome sight of not one, not two, but three plump red telephone boxes. One is only for emergency calls; the second has had its larynx torn out; the third is inhabited by a young man who has settled in permanently with his bulging address book and a mountain of sixpences.

If you have the time, energy, weather, and the shoes and are lured by the acrid fascinations of the neighborhood, you might want to take a loop walk southward in Finsbury and back, or combine it with Clerkenwell (p. 199). Goswell Road leads to Rawstorne Street and the Brewers' Buildings (1871–82) with crests over the heavy doors that call for a moat, stone flowers in the brick, and pristine white iron ornaments and spears guarding the stairwells. Then continue on through the seclusive rows of simple houses on Paget and Hermit streets, into the degrees of muteness on Wynyatt Street and Goswell Terrace, then, maybe after a stop at a fish-and-chips bar, into Spencer Street leading to an etching of derricks and fogged by distance, the unreal tall spindle of the G.P.O. Building. You may find that the elderly ladies and the little girls of the neighborhood have their hair cut by the local barber, as was the practice and maybe still is in poor streets of New York, and an open doorway—rare—blocked with bicycles and a half-dozen gleeful, noisy children.

A magniloquent pub, strewn with green and shamrocks, introduces St. John Street, which takes the second half of its curve near Sadler's Wells, opens to Chadwell Street, and that into still another square, this one Myddelton, named for the Sir Hugh Myddelton who caused the waters of the New River (1609–13) to flow into the city. Sitting around the expected unremarkable biggish church, playground, benches, and roses, Myddelton Square repeats the bright nursery-school colored doors but then confines itself to grays and whites to adorn its tan-gray bricks. The style stays in the surrounding streets in greater and lesser degrees of flakiness, to change at Lloyd Square for yet another classic variation on the square theme. The jagged, shark's-teeth line of pediments flows swiftly down Wharton Street into the gray, skinny shade of the ubiquitous Post Office Tower, straightens out on Lloyd Street, and Great Percy Street, planted with a new rich growth of green parking meters that look foolish here, particularly when they wear their weekend hoods. Nearby, the elevated green of Claremont Square whose slopes of grass and shrub hold a reservoir of the old local waterway. Immediately below it a number of buses plying Pentonville Road, and you are again very near the Angel Tube Station. However, there is still one local curio that is possibly worth noting, before you board the bus or plunge into the station. London, as indicated, enjoys commemorating its great men, indigenous and foreign, and plays no favorites. If he was a guest or a famous refugee—Freud on Maresfield Gardens, José San Martín on Park Road, an eighteenth-century Serbian educator in the City—he merits a tablet, and thus Lenin has his plaque, at the top of Vernon Rise, in Great Percy Gardens, and it gives his full name and credits: "Vladimir Ilyich Ulyanov, founder of U.S.S.R."

## ◦§ *London Is Where . . .*

In winter the hot-water bottle becomes to the adult what the little blanket is to the baby, ubiquitous, cherished, and its absence a source of anguish. Almost as important is the favorite cardigan, which sometimes acts as pajama top, as well as loving woolen arms. Then, there are the little heaters, dragged from place to place like stupid little dogs on a leash, and the "passion killers." That is the term English boarding schoolgirls use for the warm underpants no woman wants to wear or should be without in London's February.

There is, of course, the warmth of lovemaking. It is reasonable to expect a girl to respond to male charm via the traditional etchings, but it usually works better to say, "Come see my new, big heaters." She does, and the usual progress is made, until she must peel off one pull-over, then a second, and the woolen shirt, lacy and pretty as it might be, but still a woolen shirt, before she gets to the bra. Below, the boots have to be pulled off, then the patterned woolen stockings, and then the knee-length passion killers. By this time what was urgent is less so; the time is somehow not now anymore—wise schoolgirls.

On Sloane Avenue in Chelsea there is a set of apartment houses named the Nell Gwyn House which sports a figure of the gay girl herself as Spanish buildings might be guarded by a figure of the Virgin. Maybe it is the suggestive fact that she once lived in the neighborhood, but the house has, justly or not, developed a reputation for housing modern Nell Gwyns.

Among the marketmen and the coffee stallkeepers and the men who scratch the depths of Covent Garden sewers, the name of the man who built the extraordinary St. Paul's Church in Covent Garden is "Indigo" Jones.

No matter what Arts Council covenants may state, or the lists of directors, the man who actually owns the Royal Opera House at Covent Garden is the tall portly gentleman with the noble bay front and Empire mustachios, in distinguished costume and white gloves, who greets with a courtly bow the regal guests he has been welcoming to his splendid town house for many years. It is he who will hold the ticket—stalls only—of a delayed friend, and trust him to see that it is properly delivered. His proudest moment is the time he loosens his full baritone voice and, striding back and forth in the lobby, spritely but dignified, Don Giovanni inviting his guests to taste the pleasures of his house, calls, "Ladies and gentlemen, please take your seats; the performance is about to begin."

There is an immense bed-sitter (see Glossary) population, a lonely one. The foreign students manage; if they don't find compatriots in university classes, they search out clubs or institutes that wear their dress and speak their language. It is the old ladies, and some not so old, the widows on bone-bare legacies, the retired governesses on meager pensions, frightened by rising prices, who haven't the few shillings to spare for an afternoon fourth-run movie or the sour courage it takes to haunt the department stores with never a hope of buying. They read prodigiously out of the generously endowed public libraries, visit the museums, and, for the smell and breath of humanity, linger and linger over a ninepenny cup of coffee in their favorite, the cafeteria of the Victoria and Albert Museum. They rarely share a table, preferring to sit alone, their faces half-hidden by the book over which they peer at the cactus-petaled hats of a covey of matrons in from the suburbs or the coarse animation of a trio of design students. In a life filled and bounded by literature and museums, they become extraordinarily cultivated people, with no audience to show or lecture to (except when, rarely, a relative or ex-employer makes them a gift of a short trip to Italy, where their time of study and daydreaming has made of them superb guides to antique cities.

Once in a while the bleak silences of their lives become an insupportable vise, and they break out, each in her own way and always the English way. It can be as veiled and restrained as poking a fellow passenger on a bus with an umbrella. Then the apology, which serves as introduction for a discussion of the weather, the classic opening gambit good for a few moves at least. A piece of luck can leap from a map in the hands of a stranger. The desperation can be masked as a flower of politeness offered a visitor if he seems to need help, and from there, depending on the imagination of one and the haste of the other, the conversation can proliferate in several promising directions. These subtler means failing, there is the attack direct hooked onto any vagary the streets might present.

It may be one of those days when the fine rain comes down, up, and from all sides, as from a vast, gentle, invisible fountain. A bootlace trails through construction mud and is wiped and put in place on the steps of a house on Wilton Street. As the boot fixer straightens up, her eyes meet a spread of heavy, worn tweed, then an ample billow of the same tweed ending in a strip of balding fur at the neck. Above that, a broad expanse of ruddy face laden with a short stack of pastel silk dangling dismantled blossoms. The refined, careful speech that goes with the costume props that say "retired nanny" enunciates, "Are you having trouble, my dear?" "No, not ektchally [her speech forces the staunchest American vocal chords to bend to English modes; one wants to please the nanny by being a good, British child], thanks so much. Only a muddy shoelace." "Isn't it gha-a-astly, this terrible rain and the streets so filthy." (One meets this universal complaint with the usual surprise; Londoners sound as if rain happened seldom, a shocking insult in the benign climate of their imagination, the climate of sun-dappled bowers and dancing sun-drenched blossoms that their poets sing so exquisitely perhaps because they were and are so rare.) The required opening chords of weather talk established, we veer into developments with English directness, the obverse and constant companion of the famous reticence: "All day," says nanny, "I have had the feeling that my knickers were falling, and although I looked carefully in the ladies' on King's Road a half hour ago, I still have the distinct impression that my knickers are falling. Such a nuisance. Did you ever have the feeling that your knickers were falling?" "Oh, yes, frequently." "Really? Well that's a comfort. Good day, it was delightful to speak with you," and off to the next pickup.

Bus drivers are the only impatient, irritable people; watch out for their attack on traffic while you still have only one leg on the sidewalk.

If you fall down, several people will gather to pick you up, as they do in any other place. In London, the act is followed up; someone offers to find an ambulance. "No, thank you; it isn't necessary." Someone lifts you gently when you are ready to stand and eases you to a chair in the post office nearby. Someone else takes over and walks with you to the nearest chemist's, where the prescription clerk brings out water, absorbent cotton, and bandage to clean and cover your wound. Your companion insists on taking you home and is dissuaded only when you insist that you have a friend who will pick you up in a car. With a worried look and "Aren't you brave? It must hurt terribly," she leaves. You totter out soon afterward, having offered to pay for the attention and bandage. "No, thank you; that's quite all right."

The brief summertime is hashish, Spanish fly, and champagne taken in Persian gardens. After a short period of disbelief the Londoner releases the Mediterranean he has been hiding in his furled umbrella and under his bowler. The shoes come off, and the shirts; the summer dress, creased with years of lying in a drawer, donned; and everyone lies down dazed, drunk, and happy. They lie on ledges of buildings; in strips of grass fronting apartment houses, bare toes almost touching bus wheels; in barrows; on the pipes and lumber of construction sites; on the stairs of the Tate; under the wings of "Eros" in Piccadilly; in churchyards; spread-eagled on park lawns; splattered over the bottoms of rowboats on the Serpentine. Eyes no longer meet briefly to slide by each other; now is the time of the full, slow Italian strip. Women stare at their neighbors to find out—not always possible under the sweaters and coats of winter—who has begun to be skinny or fat or pregnant. Hand holding moves to waist holding and that to long kissing on buses, streets, and cinema lines. The pubs become sidewalk cafés. *Londres de Provence. Luxe, calme, et volupté.* The rains come, and the sloppy, carefree Mediterranean is locked back in his knitted brown vest.

A man in a white Sikh turban and a stylish short black plastic raincoat drinks sangría at the bar of a Spanish pub.

People are too civilized to be anti-American, but—Americans are entertaining, brash, greedy, overgenerous children, rather like the white man's burden of the Empire builders. If an unusual film comes out of the United States and has excellences that cannot be denied, a review will end with the suggestion that Americans return to the Hollywood plots they do so well. Ballet? Painting? Fine. But why must they be so American? The brain drain is a plot to sink England in its seas, very little, "ektchally," to do with low wages, high taxes, and too few opportunities for advancement.

It began life as the country estate of Sir Thomas Gresham, surrounding a house grand enough to accommodate Queen Elizabeth I and her entourage on a royal progress. The lavish hospitality—extra servants in refurbished livery, splendid new furnishing when the usual didn't suit, choicest foods in great quantities, especially devised masques—strained and broke the resources of a number of Elizabethan households willing, however, to play high stakes for royal favor. This was not likely to happen to Sir Thomas, no matter what extravagances his household indulged in. He was the richest English merchant, a manipulator of finances for the queen, the founder of Gresham College and the Royal Exchange, and a man given to pronouncing what came to be called his financial law, though it was an obvious market fact long before him. He was a forceful character, described as "more effective than ethical," eager, and certainly prepared to please the queen, to the point of rebuilding the court of his house overnight, while she slept, because the queen thought it too large, a rebuke for unseemly competition with royal houses.

After his death, the house passed from owner to owner and stopped at another point in its destiny as the proper setting for financial power. In the late seventeenth century it was taken over by Nicholas Barbon (p. 62), one of the land speculators and redevelopers who began to rebuild rapidly and rapaciously the burned face of London.

The next owner was yet another financial wizard, Francis Child, who started lower on the social ladder than his predecessors. After a period of apprenticeship, he became a goldsmith in a shop whose owner had a marriageable daughter. He married her and in time became the head of the prosperous business and the heir to considerable money left by his former employer and in-laws. His contribution to British finance was the establishment of modern banking, which rose from the need of merchants, in a period of greatly expanding trade, to keep their cash safe. It became the practice to keep it with goldsmiths, who in turn lent it out for interest. Francis Child, once goldsmith, then banker exclusively, was Lord Mayor in time, a Member of Parliament, and the founder of a line which owned Osterley. It was in the reign of two grandsons, Francis and Robert, that changes from Tudor to neo-classic were made, leaving the house as one sees it now, orderly and quiet on the outside, exhibiting the proper touch of eccentricity in Tudor towers, linked by simple stretches of façade to a temple portico surmounting a lordly set of stairs.

It is mainly the interior that is burdened and delightfully lightened with Robert Adam's talent, moving from the inspired to skillful scribbling. There are rooms in Osterley that soothe the eye like the dignified and harmonious hall, which balances graceful forms of apses with ceiling and floor designs in related patterns. The decorative panels are appropriately sized, resisting the passion for the minuscule which marks the Etruscan Room—a misnomer because the decoration is related to Greek vases, and distorted, because the resemblance to Greek vase figures seems to have been distilled through too many copies of the original designs. They appear too minute, too nervously linked by curlicues and grotesques in unattractive colors. The Tapestry Room is a curly, creamy, bouncy room, in which Adam's concern with overdelicate detail suits the Frenchiness of the Gobelin tapestries concerned with the love lives of gods and goddesses postured in a garden of cupids and garlands, the style and motifs repeated in the furniture designed by Adam, the detail supplied by French craftsmen. One returns to English-style luxury in the Drawing Room, whose silk-covered walls surround slender *torcheres* embossed with one Adam's signature, the ram's head, and fine commodes inlaid with classic motifs and medallions.

The park is an alluring "English" ramble of nature arranged to look more reasonably like nature: small waters picturesquely placed, trees isolated to give their shapes scope and drama, sudden little thickets to suggest wilderness—but not too wild.

Open April to September, Tuesday through Sunday, 2 to 6 P.M. October to March, noon to 4 P.M. Closed Christmas Day and Good Friday. Admission one shilling for adults; sixpence for children. Underground to Osterley Station or 91 bus. Also Green Line buses 704 and 705.

It was and is a dense mesh of streets and alleys, some of them too narrow for light and more than one pedestrian at a time, many of them not mentioned on any but professional—lighting, street cleaning, water supply, etc.—maps. Some of the old paths and their zesty names have gone; you won't find Pissing Conduit or Dunghill Stairs and when you find Cloak Lane or Old Jewry, time and demolitions will show you a quite ordinary business street. The famous Cheap (Cheapside) is no longer the territory of mercers and haberdashers, of seekers for casual work as it was in Elizabethan times, nor is it now patrolled by a marching watch, as it was early as the thirteenth century. Centuries have passed since the long carts brought by bakers of Stratford-atte-Bow (east of the East End, where Chaucer's Prioress lived) stationed themselves at busy corners to sell their penny wheat loaves. Nor is it any longer the western adjunct of Eastcheap, the market that specialized in meats and cooked foods in Shakespeare's time. Beheadings took place in medieval times (one of a Bishop of Exeter, whose head was cut off by order of "Citizens of London"), in Westcheap, and it saw the drama of the building, collapse, and rebuilding of Bow Church and jousting. It shared the brisk liveliness of its adjoining lanes and streets: a Bladder Street, of butcher shops which "be now divers slaughter houses inward, and tippling houses outward." Extending eastward, the market concentrated as Poultry, and to the west, as Newgate Market, on corn and meal. In the fourteenth century Cheapside was the Fifth Avenue on which Dame Alice Perrers, the mistress of Edward III, rode as nothing less than The Lady of the Sun, accompanied by splendid satellites, "every lady leading a lord by his horse-bridle," on the way to the jousting at Smithfield (p. 197). Now it is still a parade ground of a sort, of automobiles and rush-hour pedestrians, and the Ladies of the Sun are the typists who sit to catch the sun on the benches at the side of Bow Church. But Skinners Lane is still full of pelts, and Fishmongers' Hall is still near the big, swinging scales and the crunch of ice and the fans of tail and surprised flat eyes in the fish market, as they have been for centuries.

Your search might start at the Tower, the Norman mausoleum of English history, or take the tube to Bank Station, and if you are lucky, emerge via an exit on King William Street, which presents you with a plaster bar marked LIFT UP YOUR HEARTS above the winged heads of three angels and, above the entrance arch, a strong, emphatic volute. This leads to the crypt (since 1900 part of Bank Station) of the adjoining church. Next to the exit arch, a modern version of the three angels in polychrome, leading to a sweets stall and the doors of the vestry of the Church of St. Mary Woolnoth, whose mighty façade looks out from the meeting of Lombard and King William streets.

"Wlnotmaricherche" was mentioned as early as 1191, replaced and renovated through the centuries, and—it almost need not be said—destroyed in the Great Fire and restored by Wren, to be rebuilt in 1727 by his pupil, Nicholas Hawksmoor. It was somewhat marred by Victorian improvements but is still a Hawksmoor work, a profoundly serious, monumental church. It has an extraordinary Old Testament strength, built solid and square, made more solid by trios of large Corinthian columns marking an inner square that supports a bold cornice with square classical motifs. The weighty Italianate quality of the church appears in the twisted black and gold Bernini columns of the altar baldachino, in the square canopy over the pulpit shaped and carved like a big Italian box, and, around the walls, the dark sobriety of beautifully carved blackwood, once parts of the gallery. Among the wall plaques, there is one for Edward Lloyd, the owner of the seventeenth-century coffee shop which became the great insurance company, and mention of John Newton who preached here and was a great influence on William Wilberforce "Who fought and won the battle for the abolition of the slave traffic," information that suits the intense religiosity of the church.

As you leave, if you haven't noticed it before, there is a panel near the entrance that lists prices for services in 1809. Burial involved the most expensive costs—separate charges for the minister, the clerk, the sexton; for ringing of the bells at the death; for ringing of the bells at the burial; for the costs of digging and paving the grave. A parishioner could have all this and space in a vault for under three pounds, while a stranger paid six pounds. Burial in the cloisters was cheaper, while being encased in a lead coffin raised the cost by two pounds, ten shillings. Publishing banns, churching a woman, and registering after baptism all were considerably cheaper, the costliest item being "married by licence to the minister," probably not what it appears to mean. Outside the church appears a sign in French, German, and Schweizerdeutsch, marking St. Mary Woolnoth as the place for Sunday services of the Swiss Church, an indication of the need of City churches, ringed by weekend silence, to put themselves to a variety of uses.

Any direction now in the immediate vicinity opens many possibilities. Try eastward, toward the river.

At the foot of Dowgate Hill is the modern Dowgate House, at whose entrance there is a lively picture of Drake's *Golden Hind* etched into dark stone, the lines painted white, jauntily breasting very white, very curly waves. Under the ship, the legend which relates the picture to its place: Dowgate Hill was the site of the London home of Sir Francis Drake after the voyage on the *Golden Hind* and, the legend adds, a palace of Richard III; before that, the property of the city of Rouen; before that, one of the two water gates in the old city, connected by ferry with the Roman road to Dover, and, before that, named for the Celtic word for water, *dwi*.

Moving up the present rise, one comes on the west side, to the ironwork door of the Dyers' Hall, anciently of this ward, but not this precise position. Next door to it an arcade, rather like the Nash gallery off Haymarket, leads to a simple well-designed gate and a view of confident black wooden doors with carved lintels surmounted by emblematic shields. In the small yard two leaden coffers as flower boxes and the arches and sheltered walks that suggest a monastery garden. This is the Skinners' Hall, much changed but still in its indigenous place from the times when founders of the company included Edward III, Richard II, Henry IV, Henry V, Henry VI, and Edward IV, the same place which issued forth effulgent processions on Corpus Christi Day that "passed through the principal streets of the city, wherein was borne more than one hundred torches of wax (costly garnished) burning light, and above two hundred clerks and priests, in surplices and copes, singing. After the which were the sheriffs' servants, the clerks of the compters, chaplains for the sheriffs, the mayor's sergeants, the counsel of the city, the mayor and aldermen in scarlet, and then the Skinners in their best liveries." The splendid liveries are now paled to white smocks worn by gentlemen who speak Cockney or the European languages of displaced Jews, and the smells less forthright than they once were; but eyes and nose still proclaim it a skinners' neighborhood.

Under a gas streetlamp in Skinners Lane, a white-coated man sorts skins for precise matching, and below St. James Garlickhithe, on Garlick Hill, there is a dim shop hung with bundles of pelts that droop like dried moss from the ceiling. Through an arch in Garlick Hill, one comes to Miniver Place, a small court filled with the lightly perfumed, lightly fleshy scents of a fur-storage vault, and back on the hill, a place called Beaver Hall. Westward on Upper Thames Street, more signs of fur works, the odor held in the narrow walls of Stew Lane ("of a stew or hothouse there kept") and Darkhouse Lane. Walk toward the slit of river at the side of the piazza that is Queenhithe (a hithe was a small harbor for goods ships), neater and duller than it was when Henry III ordered that all London fish be sold at Queenhithe Market and that all ships from the Cinque Ports be compelled to deposit their corn there, a large royal cut obligatory. In the sixteenth century there stood a large corn storage house and a corn mill at this edge of the river. Now, no corn or fish; one walks under festoons of sacks of skins, lifted by men in trucks to the hooks which pull them onto a high platform, where one of the white-coated gentlemen calls the number of each lot as it crawls out of view. Below, a row of fancy black and white stanchions with cookie-cutter tops and much over-painted ornaments at the sides, and still the smell of furs, now mixed, if the wind is right, with the odor of coffee which lives near the furs.

Following the scent, we have gone too quickly. Skinners Lane ends at a sudden open area, bombed out, and opening to view the side of Christopher Wren's St. Michael, Paternoster Row, now in restoration. You can sit on a wooden bench, more humanely shaped than most, in flowers and sets of young trees, and look at the long, cool line of the church and the rounds of columns that are the steeple. Facing the other way, watch the buses and the taxis and the people making their way to and from Southwark Bridge, and directly across the street notice a plaque commemorating the old hall of Joiners and Ceilers (*sic*) imbedded in the house of the Public Cleaning Department, a modern building whose dark-gray walls stop for banks of flowers. From the foot of Dowgate Hill look across the river to a lone, almost skyscraper beyond Southwark and facing a sign that calls it Cosin Lane (for a family who lived here before the reign of Richard II), the view of a high, thick brick wall, ending suddenly with a raw gasp, its blind arches stuttering to an inimical black tower and spire, a Piranesi ruin imitated by German bombers.

The other side of the ruin looks onto Allhallows Lane, and the churchless tower of All Hallows the Great, also called "in the Ropery" for the manufacture and sale of ropes in the area; also *ad faenum* for the nearby hay wharf. It was described 400 years ago as "foully defaced and ruinated," an apt description of the nineteenth-century tower adjoining a nondescript brick building. Behind the gate of the tower, the dusty blackness of burned rubbish and, above, the two remaining Wren angels with black, pockmarked faces, and the hair, incessantly washed by the rain still white and strange. What is left of All Hallows the Less rests in rubble and an eager jungle of fern and thistle on a blue plaque attached to a broad stone. The plaque explains that this was the site of the church destroyed in the Great Fire of 1666, both tablet and stone broken and burned by 1940's bombings.

On nearby Queen Street at Upper Thames stands a building strange in this terrain of timid modern and rhymed black Victorian, broken teeth of old walls and wide, red-banded warehouses. The big, arrogant house, suggesting an imitation of the seventeenth-century French *palais* with its columned court behind the elaborate metalwork door, its lunettes, and swags of leaves and fruits and mansard windows, is the Vintners' Hall. You are now in the ancient Vintry Ward, where Chaucer's father worked and which had its early blossoming when the merchant-vintners of Gascony, subjects of medieval English kings, brought in great quantities of the wines of France. They flourished, and a good number became mayors of London, rich and powerful enough to offer hospitality to demigods. "Henry Picard, vintner, mayor 1357, in the year 1363, did in one day sumptuously feast Edward III, king of England; John, King of France, David, king of Scots, the king of Cyprus, then all in England, Edward, prince of Wales, with many other noblemen, and after kept his hall for all comers that were willing to play at dice and hazard. The Lady Margaret, his wife, kept her chamber to the same effect. . . ."

Going eastward from Cannon Street Station, past street signs named Red Bull Yard, Ducksfoot Lane, memorials to a more vivid life than they now live, turn down Swan Lane, the site of an ancient water gate, for a broad view of the river and an esplanade of benches, not too common a commodity on this section of the river. Above the Southwark wharves, shines the tower and clock, the serrated spires and gold flags of Southwark Cathedral; the power station tower tears into the sky like a doomsday finger. The dock buildings, hung with their amulets of cranes and elevators, nestle coveys of barges at their damp feet. East of London Bridge the giraffe cranes lean gently toward each other, bow, turn, in a slow pavane. (Incidentally, one strange and moving ceremonial gesture for Winston Churchill's funeral services was this bowing of the cranes as his body came down the river.)

Arthur Street, across from the Old Swan, will take you into Martin Lane and an annex of El Vino wine shop on Fleet Street (p. 270). This tavern was, the sign tells us, the only one that survived the 1666 fire, and small and dark and nestlike it remains. We are told, once more, that Dickens frequented that tavern, too. (What was the source of the energy—not now conspicuous—that propelled generations of London literati from pub to pub, from tavern to coffeehouse, and enough left over to produce substantial works? Were they liquor-proof, hangover-proof, sleep-proof giants, all of them? Or did others, starving teetotalers, produce the works in factories like that of Dumas?)

It is possibly a time for a cup of coffee at one of the efficient counters of a local Kardomah coffee shop—after a struggle with the Irish girl at the counter who understands you but hasn't the confidence to believe she does. Then, in from Cannon Street to Abchurch Lane, to sit on the peaceful, remote little piazza whose patterned stone walk is believed to cover a plague pit, as a number of small parks and yards in London do. The church you face, closed in and almost hidden, of dark red brick and beautifully proportioned windows, with one angel head perched over each window, is Wren's St. Mary Abchurch, not large, but massive, with its sober tower and lead steeple. On its left it is pressed by an alley, leading to another alley of small offices. On the right, a treasury of orangy brick and tattoos of pilasters and columns, four stories of them, with short, gasping bursts of columns at the top. Wedged between the busyness of banks, offices, buses, traffic signals, underground stations, snack bars, newspaper stands, one rests a grateful eye on the soothing façade and listens to the organ music coming from the open door.

The interior of the church seems square, yet is rounded by the lovely shallow dome, supported by vaulting over the clear, many-paned windows. Unusually handsome monuments are spaced felicitously about the white walls, and the carved pews are enhanced by fine grillwork sword rests. The glory of the church is the masterfully carved altarpiece of Gibbons—generally conceded to be an authentic one among a number of spurious claimants—that spills exquisite loops and wreaths and falls of carved foliage around the conventional altar tablets. Serene, rich, and warm, the church and its yard (and its frequent noontime organ recitals) make a delightful oasis, a silken piece of serenity in a hardworking tourist day.

Should you have reached five or five thirty in your day, turn on King William Street, and watch the pedestrian flow across London Bridge, quiet, orderly, brisk, a sudden strong statement of the immensity of London's population, sometimes lost in the sparseness of large squares and the unnatural emptiness of endless miles of low houses on still evening streets. King William Street offers you as well the assault of the Monument and the smell of fish, real or imagined, that wraps the immense fluted column topped by copper flames. It was built by Wren to commemorate the fire that, reputedly, started on close-by Pudding Lane where Eastcheap butchers dressed their meats and made their blood puddings. (Climbing the Monument is a temptation that can be resisted without too much regret; London is a city that is better at man's eye level.)

At the foot of Monument Street is the famous fish market, probably closed in your time of day but unmistakably its redolent self from the airs it wafts past the green ironwork and red crosses, soaring to its large stone dolphins and trident-bearing goddess. If you can stand the smell of fish—particularly vivid when the shops have closed and the ice melted on a warm day, when walls and floors and streets, in spite of frequent sluicing, breathe out the centuries-thick odor—walk a few of the local streets. Fish Street Hill will tell you its name, an honorably hoary one, long before you see the sign. The odor thins out a bit on Botolph Lane and thickens in Botolph Alley, mingled with the cooking grease of small cafés, to become lively outside St. Mary-at-Hill, the Billingsgate parish church of fine carved Wren grandeur almost lost on the cobbled, curved, narrow streets of live eels and jellied eels. Tubby Isaacs, one of the illustrious jellied eels names in Aldgate has his wholesale quarters here, and he may be one of the privileged locals who takes his ease and drink in the blood-red, hard blue and gold pub at the corner of Lovat Lane during other than ordinary opening hours. As in a few other areas of work—newspaper nightshifts, etc.—one finds the sign WE RESPECTFULLY REMIND OUR CUSTOMERS THAT ONLY THOSE ENGAGED ON BUSINESS IN BILLINGSGATE MARKET ARE PERMITTED TO BE SERVED WITH ALCOHOLIC REFRESHMENT BEFORE 11:30 A.M., the cocktail hour for wholesale market men.

The bottom of Fish Hill Street faces the blackened side of St. Magnus Martyr and its charred Wren angels and, at the side of the church wall, a row of glossy new parking meters. The tower and lead dome and mighty black clock, the strong arches, the present scrap of what must have been a larger churchyard, the double-winged angel's head and lovely fruit festoons, all dead of the black plague, the rusty aureole window with no glass, were not meant for strangulation among close ugly buildings. Rather, they were devised to mark an imposing hail and farewell to London Bridge, an approach in use from 1176 to 1831, a weight of years and use that should leave the old strip something more than a marker, a length of timber from a Roman wharf found on Fish Street Hill, and airless, sooty mournfulness.

Imbedded in the bridge that pulls King William Street across the river, there are sets of stairs that rise to the red board listing the officials of this Bridge Ward, the ancestors of gentlemen who probably lived on the river when "all the bridge [was] replenished on both the sides with large, fair, and beautiful buildings, inhabitants for the most part rich merchants, and other wealthy citizens, mercers, and haberdashers." And on the west side of the bridge, the pilastered neo-classic might of the Fishmongers' Hall, its interior splendid enough for weddings attended by the nobility and lavish charity events, its self-assurance emblemed in the large mermaid and sworded merman, holding up a crown and sharing between them a shield whose design is the shapes of fish.

As Fish Street Hill mounts, it loses its indigenous smell in the loose curves and business buildings of no obvious might on Eastcheap: one building that carries a frieze of laden camels to remind the clerks and typists who rush by of the breadth, width, and enterprise of the Empire, one large tumultuous chaos of Victorian Gothic, and the ghost of an ancient, boisterous neighbor, the Boar's Head Tavern, where Falstaff and Prince Hall, Bardolph and Pistol, Mistress Quickly, and Doll Tearsheet were as "merry as crickets." If he ever entered a church, Falstaff might have gone to a predecessor of St. Mary Pattens, a Wren church. (A patten was a sandal raised on a ring to protect feet from puddles and mud—awkward walking but an idea that can bear revival.) It is an appealing, hospitable church with a VISITORS WELCOME sign and informative labels for each singular object. Look for the seventeenth-century bench with a devil's head carved at the back and the plaques in Della Robbia colors and style and, above all, the charming eighteenth-century monuments, one, especially, of gleeful rococo wiles.

From Rood Lane you can look down to a view of the ponderous St. Mary-at-Hill clock hanging like a black sun over the narrow street and, beyond, the spires of cranes in the river. Idol Lane leads down to St. Dunstan's Alley and, if it hasn't been razed in the current rebuild-ing, a modern ruin as dignified and strange as the ancient ruins painted by Guardi, window arches, some of their divisions and stone ornaments intact, opening views of mirror image arches, the bases buried in deep weeds. The freshly rebuilt, forward-looking contrast is the Hall of the Worshipful Company of Bakers (reached through Cross Lane), which is studded with its seal of expected strong arms, scales, and sheaves of wheat, and unexpected moose.

It might now be about 7 P.M. Only the late stragglers, one or two alone, are left at the bus stops or disappearing into the tube station. The listing, burdened bridge (London Bridge is not necessarily falling but leaning dangerously) is light and fleet again, the motionless goods elevators hang like tired balloons, and the cranes rest as line drawings on the pale gold-stained sky.

If there is still time, however, you might go back to the Vintry Ward. It stands now where it indomitably stood, in one shape or another, for hundreds of years. There was a Stock Fishmongers' Row, named for the number of merchants who lived immediately north of the hall, at the time when fishmongers were of two associations, stock and salt, with several halls among them and, among them, rich enough to put on a show to celebrate the thirteenth-century victory of King Edward I over the Scots that included pageants, a parade of 1,000 horsemen, a rich image of St. Magnus, several enormous silver and gilt fish, each carried on horseback, and 46 armed knights bearing symbols of the sea—and rich enough to pay for litigation, bribes, and fines, for they were a contentious, tough crew, "men ignorant of their antiquities," and that may be why "Billingsgate" means what it does.

As was customary with rich guilds, the vintners, too, maintained almshouses and sundry charities, of which a late witness stands in Vintners Place. It is a gray-clad figure which, from the street, looks like a ship's figurehead set on the wall by someone with a taste for the accidental and incongruous. He turns out to be a charity boy, neatly and plainly dressed in the clothing of a century ago, holding a blue cap and a Bible. Under his feet a winged putto head and on his chest a big badge marked VINTNERS' WARD, 30. As you leave the boy, look across the low buildings to the lovely rise of the Wren steeple on St. Michael's, then go up Garlick Hill for a closer look at St. James Garlickhithe, dressed in new, unobtrusive restoration. The tone is modest and reasonable; the light pours in through the large windows, etching the lines of the fine carving on the pulpit and the cover of the font, resting on the scratched and chipped old tombstones preserved in the wooden floor. Since most of them are indecipherable, one can imagine them to be the tablets of medieval worthies, the lords and ladies, the mayors, the fishmongers, the sheriffs, the grocers and brewers, the vintners.

Possibly a worthy, possibly not, is an unknown corpse who earned slight fame by keeping well preserved and, consequently, was not reburied when the vaults were cleared in the nineteenth century but placed in a cupboard in the vestibule. He is not on view, maybe unfortunately, since his public presence might bring brisker traffic to a not much used or visited church. (What a Neapolitan church would do with such a treasure!) A good viewing place to see the tower, sitting on its stone lace doily is from Sugarloaf Court, another example of the use of bomb damage, the rubble flattened and covered, to make a sunken parking lot.

The neighboring tower of St. Mary Somerset is one of ten or-
phaned towers in the City. Like almost all the churches in this once
teeming riverside community, St. Mary Somerset goes back a long,
long time. The weavers from Brabant brought in by Edward III met
in its churchyard, and by the end of the sixteenth century it was old
enough to be decayed, full of defaced monuments. All that remains
now is the pleasing white rise and, on its tabletop, a complication of
small obelisks and vases, beguiling chess pieces in the course of play.

From Trig Lane comes the smell of coffee out of sacks lolling
against a wall and, at the far end of another alley, the slow glide of a
Thames excursion boat, floating in and out of the square opening.
Then the terrible beauty of ghosts, the ironwork doors with shields,
flowers, and leaves bent and their locks rusted to imprison scraped
columns and useless brick leading to a window shored up by a slant
of wood; sagging doors that line the entrance to unused yards; a white,
plump building of 1899, richly curved and ornamented, now gutted
except for webs hanging from its ceilings; a car park surrounded by
hollows and piles of debris, crowded with marked stones, ladders,
rusty wheelbarrows, broken, crazy traffic signals still calling NO LEFT
TURN, KEEP LEFT, cracked and scored concrete on burned pillars and,
on a higher section, full bursts of green bushes and the lyrical droop
of ferns.

This might be the time to have lunch at the Mermaid Restaurant
on the river, attached to the Mermaid Theater (one gets to it by the
alley at the east side of the theater), or have lunch or coffee on the
folding chairs in the lobby, and then walk out to the river and sit down
on the benches with the men wearing away the remainder of their
luncheon hours. Immediately west is the railroad bridge that rides
along with Blackfriars, a light green-gray band stippled with the red
buses; across the river, the mass of the power station; looking east,
layers of bridge and the spurt of turrets on Tower Bridge and large
flocks of tall dock cranes, dipping their heads in foolish directions
over the Thames watering hole. Immediately around, the smell of
cooking, if the day is warm, mingling with the smell of river and
random garbage left by the thick, lazy lapping of the river. A small
duck quacks happily in the viscous black, and so do three boys, rooting
for treasures in the mud, as they did in Mayhew's time.

Across from Blackfriars Station the Blackfriars pub, shadowed by
a railroad bridgelet but otherwise isolated, has ample room to show
its soft reedy lettering BRANDIES, in gilt mosaics on green, its convoluted plasterwork panels and an Art Nouveau Black Friar, both
holy and leering. The period doesn't do so well in Blackfriars Station

in its mortuary midafternoon calm. It has a somnolence of old dust, dark-green paint, squarish ironwork designs, low ceilings, a heavy clock, the smell of disinfectant, few people, one sleepy ticket collector with few tickets to collect, an empty closed-off buffet bar preserved in glass, and figures as remote and motionless as window mannequins in the men's hairdressing salon. The only color and romance of travel rise from the spread of paperback books, gaudy magazines, and sweets wrappers in a central stall and, at the entrances, the names of European cities etched into the stone of each section of the right-hand column, in every other box of the left-hand column; names or interest or energy flagged, and the listless result sets the mood of the poor unloved station.

# 22  Thames Side South

The not impossible eighteenth-century spoon in your pocket (p. 305), where do you go from the Bermondsey Market at 11 A.M.? To the Old Vic to see if you can buy improbable tickets, by a long, erratic walk, looping in and out of docks, across bridges, through tunnels, sucked into coiled alleys, spewed out into broad, explosive streets, often guided by St. Paul's in its straw basket of scaffolding across the river. (But no mews; the houses that kept stables built north of the river.)

At the top of Bermondsey stretches the length of Tooley Street, leading to the Tower Bridge, through streets named Vine Lane—whose corner pub is called Antigallican—Weaver's Lane, and Potter's Fields, leading toward a dock street whose name is Pickle Herring. Going southward, Bermondsey dips, as a number of its neighbors must in this area where streets hold up railway tracks, and becomes confused with Druid Street and Crucifix Lane in a knotting of dark-gray brick tunnel. To avoid confusion, look for the tunnel that is Shand Street, and return on it to Crucifix Lane, past the warehouses of wine and spirits, a coat of arms painted on old whitewash which might be the symbol of Pilsner beer or a private jest. On the other side of the street Vinegar Yard advertises the availability of "rough, split hides," "pinned shoulders," "pinned bellies," and the appropriate acids and chemicals for their tanning, somehow uncomfortably related to the wines that come from Jerez and Oporto lying in a facing warehouse.

Crucifix Lane broadens to St. Thomas' Street. It has a small restaurant called Guys and Dolls (not to be confused with the King's Road wonder) to match the famous Guy's Hospital. Its iron gate and classic inner façade seem to be surmounted, through an accident of proximity by a strange, bulbous skeletal dome topped by a weather vane. Next door, the Keats House (he was a medical student at Guy's Hospital), a conglomerate of Gothicky arches, Orientalish stars, Corinthianish columns, and faces peering out of the stone jungle. The building suffers additionally from the contrast with the row of handsome, simple red-brick houses, a few of them with restrained, carved lintels that lead to the old operating theater of St. Thomas's.

Hidden for years behind the walls of an herb attic of St. Thomas's Parish House, the operating theater missed the aseptic changes that

159

affected all the others. Revealed by the search of a burrower among records in the 1930's, it stands as testament to man's power to endure and withstand, including nineteenth-century medicine. The narrow wooden table was covered with oilcloth, which shed blood into a box full of sawdust, the box pushed from place to needed place by the surgeon's foot. The surgeon was dressed in an old greatcoat, stained and stiffened by an accumulation from other operations and usually left hanging in the room. The instruments lay on cushiony felt, a paradise for bacteria, and around and above the instructive display, medical students stood on a steep series of semicircular steps leaning avidly on oaken railings. (The operating room is open several afternoon hours in the week. Phone MAY 9191 for precise, current information.)

Borough High Street—its traffic, its scrubby, busy miscellany of red and yellow and noncolor houses, its railroad trestles and maws of tunnel, the streams of people rushing to and from London Bridge Tube Station—shocks and confuses after the dark cocoons attached to Crucifix Lane. Cross Borough High Street (the best way to do it is to become the core of a cluster of adroit local citizens) and, a short distance to the north through another set of dark brick tunnels, into the presence of Southwark Cathedral.

In spite of centuries of decay and nineteenth-century rebuilding and twentieth-century war damage, Southwark Cathedral (designated a cathedral early in this century) is still Gothic in essence, retaining the spirit and much detail of its flourishing medieval years. It keeps some bits of Norman stone used in the medieval arches left after the fire that destroyed the original priory of St. Mary Overie. After the thirteenth-century roof collapsed, a wooden roof replaced it, but not until the fifteenth century, and of this later time, there is a collection of lively bosses, some as skillfully made leaf decorations and heraldic symbols, some as portraits of devils and kings and personifications of the deadly sins. As the trains thunder by, rending the dark, velvety calm of the church, look for the memorial to John Gower, a local parishioner and poet laureate to Richard II and Henry IV, and a very early wooden effigy of a knight, carved *circa* 1300, much restored and lacquered, yet a piece of antiquity to be awed by. Pensive Shakespeare, leaning on his elbow, is here, theoretically a member of the parish since the Globe Theatre was located in Southwark, and a plaque to quite another sort of poet, Oscar Hammerstein II. The Jacobean John Trehearne, "gentlemen porter" to James I, and his lady, enclosed in thickets of ruffles, gaze from their tomb (she seems to be quite resentful) on the simpler Harvard

Chapel, established for John Harvard in 1907 by the Friends of Harvard University.

Before you leave the chapel, look into a book that stands immediately outside it. Whatever the written messages of your visiting day may be, some of them will undoubtedly say something like "Please will you pray for those who despair because of other people," and "Please pray for someone who is feeling dep[r]essed and is feeling life very difficlate." The unsure orthography and spelling cause the message to be doubly disturbing.

Sit down on one of the outside benches; the mixture in extraordinarily tight space, even for London, crowding in, almost crushing, the venerable church, requires a few minutes of contemplation. Looking sharply upward, you can see the top of the church tower, gay and light, its four knobbed ends begging for completion with bright banners. Walling you in at the right, the layered shadows of tunnel and railroad bridge; close on your left, the glass and iron and carrot and onion smells of the ancient Southwark (locally pronounced Suvok) produce market, and immediately before you, the narrow shaded walks of the minute gardens and lawns on which the sparrows fight over a discarded half of orange. In the trees the birds chirp and sing, piercing the broad black sound of the railroad train. A man sprawled facedown on the grass sleeps through birds and railroad and the bright clatter of the quick, doelike girls with long legs and neat, small heads passing through. Wandering oozily in their own dreams or vacuums, two unused old ladies on adjoining benches and as distant from each other as the shores of oceans: one a mindless, smiling crone with three or four stubs of teeth and eyes like overcooked peas, nodding, smiling, smiling; the other a dour, lipless crumple of old flesh sprouting a wirehaired beard; both wearing the immutable crushed once hat.

Out of the sun again and into alleys behind the cathedral, to St. Mary Overie's Dock (a faintly sacrilegious name unless you know that it means "over the waters"), a narrow strip of river with a sign saying that members of the parish have the right to land free, the privilege obviously not much used because the stone wall that holds the slip also nests a clotting of oranges, scallions, bits of wood, and a boot. Continuing to turn through alleys of warehouse under frail metal bridges that link them, one comes to a series of arches leading to darker and lower arches, just as Doré drew them a century ago, at each side of the high brick vault of Clink Street. Here stood Clink Prison from 1576 to 1593, and looking back into the dimness of Clink Street, you will see a battered wooden pillar with a round stone at its base. This, the local historian, whiling away a bit of time with his cronies at the side of an idled truck, will tell you was the old whipping post, once discarded but put back at the insistence of the local bishop, who said it was an important symbol and historical and should be restored.

Disquieting Clink Street left behind, one rises like Orpheus to the bright world of red brick and flower baskets and food and ale at the Anchor Inn and, after the restoratives, comes out to the shining tower of Southwark Cathedral and, turning one's back on it, prowls along the old warehouses with enormous studs, the immense wooden doors, and small windows (Doré depicted these very carefully also, and they haven't changed at all) into Park Street and up a funnel of stairs to Southwark Bridge. Across the bridge and down again. Behind you the metal strudel of layers of bridge and the gilded white top of the Monument. Immediately before you, men, trucks, and small cranes lifting sacks and loads and piles of brick from the barges that sway and waddle on the water like fat ducks. Beyond—and ubiquitous here—the broad height of St. Paul's dome spreading over the braids of green, cream-yellow, and sharp red of lifts that embroider the dark warehouses. Ahead, the house that Christopher Wren used when he was building St. Paul's, earlier used by Catherine of Aragon waiting to be escorted to St. Paul's and her marriage with Arthur, Prince of Wales, the frail brother of the younger Henry, later the VIII. A thread of alley signaled by an old gas streetlight (there are still a good number in London) spills birdsongs and a glimpse of green flowing over brick walls and, overhead, the crushing weight of soaring powerhouse tower; St. Paul's, always St. Paul's, beaming on the glossy, meringuelike Wren towers near the north bank of the river.

Standing on Bankside, we might peel off a few centuries to see Southwark as John Stow described it, about 200 years after Chaucer wrote:

> Befell that in that season, on a day,
> In Southwarke at the Tabard, as I lay,
> Readie to wenden on my Pilgrimage
> To Canterburie with devout courage. . . .

In his chapter on the "Bridge Warde Without, the Twenty-sixth in Number; Consisting of the Borough of Southwarke, in the County of Surrey," he tells us: "On the bank of the river Thames there is now a continual building of tenements, about half a mile in length to the bridge [London Bridge]."

In his meticulous, thorough, invaluable way, Stow lists for this ward, as he does for others, the prisons and notable buildings, in the first category "The Clinke on the Banke," next to the house of the Bishop of Winchester. The Clink was used "for such as should brabble, frey, or break the peace on the said bank, or in the brothel houses" nearby, in their turn neighboring "two bear gardens . . . wherein be kept bears, bulls, and other beasts to be baited; as also mastiffs in several kennels, nourished to bait them. These bears and other beasts are there baited in plots of ground, scaffolded about for the beholders to stand safe." Exhaustive as he was in most London matters, Stow seemed to have made a particularly minute study of the brothels of Southwark called "the Bordello or Stewes, a place so called of certain stew-houses privileged there, for the repair of incontinent men to the like women. . . . According to the old customs that had been there used time out of mind," certain rulings for the conduct of these "stews" were set down in "a parliament holden at Westminster. . . ." Stow then lists a number of prohibitions: "No stew-holder [is to] take more for the woman's chamber in the week than fourteen pence. . . . No single woman to take money to lie with any man, but she lie with him all night till the morrow. . . . No man to be drawn or enticed into any stew-house. . . . No stew-holder to keep any woman that hath the perilous infirmity of burning. . . ." And, never on Sundays or holidays, and never by English women. "English people disdayned to be baudes. Froes of Flaunders were women for that purpose."

Modern Bankside, sapped of the old spirit, gives way to two Hopton streets. The westernmost division leads to Hopton's Charity, a set of almshouses founded in 1752 and, judging from the bent backs that tend the flower beds and the fragile gait of a feeder of pigeons, still an almshouse, but like a number of others in London, they have a gaiety of design the word belies. These are low two-story buildings of tan-gray brick decorated with white stone which surround deep trees bending to lawns and rosebushes. (No one will object to your going through the gate, usually open. Ask permission and drop a phrase about the lovely roses—always a direct way to the local heart—and you will probably be invited to look closer.)

Besides Shakespeare's, there are other giant shadows to pursue in Southwark, some of them lurking in the alleys off Borough High Street. The White Hart Inn of Dickens once stood in the yard of that name, and the George Inn, the only one with its balcony intact before which plays were performed and still are (by a company that doesn't share the common acting skills of London), figured in Dickens, too. And the Tabard Inn of Chaucer's pilgrims must be here. It is, still bearing the name on a sign—not by many centuries the original— that hangs over the corner of Talbot Yard and Borough High Street. It is no longer concerned with rushing tankards of ale to reeves and merchants and smoothing the bedding for a dainty prioress. Its business now is repairing and altering men's clothing or hiring out suits and coats and, as a sideline, inglorious plastic briefcases for sale.

The rest of Borough High Street need not hold you too long. It is in the usual pattern of poor high streets pierced by innumerable dusty alleys, and another ancient shadow that might interest you, the infamous Marshalsea Prison which stood here from 1376 to 1811. Dickens wrote a good deal about it; it was here that his father was imprisoned as a debtor.

Southwark puts on a bright hair ribbon at a curve called Railway Approach, leading to the London Bridge Station. It jumps and throbs with life, after the dusty *tristesse;* people chomping on pizza or entangling themselves in spaghetti in a number of alert small restaurants; people shopping for sweets in a large, neat shop. Above, the chess-piece tower of Southwark Cathedral, the struts and scaffolds of a skyscraper, and, to the south, the odd black bell tower behind Guy's Hospital. On a summer's day, the mingled smells of peaches, melons, carnations, and roses float from the stalls at the bottom of the curve, a most pleasing breeze on which to leave and carry with you to Waterloo.

Hardworking Waterloo Station, having taken on the additional jobs of guiding to the Old Vic and to the Royal Festival Hall (and one should allow ample time for being lost between both; in spite of the signs, it is not difficult to find oneself under a train bridge, peering into dimnesses of warehouse and bumped by the barrows of wines emerging from hidden vaults as near curtain time inexorably ticks itself away), is currently concerned with expanding to serve the modernity of office building and entertainment center rising on the still surprised south bank. The fresh angularities of new sections thrust one up into curves and fantasies of modern building, onto a maze of ramps, to fresh concrete porches sitting on tree piers. From the front of Festival Hall, about where the coffee counter of the cafeteria gives on the river, a reassuring, familiar London mélange: the red-brick supports and plump lozenges of crisscrossed iron of Hungerford Bridge leading to Charing Cross; on the lawn a lunchtime reader, a dozing bearded boy, his head on a rucksack, and, with the encouragement of a patch of light between two blankets of cloud, a sun worshiper stripped to the waist, offering himself in the abandoned "take me" sprawl of the breed. Looking down on the human assortment, a row of curvaceous lamps wrapped in iron dolphins.

Eastward, the strange underbelly of a younger building, a concrete maze of ramps and slants, of patterns that simulate wooden planks supported by the tree piers and the echoes of boys' voices bounding against the sides of a diagonal well. A clutter of trucks and construction behind Queen Elizabeth Hall leads to the south end of Waterloo Bridge and the startling change to the Royal Waterloo Hospital, an Edwardian convulsion of swelling columns and heads peering out of fancies of red brick.

From the corner outside the Old Vic Theatre, on the Cut, a vista of old men like charred paper, heavy traffic, new basic housing projects and cleared areas still to be filled, and to the south a restless, narrow street that looks, in the open anonymity of the neighborhood, like a crowded high street of a medieval village, the market of Lower Marsh. One market tune is called by HYMIE who proclaims himself in large letters as a supplier of ready-made and bespoke clothing. He leads into, not the most colorful market in London, but one with the slightly other flavor and speech of South London (a breed apart, and pleased to be) and, above all, a fair sampler of its kind. Besides the fish and meat and vegetables and dry goods shops, it encloses several of the street-market standards: the lady vendor with multicolored hair arranged in a high pompadour that rises like a waving banner, big strands of pop pearls on her neck, and a cigarette pasted to her lip; the jumpy, energetic callers in soft caps; rows of paperbacks, secondhand and sexy; the indispensable stall of cut-rate toiletries and watchbands; the bronze lady holding a lamp; a betting office; two large pubs; a newish coffeehouse and a few sad cafés where sausage, potatoes, and peas cost four shillings; splendid new toilets; and a big, well-stocked public library.

# 23   Four Bloomsbury Museums

## Thomas Coram Foundation for Children

The matter is of foundlings, hospitals, and a humanitarian sea captain, Thomas Coram; the interpretations are by people like Hogarth and Gainsborough, and the house itself set behind immense playing fields of dozens of waddlers and toddlers and runners and fallers and their Mums knitting and talking. The combination of art and life and homage to a kind man who was appalled at the common sight, in his time, of abandoned infants is worth an hour or two of your time.

The original foundling hospital (shown as of 1746 in one of the series of London hospital paintings, of the eighteenth- and nineteenth-centuries) stretched along through what is now the playing fields, leaving for the present day only parts of its colonnades, the niche which received the unwanted babies on Guilford Street, and the committee room, moved from the old into this newer building. The rest is foundation offices and gallery, limited to its few chosen subjects. The nautical life of Captain Coram is represented by a huge Trafalgar battle scene, an explosive painting of rent sails and gunsmoke, flags flying, waves dashing, sailors drowning and being rescued. "The Siege and Relief of Gibraltar" by J. S. Copley is again a water hell scene of sinking and burning and dying in its left section and, to the right, careful portraiture of a group of commanders.

The captain appears as a number of people saw him: One large glowing portrait is of an intelligent Father Christmas with ruddy cheeks and long white hair. A more naïve portrait, more modest in size and manner, shows him militant, though still kind-faced, sword at hip and scroll in hand, pointing his stick at a foundling in a basket. Not surprisingly the most telling, a superb engraving by Hogarth, leaves him the benign white hair but adds strength in the vigorous nose and generous mouth and alert eyes.

The hospital theme is much less dull than you might think, lightened by the English talent for landscape painting, its taste for the anecdotal, and the skill of its practitioners. Greenwich (p. 184) is shown as the beauty it still is, fronted by a romantic flight of sailing vessels. The miseries and shrieks and dungeon confinement of Bethlehem (Bedlam) are soothed and silenced in a very serene portrait.

166

Gainsborough's painting of the hospital at Charterhouse is somehow less appealing, possibly because it is more straightforward than the hospitals from less mighty hands, like the elegant Chelsea Hospital, painted in 1746, showing the Wren buildings adorned by ladies in conversation on the lawn, while nearby a gentleman in a red coat with a bright emblem on his sleeve rows a boat.

The foundling theme is treated in copies of Murillo children and the heads of putti that crop up here and there and an enormous painting of that early, most famous foundling, Moses. He is a blond curly-headed little boy, quite like a number you may have passed in Coram's Fields, and the pharaoh's daughter, too, is an English beauty as fresh and pink-cheeked and satin-lipped as a Lawrence lady. The pride of the collection—and in its way a gathering of several appropriate themes—is the "March of Guards to Finchley," painted by Hogarth in 1750. A number of the soldiers in the crowded canvas are thoroughly drunk; one soldier is restrained by a girl who presses his hand to her round belly as if to compel his return; a companion makes his farewell with a squeeze of a handful of breast; still others kiss their babies, possibly potential foundlings, good-bye.

For contrast with the noisy humanity of Hogarth, there is the cool remote Chinese porcelain of the Percival David collection or the sunny Impressionists at the Courtauld or the somber antiquities at the Jewish Museum, all nearby. (It makes geographic logic to combine this group with the British Museum, but don't try it. Nothing should be combined with the British Museum, except rest.)

40 Brunswick Square; Russell Square Tube Station, or bus 19 or 38. Open Monday and Friday 10 A.M. to noon, and 2 to 4 P.M. Admission 1 shilling.

## Jewish Museum

The museum consists of one crowded, significant room in a building devoted to Jewish relief and welfare organizations seen to by absorbed people. Sometimes the person in charge forgets to open the museum in time, and you must go from office to office, finding someone who will willingly look for someone who will know who has the key. But everyone is helpful and eager, and it is never any trouble. Essentially, the room is a set of cases displaying ceremonial objects which were once fairly common and, since Hitler, have become rarities. With the destruction of Jews went synagogues, centers, collections, and houses in all parts of Europe. New objects, some of them extraordinarily beautiful, are being made, but the search for old Hebraica is a frustrating and often fruitless one.

The early English kings made it a habit to borrow from the Jews, then took the rest by fines and exile, encouraging the route by having spread stories of young Gentile blood used in Passover ceremonials, as in Chaucer's "Prioress' Tale." John Stow tells us: "Richard I forbad Jews and women to be present at his coronation, for fear of enchantments; for breaking of which commandment many Jews were slain, who being assembled to present the king with some gift, one of them was stricken by a Christian, which some unruly people perceiving, fell upon them, beat them to their houses, and burnt them therein, or slew them at their coming out."

That attitudes began slowly to improve is demonstrated in Shakespeare's curious treatment of Shylock—the approved, toothsome prejudice and the humanity, possibly prompted by the presence of eminent Jewish physicians in Elizabeth's court. The same ambivalence is demonstrated by Stow who repeats the classic charges of usury, "clipping of the king's coin," murdered Christian children, and yet is distinctly indignant, if not horrified, by the inordinate injustices.

There is nothing, of course, in the museum that goes back to medieval times; the treasures stem from the Renaissance and later, one of them a graceful Italian house mezuzah of the fifteenth century. From Italy, also, several of the wedding rings of gold and enamel, surrounded by tiny houses and inscribed with the symbols that say "Good luck." Beautifully illuminated scrolls of the story of Esther roll out of embossed silver cases, and a later book of the Passover service (the Haggada) is enchantingly decorated with realistic, primitive panels that describe the ceremony. The collection continues on through the traditional objects—scrolls, ceremonial utensils, candelabra, several rich Torah mantles of varied provenance, and the bitterest time, possibly because it was a "civilized" time—represented by the infamous Yellow Star and the currency that stood for money in Theresienstadt.

The show, like the subject, is necessarily pan-European, but the pottery figurines bring us to the specifically English, one of them an early-nineteenth-century Derby figure of a Jewish peddler in a tall black hat draped in an apron of cloths and buttons and reticules and lengths of material in a lively fall and swirl.

Woburn House, Upper Woburn Place, Euston Square Station, or 14 bus. Open Monday to Thursday 2:30 to 5 P.M. Friday and Sunday 10:30 A.M. to 12:45 P.M. Free.

# Percival David Foundation of Chinese Art

The Percival David Foundation of Chinese Art (School of Oriental and African Studies, University of London) is a gathering of masterpieces, a number of them exceedingly rare, of the porcelain and pottery of China from the tenth through the eighteenth centuries. One starts by staring in unbelief at the soft gray-blue Ju ware, made in Honan Province for a period that lasted no longer than twenty years, early in the twelfth century, some of it inscribed with the antique calligraphy that gives date and provenance. Similar southern ware, misty gray shading to green-blue grays, was developed in the later twelfth century, after the court was driven south by invasions of Tartars and Mongols. One vase of this group was held in such awe that a later inscription describes it (to quote a quote in the pamphlet) "solely for imperial use, nor ministers nor people dared to pass or gaze thereon."

With time the colors change, but remain subtle, and the shapes more varied, beginning to include petal forms and sculptural shapes. One is introduced to superb specimens of celadon ware, commonly used in the medieval world. Its range was wide, and duration long—the collection has examples that go back to the tenth and eleventh centuries— one reason for its popularity being its reputation as a poison detector. On to cases of white ware, much of it with darker edges, incised or raised, of flowery, rhythmic designs, some of it as early as the tenth century. Experiments in technique produced some curious and charming variations such as "hare's fur marking" that appears like spots that have run and, sometimes, like silvery stippling.

The second floor brings us to the forerunners of some overfamiliar matter, the blue and white of ubiquitous later china, still sold, as it has been for many years, not only from China but out of porcelain factories everywhere in the world. It is interesting to see it as it originally was, shortly after fourteenth-century craftsmen began to experiment with cobalt blue decorations. Two of the most extraordinary pieces in this altogether extraordinary collection are two large temple vases whose inscriptions give their dates as mid-fourteenth century, believed to be the earliest dated specimens of this ware and marvelously decorated with fierce, windy, tossing branches (or waves?) and the spiny, flamelike coils of dragons. Later the blue and white varied in intensity and freshness, combined with other colors and then still more colors, much of it applied as enamel to produce frail, deftly etched flowers and fruits, fish, small ships among serene baby waves and large water blossoms, and the graceful, strong-tailed Chinese chickens. One unbelievable and lovely example is a bowl called "The Dream of Lord Kitchener" who desperately wanted but never got it to add to his collection; it holds tendrils of grapevine and three small butterflies, separately applied inside and outside the bowl. Held up to the light, they align and meld awesomely.

On and on through elaborations of color, of refinements to gossamer delicacy and sophisticated shape, through polychromes and monochromes, through peach blossoms and dragons; from enormous bowls painted with fish and dragon-spewing waves to cups like the frailest of shells, a remarkably modern monk's cap jug of the fifteenth century, specimens of openwork like lace, and eloquent figurines.

On the street floor, the ceramic work is that of more recent and familiar types, dating from the apogee of enameling reached in the late seventeenth and early eighteenth centuries and occasionally showing the influence of foreign design, as in one bottle clearly derived from the Persian. The elaborations are joyously colorful: cherry blossoms bursting through the porcelain of a large platter; ducks and storks and round, plump birds; a great platter painted with peach leaves and blossoms and full, blushing fruits whose juices one can feel in the mouth; pieces made for European trade, like a haughty shepherdess with very curly sheep and European ladies and gentlemen (not all of them successfully round-eyed), and always, the brilliant techniques and adroit, lively draftsmanship.

Open Monday 2 to 5 P.M.; Tuesday to Friday 10:30 A.M. to 5 P.M.; Saturdays 10:30 A.M. to 1 P.M. Free. Russell Square or Euston Square Station. Many buses on Euston Road, Woburn Place, Gower Street.

# Courtauld Institute Galleries

Although we live in an avid time which says that there is no such thing as too much art and so one tries to stagger through too much in one muddled, breathless day, the Courtauld in Woburn Square should appeal to the viewer of normal endurance and receptivity.

The works reach back into uncertain time with fourteenth-century attributions to the workshops of Simone Martini and Bernardo Daddi, through "schools" and the anonymity of "masters of" and "followers of," among them northern works that include a number of early English paintings, not commonly seen.

The later Italians take over with a Veronese, and a stretch of blue and white Della Robbia figures, one Bellini version of the "Assassination of St. Peter," and a "Toilet of Venus" which might be Veronese or Titian and panels from Renaissance *cassoni,* the masterfully painted chests in which the trousseaux of blooded Italian brides were stored. A religious work of Botticelli, "The Descent from the Cross" by Rubens, and what might have been a preliminary trial (*modello*) painting of the Philip IV equestrian portrait in the Prado by Velásquez, from the studio of that painter. In the same room, a Tintoretto portrait, one by Goya, and a Crucifixion by Van Dyck, and in this gallery, as well as the others, furniture of the appropriate periods.

Most Londoners go to the Courtauld for the French paintings of the late nineteenth and early twentieth centuries, paintings with the thunderous names, starting with one of Daumier's strong "Don Quixote and Sancho Panza" paintings, a version of Manet's "Le Déjeuner sur l'Herbe," and one of Eugène Boudin's lovely beach miniatures, through the time of a many-patterned Vuillard interior (1912) and a glowing Modigliani nude, painted in 1917. And in between, one of the terrible earless self-portraits of Van Gogh, the magnificent "Bar at the Folies-Bergère" by Manet, a few lyrical Sisleys and vigorous Pissarros; Degas, Renoirs, Monets, a surprising number of Seurats; a few from the poisoned brush of Toulouse-Lautrec; of Gauguin, the dreamlike, threatening "Te Reroia" and "Nevermore" (once the property of the composer Delius who had known the artist), and Cézanne represented by eight canvases.

Although Roger Fry acquired a Seurat, his contributions to the collection covered a later time: Bonnard, Derain, Dunoyer de Segonzac, and a number of Rouault gouaches. Reflecting an interest of his time, he, too, collected primitive sculpture, of which there are some examples here. The rest is twentieth-century English painting, mainly with examples from names you may know well, like Sickert and Vanessa Bell, and a number from the hand of the donor.

The furniture and pottery you will see in the Roger Fry Room is related to a number of the artists represented in the paintings. It was they, and others, who designed the crafts objects to be made by the Omega Workshops organized by Roger Fry before the outbreak of World War I, an echo of the pre-Raphaelite yearning for the integrity of the handcrafted thing and nostalgia for the cottage pre-Industrial Revolution days.

Weekdays 10 A.M. to 5 P.M.; Sundays 2 to 5 P.M. Free. Euston Square or Russell Square Station. Many buses on Euston Road, Woburn Place, Gower Street.

# 24 Kensington: Victoria and Albert Museum, Aubrey House, Leighton Theatre Museum

The royal borough of Kensington, whose name suitably derives from the Saxon for "king's town," follows the story of a number of London suburbs in making a sizable leap in population following the Great Plague of 1664 and the Great Fire immediately after. William III, whose asthma could not brook the damp of riverside Whitehall (p. 82), moved his court and residence to Kensington, spurring on the development of fine houses and shops in the area. The greatest catalysts, or at least those who left the most conspicuous buildings, were Queen Victoria and her Prince Consort Albert, who set the Exhibition of 1851 in Hyde Park, caused museums and educational institutions to be built, and studded them with the remarkableness of the Royal Albert Hall and the astonishments of the Albert Memorial.

Kensington, originally clustered around the south and west of the Hyde Park-Kensington Gardens area, has proliferated and added to its prosperous houses and mews sets of incongruous adjuncts that make of the borough a patchwork of satins and coarse rag. Beginning at Harrod's, by now as much Kensingtoniana as the Victoria and Albert Museum, one can explore the beguiling smooth-skinned, flower-hung web of Trevor Square and Place, flowing into the Montpeliers and Cheval Place, the Rutlands separating, twisting, and coming together again, and the family of Ennismores, all between Brompton Road and Kensington Road. Somewhere on Kensington Road you may have seen a sign signaling the fact that John F. Kennedy lived here when his father was ambassador, and on the south side of the wedge sits the incomparable Victoria and Albert Museum.

No halls of Greek friezes, or wealth of Sumerian and Greek jewelry, or reconstruction of Egyptian dynasties here, yet the Victoria and Albert is as terrifying as the British Museum for its size and complexity, the expertise in its many broad fields of treasures, and how is one to see it all or that which is most significant? Like all London

172

museums, the V and A is sympathetic and humane. Therefore, among its many publications one finds a *Brief Guide* that lists sections and a few noteworthy objects in each and a booklet called *100 Things to See in the Victoria and Albert Museum*. (Both booklets include a couple of back pages for notes, a compliment to your informed interest and critical acumen.)

The booklets lead to early Christian art, including exquisite ivories and rare English alabasters. Or one can begin with the enchantment of the arts of Islam or India, the latter including the mustachioed, Greco-Roman draped, Eastern-fleshed Gandhara figures, wonderful bronze gods and delicate Rajasthani miniatures.

To follow that, you might find your way to Gothic glories of tapestries and church art, the sculptures of the Italian Renaissance and Raphael's cartoons for tapestries designed to adorn the Sistine Chapel. The incomparable crafts sections show quantities of stained glass and the examples of glass for household use from ancient times through the skillful production of more modern English glass. As for ceramics, the Italian majolica is considered one of the best collections in the world, as is the representation of English ware. Furniture? The Jones Collection is a gathering of the curly goldenness of seventeenth- and eighteenth-century French furnishings, whipped-cream paintings and papery, flowery porcelain. English furnishings going back to Tudor times fill room after room with charmers and oddities like the great Bed of Ware mentioned in *Twelfth Night*. It is a community bed, eleven feet by eleven, which inevitably found its way from the great house for which it was ordered in the sixteenth century to inn after inn, where it slept as many as eight at a time—not so bad an idea for cold, damp English nights in a not too fastidious time.

Then there are the corridors of Victorian furniture, the triumph of craft, small inventiveness, and magpie acquisitiveness over art and taste. A vase, already cocooned in flowers and fruits and vines, branches and oakleaf protuberances around a romantic landscape, adds on three white clawed feet with gold nails and, as pinnacle, a gold rhinoceros. A purple couch of papier-mâché is dotted and spotted with mother-of-pearl and covered with floral panels and, so that it may not feel cold and naked, marked in whatever space is left with fine gold arabesques. The busy Prince Albert contributed the design for some of the ripest blossoms of Victoriana, one of them a centerpiece combining a lion and a unicorn, four dogs modeled after the queen's pets, a dead hare, a dead mouse, a mouse in a little trap, and, for some arcane reason, two double shells. It moves upward as a square shaft with boys swinging in the openwork and upward again to lionlike heads flanked by fruit and flowers and still upward to another set of burdened little boys who hold the lower edge of a vast bowl.

The displays continue on through some of the productions of Morris and his friends and cooperators—the famous chair, stained-glass panels, rugs, wallpaper, and curtains designed by Morris, as well as some pieces of furniture and the beautiful lusterware of William De Morgan. One soon begins to observe the changes to the lighter and more livable-with: of 1900 a sideboard, still elaborate, but more playful and airier with semiabstract floral motifs; an ample, beautifully proportioned sideboard with brass pulls and hinges. The flowing organic lines of Art Nouveau begin to appear in lovely decanters and silver vessels; and at the end of the galleries, astonishingly modern designs out of Glasgow that include an extraordinary plaster frieze (1904) and candelabra that might have been designed right now.

It may not be your cup of tea at all, but the William Morris Room, quite separate from the rest of the furniture displays, represents an interesting development in English design, literature, painting, social history. Back on the main floor, through an Italian doorway, flanked by two pieces of fifteenth-century Italian ironwork and neighbored by two Crivelli paintings, one enters to walls of soft blue-green with an all-over relief pattern of leaves, blossoms, and fruits. Below the fruited bower, a border of more fruits and leaves on gold, interspersed with floating, sad pre-Raphaelite giantesses, the nudes less alluring than the girls in robes like freshets of tears. The stained-glass windows by Burne-Jones show more of the Niobes, this time surrounded by pale-yellow disks of glass.

This Green Dining Room, the only Morris interior that remains intact, seems to lack a table, the normal place for that absorbed by an enormous, buoyantly designed piano of oak covered with gold and silver flora and ornaments designed by Burne-Jones. The Morris chair is present and a Morris carpet and, of the same hand, an embroidered screen of three queenly figures with big falls and bursts of hair in the approved pre-Raphaelite auburn tone, the whole a blowup and distortion of dainty medieval ladies in a Book of Hours. The taste for the medieval is repeated in a huge, strange cabinet with a lectern top, a cooperative effort of William Morris, Ford Madox Brown, Burne-Jones, and Dante Gabriel Rossetti, all of whom had a hand in its painting.

In the miniature galleries you will find the portrait of Anne of Cleves painted by Holbein the Younger at the behest of Henry VIII, who wanted some idea of her looks before he committed himself entirely to the political marriage; the miraculous miniature of a Mrs. Pemberton painted on a ground of blue enamel; and a larger, sonorous portrait of a Hans of Antwerp. Isaac Oliver, working in the late sixteenth century, painted two delightful little girls, a lovely "Lady in Masque Dress," and a meaningful portrait of a Lady Hunsdon. One of the great masters of the miniature, Nicholas Hilliard, Queen Elizabeth's carver, goldsmith, and limner, is represented by a group of vivid, elegant little portraits, full of verve and movement: one delightful one of Arabella Stuart; another of Queen Elizabeth, not quite as good, but the case and cover of pierced gold and enamel set with precious stones is a magnificent display of Hilliard's high capacities as goldsmith. His "Elizabethan Gentlemen" is the famous languid beauty in long white silken hose, black and white jerkin, a white ruff, short cape swinging from one shoulder. He leans against a tree and is screened by perfect sprays of green leaves and delicate pink flowers which discreetly pattern his clothing and leave free his pale, round face and careless, curly locks.

The collection is endless and, fortunately or unfortunately, much of it imposing enough not to be neglected. One can go from Italian Renaissance arts to the whole rood loft from a Netherlands cathedral of the seventeenth century, complete with plaques of Biblical scenes, and minute crowds of sculpture, pillars, saints, and garlands; English window tracery of the fourteenth century; the sixteenth-century dormer window of a French chateau; ultrarealistic German; crude, primitive Spanish; and more and more and more. And what is not in the original is in a huge, forbidding gallery where plaster casts of famous monuments stand, including the shocking immensity of Trajan's Column cut, because the gallery height is limited, in two.

Among the bountiful plenty, there is a delightful costume section, priceless embroideries, and rugs on the stairways and in the halls, and, most important, a remarkable collection of Constables. As you leave, look into the case of the New Acquisitions Room near the entrance. A number of the pieces are marked IN LIEU OF RATES (taxes)—one was, some time ago, an invaluable collection of Mogul prints from the estate of Clive of India—and this particular mode of settling for taxes has released an impressive tumble of gems. Imagine what may still be hiding!

Open weekdays and bank holidays 10 A.M. to 6 P.M.; Sundays 2:30 to 6 P.M. Free.

West and north, flanked by the stones of Exhibition Road and the dreary repetitions of Queen's Gate, there are ponderous masses of

Victoriana and borrowings, growing more avid as they go northward to an immense tower—Egyptian? Florentine?—and the Royal College of Organists painted all over with heraldry to match the magnificence of the frieze that circles Albert Hall, the figures once of gold leaf.

Cuddly Kensington continues on as pretty ribbons of streets called Cambridge and St. Albans and Victoria and Thackeray, leading down to the controlled lustiness of the streets that surround the Gloucester Road Station or, northward, to Kensington High Street, a more impersonal shopping street, and its meandering silver, china, antiques annex, Kensington Church Street. By turning into one of the openings near the church at the corner of Kensington High and Church streets and wandering northward toward Notting Hill Gate, looping between Kensington Church Street and Campden Hill and the Aubreys, one comes on small movie-set houses on bosky paths, and, on Campden Hill, Victorian bumps and grinds houses, almost licentious in their bulges of excess. Near the top of Campden Hill Road, in the shadow of the water tower, there is a house behind a gate and the information that it is Aubrey House, of the late seventeenth century, one of a few mansions left on this airy, aristocratic hill. It once had an Adam ceiling, now gone; some of its grand length has been cut into flats; it suffered bomb damage and repair. Yet old charms still cling in the hidden park of long greens and rose beds, and inside the house, vistas from room to room that sketch out a Great Hall, not so great as to overburden a mellow, humane house.

Much of the Oriental collection once in the house was given to the Victoria and Albert and the British Museum some years ago, but there still remain superb Oriental animal figures and chests, fine, frail English bookcases like wood filigree screens, invaluable books, and—the glory of the house—a judiciously selected, not too large group of paintings. Rembrandt, Goya, Hals, Guardi are represented, and lesser masters in several fine portraits, the paintings an English gentleman of taste and means would have collected, except that this group conspicuously lacks English paintings. An omission by chance or choice? One does not know.

South and down in the economic and taste scale, through the endless rows of small hotels and bed-sitters peering out from behind their sentinel columns charging the traffic of Cromwell Road, to the "home away from home" clubs and pubs and the tinny jubilations of Earl's Court (called Kangaroo Court for its Australians) and its

enormous, plain exhibition hall. Then north again, to Holland Park
(p. 250) and, near it, Leighton House and its Theatre Museum.

Frederick Leighton, the highly esteemed Victorian painter, president of the Royal Academy, a baronet, and, for one day, Baron
Leighton of Stretton—he died the day after the ceremony—built
his unique and sumptuous house as a showcase for his work, his
treasures, and his elegant life, in 1866. For his house he collected a
prodigious number of antique Persian tiles and, with tiles of like design worked by the master ceramicist William De Morgan added to
the ancient, created an Arab hall, a corner of the Alhambra in Kensington. It is a Moorish sampler of the deep, velvety blue glow of
tiles, the intricately carved woodwork of harem screens, and, for
completion, the plashing of a small fountain.

Several studios in the house display a number of fine drawings and
for our tastes heavily literal, not too fine, paintings on classic themes,
one of them a large, vapid painting of Clytemnestra with drapery like
boiling pasta and a curious anatomy that places her breasts where tonsils
would more normally be.

The British Theatre Museum housed in the Leighton mansion-
studio is surprisingly new, established as recently as 1963, after considerable loss of the memorabilia accumulated by the ancient, busy
craft. Surprising, moreover, is how much there is left to display of
letters and playbills, promptbooks and souvenirs, and more fully
represented, the more nearly contemporary theater, with complete
sections devoted to plays and productions of plays of James Barrie
and an area set aside for the Old Vic. David Garrick is represented
by his waistcoat and dagger, a dressing table that probably was his,
and the copy of a playbill that announced his first appearance. A
playbill of 1812 displays the theater's generosity in that time: a
double feature of *Hamlet,* followed by a musical farce called *The
Devil to Pay.* A panel of miniatures, etchings, watercolors, and photos
records theater faces from 1564 to 1879 and, of a later time, many
photographs of Mrs. Pat Campbell—alone, with Sarah Bernhardt,
and as caricatured by Max Beerbohm, along with Bernard Shaw. One
sketch of the famous pair is titled "How They Respectively Appeared
to Themselves" — both young, lovely and lyrical. In the companion
drawing, "To Each Other," she appears large, round, and haughty
and he tiny, shriveled, and enraged.

One can find out how much Ellen Terry was paid and how much
Henry Irving paid for leasing the Lyceum Theatre and the costs of performing there, an impressive sum for 1887. One can read the corre-

spondence of Irving with Whistler (signed with the butterfly symbol) and the passionate notes from Bernhardt in French and equally passionate notes in her *sui generis* brand of English. More recent theater history rests in costumes and the pipes of Pan used in the first production of *Peter Pan,* a manuscript of an Osborne play, and, in the Old Vic section, the sword used by Michael Redgrave when he played Hamlet and of the 1937 season, Edith Evans as Rosalind and Redgrave as Orlando; Vivien Leigh, incandescent as Titania and the young Celia Johnson and Alec Guinness in *Saint Joan.* And back in time, again, the necklace worn by Ellen Terry as Imogen, a death mask of Kean, the makeup table used by Sarah Siddons.

Although the house may be viewed every day but Sundays and holidays from 11 A.M. to 5 P.M., the museum was open (at this writing) only on Tuesdays, Thursdays, and Saturdays during the same hours.

Kensington has the distinction of running up to one of the most turbulent and colorful areas in London, Notting Hill Gate, where the city's only race riots took place a few years ago, and the entrance to the area of slum housing (some of it rapidly improving) that runs northward, surrounding tourists' Portobello Road and, more grimly, the northern indigenous section of that market, where a population which might be called cosmopolitan if it were far richer than it is makes its life. Kensington Church Street shares buses with its poorer northern neighbors, Negroes, Indians, Cypriots, Spaniards, and Italians.

The meeting of north and south of Notting Hill Gate at bus stops makes telling juxtapositions. On the same queue there stood, one afternoon, two Madonna and Child compositions. One consisted of a stout young woman in a sensible short bob and a cotton housedress and brown saddle shoes, no particular expression on her face. She carried a neatly combed, cleanly dressed baby, whom she held firmly and dully. Her Hebe was a six-year-old as quiet, neat, patient and dull as Mama. Madonna Two was in a purple microdress shot through with whirls of dusty orange and purple brown. On her head a purple corduroy cap, four-inch plastic hoops bouncing from her ears, and on her feet, pale lavender pumps of plastic. Her child was a dirty cherub in a pink velvet cloak—probably improvised of a strip of old drapery—with Struwwelpeter blond hair and a dirty face. The kohl-eyed face and whitened lips of Mama kissed the smudged little face constantly; she let the child stand, picked him up, let him crawl and sprawl over her as he liked; she stayed immensely pleased with him. Her St. Anne was a skinny little woman in a lacy child's dress over her reedy legs; her hair was long, jagged fronds, into her eyes; the nursing bottle she held looked as much hers as the infant's. The idea occurred: Maybe the "beat," the "flower people," with their principles and conduct of permissiveness and affection should bring up the world's children. That might be their contribution, the place to put their imagination, goodwill, and what must be a huge, tamped-down reservoir of youthful energy, for which they are searching.

Having exhausted the shopping El Dorado of Kensington Church Street, one steps down with French, German, and Spanish dealers and tourists from everywhere to Portobello Road via the Notting Hill Gate Tube Station or bus 52. The vendors in this and other weekend markets are often keepers of shops in other parts of the city, and knowing, so you will not, in all likelihood, pick up a Giorgione painting for a few shillings or two forks of solid gold from a ducal house. What you will find is a great, robust crowd on Saturdays mashing itself happily against street stalls and stumbling through the endless warrens of arcades. As in other fields, and antiques particularly, several forceful influences, pushing an oversupply of hitherto neglected items, can make a trend. The latest, in overabundant supply everywhere, is "Victorian," lachrymosely "twee" or heavily threatening, its contortions brightened, but not beautified, by the shine of mother of pearl inlay on black lacquered papier-mâché. Mixed with the Victoriana, the later Edwardian (but still labeled for Mama) and the organic ebbing and flowing of Art Nouveau. Add to that the passion for early machine models, tattered policemen's capes, and balding shakos. For the girls, white cotton petticoats, camisoles, and children's dresses of fifty years ago and the beaded dresses of thirty years ago. Big bell jars closed around stuffed birds in landscapes of inept Surrealism round out the roster of the major motifs of present-day London "antiques" markets. But they don't fill, quite, all the space of these few dense streets where you will find a multiplicity of objects in metals, including Indian brass figurines; strips of beading; books; bad prints, good prints; Edwardian photo albums with pictures of the cushiony pinups of their contemporaries; scent bottles, some of them antique and expensive; tiger-sticking knives; furniture—old, elderly or just sick in the older and newer senses of the word—snuffboxes; mandarin gowns; writing tables; plumes; mangy furs; silver; fitted opium boxes complete with heater and tweezers; some good pieces of jewelry and much that is mediocre. And watch out for the word "Georgian"; there were four Georges spanning a long stretch of years, and the word doesn't always justify the shadow of antiquity and the commensurate cost. The road is, incidentally, not the whole of "Portobello," less frenetically busy also along Westbourne Grove and streets called Pembridge Road, Chepstow Road, and Ledbury Road.

Sharing some of the walk and soon taking over altogether, the oranges, cauliflowers and tomatoes, the butchers, bakers and chemists, which give room, northward, to the flea market's flea market, a discouraged path of old work shoes, cotton skirts for five shillings, second- or third- or fourth-hand coats, and bits and pieces of defunct machinery and furniture. The one gaudy "Portobello" annex is at 293. It calls itself I Was Lord Kitchener's Valet, the sign in yellow, green, orange, and a comic-strip military face. The cloth-clouded dark interior looks very much, *au fond,* like secondhand clothing anywhere, but the areas near the door and outside show aged capes, uniforms, old dresses dripping chiffon panels and loosened beadwork; plaid trousers, red jackets, braided and brass-buttoned—moribund, most of it but, if the fashion has hit your young, probably an inspired hideous gift. (The Valet has grown prosperous enough to expand to the Antiques Supermarket on Barrett Street and to Foubert's Place in Soho).

Push along with everyone else, listening to the babel of languages, including the diversities of English. A concentration of the young personae gather in the big Henenky pub at the corner of Westbourne Grove and Portobello in the fashion parade of what is not only approved, but *de rigueur* right now, while Finch's pub a few blocks north holds up the hangers-around of a shaggier breed. Get an Olympian view from a seat near the edge of the outdoor upper-level snack bar of the Portobello Antique Supermarket diagonally across from the first pub, and look down at the revival—or maybe it never died— of a medieval fair.

One Kensington day, you may be dizzied by the silver on Kensington Church Street, eyes strained from peering into the matted dimness of Biba's (p. 323) and ears throbbing with its high-decibel recordings, feet growing reluctant, the pubs are closed and you can't drink any more tea. Go to Derry and Toms department store on Kensington High Street, take the lift to the top, pay your shilling, and walk out into the peace and ease of gardens, one and a half acres of gardens— Old English, Tudor, and Spanish. The roof gardens offer a view, unfortunately mainly of railway lines. It is better to linger among the waters, running, splashing, filmy for ducks to eat in or streaked with goldfish.

The Spanish gardens are the most elaborate with tall palm trees in a lushness of flowers and tiled roofs, grillwork and Moresque arches, columns and an aviary. The Tudor gardens meander through brick-walled, low-arched areas, ivy-draped and trellised; orderly, yet with that touch of the old and overgrown, a little more careless than the modest, quiet, orderly beds of the "English" gardens. As if to include as many garden pleasures as possible, this astonishing space encompasses, too, bits of lawn for the ducks to nibble at, a baby waterfall tastefully surrounded by fern and rocks and water weeds and pads of water lilies. It is English gardening at one of its skillful apogees and one of the few places in London where you will find a PLEASE KEEP OFF THE GRASS sign.

NOTE: It was possible, and then not for a time, to have tea or lunch in the gardens. The service may have been restored.

# 25   St. James's

On one Sunday morning, at about eleven o'clock (if you choose to skip the changing of the guard at Buckingham Palace), leaving Green Park Station, keep to the eastern edge of the park and follow the lines of proud houses, some modern with long glass windows, one pillared, pedimented, and topped with the icing of classic ladies and vases. While you are examining, listen for the strains from Buckingham Palace, whose music can be impressively unmartial, showing a tendency to operatic arias, flamencoish music, and the tunes of the dear old days, like "Margie." At the end of the row, back of Lancaster House, a palace of the early nineteenth century that led an interesting life of royal visitors and revolutionaries. (There is a room named for Garibaldi, who was a visitor here, visible on occasional weekends, when the house is not used for conferences.) Lancaster House and its rather typical garnish of porticoes, long windows in yellow-white stone, and a balustrade of vase shapes holding pedestaled lamps, leads to the Tudor—primarily—maze of St. James's Palace whose dark brick façade, embellished with sentry boxes, presents itself at the end of St. James's Street.

In its place, 800 or 900 years ago, stood a leprosarium, at that time a safe and long distance from both the ecclesiastical city of Westminster and the merchants' City of London. It probably remained church property until Henry VIII took it over and had the present palace built, reputedly on designs by Holbein, while Whitehall Palace (p. 82) was taking shape. Here a number of seventeenth-century sovereigns were born, although the center of courtly activity remained Whitehall. When that palace was burned down, in 1698, St. James's became the official royal residence until Victoria came to the throne in 1837. After that time major court activities took place in Buckingham Palace while St. James's continued in limited court uses until the outbreak of World War II.

At the side of the Ambassadors' Court—a yard of black-red brick with lighter brick frames (late seventeenth century), many-paned white windows, old lamps over the doorways, guarded by one uniformed man carefully walking a marked path, back and forth, back and forth, before a sentry box—is the Chapel Royal. Under its English Renaissance ceiling, attributed to Holbein, Charles I knelt to take the sacrament on the morning of his execution, and some two centuries later, Queen Victoria and Prince Albert were married.

Have a close look at the beautiful linen-fold doors and their guards in the famous black busbies and red coats on the Pall Mall side of the palace; then go around to Marlborough Road, for a small, intimate view of the palace: a dark low Tudor arch, crenellations, and the engaging chimney pots in assorted groupings—one alone, a pair, a cluster of four, a bouquet of six. If services have not yet begun (eleven fifteen) in the Queen's Chapel, see if you will be allowed a look in, since it is not open to visitors at other times. It is a remarkably beautiful work of Inigo Jones, finished in 1627, its classical, uncomplicated presence dressed in a superb coffered ceiling, a courageous building for a time when churches clung to the heavy, dark complexities of the Gothic.

Out in the yard, the single guardsman stamps, wheels, and turns inexorably, mechanically propelled on his cement track, and is joined at noon by a group for a short stamping and turning ceremony. In the yard and under the protective arches (it has begun to rain) little boys march, turn, swing their arms, and strut with the rhythms of the group, one little redhead with a broad face and sturdy legs already a Beefeater. The toy soldiers separate to have their photos taken by tourists and then mount enormous modern military trucks and, having changed their busbies for caps and covered their red, form-fitted, silver-braided uniforms with dark blue cloaks, drive out of the dark-brick Stable Yard.

# 26  Greenwich

From an early historian:

. . . King Henry VIII . . . on May-day in the morning, with Queen
Katherine, his wife, accompanied with many lords and ladies, rode
a-maying from Greenwitch to the high ground of Shooter's Hill, where,
as they passed by the way, they espied a company of tall yeomen,
clothed all in green, with green hoods, and bows and arrows, to the
number of two hundred; one being their chieftain, was called Robin
Hoode, who required the king and his company to stay and see his
men shoot; whereunto the king granting, Robin Hoode whistled, and
all the two hundred archers shot off, loosing all at once; and when he
whistled again they likewise shot again; their arrows whistled by craft
of the head, so that the noise was strange and loud, which greatly
delighted the king, queen, and their company. Moreover, this Robin
Hoode desired the king and queen, with their retinue, to enter the
green wood, where, in harbours made of boughs, and decked with
flowers, they were set and served plentifully with venison and wine
by Robin Hoode and his men, to their great contentment, and had
other pageants and pastimes. . . .

Shooter's Hill still exists as the official division between Greenwich
Park and Blackheath. One of the paths leading into Greenwich Park
from the east is Cade Road, named for Jack Cade (*Richard III*), the
rebel leader of 1450 whose bands rested on the immense green before
they made their way to the city. The Saturday market on Trafalgar
Road is studded with delightful flower and fruit stalls at corners with
small streets, one of them Tyler Street, to commemorate Wat Tyler, one
of the leaders of the peasants' revolt (1381), who also camped on
the heath. In 1415 Henry V, back from France and the triumph at
Agincourt, met at Blackheath with the eminences of London for the
ceremonial return.

Holding onto images of invading armies of Danes and rebels, of
Robin Hood and riding out for Maying, and of busy shipbuilding
yards, one might start a South London trek on the 188 bus from
Waterloo Station waiting at the stop with a group of the indestructible

184

Lambeth ladies, either very thin or very fat, either toothless or flashing an army of white glossy identical shields provided by the dental clinic. Two bobby pins make a coiffure or a wide wavy flow of very blond hair, like that in Renaissance paintings of Venetian courtesans. Coats have the high Joan Crawford shoulders of the thirties, and always the conversation hooks into a younger woman—a daughter-in-law, a shop attendant, a coworker—who is "saucy and cheeky," "cheeky and saucy," repeating and repeating the satisfying, hard-rhythmed phrase with full pleasure.

The bus roots its way into working-class markets and shops and an ebullience of shapes and prams, hair color and market baskets, insubstantial temporary housing, and the not yet replaced scruffy tenements. The neighborhood mixture of warehouses, tall housing estates on scratchy lawns, new shopping centers, and the fragrant caves of old greengrocers turns, at Creek Road, in Deptford, to a forest of stacks and the flanks of ships resting in the long, snakelike creek. Beyond, a coalyard with immense chutes and a dark-red crane looming over the sparkling black, and at the corner of Creek Road and the Stowage a companionable pub, the Hoy (a type of sailing vessel), where the conversation among the officers of freighters is less "Ole Davil Sea," brothels, and blasphemy than you might expect; the talk is often political, fresh and sharp, and embarrassingly well informed. At this point, you are close to two distinctions of Deptford: the imposing Archer Church, St. Paul's, superbly set in its green rectangle, and around the corner, on Albury Street a dimmed row of eighteenth-century houses with remarkably carved doorways.

One of the victims of the Danish invasions was the martyred St. Alfege, once Archbishop of Canterbury. On the site of his martyrdom in Greenwich, a church was built in the twelfth century. The church seemed to have held up through the baptism of Henry VIII, but its decrepitude was blown to stone and rubble by a gale in 1710, and the Parish Church of St. Alfege was rebuilt six years later by the architects John James and Nicholas Hawksmoor. Anyone who has seen one Hawksmoor church will recognize the monumental, intense style, here expressed in majestic exterior arches and a few weighty urns. Around the side of the church and through a small green, neatly bordered by tombstones, is the entrance to the surprisingly modest interior, maybe planned that way by James or possibly simply restored after the bombings of the early 1940's. A mimeographed sheet—you can have it in English or French—attached to a broad paddle informs you that General Wolfe was buried here, and where to find the keys and stops of an organ that belonged to Thomas Tallis, the "Master of Kings Musick at Greenwich," the same organ on which Elizabeth I and her sister, Mary, learned to play.

Leaving via a street named for Nelson, one arrives at the *pièce* of Greenwich, Greenwich Park and its Royal Observatory, the National Maritime Museum, and Royal Naval College.

As you look up from the road, along the upslant of steep green and old trees, searching for the momentous zero meridian line that you think should blaze across the sky and doesn't, you see instead the long neoclassic colonnades of Christopher Wren's Baroque Royal Naval College, Inigo Jones' Queen's House, and at the summit, Wren's Royal Observatory buildings in domesticated red-brick and white style, at that distance like a toy castle surmounted by pretty bulb domes that once opened for astronomical observations.

Over the long slow building and rebuilding of Greenwich, a number of hands and tastes were involved. Wren was past sixty at the time of the building of the Naval College, and a considerable amount of the work was supervised and certainly modified by Nicholas Hawksmoor and John Vanbrugh, and even the most casual of amateurs can experience the difference between them, although they worked at about the same time and were confined to the same master plan. One of Hawksmoor's sections is powerfully controlled and sparse, suggesting the Louis Sullivan of two centuries later, with its shallow arches, repeated in differing curves along a simple, flat side while the Vanbrugh buildings are sententious English Baroque at its bulbous clumsiest.

Erase the present panorama, and somewhere in the middle ground put the fifteenth-century palace called Bella Court by its owner, Humphrey, Duke of Gloucester, and where the observatory is, the high point, his tower fortress. In this stronghold on the river Humphrey established a court of international learning, like the Renaissance courts of Mantua and Urbino that he had come to know in his Italian travels. Later the palace passed from owner to owner, at times decayed, at times improved, until the advent of Henry VII, who settled in and brought forth Henry VIII, who caused the palace to shine and the river to sparkle with his effulgence as he rode, dressed magnificently, in his royal barge between Greenwich and Hampton Court, and Greenwich and Westminster, and to nearby Deptford to visit the shipyard he had established there. On the crest of his hill he built a watch tower, and below that, armories, which employed a good number of imported craftsmen and amassed a large collection of superb armor. Near the armories were his tiltyards and the stables, and beyond, the guest rooms, tennis courts, gardens, orchards, and the apartments of both his queen and his mistress Anne Boleyn. When it was Anne's time to be discarded, it was from Greenwich that she was taken to the Tower to be beheaded, leaving the disappointing girl child, Elizabeth, who had been born in Greenwich four months before. After her tormented childhood and her emergence as queen, Elizabeth used Greenwich and its waters and orchards and greens as playground, as well as for state business. Here it was that she welcomed Sir Walter Raleigh, who came as a messenger of conquests, and it was here, the legend goes, that he spread his cloak for the queen to walk on.

After the reign of Elizabeth I came the altogether different James I, whose one important act, in our immediate context, was to order a Queen's House (for Anne of Denmark) of Inigo Jones, the inventor of the proscenium arch, the innovator who enriched the theater with his designs and inventions for masques, the architect who pulled English building out of the low heavy Tudor of small rooms and medieval great halls into Mediterranean grace and light. But before the house was finished, the queen died, and it wasn't until ten years later that Charles I ordered Jones to finish it for his queen, Henrietta Maria. Surrounded by more ponderous buildings, the Queen's House seems a miniature, and that is part of its immense present charm, a charm that named it the House of Delight when it held the superlative art collection of Charles I.

In 1675 Sir Christopher Wren was commissioned to build a royal observatory on the site of the earlier watch tower fortresses for the use of the first astronomer royal, and some twenty years later he was asked to design a naval hospital. For this he was prepared to raze what was left of the old buildings, including the Queen's House, but Queen Mary was adamant that it be left, and sufficient uncluttered ground to give it the air and space it needed.

The wounded sailors began to arrive early in the next century, and with them governors of the hospital, who took it for granted that the Queen's House was theirs to live in and reshape to their convenience and to accommodate an increasing number of pupils of the Royal Hospital School. It wasn't until the Royal Hospital School was taken out of the building (in 1933) and restorations of what could be restored were made that the house returned to something of its early harmonious beauty.

The little palace functions as part of the Maritime Museum now with precise ship models, dashing portraits of maritime worthies, and great seascapes and portraits of noble ships, but there is much seaworthy matter elsewhere in Greenwich. The house deserves attention for itself, for the grace of its small, lilting double-entrance stairway and the fine turns and curves of its Tulip Staircase, the columned loggia, the details of the balcony ringing the Great Hall, the masterful plasterwork in the ceilings, and the utter felicity of what the whole must have been, if these surviving parts are honest witness.

There is a wry logic in going from the Queen's House directly to the Painted Hall, a study in changing tastes, in this case within a century. It is part of Wren's Royal Naval College and now serves as dining hall for as many as 400 officers. What you will see are long, long tables and many small lamps (when the plate is out on the tables—Londoners mention a solid gold service or, at least, silver— and the hundreds of lamps are lit, and the medals and braid on dress uniforms glitter, and the amber and ruby of wine glow in fine stemware, is not, unfortunately, a public time) and some incredible painting, highly thought of in its time and, to our tastes, somewhat ludicrous. In great stentorian sweeps, Sir James Thornhill frenzied the hall with a hierarchy of allegorical figures storming around the Olympian figure of Queen Anne and Prince George of Denmark and, similarly threatened, William of Orange and George I separately making landings, to keep the watery motifs going. You will have seen better painting in any number of halls and salons but rarely quite so much, including the grisailles and trompe l'oeil confections dear to the hearts of eighteenth-century art lovers.

The Chapel, on the other hand, is a gay, playful jewel box, the rhythms of its window arches repeating in variations of transverse arches that look like swaths of silk, the architect's art borrowing, successfully, from the jeweler's and the dressmaker's crafts.

As in almost every British museum there is a plenitude of interesting objects: a Print Room with thousands of marine drawings and a remarkably replete iconography of Nelson, a strong painting of Captain Cook, a painting of his death and the views of Tahiti as he first found it, sketched by William Hodges, the artist who accompanied Cook on his second voyage. An immense gallery is devoted to ship models of all ages and sizes; smaller galleries are concerned with the Battle of Trafalgar and various wars, each in its own section.

Navigation instruments going back in time make fascinating displays; quadrants and sextants and astrolabes and compasses, some of which look like the high achievements of master goldsmiths and clockmakers. The instruments of the first royal astronomer, John Flamsteed, were removed by his widow, but those of later royal astronomers, including the famous Halley of the comet, left instruments and testaments of their work.

One of the turrets of the building sports a dented ball which dropped at precisely one o'clock each day so that ships, to which it was visible on the river, could correct their clocks. It still drops but as a cherished antique gesture.

The illustrious companion of battered-ball Greenwich mean time, zero meridian, is even more modest, a line out of the observatory and into a clump of bushes, and that's it. Not to feel cheated by the frailty of the casual line, visitors follow it the short distance allowed them, teetering on it as if it were a high circus wire, and stumble into the shrubbery with a satisfied, laughing sigh. They had actually walked zero meridian, and the fact that it hardly exists to the eye must not spoil the pleasure.

Open weekdays 10 A.M. to 6 P.M.; Sundays 2:30 to 6 P.M. Closed Christmas Eve, Christmas Day, and Good Friday. Free. Restaurant.

Since the Naval College and Maritime Museum present an uncommunicative green stretch along Romney Road as it moves toward Trafalgar Road, pay the four pennies for a bus ride past side streets of cottagy houses, shadowed by the giant stacks of the power station, to the stop near the Greenwich Baths on Trafalgar Road, and then walk through the row of provincial shops reluctant to part with the carving over their doors, serving the Indian and Pakistani families come to work at the local plants, people necessarily more interested in the cost of lentils than carvings. An old type of general store, out of use in most urban areas for fifty years, still exists here and calls its collection of dish towels, socks, blatant cheap rugs, dishes, trousers and jewelry, the General Salesman. Opposite the omnivore, a large Edwardian pub that doesn't have to be made "period," and immediately beyond, a reliable symptom of the working-class status of a neighborhood, a storefront surgery listing the names of several doctors.

East Greenwich begins to meld into Woolwich with the curve of rudimentary two-story houses on Old Woolwich Road and Whitworth Street, with the flower stalls already mentioned on Earlswood Street and Colomb, as well as Tyler, and an enormous supermarket which (at least the handsome young curate in a hand-me-down-ragged-gown at St. Alfege's Church said so) is dragging the trade away from the shops of West Greenwich, causing them to wane and perish.

The 108 bus makes a stop at Woolwich Road and travels by insubstantial stucco bungalows and endless rows of clumsy little Victorian houses to the green grass sea that ebbs off Shooter's Hill. On a normal, misty London day, it is a lovely thing to come on after the dispiriting ride. A Blackheath boys' school sends its scholars out for cricket, to shape a restless Kandinsky of green, blue, orange and red jerseys, stopping, darting, colliding, before the church that sits as important and isolated as Mont-St.-Michel in the foggy distance. The houses of St. German's Place lead into a ramble of deep greens, roads marked "private," and a miscellany of houses, all labeled "Morden." The excluding gatehouse of Morden College and its Frenchified eighteenth-century landscaping hide a set of what should be, according to Professor Pevsner's description, a distinguished set of almshouses. It was, according to Pevsner, built in 1695 by a Turkey merchant (the master of ships that carried cargo to and from the Near East) for the shelter of "decayed Turkey merchants," each apartment obviously more spacious and comfortable, with one bathroom for each pair of small flats, than much of extant London housing.

Morden Road, bordering the college, is an assemblage of large houses of several styles, including modern horizontal, a large glass and cement shoebox squeezed in too tight a space, its asphyxiating position fortunately semihidden by the tall trees that shield the road. (One would like to know how Charles Gounod found his way to this hill in a distant corner of London, as he did in 1870, and left a plaque to prove it.) Rounding a southeastern corner of the heath is a beguiling crescent, the Paragon, alternations of six tall windows behind white colonnades with sections of three-and-a-half-story square brown houses softened by mansard roofs. The handsomeness continues on South Row, which also shows off a pond, almost obscured on weekend afternoons by young men and boys and their miniature sailboats and motor vessels spluttering across the miniature ocean.

The luster fades on Montpelier Road and Vale, as it runs down, carrying with it a few small hotels to meet with Tranquil Vale, both thus shaping the high street of Blackheath. The antiques and junk; the shops for imported delicacies; the homemade cakes baked, served, and sold in a picturesque alley; the ladies' and children's clothing shops with clever names and creamy, confectioner's colors; a tiny, flowered square peeping out of an alley; a trattoria; the bookshop; the rise and fall and curve of the streets; and the preposterous traffic will remind Americans of summer-house towns, lumped together as "New England." A Londoner would probably say it resembled Hampstead, but not so determinedly *avant*.

Going northward on Tranquil Vale (noticing that the parish church has turned to welfare work and ballet classes) past ugly houses with Edwardian mumps sitting at the side of the smooth, endless green, one comes on the enormous adjunct green that stretches between Lloyds Place and Grotes Place, and on its inner border rows of eighteenth-century houses. Eliot Place moves northward with some good houses, others not so good, and two of them (one no wider than a window and strips of supporting wall) with pairs of Oriental pigeon-breasted lions sitting on the roofs of their porticoes. Beyond, the lovely fan and wide pediment that stretch over the ivy-covered bays of a Regency house, and soon after, the large, white, classic, colonnaded, and bow-windowed Heathfield House.

The suburban villas begin to cover themselves with denser stands of trees and shrubs, trying to be country, as the terrain dips off the heath, into Pagoda Gardens or settles into total country quiet in the Orchard. Here, no more than ten minutes' walk from the frenzy of Tranquil Vale and the trains rumbling in and out of Blackheath Station, only the sound of one blackbird cawing.

The heath gathers its flat green silk into hillocks and plants trees on it and spills its southwest corner into Lewisham Hill. To the north it becomes Dartmouth Row and its early-eighteenth-century houses. To the south, middle-class villas becoming ragged and slatternly as the hill descends to a Victorian obelisk whose legend has been defaced by weather and the ubiquitous shadow of a railroad bridge, this time at Lewisham Station.

Innumerable British Railway suburban trains substitute for the underground system these parts of London lack, largely because the land is too marshy. Cross to the other side of the bridge, past Silk Mills Path—and who knows how old that name is—to a narrow walk that hugs the side of the bridge and rises to the station. The strange sounds you may hear will be the voice and steps of a gray mule that begs from the greenery on the other side of the wire fence. He soon gives up, barred from the strip of canal that suddenly appears far below, the decorative waters for a group of brilliantly colored brick cottages, sitting up to their eaves in growths of well-fed, tall flowers and garlands of wash. This colorful little lost hollow was made for Sickert to paint, if he were alive, and if he ever walked the path to Lewisham Station.

Boarding and sitting down with the thin, tough little charmers of Lewisham in their pink hair and stiletto heels—let those Chelsea fools walk barefoot or, worse still, flat-shod—listening to their pink tongues flicking poisonously around the other girls in the filing department, you may have quite another London from that the tourist buses offer. The train touches on the terrible emptiness, the pathetic scalloped edges and glass eaves of what is left of London Bridge Station, flows into walls of skyscraper, brushes by Southwark Cathedral into splintered views of St. Paul's, then on to blanks of factory walls and bleak flats east of Waterloo Station. Still another view of the modern fantasy of the Festival Hall enclave, the stuttering images of Parliament through the crisscrossed bars of Hungerford Bridge, and you are in the familiar confusions of Charing Cross Station.

# 27   Museum of British Transport

Via one of several buses—possibly the 88—one arrives at the small, fat-domed tube station at the northeast corner of the abundant Clapham Common, and just before the station, on Clapham High Street, the Museum of British Transport.

It is a railroad station of the time of St. Pancras or Victoria, crammed with trains and sections of trains surrounded by buses, signs, prints, pieces of machinery, recorded narrations, and appropriately, little boys who explain it all intelligently to their mothers or, unaccompanied, as twos and threes leaping and darting among the vehicles, exclaiming, "Cor!" (This is the sort of museum which one should see with a little boy.)

There is some vague order of chronology here, but unless you are making an evolutionary study of trains and buses, it doesn't matter how you attack. You may enjoy the most splendid first, beginning with the royal saloon of the Great Western Railway, finished in 1874 for Queen Victoria's use, equipped with satinwood and tufted silks and, to deaden the sound, a cork floor laid on double boards and then covered with felt and carpeting. There was a little gadget she could pull or push to slow the train if she wished. Edward VII's saloon, of 1903, is finer, with a tiny sitting room, a splendid bathroom, and, near his bed, a thicket of bells. Of earlier, pioneer times, there is an 1869 saloon used by Queen Victoria—soft, puffy, fringy, and lacy and gilded, with blond doors carved in Gothicky designs.

For a demonstration of how later *hoi polloi* (not very) traveled, there is a dining carriage of 1914 which one may enter. It is strange; the light is eerie, and the quiet uncomfortable in the coffinlike enclosure of frosted windows and darkened woods and the decayed elegance of Art Nouveau patterns. For the much lower classes, those that never used a dining car, there are the coin changers, ticket punchers, an old green iron machine that disgorged pieces of Nestlé's chocolate for a penny, and a machine that gave up a platform ticket for one penny (it now costs three pennies to buy the little antique). Old railroad posters show "places of interest" that the expanding lines were unfolding to view and signs, countless signs: IT IS FORBIDDEN

193

TO SELL RETURN TICKETS, HURRY ON FOR THE LIFT, and MEN EM-
PLOYED BY FARMERS MUST NOT CROSS THE MAIN LINE TO FETCH
MILK CANS.

Along with the posters, the signs, the brass nameplates, the instruction books for signalmen and engineers, the lithographs of river
bridges and stations and packet boats, the maps, the bundles of old
tickets, the lanterns and whistles, the caps of railroad personnel, and
exquisite models, there are legendary beauties of railroad design. One
is a locomotive of 1893 as confident and dazzling as an Elizabethan
gentleman in gleaming green. Another is a siren of *café au lait* with
green edges and bands of black, fine red and white lines to echo
contours, brass and copper fittings, and a copper-hatted black smokestack. She is small, enchanting, and was extraordinarily durable; built
in 1880, she swept her pretty skirts back and forth on the London
to Brighton Line until 1947, when she was put out to pasture.

The companion category, public buses, is equally full and engaging,
moving from a flower-wreathed omnibus, bright, dainty, and horse-
drawn (1829), through the discomforts of the knifeboard horse
omnibus of 1851, whose upstairs passengers sat unsheltered on tight,
narrow benches, back to back, sharing a slat as backrest, and another
open-topped, horse-drawn omnibus covered with ads that proclaimed
—between Victoria Station and King's Cross—the efficacy of Pear's
soap, Sanitas disinfectant, Oakey's knife polish, Horlick's malted milk,
a lung tonic that never fails, Heinz pickles, and Carter's little liver pills.

Nothing in the way of public transport seems to have been omitted,
including a cable car that climbed the hills of Highgate and a gay
tramcar with little folding benches and open sides and a lumbering
behemoth, a perilously tall tram that was actually one full-sized car,
lacking wheels, set on top of another.

If you find you've had enough of vehicles, their innards, trimmings,
and accompaniments, you might make the journey through underground posters and old photographs and panels that take you from
transport by foot to Roman litters, to sedan chairs, to steam carriages
and omnibuses, to motorbuses, to the first underground (1863) and
the tubes proper, in 1890.

Have a cup of coffee or an ice cream at the inexpensive snack
bar, and if your interest holds, go out to the yard and into a new
building of "small relics," which means seals and insignia, glass,
china, silver, pewter, silk banners used in royal trains, more tickets
and timetables, a gallery of portraits of famous British railroad giants,
and wonderful prints on railroad subjects. And don't forget to look

for a royal washbasin, thickly, luxuriantly sunken into a pillar of padded silk, that the lurch of the train might not offend royal flesh.

Weekdays, including Saturdays, 10 A.M. to 5:30 P.M. and bank holiday Mondays. Admission: adults 2 shillings and sixpence; children one shilling and sixpence.

Where Farringdon Road becomes Farringdon Street, there is a lifting of mood that comes from the wine shops and the heaps of fruits and vegetables, the glistening fat and pinks and reds of meat from the retail butcher shops, and from the Smithfield Market the voluptuous odor of meat. To add to the explosion of color, 'the dark-red iron bridge—curved, statued, and shielded—that holds up Holborn Viaduct and, below, public toilets recently redone in bright conveniences blue.

Before you go into the well-organized, comparative quiet of the market, try to imagine the stench and noise of the time, before the present market was built (in 1868), when it was the largest live-animal market in the world, surrounded by numerous slaughterhouses. If you don't think of it as death and the spurt of blood and the sag of flesh, all for cramming into your guilty maw, the Smithfield Meat Market is peculiarly beautiful. The best section is Victorian, hundreds of close arches and pillars and coils and arabesques of fancy grillwork, the requisite ornate steeple outside, and inside, to soften the black and green ironwork, the light of old, white lamps.

For the clutter and clatter and ham-handed market humor, the early hours are, of course, best, but the hours of easing off, at about ten in the morning, bring a hypnotic hieratic mood. The white-coated and capped butchers move more slowly and speak more tiredly; the porters in blue stroll along with their barrows as if they were prams; the sound of the wheels and the whine of electric knives sawing through bone are lost in the sawdust. The rows of empty hooks shine and bristle like armored troops, while others hold large surrealist bouquets of clustered lungs, livers, hearts, and windpipes and pink, smooth halves of piglets, and, suspended like a display of market baskets, big bags of beef hearts. Under the silvered sky of hooks and immense scales, in gardens of gold and red signs, hang the walls of beef from Australia and New Zealand and Scotland and the Argentine and, excised from the protective flesh, the neat design of cages of ribs.

As you walk through a newer, less ornate section, a barrow trundles by, laden with big strips of suet, carefully folded, as folds of wool might be. The huge geese and rabbits, hanging at full, dead length, begin to resemble attenuated Gothic ornaments, the feathers left on the chests of the stripped turkeys become white peonies, and the mounds and heaps and mattings of chicken, exotic carpeting. It all has become unreal, bloodless, and lovely.

The "smooth field" on which the market stands had as its priory St. Bartholomew, founded in the twelfth century by one Rahere, who, recovering slowly from a fever contracted while he was on a pilgrimage to Rome, had a set of terrifying visions and, finally, a consoling one in the shape of St. Bartholomew, for whom he built a church and a hospital when he returned to London. A half-timbered sixteenth-century gateway house leads through much older arches into the Norman Church of St. Bartholomew the Great, which suffered much change before and after the dissolution of churches but has kept its Norman arches and vaulting that combine felicitously with the fifteenth-century Gothic windows and the almost unadorned font of the same time. It shows several noteworthy monuments of the sixteenth and seventeenth centuries, one of them erected for the founder, Rahere, and enough of its very early sections to make it one of the oldest edifices still standing in London. It is, however, the remoteness, the retiring quiet, of both church and neighborhood that seem so singular, particularly when the market noises have ebbed away.

It is difficult then to believe that here scholars from St. Paul's and St. Peter's at Westminster, as well as other ecclesiastical schools, met for "the arguing . . . about the principles of grammar." In the fourteenth century plays of considerable length (one went on for three days) were performed in Smithfield, often viewed by royalty. There were tourneys in Smithfield where the knights showed off their prowess to the king. Smithfield was a hanging place and the place where Wat Tyler was beaten and stabbed and then beheaded, and it was the site of a great annual cloth fair (remembered in local street names) to which "the clothiers of all England, and drapers of London, repaired." Hogarth was born in Bartholomew Close and baptized out of the old font; Dick Whittington's money helped repair St. Bartholomew's Hospital. Possibly too much has happened; the area is old and weary, given life now only by the brilliance of the market and the young doctors dashing in and out of the hospital.

North of the market, follow St. John Street, into the small hammerhead shape of St. John's Square.

"The Gate Houses of the Grand Priory in the British Realm of the Most Venerable Order of the Hospital of St. John of Jerusalem." If you write for an invitation to visit, the letterhead stamped with the strong Maltese cross carries this title in type that suggests Arabic script and the medieval lettering of Irish manuscripts. The gate is the only extant piece of antiquity (early sixteenth century) of a much more antique order, which you may know as the Knights Hospitalers or the Knights of Malta, who owned and controlled that strategically important island from 1530 until Napoleon took charge in 1798. It was a thriving order in England until Henry VIII took his anti-Papish broom to church holdings, demanded that the order be dissolved and its church destroyed, in 1546.

It wasn't until 1874 that its gate was returned to the order, and after changing the gateway and taking down two taller towers that flanked a pub, the order took on new life and attracted new members and continued to grow, translating its ancient hospitalers' function to a variety of modern medical services. Slowly, slowly, the revived order began to gather treasures for its library and, for its museum, began to search out testaments of its past history.

The crystal chandelier in the council room, solidly hovered over by the elderly Victoria in her tiny crown and falls of lace, holding the charter she granted the order, is out of the Farnese Palace in Rome. One passes an intricately made seventeenth-century Portuguese chest, one of those with hidden mazes of secret drawers, and beautiful Italian jars, once the possessions of the order in Malta, and in the chancery, seventeenth- and eighteenth-century silver and gold plate made by Italians and a belt of coins minted by the knights in Malta.

A unique circular stairway of wood, much of it in the original material, leads to the library that contains, in many languages and stemming back to the fifteenth century, books dealing with matters of the order, one prize the extraordinary illuminated Rhodes Missal presented to the order by a French grand prior.

Documentation of the order continues on in the museum: lists; descriptions of sieges; very early record books; and momentous documents like the bold, dizzying script conveying King Henry's order that the Grand Priory Church be destroyed (1546) and an earlier complaint of 1307 made by the mayor of Waterford because the knights were pushing too far their rights of "murage, pontage and panage." There are great salvers, and chalices and beakers and magnificent rings, chain mail and later armor, chests and paintings that speak of mighty ancient history, and the rituals still echoed in present-day meetings. The gentlemen sitting at services in the adjoining church, under banners that duplicate those carried by Crusaders, or carrying the staffs and pacing the solemn ceremonies, wearing the medal of the order around their necks and long black capes dramatized by the Maltese cross (the legendary animal symbols rampant in its triangled arms), become, in the aura of antiquity and the romantic English yearning for pageant times, medieval knights.

Clerkenwell Road calls its candy stores Tuck shops and, as a working-class citadel, maintains a Karl Marx Memorial Library. Where Rosebery Avenue meets Clerkenwell Road, there is St. Peter's Italian Church, which serves the waiters and Soho dandies who come as migratory workers and settle in this area and nearby Finsbury, where they hold a spring gathering of the clan in a *ballo di primavera*. Clerkenwell Green angles out of the road and into a little, irregular close, which rises just enough to make an eminence for the parish church of Clerkenwell, St. James's, here in one shape or another since the eleventh century. Out of the close, meanders with names like Pear Tree, Bowling Green, Vine Hill and Vineyard Walk, names that cling to a heritage of suburban pleasure grounds now belied, wander in and out of Farringdon and Clerkenwell roads. Together they share tenements with poorly protected balcony stairways and dark courts like the Victoria Dwellings on Clerkenwell near Saffron Hill (a famous thieves' nest in past centuries), a dour pile of dark red-brown brick with obdurate obtruding sections and square battlements. What the neighborhood has to sell lies on Farringdon Road, across from the Daily Worker Building at the corner of St. Cross Street, a market of nails, bits of tools, brushes, and books, maps, and prints (p. 320).

Following Clerkenwell westward and taking the diagonal of Hatton Wall which leads into Hatton Garden, you will find yourself among a street of no distinction whatsoever except that it has a good number of silver and jewelry shops, few of which sell at retail, and above them behind the nondescript windows, hundreds of men (many of them refugees from Central Europe) who are engaged in the meticulous, patient craft of cutting and polishing diamonds. London is not one of the major cutting centers; but it is the world's leading rough diamond market, and although you may not know it, on the second or third story of the building you are passing, there may be a legendary diamond passing from hand to hand in a conclave of the world's diamond merchants, who meet here several times each year.

Back on Clerkenwell Road, where it meets Leather Lane and where you might be waiting for the odor of leather, you will have instead the pleasant molasses smell of tobacco curing that emerges from a factory on the corner. On Leather Lane itself there is a market smell, that which is given off by old electric fans, secondhand tools, packaged groceries, mushrooms, and watchbands (a big item in all street markets), bronze equestrians, soap, sweaters, garbage cans, plastic toys, sweets, bathmats, and paperback books with curved corners.

Not far from here, via Roger Street, is the Dickens House on Doughty Street: fascinating, breathtaking, absorbing, thrilling if you are a devotee of Dickens; a house of books and impersonal mementos if you are not. Better yet, stay in the area awhile.

Oldborne, or Hilborne or Holeburne, was already in Elizabethan time an integral part of London. It was in Oldborne that one of the new grammar schools (1447) established by Parliament was erected. And through Holborn, in 1539, Henry VIII marched with a "great muster . . . made by the citizens . . . all in bright harness, with coats of white silk, or cloth and chains of gold, in three great battles, to the number of fifteen thousand" on his way from London to Westminster. Centuries earlier, on what is now Ely Place, a spur off Charterhouse Street, the bishops of Ely maintained manors. One of them, Thomas Arundell, built luxuriously: "In this house, for the large and commodious rooms thereof, divers great and solemn feasts have been kept, especially by the serjeants-at-the-law." One feast in this palace was attended by King Henry and Queen Catherine and the Lord Mayor, knights, esquires and gentlemen, who consumed "one hundred fat muttons . . . ninety-one pigs . . . capons of Kent, nine dozens and six . . . cocks coarse, fourteen dozen and eight . . . swans fourteen dozen, larks three hundred and forty dozen" and much, numerous else.

Although Ely Place stands behind a gate marked PRIVATE, passage during the day is open to allow access to the business conducted in the neat eighteenth-century row and to the remains of the palace of the bishops of Ely, its chapel, now the Roman Catholic Church of St. Ethelreda, one of the few churches taken in the Reformation to be returned to its original faith. A broad tree almost obscures the façade, the depths of whose arches and windows, substantially below the present street level, betray its age, something less than 700 years. Its crypt, still used for winter services, is said to be of an even earlier time, and the elements of which that was built, earlier still.

The entrance to the church is by way of a side hall that shows more sunken arches and through the wooden door that was the bishops' entrance, as they emerged from their house. On the right, a pleasing screen of wooden roses bound in iron and on the left, a new window dedicated to English martyrs who resisted the Reformation. They appear again more convincingly (because more simply, perhaps) in niches adorned with restrained Gothic tracery, and set off by the chaste wooden roof, close to life-size and wearing the costumes of their metiers. Four were executed in the city abattoir, Tyburn: a lady-in-waiting (1591), a seamstress (1601), a Thames waterman (1588), and a prior (1535). Three—a friar, a secular priest, and a schoolmaster—were kept to die in the locality, Holborn and Smithfield, possibly with the dispatch not afforded the priors of large, influential abbeys who, to quote Garrett Mattingly, "were drawn on hurdles to Tyburn, there hanged, cut down while still alive, their bowels and hearts ripped out, and their bodies hacked to pieces and impaled on spears, all this carried out with a singular brutality upon one victim at a time, while the others looked on. . . ."

Off Holborn, inside Staple Inn, welcoming benches in a small brick court, a few trees and the information that Staple Inn Hall was destroyed by bombs in World War II and subsequently redone, with original materials, to the original sixteenth-century design. A farther arch leads into a yard studded with a recently burnished eighteenth-century clockface and an elaborate eighteenth-century doorway facing an arc of Fauvist flowers surrounding a vaselike fountain. Its stairs lead up into a close, threatening new structure, angled with monstrous, clutching arms over the delightful garden and the breathless paths that lead out again to Chancery Lane and Holborn. Brooke Street, across from Staple Inn, where Thomas Chatterton died in 1770 (the number is 38–39), is a return to the modest uniformity of old shops that lead to tenements, a few trees and benches, and a scraped sign that calls it Brooke's Market, an adjunct of Leather Lane. Turn into the doorway that leads to the minute yard of St. Alban the Martyr, then to its Victorian Gothic chapel and an enormous, light, modernish church, bombed out and reconstructed. The church is the usual calm, antiseptic, pleasing modern except for an enormous altar painting, a latter-day suggestion of El Greco transfigurations in nervous, chalky colors that seems to have no relationship to the simple boxes that mark the Stations of the Cross or the unassuming organ case. With a moment's pause at the Brooke House Hotel to wonder who, why, and how much behind its lace curtains and to say hello to a child with a running nose and dirty face, walk through Brooke's Court, whose tenement walls mewl FOREIGNS GO HOME, then into Gray's Inn Road. A few minutes in alleys called Fox Court and Holborn Buildings with their pushcarts and forgotten garbage and silent, invisible people will be enough.

Sir Francis Bacon, with the essential, ubiquitous sparrow on his head, is easier to take. He stands in South Square of Gray's Inn (across the road) facing out to the side of the great Tudor (and much rebuilt) hall, which fronts as well on the gardened Gray's Inn Square in which three students—they look Indian, Malaysian, and Japanese—babble along about their law studies in oddly cadenced English.

The gentlemen of the law here took the air and their ease, as did the gentlemen in the other inns, but Gray's Inn seemed to be a shade more *sportif* in its early years, devoted to archery practice and more strenuous sports than ambling and talking. The athleticism became valuable practice for a brick-throwing contest with the workmen hired by Dr. Barbon (p. 62) who was eating up their fields. Nor did they neglect the arts. They were lively participants in the masques frequently staged at the inns, going too far once in the time of Wolsey, who insisted that he had been insulted by the words and actions of one such entertainment and had the leaders committed to Fleet Prison. That they were aristocrats and always mindful of it was not only attested to by their luxurious entertainments, but by the fact that when there was an apprentice's riot, the gentlemen of the inns were called on as volunteers to quell them, although it was Sir Thomas More and his patient persuasion and a few executions ordered by Henry VIII that successfully subdued the lower classes.

The square leads out to the early nineteenth-century and attractive Verulam Street buildings behind the protecting wall of Gray's Inn Court and into a London contrast. Portpool Lane is a street of unimposing recent buildings with an older alternation of white pilastered tenements, next to colored houses with an extra level of mansard windows, a satisfying play of contrast in color and height. The low, broad arches serve to give glimpses of the depth and complexity of the estate, of the large lockers in the yard which might still be outdoor toilets, and of the fenced-in bomb damage that substitutes for garden; on the windows, the symptom of working-class respectability, lace curtains, some of it in fuzzy printed patterns on net, some of it in swaggering bold designs, some of it retiring, all of it clean, like the little boys who own the street at six thirty on a fair evening.

Lincoln's Inn was not altogether successful in keeping its park inviolate, especially with the rapid growth of the City and in particular, the destructions of the Great Fire of 1666. But the Society of Lincoln's Inn kept a careful eye on developments, winning a decree from the House of Commons that building be limited to the periphery of the large rectangle as one now sees it and that the buildings be well and harmoniously designed.

By and large, they *are* harmoniously designed, although no ruling made in the seventeenth century, followed by a great plague, a fire, land speculation, wars, and destruction, could stay frozen. The earliest stately buildings were built during the reign of Charles I, about 1640, and show his taste for the Italian as designed by Inigo Jones. It is still disputed, but one house which might be specifically Jones' is the smoothly rhythmed Lindsey House at No. 59–60; next to it is a Palladian copy of 100 years later, when the style came back into fashion.

At No. 13 on the north side of Lincoln's Inn Fields, stepping out of the building line like a classical hero striding to the front of the stage, stands the Soane House, now the Soane Museum. Built in 1812 by Sir John Soane, the architect of the mausoleum and art gallery of Dulwich (p. 217) and the Bank of England (some of his halls still extant) in a wonderfully romantic style that reveals of its time the love for things Greek, usually in Roman translation, dark Gothic meanderings, a passion for brooding over strange exotica from far lands and times. The interior and its contents, one of the most fascinating and greedy collections in a city of avid and often eccentric collectors, reveals a great deal of the man who, Sir John Summerson, the curator of the Soane Museum, says "was a curious, thorny, intricate personality. The leading trait in his character was, without the least doubt, a consuming ambition. He had been a poor boy; by his own endeavours he climbed out of poverty into the ranks of a respectable profession."

In rooms richly furnished with rare pieces of furniture, handsomely bound books in stately bookcases, under niches housing classical figures, one comes on an astonishing diversity of objects. From nymphs and cupids on wall medallions, one turns to a bust of the painter Sir Thomas Lawrence and, one of the leitmotivs, architectural details from many, far-flung places; models of architectural projects by Sir John; objects of antiquity, authentic and "after the manner of." The dining room and adjoining library hold several dozen vases, Greek, Chinese and Wedgwood, a few of which were bought at Christie's auction house. Flemish, German, Italian, English, Roman, and Greek objects (among them some fakes), in bronze and ivory and wax, whole or as shards, and a corridor heavy with casts of details—capitals and friezes and ornaments from classic temples.

It is, however, the Hogarth paintings that are the lure, housed in a room of hinged panels, apparently a device originated by the architect. Mrs. Soane bought the eight "Rake's Progress" paintings from Christie's and paid for the set five hundred and seventy pounds, a great bargain even for the money values of 1802.

The four paintings of "The Election" by Hogarth were originally sold by the painter to David Garrick, the actor, and bought by Soane in the sale (1823) of Mrs. Garrick's possessions. Crammed with contemporary allusions, the canvases explode with movement and caricature: the drunks, the musicians, the bribers and the bribed, the banners, the peddlers and women; cobblers and carpenters; the maimed, the blind and the dead; pigs, a donkey, a bear, monkeys—in short, the Hogarth riches rendered with consummate skill, his fearsome eye and slashing contempt.

Hogarth by no means monopolizes the room. He is accompanied by architectural drawings, many by Soane, a superb set of wash drawings by Piranesi, a watercolor by Turner and two Canalettos, in the assortment of paintings which leans toward romantic landscapes around melting ruins.

Soane's passion for the dark, monastic Gothic appears most startlingly in the basement of the house, where one turns first into a "monk's" apartment, properly gloomy, housing many things medieval, mixed, Summerson tells us, with "samples given to Soane by stucco and artificial stone manufacturers." One looks out of the parlor into the monks' yard through authentically medieval arches taken by Soane from the ancient House of Lords in Westminster when he was working on one of the numerous rebuildings of the old magnificence. Near the opposite end of the basement, ancient Rome takes over in a room still called the Catacombs because it was once lined with cinerary urns, and next to it an anteroom hung with the ubiquitous casts and ornaments in plaster, along with a human skeleton, two dried cats and a rat, souvenirs of demolition in Soane's time. Why he kept them here with his treasures can be answered only from the grave, if Sir John Soane, who could be a taciturn man, would answer.

The necrophilia—in the main esthetic—goes on through the Sepulchral Chamber, which surrounds another important Soane possession, the sarcophagus of the Pharaoh Seti I, and on to memorial tablets in the crypt and forests of plaster casts of figures and columns. You have surely, by this time, stopped looking at the plaster forms, but try to rivet your attention on one more, a white and beautiful Apollo that was made to adorn Chiswick Villa (p. 206) and discarded in the course of alterations. It was given to a Mr. White, who presented it to Sir John, the gifted magpie, who reshaped the room to give Apollo his deserved space.

Much, much else to see, and though graveyards full of plaster casts may discourage you and you've had the little that is enough of antique and medieval gloom elsewhere, keep in mind this is a remarkable house, that it contains brilliant Hogarths, that it holds an invaluable architecture library, and that it sits on a generous history-ladened square.

Emerging on Holborn once again, you might be near Staple Inn, once one of the law inns, still largely Tudor, leaning on timber crutches, weak-kneed and tired. There have been many rumors about this last of London's Tudor (sixteenth-century) houses: that the city was going to demolish them; that rich America was going to buy them, but London refused; that London had offered them, but the United States had refused, etc., etc. But there they still stand, jostled by the passersby and bewildered by the traffic.

South of Staple Inn, walk along Fetter Lane, not as one might imagine named for horses or people hobbled but because it was a hangout for "fewters," or idle people, derived from an old French portmanteau word which covered thieves, drunks, and prostitutes. No amount of lingering will uncover lost and forgotten sin; you may as well continue down to Dr. Johnson's house, in from Fleet Street, and have lunch at the Old Cheshire Cheese, one of Dr. Johnson's inns, and that of most tourists, directly east.

About halfway between London's large, truly international airport and Trafalgar Square, beside an anonymity of houses and factories strung along the swooping curves of a major highway, stand the country houses of two eighteenth-century Londoners, within a short distance of each other, in a propinquity (one might almost consider it deliberate, given London's taste for evocative contrasts) that links a singularly antithetical pair: William Hogarth and Richard Boyle, the third Earl of Burlington.

Hogarth, the younger by two years (born 1697), was brought up in the ancient shadow of St. Bartholomew's (p. 197). It was a poor neighborhood, offering only a minimal amount of schooling, particularly to a boy who preferred drawing. He was early apprenticed to an engraver and, by the time he was twenty-one, had set up his own shop for ordinary commercial engraving, which gave him the means and leisure to spend time on painting and the development of his "moral," acid series of the sociology of his times. The prints of some series became successful, and he was able to move to improved quarters in Leicester Fields (now the breathless movie, pinball machine, quick-fried-meal Square) and a country cottage near the Thames in Chiswick, continuing his contentious, cantankerous battles—economic, esthetic, legal, satirical—from both centers. One of his targets, poisonously etched as "The Man of Good Taste," was his neighbor, the Earl of Burlington, and another was the earl's protégé and assistant, the designer-architect William Kent, for whom the Hogarthian brew of envy and malice began to simmer early, in a drawing class they both attended.

By the time Lord Burlington was ten, he had succeeded to his title; at twenty he was an important government officer in a number of capacities, one of them as Lord Treasurer of Ireland. Twice before he was twenty-five, he made the leisured cultivated gentleman's grand tour, the second to Italy alone, where he became enamored of the neoclassic architecture of Palladio and, back in England, the Palladio-inspired designs of Inigo Jones. The great palace he had inherited in Piccadilly had been changed and expanded to incorporate the Italian's principles, and near his Jacobean country house in Chiswick he began to build a Palladian villa, something like Palladio's Villa Capra, near

Vicenza, with adaptations from Inigo Jones drawings in the Burlington Collection. It was a villa not so much for ordinary living but to serve as an annex of Olympus, where the refinements of art, letters, conversation, and graceful dalliance could consort; composed, orchestrated, conducted, and paid for by the golden lord, who had no trouble seeing himself as an eighteenth-century English version of a Renaissance intellectual and patron of the arts, a latter-day Pico della Mirandola. Pope, for one, was a frequent visitor and dedicated to his host one of his *Moral Essays,* "Of the Use of Riches."

After Lord Burlington's death in 1753, the land and houses passed by inheritance and marriage into the hands of the dukes of Devonshire, one of whom caused the older house to be torn down and the Palladian villa expanded. The intellectual life, in varying shades, continued, as well as the luminously social, particularly in the glow of the redoubtable Georgiana, Duchess of Devonshire, who was supreme social ruler in the latter half of the eighteenth century. In the nineteenth century the villa turned entirely to the social, housing royal guests, both foreign and native. Later the classic house seemed no longer useful or pleasing, and just before the turn of the century it served as shell for a private Bedlam. More recently it became a ward of the government, which restored the house to very near its Burlington image.

As it stands now, a splendid, gleaming anachronism, divested of most of its furnishings, protected by formal rows of termes and *allées* and bosky English park from the busy twentieth-century colorlessness around it, it seems like a beautiful, regal orphan, inadequately sheltered and incapable of sheltering. Classically columned and pedimented, surmounted by an octagonal dome lined with coffering, enclosing royal portraits and classic busts, white and blind, under the noisily colored populace of gods, cherubs, and allegorical figures bounding along Kent's ceilings, it is still an enchantment. The two-story house is divided into handsome chambers on the upper piano nobile, and below, the library, where the current interest is, mainly, the harmonious distribution of space and the displays of sketches and plans for the villa. From the domed saloon, the focal center of the upper floor, one moves into the Red Velvet Room, the Blue Velvet Room, the Gallery, through superb doors and arches surmounted by rich garlands, under coffered semidomes, and deeply curved pediments; past elaborate fireplaces and ordered thickets of garlands and drupes, scrolls, and rosettes; toward long, lordly windows that give a glimpse of stone acanthus on classic pillars. The park is a beguiling amalgam of strictness learned from the French model set by Louis XIV's Lenôtre and released from that strictness in English meanders that turn to a Doric column, an

Ionic temple, an obelisk, a "classical" bridge, and, leading to the formal gardens, a stately Inigo Jones gateway.

No splendors whatsoever rest on the Hogarth House, a simple three-story country house whose only singularity, and that not very singular, is a hanging bay window extending from the upstairs parlor. Its furnishings are sparse, a few tables and chairs (copies of the originals) and a piano reputedly made by Clementi (he of the sonatinas and exercises everyone struggles through) bought from a local inn. Other than these, only Hogarth works, in their variety and number covering the walls of room after room: the brilliant, the not quite brilliant, portraits; London scenes; the world-famous "Election" series, "The Harlot's Progress," "Mariage à la Mode," the group illustrating Don Quixote, the "Industry and Idleness" series, and the "Rake's Progress"; the religious paintings; part of a heroic series of "historical" paintings which were of driving importance to the painter, but not his true metier or very successful. And to carry the line back, between brick cottage and Palladian villa, "The Man of Taste," satirizing Lord Burlington's laureate, Alexander Pope, as busy dwarf in an immense wig, and the despised enemy, William Kent, Lord Burlington's Raphael, as a large figure of imperious stupidity.

Tube to Hammersmith, then 71 bus. Admission one shilling and ninepence for adults; ninepence for children. Open 10:30 A.M. to 7 P.M.

At the far end of Melcombe Street, as one stands on Baker, the ordinary street view ends in a filigree of white arch, suggesting the roof of a distant greenhouse. Closer, it presents some of the finest ironwork in London, leading to the not much used Marylebone Station. In spite of the commerce-station-traffic furies on nearby Baker Street, the square of Marylebone Station has a remote, summer-house feeling, especially when a wind fans the trees out over the shallow glass galleries. They flow to the station in a descending scale of width: Papa Arch, Mama Arch, and Baby Arch, as awnings of Victorian lace with little iron flowers reaching down and standing up and rosettes on the crossbars. The building proper echoes with real flowers set in semicircles of cement, welcoming to the warm reddish brown wood of the hall and its soberly carved, enormous, and frequently closed ticket office, like a huge confessional. The train section is of gentle, pink-orange brick, the roof a play of parallels and oppositions on shallow angles and crossbars holding glass blocks that make a fleeting dynamic rhythm, reminiscent of more modern art.

Most areas and even full boroughs have their stamp. Soho is prowling in tinsel and cheap satin evanescence; Stepney means docks, new housing, and scowling rows of old housing; Hampstead a self-conscious adorableness, sitting on hillocks and lakelets and meanders of heath. It is more difficult to define St. Marylebone, which encompasses in its diversity the lively international restaurant village of Charlotte, Goodge, and Percy streets and the west side of Tottenham Court Road, a raffish, slouching street that has not yet lost altogether the brutality of its ancestor, the immense field where one of the favorite amusements was to throw a cat into a pond and set dogs to terrify her until she was drowned or torn apart. While mansions were being built in Marylebone by Robert Adam and the palace erected that ultimately housed the Wallace Collection and later, while John Nash was setting up his chill classic terraces (enough of them seen consecutively give the sense of examining an enormous warehouse of high-style freezers), an Irish rookery of poverty and drunkenness, of eight and more in a room and all-night battles, of prostitutes and typhus, seethed on Orchard Street near Portman Square. Yet the Marylebone workhouse infirmary was one of the first to insist on impeccable cleanliness and fresh air as deterrents to disease, and it was one of the parishes which early stopped abandoning its destitute young and infants to murderous "nurses" whose tranquilizer for a sick, hungry infant was gin poured down its throat. (If the infants managed to survive, they were given as apprentices to masters who would send a five-year-old up into a burning chimney and provide him with no bathing facilities so that he was not only a charred, ragged, smelly little pariah, but soon covered with skin cancer.)

Marylebone owns the stately shops on Wigmore Street of antiques and jewelry, books and records, dignified clothing, and Frenchly stuffed rolled veal. It owns, too, striving and collapsing, sharp and careless, alert and sluggish, Edgware Road. In Marylebone one can shop in the dedicated sobriety of taint-free, pure and wholesome foods on Baker Street, among the neat rows of ribs in gold-glass-wood butcher shops and tall slopes of greens and fruit on Great Titchfield Street, in the bawling and banter on Church Street (p. 304) or in the dignified upper middle-classness of Marylebone High Street.

Where to plunge in? Perhaps just outside of Madame Tussaud's, near the distracted Baker Street Station. It confronts the Portman Mansions, one of the apogees, and as much as you may ever want to look at, of turn-of-the-century Ugly Duchess housing, the dauntless cliché of red brick and white bowed windows, topped by a menagerie of angry heraldic animals howling into the sky. A sharp alteration from the tall, broad, and showy hides in the St. Andrews Mansions on Dorset Street, off Chiltern Street. Its porter's bell and sentry box are no longer in use; the supply of porters, particularly for small houses, has dwindled, but inside the gates, the enclave of ivied brick and balconies spilling flowers still has the retiring, proud appeal of an old-fashioned flower shop run by a bluestocking of impoverished nobility.

Chiltern Street presents orange-pink brick that once housed workers' tenements, recently redesigned as flats with private toilets, and other modern amenities and confusingly renumbered. Except for shining up the brick, not too much has happened to the shells of the houses, still crazed with chimney pots and a bearded river-god whose enraged mouth spews water pipes. The street's uniformity of small grocers and snack and sweets shops helps hide a few specialist's shops, and, behind a screen of brown paint, the shops that restore the royal paintings. The precise Victoriana winds up in a glory of red fire station with engines emerging from arches, little perpendicular sharpnesses on a stutter of narrow windows, and, holding up a large window, the dedicated heads of firemen in their helmets.

Southward lie the unobtrusive pleasantness of Blandford and Manchester streets, the antiques and galleries of George Street, the superb Wallace Collection on its suitable square, the dignities of Wigmore Street and in Barrett Street, one of London's many antique supermarkets. West of Baker Street, York and Crawford streets and Seymour Place continue the displays of George Street along with a bit of dust picked up from nearby Edgware Road; then the peaceable uniformities of Bryanston Square and Montagu Square, and immediately to the north of these, again, the iron lace doily of Marylebone Station.

On the arbitrary assumption that you might be approaching Marylebone (not, incidentally, derived from some French saint whose name was Mary the Good, but from St. Mary's on the Bourne—the Tyburn River—which ran through the area toward Marble Arch) from Bloomsbury across the border of Tottenham Court Road or Soho, make your entrance with a short walk down Tottenham Court Road, for its slapdash flavor, then turn into Percy Street, and then Charlotte Street, primarily Levantine, with a small Akropolis restaurant and a big one, a Hellenic Provision Store, kebab, felafel, and taramasalata houses, but accompanied by an immense German delicatessen and its restaurant, Italian grocers, a Spanish provisions and artifacts shop, and a few French restaurants. To keep the intellectual franchise, the Scala Theatre and a bookshop that concentrates on art books; to mark the international quality of the neighborhood, a chemist that explains itself as "Apotheke and Pharmacie," and, the sign of acculturation, a neighbor on Whitfield Street that combines its kebabs with fried fish-and-chips; for chic a funny, unconvincing row of wigs; for modernity, a set of glass boxes bordered by a frieze of young men admiring the girls at the ground-floor stencil machines.

And it all leads into the ebullience of Goodge Street which appoints itself the high street of East Marylebone, heavy-lidded and dull at night, as are most London streets, and a carnival street during the lunchtime hours, when the people who work in the local offices and shops crowd the snack bars, the spaghetti houses, the fish bars and Greek restaurants, the Indian restaurants and pizza makers, the bakeries for a bun, the sweets shops for a lunch of chocolate, the pubs for beer and a sausage, a plastic-lamp-hung hamburger palace, and a small English restaurant for the staunch aberrant who insists on beef and kidney pie in a plain place that shines with the name of Glory. The hardware shops are busy, and the quick shoe repair; the flower carts on Charlotte Place move their thick-stemmed roses for sixpence apiece; the evening's meat and groceries are arranged for, and the pack of cigarettes for watching the telly. The girls explore the inevitable Carnaby Street offshoot, here called 50 CiDiCi (or maybe not, but that is what the sign *seems* to read). The most judicious purchasing, slow and measured, is done at the Heath and Heather shop at the corner with Whitfield Street, dedicated to HEALTH. It will sell you the granules and syrups, the oils, grains, and honeys that make and keep you strong and, near booklets that tell you food dyes cause cancer, sweets made of nuts and fruits, unseductive to look at, with equally unseductive names, like Nutade. The magic of rose hips and bran, maybe taken with Scandinavian hardtack, are yours for the buying, and if you hadn't been careful before, eating any old poisonous thing that appealed to you, and are now in deep trouble, there is Heatherclean to restore internal cleanliness. Hypertension, acne, and nervous debility are taken care of, and coughs stilled by a syrup called Balm of Gilead, and one wonders why liquor companies and tranquilizer manufacturers haven't already used the name.

Bordered by the dark walls of Middlesex Hospital and threatened by the technological shields and disks that seem to be falling off the Post Office Tower sits Cleveland Street, of no remarkable importance but a fine example of a street that has been left behind and contented to be, the attitude of a good number of London streets. A finger of Cleveland Street, Tottenham (not the road), has an Indian spice center that washes the air with the odor of curry and brightens it with soldierly rows of detergent, and near Foley Street it sports a set of houses that manages to combine and distort Victorian Gothic, Art Nouveau, Tudor brickwork, and Italian Renaissance design. Cleveland then stubs its toe on the base of the tall hypodermic tower and its inevitable souvenir shop of hectic clichés, then escaping via Grafton Way, cools off at Fitzroy Square.

The east and south sides of the square were planned by the Adam brothers at the end of the eighteenth century as classic, chastely ornamented units. No. 29 is an address usually associated with Virginia Woolf, but the blue ceramic plate states that George Bernard Shaw lived there from 1887 to 1898. Several publishing houses live on Fitzroy Square and, behind the garlands of the once destroyed, since rebuilt south side, the London Foot Hospital. Quite another brand of science is the terrain of the Scientology Offices, around the corner, at 37 Fitzroy Street. Its signs deplore the state of the world—an easy matter—and offer remedies, vague and boundlessly ambitious, also easy if you will subject yourself to its dianetics testing and classes;

schedule listed. Should you be bashful of walking in cold, another sign YOU MAY TELEPHONE HERE (probably brought from Ireland, where they abound) supplies a neat excuse. The neighbors offer only the balm of smiling stone faces above their doorways.

With a look at Greek exuberance that blazes Maple Street, turn back into Cleveland Street and its peaceable faded charms: the Greek groceries and small greengrocers; small sewing establishments behind storefront net curtains; leathers and guns and buckles; a sign that Samuel Morse lived at No. 141 from 1812 to 1815, another that the sculptor John Flaxman lived and died at No. 7 on Greenwell Street (a sprout of Cleveland Street); an Indian restaurant that prefers to call itself Volga; a spidery iron griffin left of an old shop sign; Indian families and young indigenes; and the pride of the neighborhood, Louis Koch's fine furniture at No. 106, displayed behind a lovely bowed front and guarded by two life-size stone dogs.

The southern end of Cleveland Street takes you back to the complete neighborhood of Goodge Street. It assumes an angle, a new name (Mortimer Street), and begins to dress like West Marylebone. Its Indian restaurant, at No. 81, a branch of a famous Indian chain (Gaylord's), is bigger and whiter in the table napkins, the pubs take on splendor, and the houses grow taller and wider. One of them, at the corner with Nassau Street, is a many-paned, long-windowed edifice that is a touch *Belle Epoque*, a bit Louis Sullivan, and, contrasted with other houses on the street, a fine example of what holding back at the right point can achieve. Absolutely without restraint, piling decorations on with omnivorous greed are the St. Andrews Houses at No. 27–29, groaning with keystones, two kinds of bowed window, scrolls on broken pediments, a roof both pedimented and mansardish, the whole sundae syruped with heroic floral bands. It has its tasteless age for excuse, but what can have possessed the builders of a 1914–15 building, a *Madwoman of Chaillot* confection called Radiant House, a distracted collected of blue tiles, iron coils, and stone bosks; columns, beading and bowing in nervous divisions.

If you like this sort of thing, and there can be a funhouse pleasure in it (although there is a recent movement to view all Victoriana solemnly) walk up Great Titchfield Street to its meeting with Langham Street for Gothic Tuscan in a dizzying black and white of stripes, zigzags, and checkerboard. Langham Street finishes in a distraught flurry of the huge melting and pitted cheese of the BBC building combined with John Nash's All Souls' Church, whose rounds of columns were meant for a graceful melding of his Regent Street and Portland Place, to lead to the royal enclave of the Regent's Park area.

As if to maintain the design, Great Portland Street Tube Station repeats the roundness and then leads into the business, mainly "rags," of Great Portland. Glance at the taciturn face of Gosfield Street, unexpected in this open, placid neighborhood, look at the tall arches and slender menorah of the synagogue, and picking your way among the bolts of cloth and racks of the finished dresses, flying in and out of the trucks on Margaret Street, find All Saints' Church. This extravagance of Victorian Gothic shows clusters of marble pillars something like Westminster Abbey, capitals suggestive of pre-Raphaelite designs, sections of ceiling remotely Tudorish, tiles and stained glass Burne-Jones figures, and where there aren't people, Byzantinish abstractions of all-over design and a tremendous carved reredos in what might be Flemish style. The pulpit of much many-colored inlaid stone returns to the Italian (one looks for the stone Toscanini-faced lions that rest on just such short marble pillars in Ravello) and back to William Morris in a golden, grape-patterned canopy. That which could possibly be done to the interior of a mid-nineteenth-century church in the Gothic mode was done, for awe and pleasure in its time, for the envy of such abandon in ours.

The restraints of an earlier time greet one north of the great, clanking, roaring maws that are eating out a tube system under Cavendish Square. Chandos Street begins to hum a minuet that paces and bows toward a lovely set of houses, one at the bend of a corner into Queen Anne Street—a regal delight of beautifully spaced windows and columns, fine ironwork rising to graceful lamps, and, on the portico, a frieze of ram's heads and garlands, an Adam signature. The handsome houses of Queen Anne Street with their broad fans and careful doorway detail begin to descend into eccentric compromises with the style, and then at Welbeck Street and its tangents become again unexceptionable Marylebone, picking up color where Marylebone High Street presents the glowing size and bulges of The Old Rising Sun pub (1866) at its corner with Paddington Street.

Before you take your ease at this pub, you might prefer to approach Marylebone High Street by a series of short, undemanding loops, walking into Wimpole Street for its collection of styles, from château to frenzies of turrets, temples, pediments untouched or broken, wide urns, and the omnipresent scallops of balcony. Then the steely charms of medical window displays in New Cavendish Street (that binds itself even more closely with nearby Harley Street by sporting a "Doctor's" restaurant) and the meanderings of Marylebone Lane, which followed the curves of Tyburn Brook on its way from Hampstead to the Thames. After a glance at the pictures being shown by the Picture

Library of the BBC publications building at No. 33–35, wander in and out of the network of small streets that border Marylebone High Street. Look, for instance, at the strange houses on Beaumont Street, where there was once a famous pleasure garden, and, on Nottingham Street, the splendid Prince Regent pub of etched glass, carriage lamps, gold Regency beading, and, to do the bawdy monarch full homage, a large niche for a bust of the regent, protected by iron bars.

Peer into Oldbury Place: garages, a Nature-Cure Clinic, and a house in "mews" dress of nursery pink trim and pink geraniums on white over a delicate fall of greens, and for the full treatment in candy-box mews style, Devonshire Place. Nottingham Place, a strict row of red brick and grayed yellow brick has made itself pleasing by spacing its windows well and introducing bright green and dark green, blue and white on sections of its ironwork. The street seems to be dedicated to small hotels with service suites and flatlets and equally dedicated to missionary work. The Royal Mission to Deep Sea Fishermen is here; across from it the London Bible College; on another corner, the Methodist Missionary Society and, quite close by, the enormous Friends Building on Marylebone Road. Paddington Street a little self-conscious (a fish shop calls itself Fishmonger), has a secluded park that now stands where there was an old people's home, still inhabited by the elderly of the neighborhood, and a beguiling figure of a street orderly (cleaning boy), his twig brush under his arm, examining a find.

Marylebone High Street and Road meet at St. Marylebone Parish Church. The first church of this community of Tyburn was built on Tyburn Road (now Oxford Street) early in the twelfth century. The area began to decay, the church was isolated and robbed of its treasures, and the parishioners petitioned for a new church, soon built on the site of the present graveyard (about 1400) and dedicated to St. Mary. It was this small church that Hogarth used in one of his "Rake's Progress" series, the pew inscription of the painting still to be seen in the church. The name "Tyburn" with its echoes of hanging was gradually replaced by the name of the parish church to designate the district. (Tyburnia moved westward as the Victorian name for the Paddington-Bayswater area north and west of Marble Arch where the ancient, many-fruited Tyburn Tree gallows stood for six centuries.) A third church of the eighteenth century was replaced in 1817, redesigned toward the end of the century, severely damaged in World War II, and again restored, the clear windows now bordered by fragments of the Victorian glass.

The church enlaces a compendium of names: Nash built the

columned portico, possibly to blend with his Regent's Park walks and terraces, and Elizabeth Barrett, spinster, and Robert Browning, gentleman, were married here after their long romance compounded of letters, poetry, high romance, and pathology. The church once planned a large Browning Chapel but, discouraged, contents itself with showing the marriage certificate and portraits of the Brownings, a table from their house in Florence, angels from their Venetian palace, and, from the Browning Study Group of Winnipeg, a window in the present small Browning Chapel.

The arts and literature had earlier representation as well. Sheridan was married here, and Byron, whose family lived in fashionable Cavendish Square, was baptized in St. Mary's, and so was Nelson's daughter, Horatia. In the little graveyard, where the second church stood, lie Gibbs, the architect of St. Martin-in-the-Fields; a composer; a sculptor; painters; a lady engraver of the early nineteenth century; the "according to Hoyle" Hoyle, the writer on games; and Charles Wesley, the brother of John, also a preacher and the writer of a number of famous hymns and the husband of a lady who, in spite of having left a prosperous home to share the meagerness of a preacher's life, lived to ninety-six. Diagonally across from the graveyard, next to a pristine case full of this year's auto models, there is a funeral parlor that still bears the name of the parish clerk of St. Mary's who appears in Dickens' *Dombey and Son*. Dickens lived in Marylebone and there wrote a considerable number of his books, in which local shops, houses, and people figure, people who appear again, sculptured along with their author, on the wall of a modern building, east of the church, where Dickens' house once stood.

Follow Nash, now, in his rhythms of terraces, with friezes and without, or surround yourself with the blandishments of Regent's Park, its Canal ride, the Zoo, and especially the luxuriant rose gardens.

# 3 1    Dulwich Gallery

Twelve minutes by train out of Victoria Station, or about forty-five minutes by bus, and a short walk bring one to the village of Dulwich, a name obscure to most of the world—except for connoisseurs of classic painting—until there occurred a spectacular art theft from its gallery, mysteriously achieved and as mysteriously restored after a few dialogues between the police and the underworld.

Among appealing London anachronisms, Dulwich shows a choice few. There is the countrified village itself and its Georgian houses. It owns the only working tollgate left in London, a set of ancient almshouses, a highly respected college in St. Pancras Station style, and the Dulwich Trust, which controls gallery, college, and almshouses, is still called Alleyn's College of God's Gift. And were you inclined to offer what elsewhere might be called a pledge of support or become a financial friend, you would have to, in Dulwich, commit yourself under the Biblical thunder of a Deed of Covenant.

Immediately out of the center of the village, a gate leads into gardens and the wings of the white almshouses, used originally as the college buildings. The almshouse chapel is in the original Elizabethan-early Jacobean style (unobtrusively redone in the nineteenth century), a dark golden room of oak, with simple and well-carved ornaments, such as the supple small animals and acutely drawn heads that appear on the armrests of the pews. A back door of the calm, restful room leads to trees and lawn and the dark yellow brick of the gallery.

The core of the collection is quite old, the gift of Edward Alleyn to the college of which he was the founder. Alleyn was a popular actor of Shakespeare's time and well enough paid to retire at forty with the ten thousand pounds (Elizabethan value) that bought the Dulwich estate. The next donor of art to the collection was also an actor, William Cartwright, who lived later in the seventeenth century. One hundred years later a noted art dealer named Noel Joseph Desenfans was commissioned by King Stanislas of Poland to assemble a collection for him, but before he received his paintings or paid for them, the king abdicated. Desenfrans offered the potential royal collection to the Crown and Parliament as the beginning of a national gallery, without success. Ultimately, he sold some of the paintings, kept others, and bought more in the normal course of his enterprises. On his death the pictures became the property of his widow and a friend, Sir Francis Bourgeois, a collector and painter in the court of George III, who bequeathed his now augmented collection to the college. In 1814, Sir John Soane (p. 203) built the gallery—the first in London for public exhibitions—now seen in faithful reproduction, risen from the shards left by bombing. The building and its mausoleum for Mr. and Mrs. Desenfans and Sir Francis are singularly accomplished and original, beautiful in themselves and like nothing else except the Soane House and Museum in Lincoln's Inn Fields.

The news releases concerning the robbery mentioned the great names—Rembrandt, Rubens, Van Dyck, Tiepolo, Raphael, Van Ruisdael, Gainsborough, Lawrence, Reynolds—of whose work there are here a number of important examples. Rembrandt's "Girl at a Window" and a portrait of his son, Titus, though paintings of young people, enfold one in the Rembrandtesque mist of morality. One finds clean, small Dutch landscapes of broad trees and infinite skies hanging over modest houses and calm people; the allegorical ladies, the sainted ladies, and the fashionable ladies of Rubens, all edible, like big, fresh-baked rolls and mounds of butter. Van Dyck is represented by several paintings (along with some marked "studio of" and "copies after"), one a portrait of Emmanuel Philibert in rich armor and a high ruff, as direct and sharp as a Velásquez and another, a fascinating "William Russell, Fifth Earl and First Duke of Bedford." He wore his hair in a long, shaggy nonbob, as in present-day Chelsea, chose to have himself painted in the romantic satins favored by Belgravia's young bloods, cherished and showed his pretty hands as they do, and cultivated, one way or another, the tired eye and slightly puffy pallor the anaerobic present young like to sport as symptoms of their decadent lives. The Italians are here, often as "copies of"; Velásquez and Murillo appear, sparsely; and of the French, the donors seemed to have found Poussin most interesting and amassed a sizable number of his works. And if it was Sir Francis Bourgeois who bought the Reynolds and Gainsboroughs, he showed sturdy confidence in adding a large number of his own works to theirs in the English collection.

Hardly as lustrous as the famous mentioned above are the nevertheless stimulating unknowns, particularly those who executed ineptly or cleverly a variety of portraits, mainly English, creating a minor annex to the National Portrait Gallery.

Glance down from the paintings occasionally to look at the pieces of furnishing here and there, fine chests and chairs and one amazing table that sits on a gilded dolphin and is encrusted with shells bearing miniature paintings. Then look again at the interior design, the remarkably advanced skylight and the repetition of arches, touched with gilt and modest flower patterns, that flow like music from room to room.

Free. Open weekdays, except Mondays, 10 A.M. to 6 P.M.; Sundays, 2 to 6 P.M.

Hampstead is an amorphous shade that can, if one chooses—and many do because there is glamor in the name—cast its aura on the large courts of flats in St. John's Wood, bordering Regent's Park, on the serviceable unlovely Swiss Cottage Station, on an infinity of two-columned white curves of houses called Belsize, on red-brick villas of sixty years ago, some of them extraordinarily fanciful in their time and to our taste forbidding houses for Ushers to decay in, for rotting loneliness and people administering slow poisons to their loved ones. Its more specific meaning now is the steep—for London—village near Hampstead Heath, isolated for merchants' country houses and spa gardens in earlier times and still isolated by a paucity of buses and underground meshwork. The pure white beam of liberalism shines steadily on Hampstead and occasionally casts one singular ray. Sometime ago one could read a sign outside a church on Rosslyn Hill which stated that: "If the claim is made that certain theological beliefs must be accepted without question or the right to doubt, then this chapel denies that claim. The right to question or doubt is the right that enables truth to grow."

Buses approach the center of Hampstead, but don't venture the presence itself. However, the 45 bus stops very near the house in which Keats lived, next door to Fanny Brawne. It was originally two semidetached houses built with Regency grace and the subtlest adornments by Charles Dilke and Charles Brown, both gentlemen involved in the literary arts, the first as critic primarily, the second as writer.

In the sitting room or bedroom, still as they were in Keats' time, or in the modest garden near the ivy-wreathed door, Keats wrote four of his greatest odes, his "La Belle Dame sans Merci," a number of sonnets, and much of "Lamia," and probably discussed with his friends and her mother plans for declaring officially his engagement to Fanny. Early in 1820 plans for a luminous career and marriage came to a dreadful halt. Keats suffered a hemorrhage, and trained in medicine and having lived with a consumptive brother, he could not deny its meaning, in those days, an early death. After a convalescence in Brown's sitting room, Keats began to try to live again, writing, visiting, but fell ill, first cared for by Leigh Hunt and later by Mrs. Brawne and Fanny, who prepared his clothing for the trip to Italy when it was decided that only the Italian sun could revive the poet. The Italian sun failed him, as the Mediterranean failed Shelley and the warm Greek soil failed Byron.

From room to room, modest memorabilia: locks of Fanny's hair and bits of jewelry; a gold brooch in the form of a lyre; the strings made of Keats' hair; Keats' engagement ring to Fanny; portraits of the poet by Joseph Severn, the friend who went with Keats to Rome. The Chester Room is a small museum of display cases in which one finds the handsome medallion containing the poet's hair made for his sister Fanny and bequeathed to the collection by her Spanish grand-daughter. Here and in adjacent rooms early editions of his poetry, the books he owned, his medical notebook kept in a minuscule hand, his letters to Mr. Dilke and love letters to Fanny Brawne, miniature portraits of his friends, a facsimile of the register of Guy's Hospital on which the name of John Keats appears and his certificate to practice as an apothecary.

The house is irresistibly moving, certainly as a frame for the high, swift shower of gold that was Keats' short life and for its own sim-plicity, sparsely furnished and decently commonplace except for the aura that shines through the rooms of boundless devotion and affection for the doomed young poet.

Immediately next door, a very similar house acts as the local public library, and hidden where rays from the skylight cannot fade it, a world-famous collection of Keats' material, as well as invaluable material concerning his contemporaries in the rich blossoming of romantic poetry.

Because Hampstead still makes its geography of a maze of eight-eenth-century alleys, more, probably, than any other part of London, there is no specific route to follow. Perhaps down Pond Street and the loop of Hampstead Hill Gardens and then up Rosslyn Hill as it becomes Hampstead High, the neighborhood flavor emanating from a French bookshop, a NO PARKING sign prefaced by POLITE NOTICE (not unique but apt to appear only in refined areas), and, inside Pilgrims Lane, a line of cottage houses and red-brick houses with windows that try to look like Christopher Wren's. Beyond them, two pieces of Hampstead individuality, a huge ship's figure lady jutting out of a house, and immediately next to her, the blondest and most horizontal of suburban modern house and garage. Follow the threads of Rosslyn Mews and Pilgrim Place, glance at the antique shops and bookshops that sell old maps and prints from self-effacing shelves and bookshops of sunny newness and posters advertising "Rubbish at the Round House" (p. 117), yet another exercise in innocence by bearded infancy. Gayton Road surprises and shocks in the ramble of prettiness by being as grubby and uniform and sodden as houses on dock streets, but the mellow tones of country village charm sound clear again in the mazes and turnings and wriggles off either side of Heath Street as it climbs to the Heath.

West of Hampstead High and Fitzjohns Avenue a set of neat, fine houses that constitute the famous early Georgian (1720) Church Row. Continuing in a westerly circle through the shrubs and country green of Oak Hill Park and Oak Hill Way, one comes on gardens, mansions, and solid, rangy suburban houses that descend to the blank of Finchley Road. Northward along Hampstead Grove one finds oneself in the hollow of Admiral's Walk, bordering the heath, where Galsworthy lived. Holly Hill, separating from Heath Street, marks that event with an effulgence of red Victorian fire station and ambles in its own northerly direction, carrying eighteenth-century houses and sudden slits of view up and view down. From its peak at the Holly Bush Pub, George Romney's studio, and Fenton House, it rambles down via fans of stairs and slopes to little Golden Square, the place of a sandpit when Elizabethan Hampstead held 200 people, inhabited for a long time by a prolific family of Gouldings, and now, like so many diminutive London squares, a pretty little girl dressed in a flowered hoopskirt.

Fenton House, mentioned above, is referred to by Professor Pevsner as "the splendid Fenton House of 1693, the best house of its date in Hampstead." Built by an anonymous architect, Pevsner suggests, it had no official name until a century later when it became the property of a "Riga merchant" named Fenton. The house was sold in 1936 to a public-minded citizeness who gave it, with its furnishings, to the National Trust.

Besides the chaste, paneled stateliness of the house itself and its furnishings, there are in a number of the well-proportioned rooms rare pieces of porcelain, in appropriately designed cases and cupboards and on fine tables and curved shelves. One room may be devoted to English porcelain and the elaborations of Meissen ware, another room with Chinoiserie effects shows a collection of early Korean and Chinese bowls and figurines and a number from a later time. The drawing room is the place for a rich dark-blue Worcester set, painted with flowers and birds by two Sèvres craftsmen.

If a dozen porcelain bowls and figures look like 400 others to you, you might explore the musical instruments that fill the rooms not dedicated to porcelain. They were the property of an archaeologist and a purist who hated to hear harpsichord and clavichord music played on the piano which, he believed, distorted it. *Ergo,* he collected the early instruments and kept them in working order, and Fenton House maintains them for the use of students and to show: big and little harpsichords, English of the eighteenth century and Flemish of the seventeenth (on loan from the collection of the Queen Mother); an English virginal of the seventeenth century and one from Italy 100 years older; transitional forms of harpsichord cases around piano strings; and the small rural organ, collapsible to resemble a Bible, used by traveling preachers.

It is not rare to hear a soprano practicing to the frail sounds of a harpsichord the piece of seventeenth-century music she will sing at next week's recital. Having paid an extra shilling for hearing her from the garden, at the top of the city, you have also bought the privilege of sitting in a sheltered place of an early sheltered time (if it weren't for fires and plagues), your drip-dry shirt become beruffled satin.

The heath and its high street are bound together by the intellectual, old-fashioned gentility of Well Walk and Flask Walk—both names reminders of the health-giving waters that were drunk here—Perrins Walk and New End Lane, which leads to the local hospital and a pub with a large, raised terrace for its young doctors and neoromantic young neighbors. Elm Row and Hampstead Square present the traditional Hampstead face of eighteenth-century winsomeness, brilliant handkerchiefs as gardens, and on the baby stairs, tubs of flowers; at one corner of New End, a soup kitchen and dispensary established as thanksgiving because the parish had been spared from the cholera plague of 1849. Under the heavy shadows of jutting angles and rounds of the hospital lies Streatley Place, an interim strip that leads to and from enmeshments of alleys. It should (unless the zigzags, spurts, and disappearances of Hampstead's erratic paths have twisted you to immobility) lead to Mansfield Place, a pathway marked by a school, and, suddenly, an obscure hamlet within a hamlet. It is a court of narrow gardens hung with clothing and roses, aspiring fruit trees and vines reaching into the doorways of modest two-story houses, whose low shapes and passionate gardening suggest craftsmen's cottages of 200 years ago, worth searching out as still another, coarser note in the Hampstead saraband.

It takes a map and determination to avoid Heath Street; any turn will throw you into it, and in any case it is one of the most attractive of high streets, glittering and posturing and cajoling with Spanish imports, high-style (and good middle-echelon) clothing, books and records, wines and groceries, snacks and "ministeaks"; late coffeehouses and restaurants with Continental names, antiques "in" shops and an "antiques" supermarket—international crafts, vegetarian salad bar, honey and wholesome grain, Indian silks, Mexican bags, furniture, china, silver, and homeless objects that defy categories, housed on fresh blond shelves. Heath Street is stopped by a roadway, a dip to the right into tall grasses, a pond for little boys to sail boats in or swim, if mothers and local authorities permit it, and ahead, the vast sprawl of green heath.

The horizon of sailboats and cars, golden boys' heads, and one horseman blocking the sky waiting for his horse to drink or cool its hooves dips to a congenial pub crawl in large old inns with spreads of outdoor basking space and indoor details suitable to their history as highway taverns and coaching stops. First, Jack Straw's Castle, still dressed in some of its eighteenth-century wall; to the north the Bull and Bush, then northeast to the Spaniards Inn. Northeast once more, into Hampstead Lane and the wooded park, the rolling lawns, and the extravagant flower beds of Kenwood, Hampstead's museum of art, one of its concert grounds (indoors and out) and the most palatial of its houses.

The first records of Kenwood as a house go back to the early seventeenth century, but it takes its present shape from the time of William Murray, who became the first Earl of Mansfield, a noted English barrister and ultimately Lord Chief Justice from whose pen flowed many historic decisions in English law. After his house in Bloomsbury was burned down during anti-Catholic riots (he had announced a judgment favorable to a Catholic), he established himself at Kenwood, which had been his country villa, saved, according to Sir John Summerson, by the landlord of the Spaniards Inn, who fed the rioters enough liquor to divert them.

Some years earlier he had contracted with Robert Adam, at the height of his career as architect and designer, to redesign the house, the classic columned villa one sees now, flanked by later, darker wings, added by a descendant. The palatial house stayed in the family, not much used until World War I, when it was threatened by transfer to land speculators. During the years of struggle between owners and groups interested in preserving the house and the extensive grounds, the Adam furniture, French furniture, and a number of paintings were taken to the family seat in Scotland, and others sold at auction. "Iveagh Bequest" coupled with the name "Kenwood" refers to the purchase by Lord Iveagh, Rupert Edward Cecil Lee Guinness, in 1925 of the house and a portion of the acreage. He refurbished the house with his collection of paintings and bequeathed it all to the public after his death.

One learns to recognize and enjoy the Adam style quickly, the playful, delicate classic patterns repeated as exquisite, gifted doodling, the filigree grace, the suave color combinations interlaced with gold tracery and arabesques in light soprano trills. Before entering through his temple portico, one should, however, stroll through the gracious eighteenth-century park, its ramble of curving paths through a magnificence of blooms and calm sea of lawns. Then the house, with its shallow arches and columns, the ceiling panels and plasterwork friezes and ornaments, adorning the spaces above a characteristic and distinguished collection of paintings, mainly English and most of the rest Dutch. By far the most beautiful room is the library, a magic of curved ceiling etched with fine plasterwork around painted circles and semicircles and lozenges, patinaed bookcases in arched niches, warm, yet gentle color, and suitably furnished with chairs and tables on loan from another great eighteenth-century house.

From eighteenth-century grace and silk, you can walk southward to the height of Parliament Hill and down again for the unexpected view of bathers in the southernmost Hampstead ponds and a few houses that seem to stand knee-deep in the waters, a Hampstead touch of Venice. Or board the 210 bus for Highgate Village. Highgate shares hills and ponds with Hampstead and then slips to its own village. Highgate High Street for renowned polite pubs where *au pair* girls meet with their dates on Saturday night. (It keeps to itself a few impolite pubs for Saturday night release of noise, bonhomie, and obscenity.) Highgate is wooded with a miniature forest, cricket grounds and benches for spectators, and, to keep the children off the grounds, a large, well-furnished playground. It hasn't the picturesque appeal of Hampstead, but it does have its own famous cemetery, divided into old and new sections.

The old section is an unkempt, haphazard wilderness, where birds roar and spring blossoms of lilac and cherry rain petals onto graves half-covered with crawling vines, where the frowning leonine rhododendrons are fiercer than a big, sad mourning lion that sits over the tomb of a "menagerist." The appropriate in funerary decor is demonstrated again in the tasteful arrangement of crossed tennis rackets, clusters of tennis balls, and a design of cricket bats on the grave of a "sporting goods manufacturer." Mourning ladies hold vases covered with mourning cloths, near an astonishment of "Egyptian tombs," lower than the rest, behind an entrance of bulbous Egyptian pillars flanked by two obelisks, and, around the entrance, what seem to be gigantic stone worms, or maybe bandage coils, for embellishing the spirit of decay.

The new section pays tribute to two great men, he who invented an essential elixir of English life, Hovis bread, and Karl Marx, represented by a huge head, inscriptions of sentences from his works, and a respectable number of wreaths and flowers. A genius who died young, at the age of thirty-five, takes us back to the specifically appropriate, here a grand piano in stone and an inscription of a quatrain by Puccini.

It goes on—as cemeteries have a way of doing—and on, through new neatness and the picturesque tangles of the old. Following communion with the dead, you might go to the top of the park, and if the weather and hour permit, bask in the local conversation on the yard benches, or find your way to North Hill Road pubs for more earthy conversation.

Hampstead was supremely lucky for its fair with sun bright enough to paint noses and napes bright pink. White Stone Pond at the top of Heath Street was a toy ocean of toy boats, and the supply stations of ice cream kept sustenance lines going briskly. Families with baskets of sandwiches and orange crush and, somewhere, an umbrella (the Londoner's third leg) poured out of the tube station and spilled from the buses. In luxuriant grass that dips from the side of the roadway across from the pond, bikinis and bare earth-worm-colored chests spread and turned and opened themselves in D. H. Lawrence abandonment to the sun, crushing out grass odor to mingle with the smell of suntan oil. On a rise above the bodies in the deep green beds, several hundred children, neatly arranged in a square, were taking instruction for a treasure hunt from a leader in glasses, hairy legs, jaunty tam, and a Scout suit. First clue given out, the children rose like a swarm of locusts, the long-legged and practiced forging ahead down the paths, leaving a trailing line of the bewildered too young, whimpering with anticipated defeat as the giants roared ahead, worried about the forests of twelve trees that loomed and reached for them at the bend of the path, prone to scraped knees and a wild yearning for Mama.

While the children run, the parents stroll to meet them at the designated point at the bottom of Parliament Hill. Before that, there is time to climb the long slope to the top of the hill to see the mounds and dips of Highgate accordion-folded to tableland of houses and an unambitious spire; an amiable, old-fashioned, house-ridden set of views.

What is best on this day are the closer views, looking up to the small figures walking and standing on the crest; their movements vague in the distance, the still figures very still, their shapes reduced to small cutouts dotted with a spot of red shirt or a brilliance of yellow sweater. Against the wide sky and soft line of the hill, as if it might be a line of beach against pale water, the figures look like the calm, quiet people in a Boudin painting. Closer to, a naked baby examines the surrounding terrain, cutting erratic, unsteady paths to the guitars, drums, beards, and shabby brocades to one side of her. Soon bored with the thump of one beat and four chords too long repeated, she weaves her way to a display of biscuits and soda pop guarded by a handsome array of well-dressed locals, who share with her, as she expected. The next goal is a group of office girls in bikinis and their dates, giving their backs to the sun and nibbling sweets, which they don't offer her. She toddles on, through the blue jeans, the peach-pink cheeks, and falls of gold on adolescent heads, the yellow and orange and purple of sweaters spread on the grass, past little dogs whom her nudity unnerves and large collies who turn from her in quiet disdain, picking up a crumb here and a crumb there, very happy in her pilgrimage, as long as she can cast an eye back to the home base of pram and mother.

From the base of the hill, a sudden shimmer of movement, and the sky fills with blue tagged balloons to sit in the trees or to float off and win a prize, as the farthest roaming, for the child whose name appears on the tag. As a balloon makes it through the Scylla and Charybdis of kites and trees and disappears into the sky, one hears, "Mine's going to Spain, I think." "Oh, I think mine will reach India." "Mine is going to China, but will they know how to mail my card back? Do they have post offices, and can they read English names?"

For the tenth time, a voice asks that all people leave the large marked-off area from which the balloon ascension, for which the crowd has gathered, is to take place. People remove their children from the spread of lawn, and the photographers choose positions for action. The immense orange and gray globe, puckered at its gas-eating mouth, and its straw basket sway and turn in the light breeze, like the Fat Lady trying a few dance steps. The banner of the balloon is raised and gives itself to the breeze, to the applause of the assembled; bands of cord are pulled down, all but one twisted strand. An intrepid figure clambers up the ropes to disentangle it, again to warm, universal applause. The basket is crammed with people, the sandbags that held it set to one side; only one rope, held by a pack of stalwarts, keeps the Fat Lady earthbound. A stillness covers the slope, every head turns

to the balloon, and "She's off!" She rises, sways, spits another load of
sand and sashays to the left, and slips down with a bump; rises, soars,
sidles to the right, touches down lightly, and swings off for a heavy
thump. The passengers in the basket change (there is talk of buying
tickets for the ride, but no frantic rush is visible) and go through
the same faltering, mindless motions of a restless, but lazy, psychotic
bird, always held by her tether.

By now it is after five; there are no vendors (a difficult and estheti-
cally comforting fact) to sell the children the drinks they need and
the ice cream they know they deserve; the balloon scheduled to soar
over London clearly won't nor will its red, white and blue companion,
not yet inflated or likely to be. The crowd rises and starts for the ice-
cream wagons down the street and home dragging its yellows and
purples and oranges and blues and reds up the hill and over the other
side.

The unchilded stay on for the conducted walk through Hampstead at
seven or a visit to local studios, open to visitors for some hours during
the fair; maybe to a recital at Kenwood House, an important old film
at one of the local cinemas ardently devoted to them, and, should
they be open, dinner at one of the Hampstead restaurants (p. 292)
honoring the fair with "Gastronomic Fortnights" of especial specialties.

"And so"—to remind you of a devotee of London parks, fairs,
theaters, crowds, and entertainments of all sorts—"to bed."

# 33 Pollock's Toy Museum

Not far from the clash of noises and the frenzies of movement that mark the meldings of Picadilly Circus with Soho and Leicester Square, there is a quiet street, Monmouth Street, once an old-clothes center of London, now less shabby and less colorful, one of its few distinctions the presence of a narrow, steep little house for a collection of old and new international toys.

The street floor sets aside books and puzzles, paper theater sets, dolls in costume and denuded, for selling, and, in cases around the walls, ravishing toy theaters. Mounting the frail, tight stairs, one comes on toys made of matchboxes and matchsticks; posters and whistles and bird calls from many parts of the world; dolls in houses and outside, in various shapes and degrees of riches—an old couple, a costermonger couple blazing with pearly buttons, minute peasant dolls and prosperous Victorian doll families—furniture, miniature paintings, dishes, and domestic animals to complete each ambience. Of burlap, of bone, of wood, of porcelain, short and fat, lean and tall, minute and large, stylized and painstakingly to the life, they come from Russia, Austria, Sardinia, Sicily, Mexico, India, the U.S. Southwest, Burma, China, and Thailand.

Japan and her meticulous miniature crafts have a set of cases, the delicacy balanced by a neighboring large, robust Noah's ark; in an upper hallway, a frilly locomotive made of paper and, at the top of the house, a collection of theaters set with characters and scenic backgrounds from the French and English stage and the ballet and, in an adjoining section, early optical machines like primitive movies. In short, the perfect museum for young children, and if you have to buy your way out, it will not cost too much for unusual games and toys.

Free. Open Monday to Saturday 10 A.M. to 5 P.M.

# London Is Where . . .

One-third of a cinema show is absorbed by sweets and ice-cream inter-missions, following loud Technicolor advertisements, one of them often extolling the refinements of a gambling place on Great Windmill Street in Soho, instant membership and a low entrance fee.

It is permitted to smoke on underground trains and on the tops of buses, in most shops, some theaters, and all cinemas, while cigarettes are available in vending machines on main streets all night. Eating is quite another matter after 11 o'clock. Unless you are in Soho or Bayswater (which folds up at 1 a.m.) or near Fulham Road or one of the very few hotels which keep their kitchens open at night, you will have to content yourself with a sixpence container of milk from an Express Dairies machine—if you have sixpence and the machine doesn't balk.

You may see old balance scales equipped with varisized weights used to weigh copper, silver, and small bills standing on the counters of bank branches.

Post offices share quarters with brassieres and baby socks, or cig-arettes and sweets, or pencils and school notebooks.

Intense public animation is limited to pub discussions, great bursts of speed in running for and leaping on Hyde Park buses, and the gyra-tions in discothèques (and some of that is forced).

There is color, excellence, noblesse, elegance of spirit, a remarkable degree of certain kinds of honesty ("buy the cheaper one; it's just as good," from a salesman), wit and passion in individuals, and yet the London mass seems passive and spongy.

Heaters take the place of painting and sculpture; of all shapes and sizes, they hang on walls, stand on windowsills, above and below doors. They come as flat, futile imitations of radiators, as imitations of coals in a fireplace; they shape a versatile crafts area.

History is remembered; for instance, the d that stands for pence is the word of the Roman conquerors, denarius.

The bladder and kidneys are as highly respected as the dog. Rarely will you be very far from an underground sanctuary, radiant with freshly painted grillwork, white tiles, and clouds of disinfectant. One of the best stations, one which combines a telling number of London artifacts is immediately north of the worthies in the National Portrait Gallery. The dark green railings leading down to ladies' and gentlemen (two of these) are companioned by bright red phone booths and a glorious, multibranched, voluminously ornamented Paris Opéra type of streetlamp. On the lamp there are two signs, bearing helpful arrows and specific street names, that indicate where the public lending library is and where the public reference library. Down below, the further enlightenment of places where you can wash yourself and your clothing and rid yourself of syphilis.

If you are disabled or elderly, the public library will deliver books to your house and, if you are not, urges you to let your crippled and sick friends and neighbors know about the service.

Adults pay one penny per day (nothing for Sunday) on overdue library books, and there is no charge for children's books held too long.

It is possible to hire a ten-shilling catalogue for one shilling in the Tate Gallery when a large important show is on.

It is permitted three boys with matted hair and dirty bare feet, laden with amulets and tinkling bells, to draw cartoons for tourist sales in an empty shop entrance on Regent Street, quite close to Beak Street, where Canaletto lived in his London time.

Politeness is a lovely thing, and you may suffer from it, unable to make a point or move it, to receive an explanation or offer one. As you persist, the politeness gathers, and you are fighting a mountain of honey.

Poverty is lace-printed net curtains and columns scratched naked.

A bus conductor will call, "Thank you," instead of "Fares."

Permission was granted Royal Academy art students to decorate a field of hoardings on King's Road. They painted all night, cheered on by a small host of the curious and insomniac. The newspapers printed a picture of the results, a repetitious series of large teardrops, and reported the event with the mild, respectful interest that greets the achievements and vagaries of the young in London.

There is little pushing, except during the tired going-home hours, at bus stops or tube stations (and even that adroitly accomplished with "Excuse me"), one of the reasons London is called civilized. And it is, combining an ancient tolerance—compounded of indifference, an occasional eagerness to be amused, the admiration of a tradition-bound people for the eccentric—with the pleasanter aspects of resignation, the willingness to stay anachronistic, an unexcited, unsurprised old friendship with the vagaries of the human condition, and a strong taste for mellowness.

Among Theosophical societies, societies for reading the new version of the Bible aloud in large public squares, societies for converting the Jews, for the protection of pet ponies, for the promotion of Hellenic studies and Roman studies, for the protection of ancient buildings and new music, for spreading the knowledge of true prayer, for psychical research, of friends of wine, of herbalists and genealogists—unfortunately, no more Muggletonians—there is one for the protection of animals of North Africa, specifically, and a gallant one—eyes streaming and chest crushed by smog—campaigning for Clean Air.

If you ask a shopkeeper or a porter in a building where the nearest postbox is, he may say, "Oh, leave it here. I'll be posting some letters today, and I can easily drop yours."

Henry Moore decorates a low-cost housing estate, Barbara Hepworth enlivens the façade of a department store on Oxford Street and makes meaningful a court of government offices on High Holborn, and Jacob Epstein has put a superb "Madonna and Child" before a small nuns' building on Cavendish Square, yet household decor clings to cretonne-in-a-cottage style.

A cobbler will not tell you the price of resoling a pair of children's shoes beforehand because, he says, it may turn out to be a cheaper job than you both think, and he wouldn't want to quote too high a price.

# 34 Entertainment

## With Children

**Chessington Zoo**

An almost perfect "Sunday in the park," especially if you go with children. The well-planned and yet not too large space allows lions and tigers sauntering grounds, and there are long paths for the peacocks' parade. Among the gardens and ice-cream stalls, clown monkeys and acrobat monkeys, sad-eyed, lice-picking mothers and belligerent fathers. There are big animals for awing and small ones for petting and a cage of myna birds, dark and beady-eyed, sitting in a pointillism of blue, pink, striped, speckled, dotted, dashed little birds. One myna, apparently trained by a Chinese waiter, repeats, "Herro, herro, herro"; a companion keeps asking, "What's your naime?" while a third sheds deep, villainous laughter over their contemptible efforts.

More vigorous pleasures alternate with animal viewing. Clattery, broken music sends buses and horses whirling on a carousel next to the high lift and dip of airplanes. There are halls of mirrors and skeleton-hung cavern rides, subtle slides and precipitate slides. And an extra that comes in handy as training for pub gambling machines or at the tables of Soho, Bayswater, and Mayfair, gambling devices that respond to pennies and ha'pennies. It is instructive to see a little girl, not quite seven, breathless, flushed, demolished on a turn, flying on triumph when the machine returns two pennies, Dostoevski's gambler in faithful miniature.

You can calm your agitated young with the usual administration of sweets that beckon from many stands, or put him to a full stop by letting him stand at the door of the pub, which opens at seven (when some sections of the zoo are closed), and let him peer in at the keeper having a beer while the lion cub he has brought with him settles, like any good pub dog, at his feet.

Train from Waterloo to Chessington; Green Line bus 714. Admission four shillings and sixpence for adults; two shillings and threepence for children.

## Crystal Palace Zoo

Once part of the famous Victorian exhibition grounds, the area is now primarily used for athletic meets, but leaves space for a park for walking, boating, fishing, and a small zoo, many of the animals of the domesticated species and permitted to amble along with you on the paths. Goats with ponderous bellies and calves suckling act as demonstrations for lessons in biology to judge from the serious, patient conversations between parents and children. For paleontology, one searches out the enormous prehistoric animals, painted gray or steely blue, leering out of the greenery. They are remains of the original expositions, now more than 100 years old, and remarkably made of innumerable small bricks, their shapes and colours repaired and repainted frequently.

Free; reachable by the 2 or 3 bus and a number of others indicated on the bus map.

If you have taken your child to the Bethnal Green Museum, possibly—depending on his age—to the Geffrye, the Transport Museum, and to see the mummies in the British Museum and Queen Victoria's toys in the Kensington Palace, and it is still raining too hard in the ubiquitous playgrounds, see what the **Public Library** has in the way of films and puppet shows. And if it isn't raining, and it's summer, try the puppet shows in the parks or the weekend folk dancers and musicians on Hampstead Heath.

London, the big, plain cornucopia that spills parks for adults, does well by children, also. The many well-equipped playgrounds have already been generally mentioned, but you might like to take your young to a rather special one, that of **Battersea Park.** For young ones there is an enormous sheepfoldful of things to crawl in and on, immobile and safely teetering, and sandboxes. An adjoining room holds solace for a rainy day: games, clay, paints, and someone to distribute them and admire the handiworks that emerge. Best of all, the room contains a chest of old costumes for strutting and pirouetting and feeling much better than a wet little girl might.

Bigger children—no adults, no infants permitted—have for themselves one of the city's "adventure playgrounds." Much of the work is often done by the children themselves; in their forest sanctuary at Battersea it may mean that they had made the platforms in the trees, hung the swings from high limbs, and built a footbridge over a gully. Safe behind their fence, using their own devices, subject to none but their peers, they run and leap and roar like the kings of the jungle they have become.

If your children are, like most of the breed, dog lovers, take them to the **Sheepdog Trials in Hyde Park,** usually held on two days in late May. The demonstration of training and canine intelligence, of speed and precision of movement, black and white dogs lying in wait for, and harrying, bewildered sheep may have limited interest, but not for the London audience, which comes early and stays late. You, too, should go early unless you can keep your young perched on your shoulders for an indefinite time.

**Royal Tournament, Earl's Court** (two weeks, matinees and evenings, early summer).

It has been going on since 1880, and as long as there is a big arena, an English army, and idolatrous little boys, it should go on forever. Not as quiet as it might be—parents who want to share the joys of their youth with their children sometimes start the frightened or bored (or alternately both) at too young and weepy an age—still, the best time to go is the matinee, which starts at two thirty, but get there early to watch the busy parents and teachers corralling their hordes, the independent gentlemen of fourteen buying, with a breezy, offhand gesture, their ten-packs of cigarettes, and the little girls frantically pushing at the counters for sweets as if the whole city weren't a choc- olate-into-caries mountain.

The show proper starts at two thirty, when the competitions for jumping begin. Each rider appears from a crenellated painted castle portal surmounted by cannon mouths, sitting against a landscape that gathers beach, waters, mountains, and trees. High on a balcony of the castle sits a band that plays soft, undisturbing music through the jump- ing. The jumpers are followed by a competition of speed in erecting poles, swinging across an imaginary chasm, transporting and mounting cannons, as it was done in the Boer War, the excitements of speed and precision heightened by the shrieking boys. Then the hall dims and becomes an underwater scene consisting of an uncertain sea horse, a jellyfish, a starfish, and an octopus and a frogman who fights the oc- topus and, after finding an immense pearl, turns to his essential busi- ness of examining a sunken section of aircraft, to be investigated by a mine crew. The compere, a cheery uncle-ish voice that keeps spurring on and pointing up the drama, says, "Let's all be very quiet now. One move, and the mine may go off."

The charge sent down, the fuse lit, and, to the bangs and bellows of as much noise as the band can make, the explosion goes off. The undersea's fauna is drawn up to the ceiling to make room for the beautiful royal drive, cannons drawn at a gallop by three pairs of horses, one rider to each pair, pulling the clumsy wagons through formations of diagonals and circles, rushing past each other to the thud of hooves, the clatter of wheels, and the jingle of ornaments on the jaunty hussarlike uniforms.

Police dogs perform by walking on tight ropes, jumping, running through tunnels, tracking and catching felons and to wild applause old Judie, one of the retired Alsatians, is driven around and around for viewing in an open car like a triumphant bullfighter-film star. What seems like 100 Scotch pipers and drummers now take the stage, their loud wailing deafening and funereal, as beautiful as they are mournful in their white gaiters and jaunty caps, the glitter of buckles, buttons, and the metal struts of the drums, and most beautiful when they swing around to show the back lengths of their romantic cloaks and tasseled scarves. To music from *Fiddler on the Roof* Army recruits and physical training instructors perform an extraordinarily swift and graceful ballet of leaping over and under and by each other off a complex of platforms. The parachutist-skiers show what they can do in a competition that involves scaling walls, climbing ropes, dismounting and mounting big guns out of a jeep. The show finishes with a confusing display of modern war action, frightening to the adults and very stimulating to the boys, who shout and cheer and make their way out reluctantly, consoled by the welcoming presence of the sweets and ice-cream stands and the promise to be taken again next year.

## With or Without Children

June 10 is the official birthday of Queen Elizabeth II. On that day honors are announced; distinguished actresses and dancers become Dame, and their male peers are elevated to Sir, and their sometimes unprepared wives to Lady. Leisured lists with pictures are printed in the newspapers, feeding the still avid public who votes Labour and yet needs the shepherd-into-prince fairy tale. That is the day of the Trooping the Color, visible on the telly but necessary to go to as an act of homage and something for the children to remember and absorb as their Englishness, along with the hot porridge for breakfast, school scarves around their necks and blue knees. It is a superb show, meticulously choreographed, scored, practiced, and performed in the vast outdoor theater of the Horse Guards Parade off Whitehall, behind the gateway and niches built by William Kent where the magnificent guards in their shining casques and deep falls of tassel usually sit on their sleek, disciplined horses. Some minutes before 11 A.M. the Queen Mother, in the flower-petaled hat that is seemingly required uniform, is driven in an open carriage with younger members of the royal family and, to the accompaniment of the royal salute and "God Save the Queen," enters the building from whose draped window she will watch the proceedings, nodding and smiling from time to time. The formations of splendid guards begin to gather for the major acts of their ballet. The band plays, the lines shape, and reshape with oiled-track precision, and an extra bit of national sentiment is touched on when a shaggy and very old horse, said to be making its last appearance, walks forth with a soupçon of the old élan, bearing two heavy kettledrums. The clock strikes eleven, and the crowd begins to cheer the Queen who rides in sidesaddle (the traditional posture for the birthday parade and one she must practice, it is said, for a time beforehand) dressed as a commander of the Grenadier Guards, wearing her Garter sash and a row of royal medals. The Duke of Edinburgh in the uniform of a Welsh regiment, a high busby held by a metal strap under his lip, not quite at her side, always a pace or two back. Looking handsome in her plumed cap and serious, the Queen salutes her mother and salutes the men again through the playing of "God Save the Queen." The tune changes to "Summer Is Icumen In" as the Queen is led through an inspection, followed closely by the Duke of Edinburgh, the Duke of Kent, and other royal functionaries, moving slowly around the long, perfect double lines. Having saluted still another standard, she retires to a corner of the immense formations to watch a square of massed bandsmen marching slowly to a waltz that turns into *"Ein Festes Burg"* and back to waltz, one slow, sliding step to each one-two-three. In front of the sea of bandsmen five gloriously clad men flourish their long batons in baroque choreography. One lone drummer, vulnerable as he separates himself from the protective mass, moves out and away to introduce the next important scene. The band marches back, leaving space for the advent of a double line of guards, a few of whom act as escort to one guard, who approaches the honored flag (as old as 1680 and used in Tangier and later at Sevastopol to signal battling soldiers back to their companies) with drawn sword and then hands it to a young ensign.

The massed troops start their elaborate maneuvers of wheeling in small space, spreading into lines, single and double, turning and reforming, separating, grouping, wheeling again. The steps change from glide to short stamp, and then to a long, graceful balletic lift and pause, as the music and the space to cover dictate. When the music stops, one hears the bawling of orders (wondering how they can come clear from the small amount of face between busby and the strap) and the neigh of horses. Constantly, the Queen is saluted and returns the salutes. The banner of honor, embellished by a crown and tassels and strips naming its battles, is dipped before the Queen and brought to the front of the field. Each regiment, playing its own particular march, passes before the Queen, while single men, alone as *banderilleros*, draw fine lines among the squares and rectangles and turning wedges of men.

The last scene is introduced by the Household Cavalry in magnificent costumes, led by the kettledrums, great panniers hanging over the sides of the shaggy old horses, accompanied by long, shining trumpets. The trumpeters are on gray horses, while the rest of the cavalry are on black horses complementing the red coats, the glittering breastplates, and deep metal helmets. One trumpeter with a banner is answered by a showy response from the kettledrums, and the whole group trots in an intricate design, the helmet fringe waving to the jingling sound of bits of metal decoration tinkling on the breastplates. Through elaborate, precise arrangements, the companies begin to mass for marching off, down the Mall to Buckingham Palace, one guardsman riding out to the Queen to ask for permission to do so. She consents with a salute and rides off with the Duke of Edinburgh, saluting, to thunderous applause.

## Without Children

**Raymond's Revuebar,** Walter's Court, Brewer Street.

One of the paradoxes of London is the passion for semi and full nudity in so chilling a climate. On the other hand, it may be no paradox at all; the sight of so many women so constantly dressed as woolly bears must produce an extraordinary drive to shout, "Take it off," which is not done in London. (Any untoward noise is blamed on toughs from the Midlands, Americans, Germans, Frenchmen, Swedes, everyone but Londoners.)

Legally a club—membership is not too difficult to achieve—Mr. and Mrs. Raymond's Revuebar is actually a fair of strip, on several layers, in variously decorated rooms. At seven a member can drink and have a snack in the Golden City Room, whose walls are imbedded with bronze nuggets, and talk and dance with girls in bunny-style costumes. He may then go to the Theater Room for the performance at eight twenty or, deciding to take in the later show, up to the Birdcage, where there are more bunny girls hopping around and a singer. Some food, chaffing with the girls and a few drinks later, at about ten forty-five, the loudspeaker system invites ticket holders (about two pounds) to come to the theater. It is a largish one, conveniently sloped and tables interspersed among the seats to hold the drinks. The opening number involves a draped and plumed chorus parading, pirouetting, prancing, revealing, and concealing two girls who slip in and out of the fernery apparently looking for their bras. The chorus off, on come the strippers, one after the other in a pageant of techniques and implications, a few slowly teasing, one stripping as if she had been caught in a storm and eager to take off her wet clothing. Others start off almost nude with nothing much to do but throw away a handful of cloth. There is a haughty girl in the basic black velvet and long gloves who moves coolly, expressionlessly while she absentmindedly slides it all off. Another girl strokes a man's shirt while a record hoarsely gasps, *"Un homme! Un homme!"* and to the hot, thudding music she rolls, coils, lifts, drops, and agonizes in a display of frenzied athleticism that might make a frightening confrontation in real life. There is the caged captive in the scantiest of leopard skins who bites and bites at the cords that hold her, then licks the scars when she is free. One girl lashes herself—a few strokes—with a chain, and one girl rides a docile nag that knows how to take the girl's skirt off and lets its tail be used as a whisk for the girl's face. This number of the girl and her best friend is accompanied by music, the words mouthed by the stripper, "That's nice. That's ve-e-e-ry nice."

The big stars are a confident, sturdy girl, whose great appeal seems to be that she likes her work and doesn't cloud it with subtlety, and an "International French favorite," salacious, funny, and a careful practitioner of striptease in the leisured Paris manner. She appears fully dressed, as if for the opera, though her stage is a foreshortened bed with a headboard of shivering plumes. She begins by turning her back and shrugging her shoulders, and that reveals a jeweled G-string belt that rises out of the low cut of her high-class gown. Then one impeccably white glove flows off and becomes an amorous hand, searching and nibbling here and there. Something comes off, a long pause and clever play, and then something else smoothly disappears. It is a longish act, for a strip, given full, stately rhythm, always with downcast, sly eye and the rounded mouth sucking air to cool its mounting heat.

Behind the scenes the chorus has been changing into classic veils that suggest—remotely—statuary in neo-Palladian parks. They trail mournfully about a central Niobe, meet in graceful pairings as on Lesbos, and dissolve to appear some strips later as cancan girls. They spare neither themselves nor the flooring on the stage, and the lusty all-out effort, the derring-do of running into splits, and not having to worry about the effects of a stripper rouse a storm of applause from the assembled gentlemen and the few ladies (one of them a stout Indian matron in a sari and jeweled nose).

The entertainment is advertised as nonstop, and that is true. In the Golden City Room a girl swims and floats and strips in a glass tank. Another strips in the normal smoke-filled air, and so it goes, until 3:30 A.M., a full evening and half the night; hearty, efficient, dedicated entertainment and infinitely cheaper than gambling.

**Edmundo Ros,** 177 Regent Street. 734-7675.

The featured act might be a magician or a lady who invents and sings topical songs or a heel-tapping, skirt-whirling Spanish troupe, but three factors are constant: the only Latin-American dance music always on tap in London (interspersed with simpler rhythms for the one-steppers), good vocalists, and remarkably good food, handpicked by the affable, suitably shaped Mr. Ros.

**City Arms,** West Ferry Road, West India Docks.

It was a pub, and at times, in ways, it still is; but on weekend nights (and others, though there are blank nights) it is the entertainment that matters. Since you cannot reach the bar, the entertainment is free from the side door when it is open, on a hospitable summer evening. Female impersonators are the *pièces,* one of them a good-looking, tall brunette, often dressed in a sleek, shimmering cocktail dress, pasted onto theoretical bulges. They sing songs your mother never taught you (or if she did, they come out different here) and play word games with the local boys, neatly dressed in their sober weekend best, who try to heckle. The entertainers always win because the free imaginative quality of the obscenities they launch is beyond matching by the boys, not, normally, slouches at the obscenity game. These shafts of dirty talk are not impromptu; repeat visits prove that. However, you may find it useful to memorize a few of the quips about loos and genitalia and inversion to use at the next dull cocktail party given by your neighbors.

**Antonio,** 3 Long Acre. TEM 7911.

A Spanish restaurant where you can find an authentic version of gaspacho to be followed by a good model of the overrated paella.

Very near Covent Garden, Antonio stays open late not only to feed ballet customers but to show them, as well, how much more meaningful is the cante hondo with its Arabic keening and the furies and agonies of Spanish dancing, than the pastel ballets of silly swan girls and idiot princes, next door.

# Gambling

You must be a member of a club, but as mentioned elsewhere, membership can be arranged. Some clubs offer "temporary" memberships, others work with hotels, and still others form a group which advertises in American periodicals, suggesting a blanket membership fee, good for many clubs. There are dozens of gambling clubs, from market bingo and fruit-machine parlors to citadels mentioned in nineteenth-century novels of high life. One Soho specimen is mentioned elsewhere (p. 257). Below, two in more exalted categories.

**The Victoria Club,** 150 Edgware Road.

Enormous and enormously middle class. The restaurant is large and serves late and cheaply to the music of a good, small band; well-padded customers chomp on sandwiches and cakes between bouts of twenty-one and roulette. Upstairs a sea of card tables, and at the door, a ticket for possibly winning a jackpot, the number drawn hourly and accumulating if a potential winner has had enough gambling and gone home; between the levels and on the way to the toilets, cheaper gaming machines as brightly lit and nervous as jukeboxes.

**The Pair of Shoes,** 21 Hertford Street.

Smooth and quiet, with polished carved woods, obviously once a fine Mayfair house. A gently lit restaurant serves exceedingly good dishes, the bar is attractive, polite, and generous (and hung with keys and keys and keys), and the gaming room whispers and clicks, delicately supervised by the swift eyes of a suave, spare man in a silk suit who glides in and out of the rooms, a nod here, a murmured word there. Until a squat young man in a linen suit, surrounded by a tall entourage of men and one woman with kohl-ringed eyes and a heap of rubies at her ears, bellows and charges around the tables, gesticulating and yowling in his five words of English, all four-lettered, incessantly reiterated. It appears that he threw a check for five hundred pounds on a table in exchange for chips. The croupier suggested that he present the check and some identification at the cashier's desk. The client, a princeling of a Near Eastern oil kingdom, has never, never thus been treated and lets it be known in his precise, unadorned vocabulary. The suave, silken, gliding man murmurs at him through the roaring, repeating that it is a simple matter of a passport or a letter of credit. Still roaring, the prince, the lady with the rubies, the fence of big men leave, and the quiet sinks back to the tables, disturbed only by the fall of a chip, a tap of a finger, the whisper of shuffled cards.

## Discothèques

A discothèque is what everyone wants to open. The requirements are simple. Gather enough people to form a "club," and work out some fiddle-faddle about liquor in off hours. Get a cellar; paint it Pompeian or with big, comic-strip Pop heads; bring your phonograph from home, and hire a girl to keep nervous snatches of record going without pause. (One silent moment, and her head comes off.) It seems so simple many try it and many fail; therefore, the suggestions below are ephemeral and vague and meant to be because no assurance can be given that any particular one has staying power.

**Annabel's Club,** at 44 Berkeley Square, is of startling longevity and still a crowded place which shows its class by being more crowded during week-nights than on the weekend. One starts off by having a friend in high places; membership is fairly pricey and, according to one rumor, selective. You must take your earphone and throat lozenges to beat the incessant and loud music which will not let you converse. Then, like the paunchy gentlemen plastered with paper-thin, iron-willed dollies, the superbly dressed Italians out of Renaissance *palazzi,* the pale, attenuated *raffinés* of Belgravia, you dance incessantly, like a wound-up dervish.

The currently approved style of dancing is old Rue Mouffetard *bal musette:* The lady winds her arms around the gentleman's neck and the gentleman spreads both his hands on her buttocks. There are variations of the posture, depending on drink and the depths of inhibition, or loathing that drink cannot touch. One pair of masculine hands will enjoy ferreting under a blouse for a while and back to home base and two handfuls of buttock; one man with face frozen in agonized embarrassment is the stiff pole for an energetic woman to climb and gyrate on. She keeps placing his hands where she thinks they belong; he moves them up and supports her enthusiasms by holding her waist with his forearms and spreading his aghast hands in the air behind her. One glossy couple will confuse dance floor with bed until they are awakened by a bump from a pair who need the space for improvisations.

From a ringside seat, it is a stimulating, amusing spectacle, joined with the pleasure of the "in-ness" of it, the sense of being rich and chosen. But where has one seen this before? In old French movies, yes, but where else? Not the orgies of De Mille or Fellini movies; this is too pallid.

It comes—the pre-Duvalier nightclubs of Haiti where the merengue was danced by magnolia women and their beautiful men, in steps and postures derived from the swaying hips and irregular, mincing steps of the market women who walked down the steep hills to the town balancing enormous loads on their heads. Here, too, a borrowing from working-class style (or what is romantically thought to be) as if the vulgar, earthy gesture—relaxed, open, easy—will, by the magic of one evening, create the lusty, joyous human being they think abounds among the lowly.

There are others of the same order—**Sibylla's,** on Swallow Street, for one, and many less expensive, ranging from large dance halls to white-washed cellars. Consult recently returned friends, or try your luck with the listings in the entertainment information periodicals (p. 22).

## Exhibitions

Other than those at the great museums and in art galleries:

**The Design Centre,** 28 Haymarket, displays attractively what is new in English design from rugs to glassware, textiles to wall coverings, telephones to sink spigots, and tells you where items can be obtained. Sometimes guest appearances of foreign crafts.

Should there be, as there frequently is, a show of jewelry at the **Goldsmiths' Hall,** on Foster Lane, try to get there, not only for a chance to see the hall in ducal style, as befits a rich guild founded in the thirteenth century on the same site, with the power to establish the weight of coinage and to determine standards of excellence for hallmarking, but also to see the work of students and apprentices, who like the *Meistersinger* contestants, show their masterworks in their ripe time, some of the jewels worth space in the front window of any famous jewelry shop one might name.

## Music

Concerts are in abundant, ubiquitous supply, which makes London a music lover's paradise, plus the fact that, by American standards, tickets are cheap and can be reserved on the phone to be picked up a half hour before the performance. For the flat-pocketed music lover, there are extremely inexpensive, or completely free, lunchtime concerts that usually start at about one o'clock: **St. Martin-in-the-Fields** on Tuesdays; **Bishopsgate Institute** almost every day except in the summertime; organ recitals in City churches and on Wednesday afternoons in **Westminster Abbey**. The **Royal College of Music** and the **Guildhall School of Music,** school auditoriums and cinemas, the town halls of various boroughs, the salons of great houses, and even the **Law Society Hall** on Chancery Lane pour music. **Royal Opera House** tickets for stellar performances of both opera and ballet are as difficult to get as at the Metropolitan in New York, even though prices rise sharply when a celebrated diva joins a cast. **Sadler's Wells** is more courageous and experimental, insists on opera in English at bargain rates, and offers good salads before the performance. But it is not endowed with a riches of good voices (a few are superb and used with fine musicianship), although that does not much matter when the performance is an amusing, cleverly acted romp through Offenbach.

Everyone plays, as you know, at the **Royal Festival Hall** or in chamber-size recitals at the **Queen Elizabeth Hall.** Poetry readings, soloists, folks and blues, use the smallest of the south bank halls named for Henry Purcell.

You may want to see wrestlers, the showmanship of "the greatest flamenco guitarist in the world," importantly aided by his electrified guitar and a loudspeaker system, and the mass charm of Central European folk dancers. All that takes place in the **Royal Albert Hall,** as well as straight music, which fills the long stretch of summer prom concerts, when five-shilling standees crowd the center of Queen Victoria's vast arena. You should go, if only to see the boys throw flowers to a favorite mezzo and one or two wafted toward a pretty second violinist in a Dutch orchestra. Whether you will hear is quite another matter. There are dull spots and dead spots, so many that the *cog-*

*noscenti* instruct you to sit in only ten or twelve of thousands of seats, and while you strain, fearing sudden deafness, from a seat in the musical desert, you look down at all the empty seats, surely better than yours. No matter how popular the concert, how long the lines at the box office, how many people turned away, these seats remain empty. They belong to families whose ancestors subscribed to the building of the hall a century ago, paying a hundred pounds per seat for perpetual ownership. By this time ownership is a valued antique and, even though the offers are quite high, not readily relinquished.

# Theater

The theater, the famous London theater, is at this writing held together by Shakespeare, Restoration dramatists, Chekhov, kindly critics, imaginative directors, and, above all, acting of genius. True, many theaters are functioning, but this is in many cases due to the skill of the cast, the reasonable cost of tickets, and the enterprise of agents who arrange theater parties that fill large buses with suburbanites. (A revival of *Desert Song,* whose theater now resembles a bus stop, is—was— doing very well.) You have a choice of mysteries; farces that hang on one comic who tells incomprehensible jokes and farces that are exquisitely timed and genuinely funny; pale, milky, little plays about "civilized" marriages and that universal, repetitious favorite the black comedy.

The **Aldwych,** the house of the Royal Shakespeare Company, is given to a stimulating repertoire of some Shakespeare, modern plays from the States or Poland or Cuba and England, and the classic theaters of various countries—*No* from Japan, the Habima players of Israel, a German company, and a Greek company which presents strange modernizations of Greek classics. The **Old Vic,** of the exalted and reliable standards, does not too often have available seats at short notice; have this arranged for you, if possible, beforehand.

**Miscellaneous**

When the National Gallery closes and the Spanish dancers are not yet performing in the pub on King William IV Street, the streets too wet to walk, and you have an hour to kill before a seven thirty curtain, try the cinema presented by London Transport in Charing Cross Station. No Swedish sex or trick death-ray cars, but well made and informative, as always, and free.

## Spiritualism

The better, unseen world hiding behind today's cloud must be a universal preoccupation. Breaking through the cloud, a serious London endeavor, is acted out as gambling, first, and hedged with astrology, numerology, health foods, Souboude, a wide, bizarre range of the occult and the spiritualism that achieves the final triumph—there is no death. ("Why," argues the practitioner, "can we believe in the grave and cremation and deny messages, through our brains and bodies, from the spirit world?")

The stronghold of the **Spiritualist Association of Great Britain** is a large house at 33 Belgrave Square, whose busy counter, where appointments are made, fees paid, and pamphlets bought, resembles the desk of a good, small hotel with a clientele of middle-aged ladies. It is possible to attend individual sessions, sittings for private groups, and, for a nominal sum, public meetings, some of them double-headers—two spiritualists for the price of one. (These are usually scheduled for one evening during each week; phone BEL 3351.)

How effective any one spiritualist appears to be depends, as it does in any religion, on one's willingness to be convinced. A random shot may strike a vulnerable spot, and the eager responses will give an astute professional much to work with. For one observer, ready to fall into devotion, it will be an uncanny, shaking experience; for another, a demonstration of clever observation. All the practitioners shed an atmosphere of optimism, leaving the whole group, particularly those selected for a "message," with the promise of better things to come. One practitioner does it with her attractive, mobile face, deep-set, glowing eyes, and large, restless movements, exuding a sense of energetic well-being that is of itself an advertisement for the health-giving properties of spiritualism. Another, a large, confident lady stands as Pallas Athena: stolid wisdom and massive power. All of them, no matter what their strengths, add to that the strength of prayer and assurance, constantly reiterated, that loved ones "who have gone beyond" ("death" is a word that is never used) are standing by and always will be, with support and love. And always repeated, the music and balm of "Bless you, bless you, bless you." On some faces, as they leave, there is the look of the anointed.

**Joseph Benjamin,** a clairvoyant, clairaudient healer, works alone, with a platform of adherents for minor assistance, for recording and encouraging and to provide preliminary information and entertainment.

He works to a large audience in two halls (details below) the majority working-class, thin, thin men and bread-filled or absolutely flat women, with a sprinkling of people from other economic and intellectual strata and, surprisingly—for people who have their own busy practitioners in Shepherd's Bush and Brixton—a number of Negroes.

After a few preliminaries of announcements, hymn singing, and entertainments, Joe Benjamin takes the stage. He is a prodigious man, whether you see him as showman, clairvoyant, healer, or all three. The neat, small head, the low-slung, wide paunch and fine hands, the Whitechapel (Yiddish) Cockney as broad as the avenue on which it was born, evoke a direct response. He has warmth, humor, intelligence, independence, and a confidence that is lightly cocky at times and dropped entirely for concerned sensibility at others.

His hands clasped to his temples, he calls, "I've got a message. It's about someone who is very sick in hospital, and there is a letter, I see a letter, about it. You, lady, I think it's you. No, the lady sitting near the wall in the brown hat." She acknowledges that she has such a letter, and it deals with illness. "Don't tell me anymore." He clasps his abdomen. "It's in the intestines, around here, I can feel it. It's very painful." She acknowledges that fact. "Bless you, dear, bless you. Your spirits are near to support you in this difficult time. I have information for you. It's not good. Do you want it? Are you sure?" After a nod from her: "She will feel better for a while, but she will go, of cancer. Bless you. The spirits will give you strength." Turning away, after a pause; "I see Brighton, the vicinity of Brighton—Hove, maybe, or Bognor. Anyone here planning to or strongly hoping to live there?" Two hands rise—a middle-aged couple, the man with a misshapen nose. "You'll get that house, not right away, but you'll get it. And that disappointment, it'll turn out fine; it had to happen that way to be as good as it will be. Somebody is in trouble—I see lawyers, courts, police." The man acknowledges a brother in trouble. "Who drives a taxi? Not you. Someone in your family." The woman says her nephew is a taxi driver. With full urgency Joe (the intimacy he creates and the persuasive control makes it difficult to think of him as Mr. Benjamin) stresses, "He's going to have an accident, a bad accident, if he isn't very careful. Warn him, will you? Please warn him. And"—turning to the man—"you've had three operations on your nose. Stop it. If you come to me, I'll fix it. Keep away from the hospitals, you've had enough."

Another pause, very short. "Somebody in this hall has a letter in her purse about a will and money. Who is it?" A hand goes up. "It's got to do with a male relative, an Italian." "Well, Corsican," the woman answers. "Corsican, Italian, same thing. Let me tell you, dear, drop it. It's not as much money as you think; it will be spent on solicitors, and it isn't worth your trouble, forget it. If you want the satisfaction of trying, waste five or six guineas on a solicitor and have him answer the letter. But I say, forget it, put it out of your mind. Or do you need the money? Are you doing all right? Eating regular? Paying your rent?" She laughs. "Oh, sure." "Okay, leave it alone, it's a nothing."

After a dramatic, deeply sympathetic moment or two, with a woman to whom he brings a message from a recently "passed" husband, whom he describes accurately enough to make her weep, and soothing, consoling words, he puts his hands to his forehead. "I see a nurse, good-looking, in a cloak and one of those bands that holds it together. Nice girl, she appeals to me; if she asked me, I'd be glad to go to the Corner House with her. She is from St. Thomas's Hospital. Anyone here got someone in St. Thomas's? The lady in the blue coat? Madam, she came to tell us that tonight is the crisis, and your patient will be better tomorrow and will continue being better. She's very real to me, that nurse—she just told me *I'm* not real—and her name is Mary Reid—spelled *R, E, I, D*—and she died young, of cancer. You might check that in the hospital register. You'll find the name; it was sometime ago."

In a session—performance?—that lasts something over an hour, he touches on twenty people among the several hundred, mentioning full, specific names, describing a life with skillfully selected, vivid detail, offering flat, sure advice—"Shut the door, get out—you'll find the strength—but make sure you get half of the house. You understand me. Out. Now. Finished. Final. And take what's yours,"—with humor, sympathy, and the direct, full impact of a superb performer. It may be extraordinary powers or the careful organization of planting and rehearsing twenty people who must also be greatly talented actors to express the astonishment and awe and weep the tears directed by the superhuman memory and histrionics of Joe Benjamin. If it is all a con game, it is the most brilliant in London and eminently worth the two hours, two shillings (and a small contribution) you will spend.

Sundays at about six thirty at Alliance Hall, Palmer Street, Westminster, S.W. 1 (St. James's Park Station). Tuesdays at seven fifteen at Foresters Hall, 5 Highgate Road, Kentish Town, N.W.5 (Kentish Town Tube Station). Go fairly early to get a seat, and for private meetings phone SPE 5737.

## Summer Evening

To the lifesaving illusions that spur the rest of humanity to rise in the morning—love will not wither, nor life ever stop—the Londoner adds the persistent dream of long, pastel summer evenings when redbrick houses and chimneys and blue sky fade in a melting of golden sun. Never any rain or colder than can be answered by a light cardigan.

Year after year the local councils and the Greater London Council and optimistic others arrange series and festivals of plays, dance recitals, and concerts as if London were a tropical city which has its predictable summer showers at three to four in the afternoon. Or it might be the gambling instinct and certainly a goodly portion of stiff upper lip that keeps the planners planning and the audiences going (chanting inwardly the lament of the Anglo-Saxon Deor, "that which they have endured, I too can endure"). The results are stimulating and a stern lesson to flabby spirits from overseas, who might avoid slogging through the dripping funerary greens of Holland Park to show their protesting wet children the Spanish dancers, who have, like sensible Latins, decided not to perform in the water-logged outdoor theater. The soaked shoes and weeping hair trek back to the bus stop and home, to try again the next night.

The garden at **Fenton House** is set up for a concert, accompanied by dancing, of Baroque music. Seats have been set out, and because the day had gone through some mercurial changes, a canopy was placed over the musicians' stand. About a half hour before performance time, the August temperature drops to November levels, but still they come, dressed in sweaters and mackintoshes, carrying umbrellas and blankets, and sit down in happy anticipation on the narrow metal chairs. The conductor emerges in his starched shirt and tailcoat, is vigorously applauded for his valor, and begins to conduct from the grass, unprotected by the canopy. The cold rains slant down; the macs are pulled tighter, the blankets draped around shoulders and across legs; the umbrellas go up; a few brandy flasks glint in the paling light. The rain flattens the conductor's hair and runs into his collar and blots the high polish on his shoes. The rain provides additional tympanic effects as it beats on the canopy. And still they play, and well, the spirited, symmetrical tinkles, and the audience sits under its clashing umbrellas and applauds as vigorously as gloved hands can. No one gives up in this endurance contest until the rain begins to search under the canopy and attacks the frail woods and strings of the violins. The conductor, now shedding water like a duck, apologizes, is again warmly applauded, and the blanketed, umbrellaed crowd moves out, if not altogether satisfied with the aborted concert and disappointed because the dancers didn't try at all (an unreliable, pampered lot), certainly satisfied with themselves and their heroic peers who lasted it out with them.

But let us assume that the not impossible dry evening shows as reality; it happens sometimes. You have seen the play at Regent's Park and gone to the concert in Holland Park and the jazz in Battersea Park. The dockside pubs your London friends take you to have turned out to be always the same two or three.

The maps that you carry along with your express checks and passport, and as indispensable, will guide you to **Hammersmith Bridge.** The bridge has a certain elephantine coyness, close to, now that it is freshly painted and its ornaments brightened up to resemble the bosses of a restored church ceiling. Immediately west of the bridge, looking down on the sleek little pleasure craft lolling at the side of the river, a block of flats puffed and blistered with *fin de siècle* excrescences, a big screen of New Orleans-Regency ironwork flattened against its proud bosom. The pride is more muted in the smaller, very well-kept neighboring houses, balconied, too, and to keep the "little," "charming" mood, a minute bank, vaguely classic in design, rather like the temples eighteenth-century gentlemen liked to place as white surprises in dark-green dells. The houses soon turn ordinary and even dour, except for the decorations of the summer night, leaning against the river wall, sitting at tables, standing, strolling, perched on the wall outside the pubs of the Lower Mall.

The guitars are out, two working on a complex duet of blues chords; the girls are out in their jeans, the boys in *sportif* Aran sweaters or in open shirts and a twist and fall of brilliant scarf. One languid magnificent pair, reminiscent of the Elizabethan gentleman painted by Hilliard, wear white linen suits of narrow trousers and long Nehru coats with high Regency collars and, under the coats, beautiful lawn shirts of bright, flowered patterns. A few middle-aged members of the community cluster together, as if in mutual protection against the fauve young, except for one couple who appear to be quite "in," a middle-aged woman in trousers and man's shirt, close-cropped hair, and a pencil behind her ear, her back the bent back of an old tailor. The companion for whom she brings drinks with great courtliness is a romantically swathed lady in gray veil, of porcelain makeup and baby voice and mincing steps, a gallant refusal to watch the years tear by like ravaging storms; she is still the lovely, fragile fawn girl they both need.

The darkened houses beyond give way to a jog in from the river, and down a few steps into a narrow alley that takes you to the very old Doves Inn, a number of tiny, low-ceilinged rooms that lead to a grape-arbored platform facing the river. The locals in this Upper Mall pub are, with not unusual variations, rather like those eastward, frighteningly young as a group, but not quite so showy. Yet like them, quiet, peaceable, given to music but not to talking or singing, inclined to bright clothes but no gaudy action; in amorous combinations and yet not sexy. (Maybe all London youth are becoming "flower people," as pretty, as passive, as indiscriminate, as silent.)

P.S. If you have the time and a car, stop in at one or two of the big pubs on Hammersmith Bridge Road and Fulham Palace Road and on both ends of the Putney Bridge (one pub, at the south end of the Putney Bridge, in addition to its large English self, provides a Bierkeller complete with carved wood *Gemütlichkeit,* sad songs and robust, with accordion accompaniment). They are homely spreads of wood and glass that will remind you of your grandmother's big china closet.

The sound is, at times, distorted by breezes playing with the loud-speaker system, and the airplanes are low and frequent; but where else can you sit on a green slope in a lyrical clearing as you can in **Regent's Park,** for a performance of *A Midsummer Night's Dream* or *Cyrano de Bergerac*? The stage is ingeniously arranged around rocky ledges cut as platforms and clumps of bushes for exits and entrances. The costumes—as always with London period pieces—are resplendent, the acting less so; but the actors are valiant people and not inclined to run for shelter as quickly as you do, when the rains come. A valiant crew, a bosky dell, dramatic verse, excitements of weather and as night falls, doves crooning in the trees, and all for less than the price of a movie at home, seven shillings and sixpence to fifteen shillings.

**Son et Lumière** (pronounced by the master of ceremonies as Sonnet Lumiere).

The launches leave Charing Cross Pier somewhere between nine and nine thirty in the evening (not Sundays, or after September 30), the price one guinea (twenty-one shillings) for adults; children at half price. Go fairly early, and take sweaters and gloves and a nip at the bar, which is open before and after the show. In spite of excursions and alarums and the booming of cannon and martial music and the rich voices of fine actors—sometimes heard twice, doubled by the vagaries of loudspeakers, walls and echoes; sometimes silenced by winds or the obstinacy of machinery—it is not quite convincing. The vivid pageant of history so skillfully recited remains remote behind the Tower walls that face the river; the wall, now dimmed, now lit, insists on concealing, rather than revealing. However, you will get a swift flight through salient points of history, and besides, the *lumière* on the buildings along the river makes gold-ivory *objets* of not always attractive buildings, and there are the lights of buses winging across the bridges, London's fireflies.

## Sunday in the Park— July 17, 2 to 5 p.m.

On the endless lawn back of the Speakers' Corner, the "flower people" were gathered, not for a rally—too belligerent a word—but rather a *fête champêtre* of apples and peanuts, to state their massed conviction that pot should be legalized. "Gathering" is not the precise word either; it was more a molecular flow, the floating of petals on a soft breeze. Lazy, acquiescent, they permitted themselves to be photographed by tourists, newspaper photographers, and TV cameras, British and American, and photogenic they were, gathered around their signs of FLOWER POWER and TV IS A WORSE DRUG THAN POT. The police ordered the signs down, and the amplifiers that were to spread the word of visiting poets were silenced. Except for some light booing and the chanting of "The fuzz loves the *News of the World*" (referring to the fact that the popular Sunday sheet had tipped the police off to drugs in the possession of a member of a well-known singing group), the flowers appeared as unperturbed as flowers in a watercolor—neither frowning nor smiling, encased in the invisible frame of the self-portrait each had devised.

There were the girls who did it literally, in cotton shifts painted with simple flower patterns which spilled over on legs and arms and, to suggest the fresh innocence of grass, large fields of green around the eyes, under the black strokes of lashes. There was a Mimi in a bonnet and a green velvet capelet, a Carmen in lashings of Spanish-shawl fringe; flowing skirts, flowing hair, and wreaths of flowers; a Victorian child's dress, all tucks and lace, and a great straw hat studded with fresh flowers; a girl in a sari; a girl in a newspaper blowup paper dress featuring Bob Dylan. The feet were sandaled or booted or bare, sprinkled with sequins, banded with Indian bell anklets and ribbons; the hair intertwined with flowers, flowers in the hand, flowers in hats and headbands.

As almost always, and following the arrangements of biology, the English male was gaudier and more expensively dressed than the peahen. (From Thomas Coryat's *Crudities,* published in 1608, describing the dress of Italian gentlemen: "without those new-fangled curiosities and ridiculous of panes, plaits and other light toys used with us English men. . . . For whereas they have but one colour, we use many more than are in the rain bow, all the most light, garish, and unseemly colours that are in the world. . . . For we wear more phantastical fashions than any nation under the sun, the French only excepted.") A brilliant, well-cut suit of red, white, and mauve stripes over a purple shirt; an orange jacket of cut velvet over a magenta silk shirt; a meticulously cut pair of pink trousers and a bespoke fine pink lawn shirt; a sculptured coif on a Malaysian boy in tight, wine-red velvet trousers and a transparent pale-blue shirt; sheepskin jackets and vests (the heat was intense); coats of Indian cotton and Mexican hand-loomed cloth, of Greek homespuns and Bulgarian embroideries. Anything, everything, and they may yet create a revolution, at least in dress, setting principles of no principles but fancy, impulse, the appropriate expression of a passing mood, and freedom from the chains of fashion.

The little bells and the big bells, the ropes of bells, the drooping flowers, the fading flowers, the wilting flowers, the nodding flowers, the indomitable paper flowers, and a talented tree of silver foil and crayoned fruits mill slowly and stand. A few gather around an impromptu platform from which an Irish poet recites, introducing himself as a man with no problems. From the crowd comes a voice, "You're dead!" quickly sh-sh-sh'd. (The quick riposte has no place in peaceful innocence.) The crowd is urged to sit—most do—in a vast field of color that spreads southward into the park, to await the appearance of Allen Ginsberg. One of the sitters appeals to a blocking stander, "Won't you beautiful people please sit down?" in dulcet, nursery-school tones. It does no good. A nonbeautiful exchange of "For chrissake, sit down!" and "Shut up!" is more effective. The peanuts and sticks of punk are passed to everyone in view. "Excuse me," "That's perfectly all right," "Thank you," and "Not at all," are decorously exchanged. Colors, beads, bangles, and blond hair shining in the sun, shakos of curled hair like aureoles. They *are* beautiful, inert as

Piero della Francesca's people, as dewy as Botticelli's; pretty incestuous Volsungs, the brothers so like the sisters as to erase the overt differences in sex; the twins that were Adam and Eve before the apple.

Quiet now, expectant, without excessive eagerness. The great man in his expanse of baldness, black spade of beard, shining red shirt and a string of prayer beads—a benign, smiling, round presence—rises on the platform to intone, "Ohm," and short, repetitive prayers figuring "Shivaya," to the accompanying sound of a squeeze box. The young, embarrassed police stop him—no music, please. He hands one of them a flower while the crowd chants, "We love fuzz; we love fuzz; we love fuzz." The "Ohm" continues, hypnotically repeated in the large welcoming voice. The crowd is not sure whether it should applaud or not—some do; some don't. They soon rise to their feet and wander to lie down in the sun or to dance in a circle around the silver tree or leap and shout and clap in Dionysian ecstasy. A number sit down to blow bubbles with the absorbed solemnity of the children they choose to be or, with great concentration, suck on pink ice pops; a few of the dedicated go on to Grosvenor Square to kneel in prayer before the American Embassy. A "with it" bird in a flowered mini-dress and purple plastic sandals, the sweaty makeup peeling from her withered face, totters along, supported by a barefoot, grizzled gent with tattooed arms.

Pot? The government and the newspapers and the telly will go on discussing it, unaffected by the Sunday show. The lovely mummers will go on using it or say they do. Letters will appear in the *Times* pointing out that marijuana is less harmful than alcohol, which the "flower people" don't touch; the old guard will continue writing querulous letters about unkempt, dirty, irresponsible, addicted youth being given the right to public assemblage in a respectable park. No one has gained; no one has lost; it was a delightful afternoon, and it didn't rain.

## Latter-day Music Hall

**The Player's Theatre** requires membership, but everyone has at least one fun-loving London friend who might be a member, or he in turn has a friend. Hotels can often arrange these matters, depending how good or bad the season is.

The theater, off Villiers Street, is a long slope adorned with pictures of Yvette Guilbert and her contemporaries, a red and white tentlike ceiling, curly lamp brackets, and, as backdrop, Queen Victoria in a gold frame. The compere, in natty nineteenth-century evening dress, white stick and gloves, leads the standing toast, "To Her Majesty, Queen Victoria," and everyone settles down with his schooner of beer and opens the pink song sheet from which he will chorus along with the entertainers.

The entertainers, most of them old vaudevillians, lovingly greeted and remembered, are wonderful tricksters; a lack in talent is amply filled by good timing, and brash, attractive confidence, encouraged by the unquenchable mood of the audience. A lady in Edwardian drape sings of Vienna in May and a too demanding aria from *Rondine;* she receives the same thunderous applause as do two extraordinarily funny, vulgar, beguiling girls, one tall, the other short, in aprons and preposterous hats who gambol through a slapstick sketch concerning two charladies. The response to the defiant, old favorite "I'm Burlington Bertie" is received with stamping and whistling, and so is a sentimental gem about "My Old Pal, My Old Gal."

The primary attraction, among the numerous, is for the audience to act like "Old Music Hall." That means, judging from the present revival, constant eager audience participation. "And that brings us, ladies and gentlemen, to the interval, a short pause for refreshment," is shouted by the audience before the compere can speak the words. Over the incessant ground bass of the underground walloping its way to Charing Cross Station, the compere calls for Australians and New Zealanders to rise. They do, to clapping and whistling, explosive after the compere has asked, "How it feels to be right side up?" Canadians are greeted with two classics: "Oh, so you are from the revolting Colonies," and "Here are our revolting cousins." Whistling and stamping. "Have you come for business or pleasure or to learn the language?" Wild howling although the habitués have heard it a dozen times before. Birthdays are hailed and anniversaries, and people from Scandinavia with the appropriate jokes about their willing girls; a white couple from Zambia: "I must confess you are not at all what I expected."

The zesty release reaches its peak in the group singing, loud and fervid, and everyone but you seems to know all the words without referring to the song sheet, especially a couple one might not expect to find in such a happy playground of the middle-aged—she a girl hung with bell and hair, he bearded and tonsured like St. Francis of Assisi or his friends on Trafalgar Square.

One can prolong the gaiety by dancing on the stage after the performance is over or supping—lightly—in the restaurant-bar in the company of the entertainers.

## Soho Evening

After the required Soho dinner—goulash or Wiener schnitzel, sole with grapes and cream and wine, or curry, or wallowing in any of the numerous Italian ponds of tomato sauce and garlic, or Chinese spareribs—you find yourself at about eleven o'clock, the pubs lifting glasses you haven't clutched in your hand, and the large, blond lady urging you out. On Macclesfield and Gerrard streets the new little Chinatown shapes up, one restaurant after another serving variations of the chopped-up bits and the noodles and, at their sides, entrances to houses with frightening stairways and small signs in Chinese, indicating a "club." Though these are probably meant to serve for Chinese-style gambling among friends, the doorways are held up by a good number of girls, rarely Chinese, rarely prostitutes, but not the *crème*. There is a piece of folklore among adventurous London girls that Chinese men are "better" and a winner at fan-tan should be generous. Therefore they hang around, a few of them in the miniest of skirts, one or two in the provocative tight pants and loose shirt of "is she or isn't he?" and the rest rather poorly dressed, plainish girls.

As you continue on in Soho, staring at stalagmites of salami and fortresses of cheese in Continental groceries, jostled by the tough, good-humored crowd of East End boys and wanderers from Ireland, Scotland, the Midlands, the States, looking for pleasure and a little trouble, notice the activities of Soho, other than restaurants and coffee houses and amusements. A manufacturer of bagpipes, a "Hong Kong" tailor, doorways with girls' names punched out in tin shields over small lights and policemen peering up at windows. For some of the potentials behind these windows, walk up Shaftesbury Avenue to Denman Street to read the listings on the board near the corner, not always easy because it has an admiring and constant public, which knows, even if its English is faulty, how to translate the familiar idioms. The usual French lessons are offered, and art lessons. One applicant claims skill at French polishing, and an ex-acrobatic dancer seeks a position. More advanced learning (and foreigners insist that it reflects a national proclivity—*le vice anglais,* that caning by masters and older boys through centuries of public schooling must have developed a taste for it) appears as "Coloured governess gives advance tuition," "Young titled lady has vacancies for pupils. Strict discipline," "Young American gym mistress, who throughly enjoys her calling, gives private lessons for physical culture," "Young schoolmaster will visit young pupils both sexes for private tuition and training with strict discipline," "Lady seeks a maid, uniform supplied, please phone Miss Lash," suggesting a quote from Jean Genet.

Having decided that the kiss of the whip is a taste to which you have not yet advanced, turn into Great Windmill Street for Soho-style gambling. There are gambling clubs in the locale that are as small and homely as the poor kitchen in which your immigrant uncle played poker with his cronies, although the sharp faces here and wary, croaking voices are different from your uncle's. On Great Windmill Street the clubs are open all night and day, or almost. Not especially elegant, but roomy and well kept, and membership inexpensive. They are usually chummy places, habitués and croupiers linked in togetherness that flows across the tables over the sweep and clatter of chips and the thin click of dice. The croupiers, working in the democratic domain of two- and five-shilling bets, are often French and Italian boys who never learned to wear the closed, frozen faces of the Mayfair table gods, nor do they find it unthinkable to let you chatter and eat a club sandwich over their baize while they flash the twenty-one cards. While you eat and render chips, a sudden hand that belongs to the roulette table nearby drops a pound on a fall of cards, loses it, takes the hand back for a cigarette, drops another pound on the twenty-one box, and goes back to placing roulette bets. On the stool next to you an Irish boy sits uncertainly, laden with pay and full of whiskey. Too fuzzy to add what might make more or less than twenty-one, he smiles and smiles as his pile of five-shilling chips diminishes; smiles and repeats, admiringly, "the luck of the Irish" with each swoop-and-erasure of cards and chips.

There are more glossy clubs, as mentioned, with customers to match, but few can give you the sense of being an international sport for the duration of two or three pounds in two-shilling bets.

The next piece of Soho enlightenment (although they might in chronology easily be reversed) is the strip club. Until recently, many of these places were a sort of Tussaud's gallery of nudes, quite immobile, something like turning the pages of an "art photography" magazine. Now they move, in a group of associated small houses, that use the same girls on a swift timetable, the same girls with the small suitcases and high makeup that you had decided were probably whores, and probably are not, because the dashing from club to club on a split-second schedule makes a too tired girl. On almost any street—you pick it—a gentleman with a Near Eastern accent will invite you in to see, in life, the gorgeous girls of the street-case photographs. Suddenly, his pitch unfinished, the bargaining on price (three for the price of two—it is a slow night) breaks off, and he darts back of the partly drawn curtain. He starts beating the half-concealed cashier, who, with the restless eye in the back of his head, he had seen folding a five-pound note into her bra. The last view you have of him he is swiftly picking up the scattered notes and counting them. The girl has taken her bashed face and bruised shoulders into an invisible room.

His partner in another branch of the combine is in an easier mood and condition and also inclined to the bargain rate. You walk through the door into debris, still another Soho restaurant to be built, but now disordered emptiness. Down bare stone stairs past the back of a man standing at an open urinal at the side (women are rarely expected, but not excluded) and into a small room filled with a stage surrounded by very female and very crude figures in plaster and gilt and a few rows of seats, the crowded place reminiscent of the rooms in which puppet shows were once held in Sicily. One expects to see a man selling sunflower seeds out of his apron sack and rows of solemn little boys. There are little boys here, but not quite little enough to sit on Papa's lap. These look as if they came from secondary schools, some with the rough elegance that might mean temporary release from Eton or Westminster. Recorded music pounds the tight walls, and soon the curtain pulls open on a small, sullen girl who strips absentmindedly and then moves up and down the limited stage, rolling her immature belly and soft buttocks in a back and forth of expressionless repetitions. One hand or both always shields the pubic triangle when she faces the audience; it emphasizes, for one thing, and saves the cost of a G string, for another. Since the stripping is perfunctory and artless, lacking the luxurious toying at which the French are so skilled, nudity is no climax. So the girls keep walking around, shaking and rolling, until the time comes to stop, at the end of the record. The next number is introduced as "A daughter of joy, tired from a hard day's work—all night, ha ha." She is an extraordinarily good-looking Negress stretched out on a couch, dressed in diaphanous blue, mouthing well and precisely "Love for Sale" on a hot, bluesy recording. She, too, strips down to white bra and panties, nothing fancy except that they set off her beautiful, long-legged body and the bored, silken assurance of each movement. The bra and the panties are removed as easily and simply as it might be done in her bedroom, and the magnificent body approaches the front of the stage, kneeling, the legs wide apart and the shielding, inviting hand in place. At this point one young man in the audience bows his head deeply to his lap and busies himself with the cigarette burn eating into his trousers. The woman lies down—while he assiduously does not watch her—flexing her legs, rippling and lifting, kneeling and kneading; tensing and expanding the serpentine muscles she plays the old, old games, alone. While she is rippling and thrusting, she smiles and nods a pleasant good-bye to the small Act I girl who is now rushing out in a cotton shift and bare feet to do her turn at the club around the corner.

A minute later the writhing colored woman lifts her hand to wave to a friend arriving for the next turn. It comes on, after a short interval of music, as a cool goddess, a tall girl with a high crown of hair introduced as a genius at fan dancing. She floats in wearing a black, jeweled bra and string under a transparent, wide cape covered with fluttery ruffles. The fans are set down on a chair, and the goddess fills the stage by winging her gown out and to her, a vapid, nervous smile playing on her smooth, childish face. Marching, marching, back and forth, she takes off her bra under the gown and lifts it high like a trophy of war, does the same with the G string and then plays peekaboo, revealing and concealing a body as enameled and sexless as a doll's, as her face. During her semibashful, uncertain gestures, her grimace becomes a full smile as she nods good-bye to her Negro friend, now on to *her* next job. The smile returns to grimace; the waxen, doll-like figure turns, floats, to become human when it absentmindedly pokes a finger into the tower of hair and, with pinky sticking well out, scratches her head with refined vigor. Ultimately, the gown drops, and the fans take over the peekaboo game, now in front, now in back; they make a screen and sometimes a tail; now you see them, the fourteen-year-old breasts; now you don't. The plumes keep going precisely to the beat of the music, marking the rhythms of a well-learned exercise performed by a carefully taught girl who has no understanding of what she or the plumes are supposed to be doing. And when the plumes are put aside and the unripe breasts openly revealed, the hand dropped from the neat little diamond of dark hair on the dead white body, the show is over. Except for a group of Liverpool good-time Charlies (one of them the man who found the rippling brown flesh too much and had to not look at it) who found the show too short—they had been promised a full hour and here it was, only forty-five minutes. The beater-upper appears suddenly, at the side of his partner; there is a swift muttered exchange of words and gestures, and the party sullenly moves on, cursing the cupidity of London and vulnerable to the next offer of hot girls or blue films.

# 35 Pubs: A Pause with and Without Entertainment

If you come from cities where drinking places proffer full-time sanctuary, as churches once did, the limited hours of pubs—about 11 A.M. to 3 P.M. and 5:30 to 11 P.M., as a rule—may seem an invasion of your freedoms. There is good historical reason for the limitations. In the eighteenth century, brandy and gin were sold off barrows, by chandlers, fruit vendors, weavers, anyone and everyone. With the small formality of a notice and an inconsequential fee, anyone could establish a distillery and did, often diluting the liquor or mixing it with harmful additives. Employers sold it to their workers and kept a tally which left the workers no pay to take home. Often, pay time was held in a local tavern so late that the men were quite drunk when distribution came around, and again, victimized by collusion between tavern keeper and employer, no pay. The infamous St. Giles area had almost 100 gin shops and, attached to them, "twopenny houses," the cheapest of brothels, and the usual accompaniments of thieves' dens and a brisk trade in stolen goods. A decline in population in midcentury was directly and indirectly linked with drink, as was a 75 percent mortality rate among young children. Older children could drink freely if they earned or begged the money; wrecked or dead at an early age. In short, Hogarth's "Gin Lane" was not a lie, nor were Dickens' reports a century later: "We need go no farther than St. Giles or Drury Lane, for sights and scenes of a most repulsive nature. Women with scarcely the articles of apparel which common decency requires, with forms bloated by disease, and faces rendered hideous by habitual drunkenness—men reeling and staggering along—children in rags and filth—whole streets of squalid and miserable appearance whose inhabitants are lounging in the public road, fighting, screaming and swearing. . . ."

The present-day descendant of the gin mills and taverns is among man's more intelligent, life-enhancing inventions. It is club, salon, and meetinghouse along professional or political or economic or sexual lines, or simply the communal parlor of a neighborhood. Some provide their own homegrown entertainment; others hire it, while the indigenes shunning the foreigners—anyone outside a circumference of three streets—hide in a safe, closed-off section. Printers have their pubs, marketmen, prizefighters, actors, postmen, leatherworkers, the Joseph's coat young, the blobby old. Some feed you fairly well; others make a listless gesture. Below, a very few, culled from grazing in the diversity.

There is no guarantee that what you will see is what is here described; the popularity of entertainment pubs explodes and fizzles as quickly as fireworks. A dim, retiring place may find new owners who hate the foggy quiet and displace it with combos whose strengths are speed and noise. The lemmings may have abandoned a bawdy trull of a pub and let it sink into sullenness. On the other hand, those mentioned below may be stayers and worth searching out.

**Deuragon Arms,** Rosina Street, off Homerton High Street, Hackney. At one time some of the clients were boys in tight pants and black leather jackets hung with chains and studded with metal, all the faces uniform with contained wrath; except one, in the same costume, a minister who had banded them together as a club for their reform or that of the church. Now the toughness has loosened, and the color brightened, as Hackney and a few visitors listen to the large amplified voices of local talent.

**The Prospect of Whitby,** 57 Wapping Wall, is not likely to have faded; rather, it is a tourist's must, no reason to avoid it. The warm, gleaming dining room upstairs, named for Pepys who was a customer, serves a decent, unremarkable dinner at moderate prices. But the action, particularly on Friday and Saturday nights, is down below, and the crowding and the noise augmented by electric guitars that give out Hawaiian music and Irish reels. Through the ramble of inviting rooms, if you can see them, a subway crush of groups singing in unison, or something like it; the bobbing up and down which is dancing when there is no room to dance in; red-faced shouting of conversations; and all the groups laced together by the constant movement of arms and mugs of beer—with little sloshing, considering the hazards—around and over the bobbing, singing, shouting heads.

North of Hyde Park and west of Marble Arch, in a soothing, but never dull, repetition of crescents and streets and mews of white houses painted with shine and flowers surrounding strips and circles and ellipses of London green, sits the **Victoria Tavern** (Strathearn Place, Hyde Park Square), a remarkable piece of London pub theatricalism. The main floor reiterates the velvety, cut-glassy Edwardian of current high fashion in pubs and brings it to singularity on the second floor, arranged like a theater, with seats sheltered by a red-velvet curve of loge and a miniature gallery on whose rail rest suggestive props: a champagne glass, an opera hat.

Possibly by an osmosis of mood, the clients stand and chat decorously, in nonpub tones suitable to the interval of an important play, maybe a new shocker by that Irishman Shaw or a pinwheel of paradoxes by Oscar.

At the side of the Royal Naval College in Greenwich, at the end of Park Row, sits the old **Trafalgar Tavern,** popular for oysters in Thackeray's time, newly restored as lush dining rooms and overdecorated bars, but its narrow, bowed balconies are beguiling from the river and for looking onto the river. However, it is too crowded; walk, instead, along the alley that parallels the river called Crane Street, buy a beer in the **Yacht** pub, and go out to the river view from its modest terrace. Later, follow the street of small narrow houses, probably of local dock workers, into a strange contrast of the broad horizontals of new housing neighbored by the immense black stacks with a suggestion of Tuscan turret of the local power station. Under the strident black towers, a minute strip of garden separates hardworking barges from the white toy castle of Trinity Hospital (p. 40), founded in 1616. In spite of its date and the medieval contours, it is a fancy of the early nineteenth century; you are gazing at a shadow, but not the substance, of antiquity, although some vestiges of older times remain inside the white walls. Across the river, stands of trees and stretches of dock and the immediate view ahead, quiet and remote on a summer evening at about nine, when the light is soft and not yet dark, and the cranes and elevators and platforms of steel are skeletal dinosaurs emerging from the murky water below. Continue on through high-fenced alleys hiding waste and scrap iron, minute houses, and careful gardens with a sampler hothouse on the river at Ballast Quay, and across the road from it, the Harbour Master's House, square and sure, with a yellow door placed at the side, away from the drive of river winds.

The night deepens; the river turns dark and misty; nothing sounds in the half-light but the soft thump, touch, and groan of two barges tied together and protesting. In the distance north of the river, floats of smoke screen the sharpness of stacks and spires, and the trees meet together as dark clumps of moss until the lights go on to streak them with hard greens and yellows. In the river, ovals of red paint, all that is left to see of barges. And it is pub time at the **Cutty Sark,** near the power station—old, small, plain, and what a local should be. The silent, old, toothless couple, shabby and motionless, sit against the wall; a photo of a wrestling team (including a local boy) decorates another wall. The gambling machine spills its thruppence token showers frequently enough to induce brisk trade. The customers have put on fresh shirts, their optimistic new teeth and new perms, and their cordial manners. If it is Saturday and payday, the young Salvation Army representative will come in to collect donations and sell his papers and exchange an amiable word or two with all the customers, and if it is Saturday, the boss (addressed as Guv'ner) will have put on his good suit and tie and grown pinker in the cheek earlier in the evening than usual; it is his Saturday night, too.

**The Salisbury** at St. Martin's Lane is cut glass, convoluted bronze, patterned plaster, plushy, curvaceous, Victorian (anything with fringed lampshades, preferably red). Theoretically, it is supposed to play host to a soigné theater clientele, out of backstage for a small tub of ale; just as often the red plush is covered by bottoms from nontheatrical Leeds, not quite as showy but equally vocal.

On Kensington Church Street, immediately off Kensington High Street, is the **Prince of Wales,** a shining, self-respecting pub whose distinction is a good, inexpensive, and nicely served lunch, not as common a commodity in pubs as legend would have it.

**The Tally-Ho.** In Kentish Town, wedged into the meeting of Highgate Road and Fortress Road, stands one of those large, plain pubs, the almost complete escape from the uninspired neighborhood flats and repetitions of summertime telly, cheaper than the movies and often more exotic, closer to hand and shoulder and ear. For the locals who prefer the ease of the tried and commonplace, the big, irregular public room crowded with men in a fog of smoke, the thick, flat din of conversation pierced by a call of triumph from a darts player or the shout to a bar-bound friend to bring another ale. Next to it, one public saloon, the *sala* of the ubiquitous lady with the gray, square bob devised in 1920 and never changed, planted and silent on her bench, the lady and flower of all working-class pubs. Upstairs, the lunches for four shillings and not much up; snacks—the immutable sandwich, sausage, Scotch egg—at the bar. So far, classic, except for the fact that one big room on the Highgate Road side thumps and leaps with jazz every night and on Sundays from noon.

On a fair Sunday, after the papers have been read, before the mu-

seums open or the arguments in Hyde Park's Speakers' Corner have
developed a good head of steam, and you've done Petticoat Lane and
seen enough great houses in the surrounding countryside, any large
pub—with outside space for the loungers with their faces to the sun,
the neckers lost together in their ferneries of hair, the gossips and
debaters, the gesticulators and the still, or the working-class zest in
its best weekend clothing in Kilburn, the East End and the docks,
Camden Town or Kentish Town—is a colorful and comforting place.
The Tally-Ho offers, besides the jazz, drinkers and listeners from
foreign boroughs who make a bright mosaic of "London"—the mini-
skirts and the maxiskirts, young beards and clean-shaven wrinkles
come to hear, once more, the Dixieland that was fresh and fashionable in their younger times. The faces are of Bangalore and Karachi,
of Nigeria and Harlem, of Camden Town and Belgravia, out of the
freshly painted and brainy houses of bewildered Islington, out of the
red-brick uglies of Swiss Cottage and the faceless bed-sitters of Bloomsbury; the wearers of the disconsolate old trenchcoat and the wearer
of the necktie that is a field of poppies from Carnaby Street. In each
corner a pair of lovers trying, a little too hard, to act as if it were the
corner of a *cave* in Paris.

**Swiss Cottage.** Maybe it was, long ago, an inn owned by a Swiss and
edged with pierced wooden scallops. Certainly it was notable enough as
an hostelry on a northbound road to give its name to a tube station
and appear as terminal point of No. 2 buses during rush hours. Busy
Finchley Road is made frantic at the station and pub corner, where a
number of tributary roads pour into the mother stream and compli-
cated traffic signals make pedestrians too timid or too bold, to everyone's mutual terror. In an island made by the geography of converg-
ing roads, the pub, a large ramble of rooms on rooms, and on the
second layer, little Swiss balconies from which the young gaze down
on the traffic and gas fumes as from a castle height onto the Danube.
On weekend nights they can posture against the intense *lumière* like
Juliet or Keats' knight alone and palely loitering or jolly Swiss yodel-
ers. To you, trying to get across the complexities of road and furious
traffic, it looks like a lost ferry breasting a black maelstrom.

**The Volunteer,** diagonally across from Baker Street Station, has been
refurbished in recent years to commemorate the time when it was a
tavern and recruiting station (late in the eighteenth century) for a
citizens' army to counter the threat of French invasion. The period
and mood are probably right—crossed swords and bugles on the walls,
along with military prints—but the degree of elegance probably inau-

thentic; whatever recruiting one can imagine in these surroundings would have had to be of gentlemen-officers.

It is a lush place, of dark blue-greens and bright red, a pretty ladies' parlor upstairs and its bar (unaccompanied ladies may not approach the street-level bar) and a stylish little restaurant. Or one can sit on the benches outside (ladies have to ask a gentleman to bring them a drink or carry it down from their bar) and, on a fair day, watch the traffic at the station, the babies being pushed toward Regent's Park and the girls like lilies on Baker Street.

The **Barrow Poets** may or may not be poets in their own right, but under this public name they are reciters of poetry, a violinist, an oboe-ist, and a variety of homemade instruments, thumped and twanged by the male reciter who acts as compere, as well. The merriment is of the most innocent—No supersonic-boom electric guitars, De Quinceys or Madam Goddams, not too many Genghis Khan mustaches in the audience come to be sweetly, anachronistically entertained.

Performances, sponsored by a brewery and the Arts Council, take place several nights a week in a rotation of pubs with largish upstairs or side room to accommodate the crowd that spills from benches to floors and stairways.

The program of early summer, 1967, ranged through Punch and Judy, Dorothy Parker, Campion, Herrick, Catullus (both in English and in American slang), T. S. Eliot, Shakespeare, to James Weldon Jonson; clever aphoristic poems on the London bus (one in semi-Latin); and a gloriously inept paean of praise for a stream-throwing fire wagon. The compere, easy, homely, and engaging, in the manner of a young, popular professor, introduced the groups of poems, loosely hung on one subject—"Women as Food," "Never Trust a Man," "Public Transport," etc.—and himself proved a fine reciter of verse, with a good ear and few slips, for American with a slightly Southern accent. He, too, was the player, and possibly inventor, of a long drum-like affair, scooped out to become a lyre, and a skinny unpainted bass fiddle with a drum and cymbal attachment. His companion, an equally easy gentleman, resembled the young Dylan Thomas, before the bulbous nose and melted body. His musical specialty, when the grand finale came, was tootling through a kazoo reed set into a funnel. One lady reciter (all the poetry is memorized, by the way) might have looked like Katharine Hepburn were she not visibly plumped with pregnancy, and the other lady fortyish, efficient-looking, and were you to see her on the bus, you would guess her to be an executive secretary. Frail and lovely old tunes came from the fiddle-oboe combi-

nation, sometimes pinkly charming, sometimes funny, as the duo
chirped and tootled through sentimental roulades of pre-World War I.

Go early, at least half an hour before the performance starts, at
eight thirty or earlier, to wander the pubs, all of them interesting. One
is a Regency pub, one will feed you supper, and another, the most
conveniently located, is a printer's pub, off Fleet Street, on whose walls
hang many and interesting prints that deal with newspapers and printing.

(For forthcoming programs write the Barrow Poets, 70 Parliament
Hill, London N.W.3, or see *What's On in London*.)

**The Vulcan,** 240 West Ferry Road, in Limehouse, draws—drew—a
fairly serious listening crowd of locals and visitors interested in the
jazz combos and vocalists who, at times, give way for confident, if
nothing else, amateurs. Well cocooned and separated from all that
noisy nonsense, the dart players dart and the earnest drinkers get
down stolidly, steadily, as much as they can before the dread "Time,
gentlemen."

**Waterman's Arms,** 1 Glengarnock Avenue, off Manchester Road, on
the Isle of Dogs, as free-form as a splash of beer and as welcome in
its matrix of pleasant council housing, after miles of eyeless walls and
lumberyards. The place blazes and thunders on Saturday nights (they
all do, if they are inclined to at any time). Under the great banners
of pastel crepe-paper streamers, leaning against 1900's theater posters,
rest the old regulars of an earlier, less showy time, sitting as far from
the combo of piano, bass viol, and drums as they can and only occasionally lifting a turtle eye to the buxom singer on the small platform.
As often as not, she is what used to be referred to as a bimbo, with
harsh red hair and a prizefighter's face, dressed in a tight lamé dress
and gold slippers, and, on a cold night, a brown sweater. Her singing
is hard and cold, a sort of practiced sexiness learned from Harlem
race records, quite accurate and not quite right and with a painstaking
lasciviousness that reminds one of Mae West, the great female im-
personator.

Rotherhithe Street at the southern edge of the river follows the contours of the river, at times almost lapped by it, at others breasted by
piers and pierced by the grillwork of docks. At No. 21, the well-known
**Angel,** a pub for snacks and an upstairs restaurant that serves respectable lunches and dinners (Monday to Friday) and intimacy with
the old Thames. Westward, at 117, sits the **Mayflower,** warm and darkly
shining of polished wood and glass shaped like portholes. Besides its
cordial self, it has two distinctions: It is possibly the only public house

that maintains a franchise to sell stamps and, at the back, the stairs from which the Pilgrim Fathers boarded their ship—hence the name of the pub. Not far away is the church graveyard where lie some of the organizers of the expedition and, near the edge of the river, the ghost of the *Mayflower* that haunts the gray waters on a foggy night.

**Ship and Whale** is farther along Rotherhithe Street, not yet discovered or given to gaudy entertainment except that which the locals make with the help of gallons of ale around the tinkly piano. It is a big dockers' pub, decorated as the local homes might be, in bits of trellis laced with waxed fruits and flowers and pictures and models of ships. Get your pint at the bar, and sit down wherever you can find space. The conversation will come, to reveal a stubborn pride in endurance and the capacity to survive, and although a number of the men have traveled and even lived abroad, there is a staunch fidelity to local houses lost behind fortresses of warehouse, erected over the death pits of children and wives and friends. If you were to ask about a house a quarter of a mile away, you would be told that no one knows anything about it; it is "downtown," part of the vast unknown territory of London, rarely visited and of no great interest.

Your table partners might be Jim and 'Arry. Jim is a man in his late sixties, with a ruddy, mobile face, not at all self-conscious about his three teeth. He knows he can get two full rows from National Health, but why bother? He can cut the meat of the Sunday joint small and the rest, the potatoes and buns and tea and mashes, require few teeth; the ale and whiskey none. He is a boaster, a pleased survivor of years and misfortune, still something of a lady's man. With a volatility native to him and the alcohol, he beams and puffs out his chest to assure his audience that he can and does lift 300-pound sacks of sugar, then shrinks and dwindles to an old man as he talks about the three children, of thirteen, whom he lost, two in the bombing of the docks and one as a soldier in World War II. The old courtier, the repository of remembered pleasure, appears when he addresses a barmaid or a client as "me gel," filling the phrase big and round with affection. Jim as the world traveler is introduced with the simple statement "I am an educated man" and followed with the proof of a few words—sailor's words—in a number of languages which, unhampered by teeth, sound much alike.

The sailor vocabulary in the "company of ladies," leads him back to refinements, "I comprehend" and repetitions of "I'm a gentleman," and, nudging his friend, "Hain't I, 'Arry?" Harry is younger, thinner, and probably better-toothed, although one cannot say because his mouth is closed and stays closed. To Jim's importunate question he nods slowly, viscously, then straightens his head to the absolute rigidity which is his alcoholic climate and continues to stare straight ahead out of boiled, pink-streaked eyes. Jim babbles on, and suddenly Harry is no longer sitting there, as part of the decor and fading into the wall-paper. He is floating back from the bar, light and easy, his somnambu-list face unchanged and, in his hands, two whiskeys, carefully placed before the two guests. Then back to his stiff somnambulist's posture. Not a word yet out of Harry in spite of the thanks; he sits in his blank-ness until, as inexplicably motivated as was his treat of drinks, he rises slowly, carefully, not to break the fragility of his alcoholic nest and, in slow motion, takes a photograph of a ship off the wall behind him and lays it before the visitors. It is an American freighter. Somehow, through a chink in his mist, the American accent seeped through, and around it, from some foggy distance, he shaped an acknowledg-ment and the gestures of hospitality and compliment. There are gaudier "true English gentlemen" and more talkative, but few so profoundly, unconsciously authentic.

When the Ship and Whale closes at eleven, the middle-aged weave their way home, while the local young, back from the entertainment of other dockside pubs, pour into a nearby fish-and-chips place run by a young Cypriot couple. If you don't want to eat fried skate or plaice, there is the innovation—increasingly popular—of fried chicken and the opportunity to notice, if your acquaintance with London's young was made on Carnaby Street and in Chelsea, that working-class youth still prefers to dress up on Saturday nights and holidays in its good, middle-class suit and pastel wool dress. Kink is for those who can afford it financially and socially, as these youngsters cannot.

**The Fox,** Islington High Street. A comfortable pub with casual attempts at the Edwardian, plays (or played, these matters are mutable) host on Thursday nights to balladeers, local, Irish, Islands, Scottish, and leftish, in its upstairs hall. The rumor is that it has gone Establishment, but you may still find a white-haired man of the neighborhood who sings his own songs about the different odors that seep through the sewers of Billingsgate, St. James's, Covent Garden, and Belgrave Square; about the fact that the girls look younger as he ages; about the growing satisfactoriness of a hot-water bottle as bed companion as one grows older. You may still find the boy who looks as poets should and who sings old Irish and English ballads, with his head thrown back and his arms wide, a bard singing in a great stone feasting hall. The star was a young Scotsman who sang bitter, funny, topical songs to traditional

Irish and Scottish airs. He took on the bomb, American policy in Vietnam, the royal family, the Labour government, the police, soldiering; for all of them he had a quiverful of sharp, acid arrows. The young audience, long-maned and coarse-sweatered, joins in the choruses and, at the break, calls for a song from a visiting guest someone recognizes. Sometimes it is an old song full of bygone gentility and flowers, as often a bawdy version of a classic, always listened to politely and applauded generously, but everyone is basically interested in running downstairs for another pint before the bitter Scots archer picks up his bow again.

**The George (Balls Bros.),** 379 Bethnal Green Road. A thoroughly masculine place of black barrels, dark woods, and the gleam of copper and glass on the many doors. The lunch is plain and inexpensive, served with an offhand intimacy, as if you were a regular who had defected for a while. Near the front door, the permanent lodgers in their caps and ancient coats, silent and rooted as fungus.

On a stroll through Chelsea (p. 48) look for Mossop Street and the **Admiral Codrington.** It has a garden, a warm twinkling interior, a large variety of snacks, and its regulars are among the most luminous of Chelsea's young.

**The Ship,** lost in the juncture of Gate Street and Little Turnstile, where beer-drinking students from Bloomsbury share the tables with gin-drinking ladies gathering strength for the night's work of cleaning office buildings.

**The Nag's Head,** across from the Royal Opera, feeds you a good salad near the street-floor bar and, upstairs, more formally, amid theatrical souvenirs.

**The Chandos Spanish Pub,** King William IV Street. The cellar section of a beehive of restaurants, across from the all-night post office. Sangría for two shillings from a punch bowl on the bar, much Spanish spoken, and if you can push your way in at about seven thirty or eight, flamenco dancing and singing at no extra charge.

**King's Head and Eight Bells,** 50 Cheyne Walk. Good food—far beyond snacks in dignity and cost and elbow rubbing with prosperous Bohemia (one of the handsomest of London's many guises), plus the shadows of Carlyle, Turner, Whistler, Wilde, and Sir Thomas More.

**El Vino,** 47 Fleet Street. Ladies suffered coolly; never served at the bar which just barely breathes in the crowding of casks and newspapermen. Whiskey is served and drunk, but as the name implies, this place is for wine and instructive. The next time you read one of the august local journals that speak with the voice of God and you find that a headline contradicts the information attached to it, you will remember the three wine bottles that decorated the table for four next to you and the blotter of one thin smoked salmon sandwich per each. (A branch exists eastward—p. 152.)

Past the overdecorated glare of restaurants, the dirty books, and hygienic supplies of Villiers Street, off the Strand, turn into Watergate Walk for another, smaller wine pub. And when you are in Marylebone, look for a similar place on Baker Street, north of Melcombe Street.

**Phene Arms,** at Phene and Oakley streets, in Chelsea. On a favorable Saturday or Sunday at about noon, bouquets and garlands of riverside Chelsea youth, the smooth, gardenia-petal variety.

The pubs on Earl's Court for Australians who sing loud songs, martial and nostalgic, and for Irish despair and belligerence, Saturday night near the Camden Town Station. Fulham Road pubs for anything.

Part of the huge new shopping center at Elephant and Castle is the **Chaplin** pub, one of whose walls is absorbed by a large effigy of a local boy (nearby Kennington) who made good.

Belgravia doesn't like to stain its ivory curves with pubs; it keeps them hidden in mews paths. **The Grenadier,** in Wilton Row, a mews' mews at the end of a meshwork of alleys off Knightsbridge, via a thread of space called Old Barrack Yard. Small, elderly, historic, a wee bit self-conscious, and very nice.

**Henenkey's,** on High Holborn, is vast and constantly referred to as "the last of the old gin palaces."

**Thomas à Becket,** on the Old Kent Road (south of the river), is a boxer's pub, currently a favorite for songs and fatty jokes, particularly relaxed on Sunday afternoon.

Before taking your place on line at Bloom's Restaurant (p. 270), look in at the **Hoop and Grapes,** 47 Aldgate High Street. It is generally agreed to be the oldest pub in London, on the site since the thirteenth century, and reputed to have a tunnel, now blocked, that led to the Tower.

If you are interested in the temporary purchase—or sale—of a boy or girl, try the pubs in the Elephant and Castle area. For making the acquaintance of a ship's steward, very much out of uniform and prettily rouged, sit down and look inviting at the **Windsor Castle,** on Harrow Road, off Edgware Road, near the local police station. (Weekends best.)

Anything goes, or stays, at a pub popularly known in its locality as the **Steps,** though its formal name is the **Custom House,** across from Custom House Station, off Victoria Dock Road, quite a way out. You will know it by inquiring on a main road in Canning Town and, closer on, by the pools of vomit outside, with or without their leaners against the wall. There *are* a couple of steps, and inside, a long bar in a freshly painted room adorned with a jukebox and gambling coin machines. The patronage seems neat, lightly boozy, and eminently respectable in the stiff-corseted manner of the London worker and his wife. The room makes a bend at the back and expands for a small bar and the usual tables and chairs. The barman (it is now about ten o'clock on Saturday night) is steady with the pouring hand, but his tongue keeps slipping away from his words, and his feet play him tricks when he dances with a strong-faced waitress. While he is dancing, a fat, soggy woman, in the sweater she possibly never removes, holds the fort uncertainly, looking at the jollity with slack eyes. At a table, two men in fine, roll-necked Italian sweaters, one in pearl earrings, talk with flailing gestures and dropped wrists to an exquisite boy in a Vidal Sassoon haircut and pale sea green on his eyelids. The fourth man wears no makeup or clothes in any way distinctive, but he will make it yet, judging from the admiring attention with which he looks and listens. Everybody is everybody's friend, calling inside jokes and sweet greetings to each other, from bar to tables, from tables to dance floor and to the soggy, fat lady, now animated, carrying a cloth to the table of the men. "What have you got there, luv?" "I found it in the loo. You want a smell? A taste?" She pushes it at his nose and mouth, and everybody laughs richly.

No one will bother you at all if you go as a couple or small group; if you go alone, it should be clear to you why, and sociological research is not enough reason.

(See also Chapter 34, "Entertainment.")

# ∙§ *London Is Where . . .*

In certain areas, shoes are made of "levver," and the lady known as Mum is one's "muvver."

An animated tête-à-tête is two people talking to themselves, together. "Too bad you are staying in London for only three weeks; now that the theater and music season is reanimated, there is so much to see and hear." "Oh, but I'm staying three months." "Pity you can't stay longer. There are a number of hidden nooks I should like so much to show you." "I should like to see them, and I shall be here for three months." "You energetic Americans; like humming-birds, you taste a bit and fly off to another blossom in the twinkling of an eye."

There is a restaurant called Moby Dick whose motto is "a meal so big and slick." Because it is in Soho, passersby giggle. Maybe it does actually refer to a large, smooth-skinned whale.

The queen of London department stores distributes her largesse, still, in electric motorcars.

The whole is not visibly equal to the sum of its parts. The overall is shoddy, ignoble, and has to be peeled, like an artichoke, or spied on, or lurked about, or surprised around a corner, wooed with time and shoe leather to reveal its myriad allures.

Free-form Elizabethan spelling persists in a supermarket sign: *Please do not bring in prambs.*

A construction firm calls itself "architectural ironmongers."

If you, as a stranger, offer a bus conductor full fare for a child, he will return half of it.

Belief in the perfectibility of man, somewhat muted in discouragement, still exists. London is the indelibly remembered spinster professor with an immortal cold and stringy hair who brought recordings of madrigals to class and suggested you try your hand at an Elizabethan masque while you were studying *Twelfth Night*, the one who was contentedly unmarriageable and afflicted with a falling hem. She derived her excitements from whether Raleigh or Bacon might have written Shakespeare's plays and wept over the rape of Irish forests in Elizabethan times. She had wit and a deftness of speech so fine that you did not recognize light insult until its filigreed barb hooked some two hours later. Devoted to uplift and progress through education, she found time for arranging lunchtime concerts and films, lectures, debates among churchmen and museum talks, and then more time for pleasantries and such mundane matters as how to get from here to there.

It is perfectly safe to walk alone and anywhere at night, including the most tortuous, lightless alleys. One suffers only loneliness, a sense of being severed from the rest of humanity which is in bed, a considerable change from past centuries when theater performances were held in the afternoon so that people could get home before thieves and toughs attacked them.

Men, "flower" or cactus, are more decorative, more dashing than women. Except for the girls in their startling semidresses whose superior allure is that of the Scotsman in kilts: Does she or doesn't she?

Newspapermen like to strike sparks off their classical educations. The Observer on Svetlana Alliluyeva: "lonely as Ovid on the shores of the Black Sea."

One can achieve easy immortality, if equipped with the proper credentials, by obtaining a card for the reading room of the British Museum. Should you use it, should you not, the number assigned you is yours, forever, immutably, till time and the British Museum vanish.

The balm of mutual help still exists, as in few large cities. It is a persuasive teacher. Doors are held for you, and you yield to holding doors. If you are trying to light a cigarette on a windy street, a stranger offers to cup her hands around your unsteady light; in the passing on of rewards, it becomes important for you to lift a child to the bus platform. Your bag of groceries (watch these, frequently made only of the spirit of bags) breaks on the street; a woman walking behind apologizes for her grandson, who was not quick enough to stop the rolling oranges, and then offers you a lift in her car; you look for someone to receive your responding act of kindness. It is this, and the endless exchanges of "Thank you," the aura of goodwill to benevolence that inspires a love for London, infinitely more than its ephemeral, spotty swingingness, whatever that means.

A girl appears at an art exhibition dressed only in bra, bikini panties, and a transparent shift. This demonstration of what can be achieved by the simple expedient of forgetting to put on a slip is goggled at only by American, French, and German visitors.

"God Save the Queen" is played after most performances, except in royal theaters, the Royal Opera House, the Royal Festival Hall, etc. In the cinema, after the last cowboy has faded into the mesa, it is likely to be the first few phrases played to silent standing. In Sadler's Wells, the music-inflamed audience sings heartily and through greater length. After a performance of Britten's *Gloriana*, an opera concerning Elizabeth I, the tribute soars to a mighty, solemn hymn.

Decrepit music, crusty with age and scholarship, is in high favor; the solemn organ clumping of Buxtehude and the prissiest and dullest of Monteverdi's church music, music that is dry wind in frozen branches, are sought out and attended with fervor. Enlightenment, uplift again, and the taint of Puritanism.

People "stand" for office while Americans "run," a difference applicable in a number of areas and worth a moment's thought now and then, as you ease into the London tempo.

# 36  Restaurants

## Introduction

Your *Feinschmecker* friends will say, "London? The food is terrible."
That is not altogether true or altogether false. It can be self-respecting
British of large joints wheeled to you as they might have been in a
baronial hall under soaring wooden arches, accompanied by Yorkshire
pudding that might be delicious fluff surrounded by stalwart crust or a
depressed sag of dough. It can be the English of carefully marinated
and spiced jugged hare or unidentifiables sunk in a swamp of white
glue. Chelsea and Kensington are expanding their repertoires to that
vague, promising category called Continental. Some of them occasionally slip back into nasty English habits: the famous white swamp of
overcooked vegetables, those puffy little powdered rolls with the empty
taste. Some remain sternly vigilant against such lapses. In short, it
isn't Paris, nor is it blubber and hardtack.

The famous London tolerance, a lovesome thing, God wot, and
the politeness may to some degree explain the frailties and carelessness
of many restaurants. Only coarse foreigners send back impenetrable
chunks of meat or pig's liver selling for calf. If the Londoner would
protest more often, we all might profit. Possibly the fault lies in latent
and overt Puritanism that damns cooking with the voice of high
thinking and low living. Nothing much can be done about this, except
to remind Londoners that it wasn't always so. Those who could afford
it ate—and prodigiously—and lavishly drank from the tuns of wine
that raced from France to fill the warehouses of Vintry Ward. And
as for no present food—or little—after midnight, medieval and Elizabethan markets and docks left room for twenty-four-hour cookhouses
that served anyone who could pay, at any hour, and it is safe to con-
jecture that the eating was good and robust. London was full of
Italians who worked for companies enmeshed in Italian banking
concerns that at times almost controlled the city's finances. Frenchmen held strong positions in the wine and silk trades, and Germans
who shipped to and from the Hanseatic League cities were well-fed
gentlemen; spices were a major import, as witness the search for spice
routes. What has happened since? It cannot be *all* Oliver Cromwell's
fault.

To make you grateful for the flavor of the hit-and-miss possibilities that may accost you in more expensive restaurants, have one of your first London meals in a working-class neighborhood—lunch near Lambeth Station or Farringdon Road or Southwark. In "Italian" cafés (pronounced with a long *a* and as one syllable), newly bristling with chrome and wax flowers, the menu will offer you spaghetti sandwiches and bean sandwiches; spaghetti, ravioli, and lasagna with chips, proving that *Chips with Everything* is a fact. The national touch stains even the highly spiced—or what should be—Italian foods, flattening the usual zing, graying and wrinkling the peas. The substitutes for lost flavor are bottled in a ring of condiments on each table: catsup, vinegar, and a variety of spiced sauces. Although many follow the Italian patterns of cheap and filling foods, a good number of items stay what they indigenously are, as sausages, eggs, stews—immutably with chips—or limit themselves to the famous fish-and-chips. That robust antique, cloaked in a sheet of newspaper, permits you to carry it away or take it to a counter to douse with vinegar and to eat on the premises. Improvements are marring the classic; the paper is often white butcher's paper, the once bare tables are covered with the same white paper, and the grim old frying tanks are winged with gleaming chrome vents that prevent the odor from clinging to and thickening the walls. There must even be places where you tear the skate or plaice apart with a knife, and some actually revolutionize the tradition by frying chicken as well. One hopes (but does not investigate) that there are separate frying vats.

Fish-and-chips is a subject that London writers grow meltingly sentimental about and rueful; it isn't what it used to be, too few, too modern, and, by implication, too clean. But Caledonian Road fries and sells it, as does Essex Road and Upper Street and, in fact, any high street of a working-class area, with the cultural concomitant, the jellied eels and winkles shops and stalls, traditionally best in Aldgate. Recently a few have begun to allow a bit of space for cooking hot dogs, for the children and the immigrants who are not yet locked in the charms of jellied eels.

To eat in London and often in other parts of England, a knowledge of Spanish and Italian helps. Practically all waiters and waitresses and countermen are one of the hegira river from those countries and have assimilated none, some, or much of the language. There is something moving in the valor of a waitress standing behind a counter, smiling Latinly at you and understanding not one word of what you are saying. Although she may have a slippery, small supply of English as she has learned it among her Cockney customers or ill-equipped friends, your American vowels and slurs will be a totally foreign language and paralyzing. Gestures and pointing help, but being able to explain yourself in a primitive form of her language brings you tears of gratitude and heaping portions, proving once more that a knowledge of foreign languages cements international amity.

There are minor difficulties, other than language, presented by London restaurants. One of them is that for a long time, pressed for space and made more desperate by bomb destruction, restaurants have had to retire to cellars, sometimes quite splendid, so you must look carefully for signs, not necessarily ten or twelve feet above sidewalk level, as you might expect, but often low and pointing downward. Another small hazard is the presence of cream on desserts, including even such lean fare as fruit compotes. You'll have to fight it off in some places and be glad of its mask in others.

London has "carveries" that serve first and last courses, and in between you help yourself to as much as you can manage, in any degree of cookedness you prefer, from hillocks of beef. London has hushed palaces where you must reserve two days ahead, for *haute cuisine* at *haute* prices. It has thousands of teahouses, for uninspired buns and strong tea weakened with milk, and coffeehouses with "Continental" pastries. It runs the gamut, in short, among price ranges, degrees of excellence, and several nationalities. Then, of course, there is the list your friends gave you. Below, a few that may or may not be on your list, mainly moderate in price (four to seven dollars, including the cover charge and the house carafe or a modest wine). Under that price, you may—not necessarily—be risking your taste buds and your love for London. Above that, it is plainly expensive—often worth it; once in a while not, but the Scotch smoked salmon will always be cheaper than it is at home and incomparably better.

# Museums

The word "restaurant" is a bit large for what actually serves food in some museums. In the **Geffrye** it is a small attractive and modern coffee shop, a duplication of what you might find on King's Road. In the **Tate** it is a large place that serves an interesting array of salads, cakes, and sandwiches with accompanying beverages. Both the **British Museum** and the **Victoria and Albert** have restaurants of no great distinction, but quiet and white tablecloths. It is the cafeterias, especially that of the V and A, that provide the best combination of eavesdropping, people watching, and inexpensive food.

The menu sets the tone: Among the shepherd's pies and sausages and chips listed on the hot dishes board, "epigram of Lamb" may appear. Politely amused by the academic joke, you move on with your tray and have your cheese on Hovis decorated with sprigs of cress, the heraldic emblem of sandwiches in England. Then the tea or coffee, and like everyone else, you select a candy bar and find a seat. The cafeteria is probably full of ladies down for a day in London, dressed in their skinny fur pieces and pink cement hats, Indian families and Chinese and Africans in flowing robes and silk pillboxes. The young wear the long sideburns of flamenco dancers or Orthodox Jews.

The best of the personae, however, are the eccentric old ladies who might, if they were Parisian and drunk and tottered behind improvised baby carriages full of old bottles and last week's newspapers, be *clochards*. Here they are Londoners, and no one stares or comments and, if he notices, makes believe he hasn't. One biddy who is a frequent visitor wears a reddish hairy cloak which looks as if she'd sewed it herself of hides hunted down among the cats that gather around Billingsgate. The day may be warm, and to cool herself or to look like a bird which she may imagine she is, she flaps the coat out in wings behind her as she circulates among the tables, staring, smiling, searching. She wears men's shoes and ungartered woolen stockings, falling like loose bandages along her calf. Her woolen cap is pulled into forward points, making a Viking helmet, and like a Viking's, her hair is long, loose, and dirty. Now and then she scrabbles in the depths of a battered briefcase exhumed from the depths of an even more battered brown carryall. One watches to see whether or how she will feed herself (no one will bother her if she decides to sit only for shelter) since, obviously, she must be abysmally poor. She floats, wings, pirouettes over to the counter. All right, she has somehow managed to cadge a few pennies for a cup of tea. But no, she buys cake and two cups of tea and wolfs most of the cake down on her way back to her seat. Then the flight again to the counter, where she buys two sandwiches and more tea, finishes those in a more leisured, refined way and saunters back to the counter for more. It is a relief; she is not too poor to eat, if not well, yet a good deal, and here may be one of the supreme models of the renowned English eccentric, in the flesh, in the extreme.

Sitting in the restaurant of the **National Gallery**, engulfing (it is too frail to be chewed) your sandwich strewn with Persian-miniature watercress, look out the window on Trafalgar Square. There is no square, the lions with the faces of elder statesmen are gone. The pigeons are invisible, lured and then chased by invisible children, who are chased by invisible cameras. The fountains have disappeared into tourist cameras, and the youth and its distraught hair are back in journals that freeze and examine them for sociological meanings. It all is erased by the big clean window, a "less is more" designer which cuts off all extraneous detail, leaving only the column and Nelson soaring in pure space.

## Bayswater

**Our Mutual Friend,** 10a Strathearn Place, at Hyde Park Square.

The cellar adjunct of the Victoria Tavern (p. 261), approached through facsimiles of Victorian streets and shopwindows that miraculously escape "twee." The specialty of the house is steaks of different styles, weights, and dimensions, cooked as you ask for them, followed by cheeses or one of a few carefully made desserts.          Moderate

## Chelsea, Belgravia, Knightsbridge

**Borshtch 'n' Tears,** 45 Beauchamp Place.

The studied unself-consciousness can be cute or appealing, depending on your mood (although, come to think of it, you should match mood to place or not go at all).

The menu, categorized as "starters" and "nosh proper," is Russianish, the leitmotiv announced by bowls of smetana, a very soured sour cream, also a cheese something like the Rumanian brindza combined with cream cheese. Borsch leads off, hot, quite good, and rather in Polish style, with a preponderance of cabbage. The beef Stroganoff is treated with the smetana which gives it a stronger flavor than you may be accustomed to, and the shashlik, not quite sufficiently marinated, treated with varying intensities of spices, sometimes very hot, but you can control that by a word to the waitress. You can have scampi, blini, trout, steak, stuffed cabbage, but mainly you get a warmth of proximity and sharing of other people's conversation because, like you, they are shouting to make themselves heard over the electrified guitars played by fine musicians who should be able to do without the excessive electronic aid. Usually the music is Slavic, but on Thursday nights it is *bossa nova,* Mexican longings, Paris nostalgias, and Gershwin, and the hat passed around for the musicians.

As of this writing, no reservations are accepted, but the place is open all day and quite late, doubling its cover charge after 11 P.M., maybe because food orders slope off to coffee and cake near midnight. The waitresses wear whatever they happen to see on the nearest hanger, and the customers likewise—from sweat shirt to green-velvet Charles II coat with a lavishness of gilt buttons—so come as you are, or whatever in your fantasies you think you are, *à l'anglais.*

Moderate

### 235 King's Road.

The compensation for lack of a name is streamers of French prose on the windows: INTERDIT AUX PAYSANS, LE PATRON MANGE ICI, and a paragraph to explain that the only condition of admission is that clients have a certain elegance and that they be *sympathiques.* That there be no serious misunderstanding, however, an enameled British flag and the legend "British to the core." There are no visible guards or censors to inspect for the required degrees of elegance and *sympathique*-ness; the only barrier is the line formed by the dashing, Elizabethan locals who keep the prose going on the line and from the family-style tables, in English. The repertoire is limited, the blackboard indicating which of the English and French bourgeois classics is available and, once in a while, an improvisation. The portions are generous, clearly devised by someone with intelligent taste buds, and you may share a table with the most colorful couple on King's Road, she veiled in a fall of yellow hair, wearing a minimal dress like the jacket of a Renaissance page, he in purple velvet. You eavesdrop as concentratedly as the other full voices will allow to share some of the secrets of swinging Chelsea and receive the voice of Roslyn, Long Island (the girl) and the dentalized *T*'s and *D*'s of Whitechapel in a discussion of bagels and lox.

Moderate

**Casse-Croute,** 1 Cale Street. FLA 6174. Until recently open on Sundays and still may be.

French enough and warmly lit, and the small rooms have remarkable acoustics. When the young intellectuals of the neighborhood (Chelsea) voice their many strong opinions in their rich actors' voices, you begin to wonder, once again in the numerous times, about "British reticence." The service is efficient and well mannered, and the house pâté skillfully made. Try the chicken in the style of Provence or for that matter any of the chicken variants, or if you would like sole in a heavy cream sauce, laced with shrimp, have that. The standard is generally high for the cost, the noises young and attractive, and at least one waiter beams constantly, sometimes two.        Moderate

**Rib Room,** Carlton Tower Hotel, off Sloane Street and Lowndes Square. BEL 5411.

Not even the waiters' accents (they come from Málaga or Cyprus, anyway) will betray the fact that you are not in the large, comfortable, modern dining room of a hotel in Chicago, Detroit, or Pittsburgh. The only possible giveaway is the English, constant, Yorkshire pudding, and the unchanging excellence of the quarter mile of beef that stretches before you. Go hungry and equipped with enough pounds to buy a comparable meal in the States.        High Moderate

**Massey's Chop House,** 38 Beauchamp Place. KEN 4856.
Also, 65 South Audley Street

Charcoal-broiled steaks, the essential baked potato with it, and salad. They call the long whitish spear of vegetable endive and the curly rough leaves chicory, as Americans do, rather than reverse them, as is done in England. The rooms are small, sometimes too small for the American voice-on-vacation and the heartiness induced by large slabs of meat. Quite perfect, in the integrity of its limited high quality menu, and atmosphere, for the traveling American who feels lost in purely foreign restaurants.        High Moderate

**Les Trois Canards,** 14 Knightsbridge Green. 598 0509.

In a village close near Harrod's, Sloane Street, Brompton Road. The *spécialité de la maison* is, as expected, duck. You will do well, however, with anything—the brochette of scampi or cold salmon, in season. The style, though primarily French, allows space for a minestrone and several pasta dishes, perhaps to comfort the Italian waiters, who give you peaceable, smooth service to go with the peaceable, smooth decor.        Moderate

**Alexander's,** 138A King's Road. KNI 4604.

The sign stands on the corner at the top of a set of cellar stairs that leads to a neatly arranged cellar restaurant, whose only oddity is that table candles are lit for lunch, as well as dinner. The usual translation of fish and meats into Italian and French styles appear on the menu—and flavorful Mediterranean soups. Most vividly Mediterranean are the young men who work and adorn the cellar with their smoky

locks and liquid eyes and the acquiescent, biddable Mediterranean
manner.                                                    Moderate

**Le Matelot,** 49 Elizabeth Street. SLO 1038.

There are frailties—the caneton à l'orange isn't quite—but for a
change the atmosphere doesn't strive for "difference" but contents
itself by echoing the name with fronds of fishnet and striped shirts
on the attentive, agile waiters (sometimes too attentive and agile with
a tendency to remove your plate if you stop for breath or conversation, between forkfuls). The soups—gaspacho, which is becoming a
London basic, watercress, seafood—are good, and so are the pâtés,
one of them, the pheasant pâté stiffened with plenty of garlic. Try not
to absorb too much of the French bread or the dark grainy bread
offered you out of a long basket; save some of the calorie allowance
for frozen mousse that gives off citrus airs or the especially skillful
pot au chocolat, made with curaçao and a dash of coffee, and served
with two bits of candied tangerine as lagniappe.          High Moderate

**La Popote,** 3 Walton Street. Ask DIR for telephone number.

Having meekly examined the enterprising profitable things its neighbor, Beauchamp Place, has been doing with itself, Walton Street got
into a firm girdle, plastered some fresh paint on her face, took a few
charm lessons, and—what with antique shops, dress boutiques, and
restaurants—is becoming a rival. La Popote, in mood and dress, is of
the new blossoming. Its two rooms run to pink, one pink-walled,
"pinky" lit, and small bouquets of pink roses, à la Maxim's, on the
tables. The menu is of international goodies, becoming increasingly
classic "London" for self-respecting houses. The gaspacho is authentic,
the oeufs en cocotte exquisitely flavored, and the quiche foamy and
light soufflé style. The main courses are handled with care and style
in open-handed portions, attractively arranged. The seafood brochette
has the red of a tomato, a flourish of lemon slice, and a bush of
parsley to pick up pale seafood colors. The chicken à la Kiev, its pack
of butter well contained, is fried an enticing golden-red, balanced by
the contrast of greens.

The pinks, the smiling flights of Chéri waiters, the carriage lamps,
the gold spindly chairs, fuse into a turn-of-the-century boudoir atmosphere with brothel flavor exuded by the wall picture of a girl wearing
only a cross, sweetly sad in her romantic cloud of hair, and, on the
menu, a lady in a La Goulue topknot, her nudity not at all sheltered
by the tray of apples she carries and among the apples her round
breasts.

There are some, possibly naïve questions to ask here. Why accompany the perfumed decor with growling, lady-baritone blues-rock? And why this sort of room for a clientele of gentlemen who might go to a brothel only as Proust did? And how *do* you spell avocado, gentlemen? High Moderate

**Alvaro's,** 124 King's Road. 589 6296.

Crammed after the theater with bodies whose faces you may recognize or think you should. It helps to speak Italian, not that English isn't understood, but it enhances the cordiality, usually accorded the distinguished regulars. The fettucini is fresh and seems handmade and after that, anything; the standards stay high, and that doesn't always happen to Italian cooking. High Moderate

**The Hungry Horse,** 196 Fulham Road. FLA 7757.

Another maze of cellars, with a difference, a grateful and handsome one. The geography makes for a sharing of conversations in some of the alcoves, but they are likely to be interesting; for instance, a blond flower boy trying to be open and loving with his parents down from the country and, in adroit ways, telling them nothing. The food? Lavish helpings of superb soups and salads and the rest a roaming, touched with successful inventions, in the indigenous and the continental. Another plus: It was open for lunch on Sundays; check. High Moderate

**Au Père de Nico,** 10 Lincoln Street. KNI 4704.

See what willing it will do to get you good weather, so that you can sit in the garden. Indoors is pleasant, too, for its ambience of attentive, family-run French restaurant, with a nice talent for veal and chicken. Moderate

**Chez Luba,** 116 Draycott Avenue. KEN 6523.

Sometimes gypsy music throbs; sometimes it is only the voices of guests bouncing off the walls of the narrow room. It is reported that the proprietor sings; usually he beams and talks vigorously, moving arms and tall white hat. With the goodfellowship, beef Stroganoff, borsch and piroshki, shashlik, and the butter-laden chicken Kiev. Expensive

**Daphne's,** 112 Draycott Street. 589 4257.

Dashing, jet-setty, more than a hint of theater, not in decor, but ambience. The dishes are unusual, very often, intelligently worked out and nicely served. See if you can recognize the people at the next table. (Dinners only and late.)                                    Expensive

**Parkes,** 4 Beauchamp Place. 589 1390.

No great size, no hoopla. The energy goes into steady excellence in every way. Order whatever strikes your fancy, with confidence.
                                                                     Expensive

## City

**Ristorante Pizzala,** 125 Chancery Lane.

After St. Paul's, the Temples, Dr. Johnson's House and for strength to meet the genuine excitements of the Public Record Office Museum, a dignified, calm lunch with white tablecloths in the company of law gentlemen and newspaper gentlemen, the editorial type. The menu, as is obvious from the name, is Italian, touched with the subtlety of the north rather than the garlicky earthiness of Naples. All the pasta dishes are here, of course, carefully made, and the repertoire of veal and chicken. You might settle for a large crisp salad surrounding cold seafood or meat and finish with one of the temptations luring you from the slow moving dessert wagon. The portions are lavish, but if you insist on big numerous strawberries out of season, the cost may be once again, or more, the price of your main dish.          Moderate

With a Fleet Street into the Strand exploration: the **Avery Coffee House,** Hind Court, inside 149 Fleet Street; an easy cellar place that serves secretaries and subeditors good salads, egg dishes, cheese, and coffee, cleanly and cheaply.                                          Modest

If a cup of coffee and a sandwich will do, you might take them in the **Lobby of the Mermaid Theatre,** Upper Thames Street, on the folding chairs usually used for meetings on sincere subjects. Or walk around the alley behind the theater to the waterfront **Mermaid Restaurant.** No surprises on the menu or horrors—and views on and across the hardworking, mucky, moving river. Only dinner on Saturday.
                                                                     Moderate

**Forum Restaurant,** 51 Chancery Lane.

A dignified restaurant that leans, as the name implies, to the Italian. Near the Silver Vaults and the museum that owns the Domesday Book and in the company of gentlemen who bring a weight of tradition from Lincoln's Inn and the Temple Inns, you can enjoy a smoothly paced, quiet lunch before you plunge back into frantic, thorny Fleet Street.                                                        Moderate

**Sweeting's,** 39 Queen Victoria Street. CIT 3062.

Between a visit to the Tower and St. Paul's or as a reward for climbing the Monument and enduring the summer smells of Fish Street Hill (or inspired by them), have an assortment of the seafood for which the restaurant has long been famous.              Moderate

## Covent Garden

**Boulestin,** 25 Southampton Street. TEM 7061. Open late.

Close enough to Covent Garden to pluck its vegetables off the market's carts and lorries and to feed you immediately after the ballet or opera. The menu is French, correctly and painstakingly so. One goes down and down (almost like reaching an underground platform if *those* stairs were neatly carpeted) into a dignified room of winy plush and velvet, lace curtains, and warm brown woods. The service is attentive and not uncomfortably impassioned; the hot dishes are served hot, the cold glacial; your waiter actually speaks French; the wine list and prices are honest. In short, a serious restaurant.
                              High Moderate to Expensive

**Rule's,** 35 Maiden Lane. TEM 5314. Open late.

Nothing great, not size or exquisite cuisine or service by demigods, and certainly not price, and still one of the pleasantest restaurants in London or anywhere. Sitting in coffeehouse coziness with prints of tempestuous poets, theatrical giants, sporting gents and their horses, surrounded by Edwardian froufrou that doesn't try oppressively hard, you may eat of traditional English dishes served as prodigiously large portions. Start with a substantial hill of whitebait (if you can stand the stare of dozens of tiny, accusing, fried popeyes), and go on to the jugged hair or saddle of lamb or oxtail ragout. Rule's is the place for desserts you've read about in novels: treacle tart or the famous trifle —a pastel mess of cake soaked in wine, mixed with custard and fruit, and covered with cream, a listless dish memorable only for the fact that it exists and so popularly. As a travel experience, you should have it once, but keep in mind that you don't *have* to and that Rule's makes crêpes suzettes nicely.                              Moderate

**The Garden,** 9 Henrietta Street. COV 0088.

Several cellars gutted and gaily painted and carpeted to serve post-ballet and opera audience and performers. The waiters are dashing, and so is the menu, which features bold oddities like veal stuffed with prunes and anchovies (surprisingly good if you like unexpected taste marriages) or lamb cutlets cooked with walnuts and cherries. However, one is quite safe in the British and Continental classics: grills and chops, trout with fennel, veal in sour cream, and, for dessert, lemon posset and Athole brose, a type of mousse made of cream, honey and brandy. There is a two-course menu for sixpence less than a pound; freer-ranging with an apéritif and wine will take you into . . .

High Moderate

# East End

**Bloom's,** 90 Whitechapel Road. BIS 6001.

Open and crammed on Sundays, when the line seems to start forming in the cold East End dawn, as for a Fonteyn-Nureyev performance. In Yiddishe Mamma portions, Bloom's ladles out the curls, strips and tiny pillows of Jewish pasta, the robust barley, mushroom, and lima bean soup and that substitute for love and tranquilizers, chicken soup floating golden coins of fat. The rye bread is authentically Delancey Street, and so is the chopped liver; the pickles and sausages, almost, while the corned beef everyone seems to be eating, not quite as spicy as you might be accustomed to, and masquerading as salt beef. A number of the waiters are, as usual, Spanish gentlemen who have here picked up a good number of Yiddish menu phrases. Express no surprise; as in the old joke, they may think they are learning to speak English.                    Moderate

NOTE: There is an annex in Golders Green, to the north. As crowded on Sunday, smaller and more compassionate; a waiter serves slices of salami to the lines of starving customers.

**Lon Hung,** 542 Commercial Road.

Several virtues operate here: available if you cannot get into the more famous Chinese row on Salmon Lane; open until 2 A.M., inexpensive, community tables at which you can make the acquaintance of a local prizefighter or merchant and his girl friend and hear the full, rich vowels of Stepney and its locutions. Expect no chic. The disproportionately long room is brightened only by two kinds of wallpaper and amiable waiters. The menu is the basics as you know them, except that they appear more frequently as fried balls than you might like. Ask about the mode of preparation before you design your supper.                                                                      Modest

# Islington

**Carrier's,** 2 Camden Passage, at Pierrepoint Row, near Angel Station. CAN 5353.

Robert Carrier is the man who devised the handsomely illustrated and well-boxed recipe cards, sold by category—fish, meats, sweets, etc.—and cheaply, and published the lot as a large, illustrated cookbook. Besides its intrinsic virtues, Carrier's offers two other attractions: the possibility of lunching on Saturday, after antique and souvenir hunting in Camden Passage and after-theater dining because the last orders are taken as late as eleven thirty. You *must* reserve, preferably several days in advance, because at this writing Carrier's is one of the most popular restaurants in London.

Like many London houses, Carrier's is doll-like, with a bar, a ruralish dining room, and, above, a room curtained, wallpapered, and the entrance canopied (suggesting a four-poster bed) in a soft pink French cloth of roses.

The menu is French-speaking international, offering as beginners the Greek mash of roe, tarama, or a salmon pâté, or, possibly best of all, a fruits de mer aspic to be dipped in a green sauce. One specialty of the house is broiled spiced meats as Near Eastern kebabs or kaftas, or steaks, chops, and fowl. The coq au vin is very rich and deep brown-red as it should be, or you may prefer the less emphatic boeuf à la ficelle, fillet very quickly cooked in bouillon and surrounded by vegetables. Dessert? If they have any left, the cold chocolate soufflé, one of the pillars of the house, or as satisfactory substitute, lemon posset.

The wine list is not extensive but exclusive, and if you're feeling Rothschildian, should add two pounds or more to the dinner bill (about three pounds per and worth it). One doesn't go to Carrier's to economize, but to enjoy, other than the expert cuisine, the softly bubbling gaiety in the atmosphere, the murmur of success, the happy spirits of your well-heeled compatriots.                            Expensive

## Kensington, Fulham

**The Chinese Lantern,** 4 Thackeray Street. WES 4981.

In an engaging tangle of little streets, itself appropriately little. Considering how small the stage is, the production is quite elaborate: a bead curtain shivering in the night air, arrangements of mellow lights, a willowy spread of leafage suggesting Chinese paintings, and, from somewhere, recorded Chinese music. There is no menu; you lend yourself to, and participate in, the succession of scenes. The meal opens with dumplings in a bamboo boatlet, goes on to soup from a Korean pot which steams on the table, followed by an array of small dishes of noodles, ribs, meats and vegetables, chicken, shrimp balls, ending with litchis. Tea, out of a lovely pot, comes constantly. During the eating, successive steps of a ceremony that includes the unfolding of a small bamboo screen that welcomes women with a compliment; they are "flowers in the garden." Subsequently each dish is named and the mixtures therein described in polite, ceremonious fashion. For scenery, stagecraft, compliments, and satisfying Chinese tastes, the cost is . . .                                          Moderate

**Tandoori,** 151 Fulham Road. Ask DIR for phone number.

Down a few steps, guided by a turbaned gentleman, to one of the prettiest restaurants in London: the dewlike spray of light from pierced lamps, drawings of dancing girls in panels on the wall, Madras plaids for tablecloths and napkins, discreet suggestions if you want them, independence of study and choice if you prefer that. The emphasis is northern—Punjabi—but if you'd like your curry to a southern heat of gasping tastelessness, that can be arranged. Start with the excellent chicken Tandoori (shared around if there are two or more of you), one of the best manners of handling that versatile bird, steeped in spices, one of which paints it a brilliant red; then go on to your choice of one of the skillfully made curries served in a dignified, attentive manner, considerably different from the nervous and ill-tempered, or obsequious, or intimate that at times seem to be the occupational diseases of Indian restaurants.              Moderate

**Maggie Jones's,** 6 Old Court Place, at Kensington Church Street, near Kensington High. WES 6462. Reserve.

Rumor whispers that the quality of the cooking is a shade more exalted on week-nights, but not to worry; the weekend quality can be distinguished, rivaling the achievements of its sibling, the Poule au Pot (p. 299).

The food is a promising compromise, a gratifying confusion of French and English elements. The English steak-and-something pie is here translated into very good beef, mushrooms, a self-respecting Frenchified flaky crust, and courageous flavors. A scampi dish, treated to cream and burning in brandy is as satisfactory as you'd find it in a Normandy restaurant or Paris. The soups, particularly those listed on the blackboard for the day, rove off the well-trodden paths successfully. If it is available, have the cold cucumber soup, served in a wine *ballon,* or the spinach soup, and finish with the chocolate mousse or the English sweet—the summer pudding of bread (light and sparse here), apples, raspberries, currants, and a red fruit sauce made pink by the inevitable, and here welcome, brook of cream. Along with banter with the young French waiters here to study English, the bill will be—for food, 10 percent service, and a carafe of good house wine—about two pounds per person.    Moderate

**Fu Tong,** 29 Kensington High Street. WES 8448.

A comfort because, like other Chinese restaurants, it doesn't care about going to sleep or resting on Sundays; when no one else seems to want to feed you in London, the Chinese will. Again, don't order fried shrimp balls or pork balls or any of the vapid, greasy little things. Stay with the vegetable and chicken, the beef and pork dishes, the spareribs and fried rice. Incidentally, here, as elsewhere in London, they seem to serve no duck sauce or for that matter much of any sauce. Ask for catsup and mustard, always available and, since it will be English, almost as hot as the Chinese.       High Moderate

**Nick's Diner,** 88 Ifield Road. FLA 0930. Reserve (as you should in the companion restaurant described below).

In a narrow house (it is amazing how much living and thinking, inventing and writing were done in these slots), from whose several levels there may emerge world-renowned theater figures you would not ordinarily associate with basements. The young men who wait on table sport a singular array of nonhaircuts and thoroughly informal shirts, a fact that leaves one somewhat unprepared for their sophistication about food and wine and their efficiency. The portions are large, almost affectionate, out of a limited and always trustworthy menu. After the very good fish bisque or a dish of marinated mushrooms spiced with anchovies, try the massive double lamb chops or the French saddled steak, the filet de boeuf en croûte or the gate of spare ribs, served with two sauces to mix to the heat or mildness you need. Under the immense smile of "Charlot" on a poster, equipped with a bottle of wine from the overhead racks which serve for cellar, you will do well and happily.　　　　High Moderate

**The Place Opposite,** 65 Ifield Road (opposite Nick's Diner, a very close relative). 3520119. Dinner only; closed Sunday. Reserve.

With a subtle instinct for the fine line between too much and too little informality, the waiters here (and at Nick's) create a welcoming warmth that goes well with the old books and prints, the presence of wood, and on the sideboard an array of delicacies from which you may have a sample if you don't quite know what to order and the restaurant and waiters are not yet too busy. Having selected some of the best dishes of several countries, they play occasional tricks with them that turn out to be imaginative and highly satisfactory treatments. All ingredients are carefully described, with some little contrived joke often attached (like threatening to make quiche with treacle and whiskey), which shouldn't at all mar your pleasure, nor should the inverse snobbism of calling hors d'oeuvres "starters" and desserts "puds." There is something about the ambience that makes it instantly forgivable and the fact that the lemon spinach soup and the quiche of crab or asparagus or any of the pâtés are delicious, whether they are called starters or not. But maybe you should have ceviche (the Spanish *escabeche*), not quite as spicy as you would have it in Latin America but a reasonable facsimile.

Searching the continent the Place returns to you with fritto misto, the Provençal bourride, calf's kidneys, a sturdy osso buco and the kind of beef Stroganoff your Sunday evening hostess with the new chafing dish can't quite achieve. As for desserts and wine, let the prose and your young waiter-host guide you.　　　　High Moderate

**Tamarisk,** 95 Old Brompton Road. KEN 7806. Reserve.

The complexities shared by Tamarisk and its companion restaurant is as confusing as the Hampton Court maze and more colorful. Having been guided into a decor that suggests Scheherazade and harem balconies, you are given a fan-shaped menu printed with motifs reminiscent of Persian miniatures. Reading among the flowers and birds and blossoming trees, you find listings like scimitara, okrochka, sakara, nefetiti, fawzia, Sheba's feast, introductions to the culinary terrain in which you will be wandering, the Near Eastern and North African. (If for political or tribal reasons even such a tenuous link with the Arab world disturbs you, be assured that the proprietor is a Persian Jew.) Every blending of sesame mash and aubergine, black olives and chick-peas, saffron and lentils; chopped lamb and marinated lamb, skewered or stewed; couscous and honey; curry and chili; steaks treated with unexpected herbs; stuffed vine leaves and okra; hot flat breads, as well as the desserts of thin pastry and thick layers of nuts floating in honey, is carefully described on the fan menu. The musical accompaniment you might expect would be veiled ladies plucking dulcimers, and there is a belly dancer, at times two. But the steadiest artists are a guitarist and drummer, skilled, engaging gentlemen, one of whom sings blues, French songs, and Mexican songs in confident approximate accents. As the evening wears on, he delves back to Thirties songs—Gershwin, Cole Porter, Rodgers —that rend the middle-aged heart, particularly responsive after the large meal.

Somewhere in the complex premises is a cellar which expands the musical scene with two other guitarists and singers of Mexican songs. For the price of a drink or two, if you can manage them, the nostalgia gives way to beautiful Tehuantepec dirges, alternating with the restless, driving rhythms of Veracruzana dances. It rounds out a full, and pleasantly bewildering evening, which, excluding the cost of Mexican joys and sorrows, should cost a sum that would come to . . .

High Moderate

**Oats,** 4 Hollywood Road, off Fulham Road. 352 0185. Reserve.

Closed at lunchtime and Sunday, but kind about staying open late, when it is open. A long room, attractively wallpapered (in spite of the fact that by this time one is thoroughly tired of A-t N-----u and its imitators), candlelight, and, deep in the back, a comfortable small lounge for drinking and waiting your turn. The waiters and waitresses seem to be illegally young for their jobs, but are seriously solicitous, polite, and competent. The menu is not large, and if you want the privilege of coming very late, some of the dishes may be out, but if you avoid the peculiarities of what is considered here champignons à la grec, you will do quite well with what the kitchen can turn out at tired midnight. Don't try for a snack or cake and coffee; you must go the full three-step course; worth it, if only for the proximity of young people in Mao jackets of French satins and royal encrustations, handembroidered and jewel studded raja coats, possibly authentic.

Moderate

**Trattoo,** 2 Abingdon Road, immediately south of Kensington High Street. WES 4448.

A clever designer seems to have cut a couple of houses longitudinally, left part of an upper story as a balcony, set in a small comfortable bar above and away from the eating area and hung the cool, airy space with cascades of fresh vine. It sounds and might be roomy and quiet, but it is basically an Italian restaurant and as noisy as any of its kind. But the noise here comes from the golden faces of Knightsbridge-Kensington *jeunesse dorée,* of the small satin and rosebud houses on and around Montpelier Square, Trevor Square, the Ennismores, and other tangles of mews, south of Kensington Gardens. Besides the company of the minor gods and goddesses in Dionysian mood, a well-balanced menu borrowed from a number of other cuisines and Italianized; spareribs barbecued as the Chinese do them with a different sauce from theirs; the French chicken in cream wrapped in pancakes, treated with Italian spices. You may dine (make a reservation) as late as twelve (including Sundays) and be as Italian or swinging as you like.　　　　　　　High Moderate to Expensive

## St. Marylebone, Swiss Cottage, Hampstead

**The Elysée Restaurant,** 13 Percy Street. 636 4804; 580 3988. Reserve.

The roof garden, not the high splendor the phrase might suggest, but rather a homely arrangement (and a rarity in London), offers you possible rain, a menu of somewhat "French" dishes and a few of the Greek's staples: moussaka, taramasalata, aubergine with lamb, charcoal-broiled lamb chops (three) nicely spiced. You can have your coffee downstairs, in the room with the pianist, the fiddler, and bouzouki player and a lusty, indefatigable singer. Between her rounds you can dance Latin, or try out the steps you learned in the taverns of Hydra or watching Greek movies, or simply sit and clap your hands with the rhythm while a group of middle-aged clients, accompanied by unlikely women, become the passionate, carefree Zorba. Through it all sits a meager elderly man, accompanied by blooded champagne in a bucket and a large blond girl who has the archaic disdainful profile and the regal roundnesses that might have been the Greek Helen's. They continue not to smile or grimace, or speak or look at each other, as they have not been doing through the last hour of bouncy, inexpert imitations of *Never on Sunday.*

Because it is a late place, neither forbiddingly expensive nor requiring the cost and rigmarole of membership, the entertainment section —where one can eat, too—is likely to be crowded, especially on weekends. Moderate

**Odin's,** 29 Devonshire Street, off Marylebone High Street. Reserve.

Suppress the immediate distrust evoked by a ceilingful of black and red umbrellas, the lamp made of a wooden bust with a tube for a head, and the wooden legs on the wall. The kitchen doesn't fly off into kink; it is "with it" only in the literal meaning, doing its serious best with onion soup and the creamy avocado soup; a superior rack of lamb, entrecote, and veal in various careful styles. Odin's has an un-English regard for the separate identities of cooked vegetables and serves them decoratively, with a generous hand, in the company of more than decent carafe wines. Moderate

**The Light of India,** 59 Park Road, north of Baker Street.

No glamor, no Taj Mahal inlays, or leering gods. Simply a knowing, honest way with a considerable number of dishes, a particularly interesting set of vegetables, and customers who provide a good cross section of London intellectual life. Modest to Moderate

Should you have wandered to Swiss Cottage for a drink in the enormous chalet-style pub whipped by the traffic of one of the most complex and hazardous of London crossings, or to see the beautiful Indian children dragging the shopping carts of their beautifully wrapped mothers on Finchley Road and the elderly German refugees talking over pastry and coffee in the goulash and strudel restaurants, or to have a stultified look at the dour, red-brick, lightless, airless, insane excrescences that were grand houses seventy and eighty years ago on Eton Avenue, and you want a cheap, decent Indian meal (one pound for two persons, or less), try the **New Delhi,** 13 New College Parade, a strip of Finchley Road. And don't mind the infinitely tragic stare of the busboy and the busy social life of a waiter, who may spend much of your time on his telephone. Modest

**Le Cellier du Midi,** 28 Church Row. 435 9998. Dinner only.

The room is low and heavy-beamed, the walls bulky; in fact, probably a fair facsimile of a Provençal cellar with cuisine to match, zesty, flavorful southern French. There was, at this writing, no wine on the premises, but the boys who buy it somewhere or other on this Georgian row are fleet and attractive as Mercury. High Moderate

**Keats,** 3 Downshire Hill. 435 3544. Dinner only.

In the warm, reddish glow of two rooms that resemble a rich man's plaything barn, thoughtful planning and cooking, the emphasis French in menu and devotion to the pleasures of dining, rather than eating.
Expensive

**The Huntsman,** 15 Flask Walk. AM 0796.

Go for dinner with an appetite and a palate primed for adventure. The specialties are regional hunting-shooting British. For the timid there is Scotch salmon and grills, but try what they do in East Anglia with a hare or a Scot's way with grouse. High Moderate

**Cordon Bleu Restaurant,** 31 Marylebone Lane.

Attached to the cooking school, and if what it serves to the public for lunch are reasonable samples, everyone should join. The fish mousses, the ragouts, the salads, and desserts can occasionally reach nectar spheres. Go early, as do the ladies who shop on Wigmore Street. Moderate

In addition to Indian and *Mittel-Europaisch,* Swiss Cottage has a small and surprisingly good Chinese restaurant, the **Mandarin,** and across the street from it, the **Malaysia**—both a short distance north of Finchley Road Station and both inexpensive.

## Piccadilly, Mayfair

**The Empress,** 15 Berkeley Street. MAY 6126.

A sister of the noble group that includes the Caprice and the Ecu de France (or did—these matters change), a calm, wide field for lunching among the expense accounts. The service is many-manned and devout; the array of glasses and cutlery gleams like Park Avenue skyscrapers, the menu lists numerous worldly delights of *haute cuisine.* So why, with all that attention and equipment, cannot they put creamed spinach into a dish of its own so that it may not float into and melt with the wine, cream and mushroom flavors of the fish? Or is it the belief that in "Continental" cooking, where one sauce is good, two are better? Expensive

**Martinez,** 25 Swallow Street. REG 5066.

Considering how many Spaniards there are working in London, it seems strange that there are few Spanish restaurants. Maybe Spanish waiters and waitresses are saving their money to open temples of "Inglis rosbif" and "yawksir puddin'" in Seville. At any rate, the Martinez is about as authenic as there is, in the style of grillwork, Spanish tiles, somewhere a Don Quixote, somewhere else a castle in Spain. The menu parallels the decor with paella, arroz con pollo, gaspacho, and fish in earthy sauces, to go with the satisfying—no *grand cru*—Spanish wines.                                      Moderate

**Trader Vic's,** London Hilton, Park Lane. HYD 7586.

There is a wealth of exoticism here, most of it quite good, to forage in. There are Polynesian things and Malayan and Indian and Tahitian and Indonesian, Chinese, of course, and Russian borsch, *pour le sport,* and beluga caviar (two guineas a portion) *pour les sports.* No fewer than eight styles of dressing are available for the salads and a wide range of vegetables, from Chinese snow peas and water chestnuts to potatoes hash-browned or in a style called bedspring. You probably have your own Oriental favorites, which will be supplied, or try the Malayan bits of beef, the brochette orientale, the mild shrimp curry, the almond duck, the Fiji beef, or anything from the large, informative menu that strikes your fancy and purse and seems to enter the spirit of the darkish rooms hung with Polynesian oars, Malaysian glass floats, and carved with dour Polynesian gods.          Expensive

**Tiberio Restaurant,** 22 Queen Street. MAY 3561.

By way of a bold, good-looking ornament of Italian ceramic you go down to a vast ramble and the spirited decibels indigenous to Italian restaurants. The menu is classic of the various regions of Italy, except for a few international treasures like caviale finissimo della nuova pesca, and foie gras di strasburgo. You'll find the poor man's southern dishes of bits of fried bread, plus odds and ends—and very good—like mozzarella in carrozza or carrozella alla Lucania, as well as Frenchified delicacies, such as a brioche filled with seafood, cream, and lobster sauce, with a bit of truffle in it and a remarkable treatment of tripe. Between the extremes, the full range of pastas with meaningful sauces, zuppa di pesce, treatments of liver, chicken, and the variety of veal dishes, all cooked with the skill that Joe's around the corner hasn't the help, knowledge, or time for. Joe's will charge you less, of course, but then he won't be able to afford the truffles and wines that go into sauces, nor will he know how to make an artichoke soufflé or prepare frogs' legs in hazelnut butter and crushed almonds.                                              High Moderate

**A L'Ecu de France,** 111 Jermyn Street. WHI 2837.

Glittering, crowded, and built to augment other people's conversations and muffle your own. The opening fanfare—a display of scampi the size of crayfish, a huge Parma ham, and a theatrical array of hors d'oeuvres—introduces the major themes, costly French cooking and careful service, when the waiters can move between the tables. Have the scampi (carefully, you are charged per piece), boeuf en croûte, or any of the styles of sole or duck.                    Expensive

**Connaught Hotel,** Carlos Place. GRO 7070.

The polished wood, kindly light, and maestro-type waiters and the very high reputation of the Connaught make you feel rich and decorative. Don't go on a bank holiday weekend, even though it may be one of the few places open; the waiters don't like working, nor do the cooks put their hearts into it. It is certainly not bad, but only the wine list stays *haute* and the price.                    Expensive

**Chez Solange,** 35 Cranbourn Street. TEM 5886.

Reserve. Small, busy, attractive, and French.                    Moderate

**The Pastoria Hotel,** St. Martin's Street.
Serves on Sunday evenings and well.                    Moderate

**Sheekey's,** 29 St. Martin's Court, off St. Martin's Lane and Charing Cross Road.
Venerated by theatrical locals; as plain as your hand and immutably trustworthy. Have anything that strikes your fancy among the specialties of seafood and fish.                    Modest to Moderate

# Soho

**Dumpling Inn,** corner of Macclesfield and Gerrard streets. Dial DIR for phone number.

A small room decorated with long panels of Venetian canal scenes and a menu of quite other exotica: hors d'oeuvres of jellyfish blubber, soya pig's maw, and listings of sliced belly, family style; shark's fins; sea cucumber; bêche-de-mer; sweet-sour fish à la squirrel; quick-fried pig's kidney. It is not easy to find out exactly what these enticements mean, but you will find self-explanatory items like dumplings and noodles. Fortified by such dishes and the superb chicken with cashew nuts, take a chance on the sliced belly, family style, in spite of the hideous picture it evokes, to find that it is a dish of thick sliced bacon cooked in a delicately spiced brew. For the satisfactions of well-cooked familiar dishes and adventure, the cost will be, depending on your appetite and courage . . . Modest to Moderate

**Braganza,** 56 Frith Street. GER 2706.

When other members of the Wheeler family (the stack of miniature and engaging rooms at 19 Old Compton Street or Antoine's at 40 Charlotte Street) are getting ready for closing and sleep, this Portuguese relation feeds after-theater diners. The cuisine, the Wheeler treatments of seafood with its improvisations on the theme of sole—with spinach, with a combination of prawns, lobsters, mushrooms, and wine, bedded in white grapes, etc.—have nothing to do with Portugal, but the former inhabitants did. They were a group organized by their government to publicize Portuguese wines, and that accounts for the tiles and floral panels, the presence of Vasco da Gama, and the name of the nonproductive wife of Charles II, Catherine of Braganza, who was returned to rule Portugal, instead. But of present matters: try any handling of sole, the simple as satisfactory as the complex, with smoked trout and horseradish sauce as an opening and a sweet pancake folded on fresh fruit and rum for the closing. High Moderate

**Chez Victor,** 45 Wardour Street. GER 6523.

Plainish, oldish, bistroish, and much loved by a number of Londoners who rarely leave seats empty for others. You should reserve, and expect the dishes you would find in a middle-class French household (crusty bread; coarse flavorful pâté maison; vegetables left alive; tender sweetbreads; and pink gigot), where food and wine are highly respected and frills not at all. Moderate

**Gay Hussar,** 2 Greek Street. GER 0973.

Intimate and attractive in an effortless way and popular. The *prix fixe* lunch is a bargain—Bulgar salad (sausage peeping through cabbage and beans), leading to Hungarian pork with red cabbage or a Yugoslav fish dish or chicken smothered in cream, among a number of Central European inventions. Desserts are less distinguished; have the cheese, to round out what is quite and pleasantly enough.
Low Moderate

**Boulogne,** 27 Gerrard Street. GER 3186.

Greek, Armenian, Slavic, Italian, French, an English dish or two
in a quiet, warm ambience untouched—so far—by Soho's striving
hoopla.                                                          Moderate

**La Terrazza,** 19 Romilly Street. 437 8991.

Currently one of the places to be seen and to see. Consequently
crowded, but that doesn't seem to impair its efficiency, its good temper,
and excellent Italian cooking.                          High Moderate

**La Dolce Vita,** 10 Frith Street. 437 2774.

Harvesttime in Pesaro moved to London: singers and trellises, brouhaha and "Funiculi Funicula," and, if you can find the time for them
among the distractions, Neapolitan dishes not yet vitiated by Anglo-
phile cooks.                                            High Moderate

**Mon Plaisir,** 21 Monmouth Street. TEM 7243.

Coq au vin, escalope de veau, boeuf bourguignonne, the French
basics as they might be cooked—and in the same sort of place—in the
Fifth *Arrondissement* of Paris.                                Moderate

Should Bloom's in Whitechapel be trailing a line down to Mile End
and its relative in Golders Green be too distant, consider **Goode's,** on
Berwick Street. It cannot boast a chef whom Princess Margaret tried
to lure out of Whitechapel (he refused to leave), but it will serve you
a reasonable facsimile of what Mama used to make. And if they won't
have you, order a salt beef sandwich at **Blume's,** on Foubert's Place.

A companion, **Grahame's Sea Fare Restaurant,** 38 Poland Street,
makes do with fish presented in a number of Jewish styles, although
you may order it as you prefer, always with the assurance that it is
exceedingly fresh. With the fish comes a mountain of chips unless you
hold it off, salads, pickled vegetables, potato pancakes, and, among the
desserts, one of the favorite forms of culinary bomb, noodle pudding.
This might be the place to mention the fact that gefilte fish is frequently
fried as a large round brown ball in London, a dreadful treatment for
what can be, properly prepared, a large helping of the French que-
nelle. Explain carefully that you want the uncoated, unmolested variety.

For the above the cost should be Low Moderate unless you have an
inordinate appetite for these versions of mother's milk.

## Regent's Park

**Barque and Bite,** beyond the zoo on Prince Albert Road. GUL 8137. One of the few open summertime Sundays. Reserve.

The charm of walking onto a quiet, seemingly empty boat on the canal, then descending to its innards of tables and people, would incline one to make concessions about the food. No need to. The dishes out of local and Continental eating habits are thoroughly satisfactory, the wines good, the portions lavish. For all this and the impulse—which you needn't suppress if you do it *sotto voce*—to sing on the waters. High Moderate

## Victoria

**Villa dei Cesari,** 135 Grosvenor Road. TAT 7453. Closed Monday.

The menu is a red-ribboned scroll of heavy paper roughly cut to resemble parchment, the waiters wear quasi-tunics, the decor is a chaos of Pompeian, and the dishes have Latin names. The kitchen, undazzled, sticks to the business of producing well the Italian classics like *cozzae marinorum, pollus delicatum caesarum,* and *vitellus catapultatis.* As well, a cartful of alluring *dolciorum* and seductive dance music, often produced by Latins from the farthest-flung area of Latinity, Afro-Cuban. High Moderate to Expensive

**Poule au Pot,** 231 Ebury Street. SLO 7763.

Related to Maggie Jones's (p. 288); like that restaurant, rural French in decor, affability, and the keen palates which design the dishes set before you. High Moderate

## Here and There

A group of **Friends** restaurants, all Chinese and related on Salmon Lane and West India Dock Road (via Commercial Road). For **New Friends** which serves late, as they all do, reserve (EAS 3366). If you want a Chinese feast, order it the day before. Better yet, go on Sunday for lunch with the scrubbed lovely children of Chinese families, and then spend a little time at St. Anne's Limehouse Church, of the marvelously talented Hawksmoor.                                               Moderate

Of the many restaurants that sit cheek by jowl on Charlotte Street and its neighbors, consider: among the numerous Greek kebab establishments, that at 95 Charlotte (Modest); for German food, **Schmidt's,** 41 Charlotte (Moderate); **Trattoria dei Pescatori,** 57 Charlotte (High Moderate; reserve), and, as the name tells you, Italian with a talent for seafood; **Étoile,** 30 Charlotte (High Moderate; reserve), often as French as one can get, in unaffected bourgeois cuisine, in London; **Antoine's,** 40 Charlotte (High Moderate; reserve), one of the Wheeler group (p. 297), and that means a dozen ways of dealing with sole and considerate handling of the rest of the tribe; **La Belle Meunière,** 5 Charlotte (High Moderate), again reliably French; and **White Tower,** Percy Street (Expensive; reserve), long famous and popular, mainly Greek dishes, but not bound within the national borders.

**Carrs in the Strand,** east of the Aldwych Theatre.

A breathless little place with an indefatigable waitress who runs from table to bar to an invisible kitchen, trying to press her comfortable bulk behind backs, between narrow tables, and past shoulders at the bar to serve a plate of hors d'oeuvres or a variety of salads based on veal and ham pie, crab or prawn, or smoked salmon, or chicken, or beef, or pork. If you know you'll want cheese, order it along with your salad, and if you are in a hurry, you may have to skip the coffee. Order beer, instead, because the lunchtime crush of customers, many of them regulars, makes for long pauses between each step of a meal.
                                                                          Moderate

**Yard Arm Club,** aboard the *Hispaniola,* Victoria Embankment. TRA 3011.

For being rocked by the Thames in an attractive dining room of a moored ship, with good Spanish grillwork and black tablecloths, attentive Spanish waiters, a ceiling that shines of hundreds of small lights, and the company of gulls and barges. The menu is Spanish and infinitely better than the slapdash arrangements masked by too much spice one frequently finds in Spain; try especially the treatments of fish (the cold merluza to begin with, possibly) and the stuffed peppers, the garlic soup, and any of the salads. The desserts seem to give out readily, but to balance that, the ship is open for both lunch and dinner on Sundays, as well as every other day, the presence of Spanish gentlemen at lunch for the note of authenticity and the lolling and lapping of the gray old river.                                               Moderate

Claridge's Hotel, Brook Street, serves smorgasbord lunches in its light, airy **Causerie,** for about eighteen shillings, a drink (their list) and coffee included. Not as varied or exclusive, yet quite satisfactory for its low price, a similar lunch at **Dickins and Jones Department Store,** on Regent Street.

Tea at any of the leading hotels is apt to be a decorous ritual which tends to broaden American *a*'s and, in any case, a useful meal if you are going on to a seven thirty curtain and supper later. The **Ritz** tea is currently—and deservedly—in high favor, but you might find it also diverting to take tea at the **Charing Cross Hotel**—an endless supply of tea, sandwiches and cakes and a view onto Dr. Johnson's candidate for the crossroads of the world.

For inexpensive Indian and Chinese meals, served all day Sunday, examine the possibilities of Westbourne Grove near Queensway.

For lunching in Southwark, **The Boot and Flogger,** 101 Borough High Street, whose signs tell you that they serve "Ham on the Bone," "Coffee from the Best Estates," and "Wines from the Wood, sold by the glass, bottle, hogshead, butt and pipe."

Orthodox Brahmin vegetarian meals are served in the **Sharuna Hotel,** near the British Museum.

Hamburgers, plain and fancy (one Greek café owner translates it from moussaka by adding mashed potatoes and a Near Eastern sauce to the ground meat), are easy to find. So is pizza, too frequently Anglified, and pancakes as served forth by Italian- and Spanish-staffed "American" restaurants. A newer development is the baked potato parlor (there is one on Chancery Lane and another on Marylebone High Street), which may proliferate into many that demonstrate what can be done with a spud once it emerges from the oven.

# 37    Shopping

One shops not only for objects, but also for the location of a shop in a shy or picturesque, or both, mews; the shop itself swells of old dimpled glass, black ironwork, and proud lettering or a hot jungle of kink. It might be the ripe Cockney of a Petticoat Lane vendor admiring a lady shopper with "Aooo! Wot a gowgeous faice!" and being addressed as "love" by him, or the affability of an elderly specialist, or the generosity of time and information, as if he had nothing else to do, of a leading dealer in eighteenth-century furniture. It might be the anachronistic integrity that points out a flaw where you might not have found it or a sign, as you explore Mayfair, that says, POLITE REMINDER: NO PARKING, PLEASE. It might be walking past the repeated pattern of lions, shields, and adornments imbedded in the windows and walls of Mayfair, the royal warrants—the first one recorded was issued to a clockmaker in 1692—that symbolize royal patronage and approval.

Were there but world enough and time—and money—one could furnish a sybaritic connoisseur's life out of **Christie's** (8 King Street) and **Sotheby's,** the relative of New York's Parke-Bernet (34–35 New Bond Street) auction houses. Between them one can pick up a Turner, cases of fine wines, Chinese and English porcelains, Etruscan and Greek antiquities, jewels of the Queen Mother of Rumania, a three-inch chessman for ten thousand pounds. (Incidentally the *cognoscenti* say it is better that a porter bid for you, and give him a good tip if he gets your coveted gem. This system supposedly confuses the knowing dealers bidding against you. Doubtful.)

Tributaries of the treasure streams that flow from great houses find their way to **Bonham's,** on Montpelier Street; the **Motcomb Galleries,** on Motcomb Street; **Phillips Son & Neale** and **Puttick & Simpson,** both at 7 Blenheim Street (at New Bond); **Knight, Frank and Rutley,** 20 Hanover Square; **Harrod's warehouses,** at Arundel Terrace, near Hammersmith Bridge (catalogues available at the store on Brompton Road), to mention only a few regularly listed, along with an occasional sale from a Thames wharf on Clink Street, famous for Oriental rugs.

Having bought or failed to buy a royal tiara listed as "very important" jewelry, you might see what there is to buy on Bond Street, Old and New, and its golden tangents: Grafton into Dover and

302

Albemarle, the Brutons (Street, Lane, and Place), Curzon Square, Sackville and Vigo, Savile Row and Cork Street, Conduit, Maddox and St. George; and across Piccadilly, Jermyn, Bury, St. James's, Duke Street, King Street, not to mention Brook, Davies, the Audleys, and the Moltons. It is a long ramble—through paintings, jewelry, furniture, clothing, antiquarian books, old and new silver, venerable, awesomely serious tailors—and a fascinating one, to see how rich London can seem in spite of wage freezes and layoffs and the melting pound. Time and energy lacking, you can get something of a quintessence by strolling the aristocratic, flower-hung Burlington Arcade and the Princes and Piccadilly arcades, all on Piccadilly, and of dimmer luster and great appeal, Shepherd Market, off Curzon Street.

Not for shopping, but not to be missed: About where Vigo Street of the silver and rugs decides to change its name to Burlington Gardens, facing Savile Row, one finds an unimposing, old-fashioned rural station, sitting next to the rippled glass and glossy black paint fronting a flower shop. This was the Piccadilly stop for Hackney carriages, and a sign, dated January, 1897, still measures the local distances covered by the service. Beyond the sign, one of London's numerous, persistent anachronisms, this one hiding behind the behemoth buses and shopwindows of Piccadilly, is the Albany, where Macaulay and Byron once lived. It is a private walk, but one can get a look in to see the low lantern-hung wooden arcade and the entrance to the houses, similarly sheltered with arches that echo the incurved pagodas (highly favored in the Chinoiserie craze of its time), and the long, narrow stretches of carefully kept hedge, the neat window boxes, and the water pipes that streak down between the houses, bound in vines.

Almost as rich as Mayfair but not quite as full or splendid a cornucopia are the shopping streets of the Knightsbridge area: Knightsbridge turning into Brompton Road, Sloane Street, and the double layer of boutiques on Beauchamp Place, off Brompton Road a short distance southwest of Harrod's.

Red-bricked **Harrod's** dominates Kensington and Knightsbridge and casts its stern shadow on Belgravia and neighboring Chelsea. It dominates not only with its presence and Valhalla food halls but with its legends, too; its size ("largest in world"); its bank and postal service in a large area where people have been known to sit and read comfortably for hours; its myth that Harrod's will send one egg to a charge customer at three o'clock in the morning if requested; its regal apologies for the errors which, in astonished horror, they tell you cannot have happened; the apologies replete with pinstriped bowing, conveyance by an entourage of tall, top-hatted, green-coated doormen, gestures of courtesy and pomp that translate the taxi they may pay for to sedan chair. Thus, it earns the right to be high-priced and to cloak a few of its salespeople in coats of glacial disdain.

Although they are not strictly in the neighborhood, the glamor supermarkets of antiques, *objets,* and peculiar clothing that serve Knightsbridge and its neighbor, Kensington, are the curving hill of Kensington Church Street, King's Road in Chelsea, Pimlico Road, Fulham Road, and in Belgravia, the golden web made by the Halkins, Motcomb and Pont streets.

Assuming that your Saturday 10 A.M. to 3 P.M. can be magically and infinitely stretched and you have been on Portobello Road (pp. 178–80), there is for consideration the more authentic and less self-conscious market of Church Street between Edgware Road and Lisson Grove. If for no other reason, it might be of interest because it belongs to the neighborhood in which Henry Higgins placed Eliza Doolittle by the sound of her full wailing diphthongs. At Edgware Road the market is mainly fruits, vegetables, canaries, flowers, and cheap clothing. Beyond Salisbury Street deep caverns of secondhand clothing, accompanied by derelict furniture and books, the combination arising to a grand *tutti* at its finish where two raised walks holding an incredible miscellany appear. But here and there, and more and more, a good piece of jewelry, an unusual small vase, a handsome plate stare out of the dismal heaps, and Bell Street, an adjunct of the market, is showing symptoms of ambition, indulging in fancy lettering and startling names, seeing itself an embryo King's Road. Maybe.

Among the stalls of silver, china, bric-a-brac in Camden Passage in Islington, there are a few shops that seriously concentrate, many on Victoriana, charm, elderly trifles, bead snakes, mother-of-pearl encrusted papier-mâché chairs and tip tables, frames made of small seashells—like the **Boutique Fantasque** and the **Corner Cupboard,** 14 Pierrepoint Arcade. Of a more recent time are the objects that drop, hang, and loll on the first stall in the Pierrepoint Arcade, whose shaky uprights quiver with plumes over a regal old coat of the servitor in a great house (the buttons are of hand-wrapped silk cord), a ring-closed sovereign purse, beaded satin slippers, and nearer still in time, a batik blouse.

Still another antiques market—Fridays only—is the old **Caledonian,** now known as **Bermondsey** for its street near London Bridge Station and proud of the legend (which probably is centuries old, and stems from a time when Southwark, its borough, was a refuge for thieves) that it is free of police search. The knowing will tell you that 5 or 6 A.M. is the time to go for beating out the dealers, but 9 o'clock will do for digging out a choice Chinoiserie box, an eighteenth-century eyeglass, a magnificent Japanese belt, and an African artifact that bears no resemblance to the clichés pouring out of crafts factories. Then there is the rewarding antiques supermarket on Barrett Street in Marylebone, bordered by the seclusive appeal of St. Christopher Place and its shops, and, when the weather is good, adorned by the outdoor tables of a coffee shop and a pub. Chelsea's King's Road nestles a small compendium of its works in a supermarket entered at No. 243 (a short distance beyond the Town Hall).

The greatest antiques market is temporary—the annual Antique Dealers' Fair at Grosvenor House, usually the last two weeks in June. And watch also for the Chelsea Antiques Fair in the Chelsea Town Hall.

Soho, habitually dedicated to strip, movies called *Vice Girls, Ltd.* or *Strange Compulsion,* good cheeses and foreign groceries, cheap wine from unexpected places and exporting its Carnaby Street wonders, has added what it terms antiques in two markets: a neglected drab at 22 Kingly Street and another, a bit more radiant, in St. Anne's Court. (A happier way to spend Soho time is to listen to its languages, look into its faces, watch white-coated men rushing movie-film cans along Wardour Street and, on the same street, peering into a beauty salon that neatens the local strippers and takes care of the boys—wigs and native hair—who want to be those girl strippers.)

And keep in mind that Hampstead (Heath Street) has a new supermarket, and back of four large caryatids Kensington High Street is gathering still more of old, oldish, and, maybe, ancient things.

One can, of course, forget the search for specifics and allow oneself to be diverted to a search for Londonness in the markets of Leather Lane (Holborn), off the high streets of Islington and Camden Town, flanking the Old Vic Theatre, and south of the Bermondsey market, the enormous market in Shepherd's Bush, brilliant on Friday afternoons and Saturday mornings, and that on Kingsland Road on Sundays, and Rupert and Berwick streets in Soho, all not far, but a universe away, from the visitor's London.

A market *aficionado* can arrange an early, early day, and a fascinating one, in the wet gray dawn shine and the crunch of ice, watching the barrowmen in their hard-leather billycock hats calling their mysterious, lost-in-time cry, "Up the hill," in the fish market at Billingsgate (Monument Station). Then on to the lovely Victorian ironwork, the bristling shine of meat hooks, the bouquets of hearts and lungs in the Smithfield Market (Farringdon Station) and then to Covent Garden for vegetables from Ireland, France, Spain, North Africa, Israel, the flower carts pulling up for the day's supply and the ladies in the squashed hats and black aprons disputing the cost of "raowses."

One tangent having led to another, which leads to yet another (the best way to travel), you may want to continue exploring what London eats, aware that shopping in a foreign country is to watch shopping as well. Go into any supermarket—the big one on King's Road not far from Sloane Square, possibly—to see what a large proportion of England's food is imported: butter from France, Poland, Denmark; jams from Hungary, Germany, Czechoslovakia, Rumania; oranges from Israel and Spain and North Africa; meat from New Zealand, Australia, Argentina.

Even if the customers don't reflect it immediately, you will be able to know the ethnic variety of a neighborhood by what appears on the street stalls. Plantains and yams lead into an area that speaks the soft, rolling cadences of Jamaica or Trinidad. Cans of ghee and lemon pickle surrounded by curry and papadums are for the local wearers of saris and Punjab trousers and tunics. Although there seem to be no stands specifically devoted to Central and South African foods, Sunday's Petticoat Lane (Middlesex Street and its environs, near Aldgate Station) attracts the gloriously wrapped and turbaned ladies whose sinuous gait and tall headdresses make of them tropical birds among the English sparrows.

Napoleon (or was it Adam Smith or Louis XIV?), you remember, called the English a nation of shopkeepers, apparently forgetting that a compelling French ideal was and is to be a *commerçant*. Whatever the justice of the epithet, there are a good number of shops in London, possibly more than there are in other big cities because London still maintains its villages and their high streets, each of which is a shopping center. The principal shopping centers (other than those mentioned) are, however, Regent Street, which almost matches Bond Street in housing superb jewelry, new and antique, fine modern china, highly respected men's and women's clothing, a number of good department stores and those temples. **Liberty's** and the mother store of proliferating **Jaegers,** Piccadilly, with its arcades, **Simpson's, Fortnum's,** and innumerable reputable small shops, is almost its peer. Crowded Oxford Street takes care of lower-middle class or cautious shopping in a long row of small shops and department stores. Similar in price and quality, occasionally slipping below, are the shops on the Strand.

Below, a few listings in categories that are still emphatically London, and remember, as you search among them, that like restaurants, shops contract, expand, move to new quarters, or disappear; check addresses.

# Antiquities

You will, of course, go with knowledge of provenance, styles, and probable cost, and since some of these categories lend themselves to faking, seek out only the most reputable dealers, or take an expert with you if the potential expenditures will be large.

If anyone is showing an authentic Cycladic figure, it will be **Spink and Son,** 5–7 King Street, the medalists to the royal family, which recently struck medals commemorating the Great Fire of London (because of gold restrictions the medals were made of platinum at five hundred and ninety-four pounds the pair). This activity did not prevent the firm from collecting and showing Roman mosaics, magnificent jades, Greek coins, exceptional pieces of furniture, in their variety of superb antiquities and antiques.

If you must have the head of a horse from the Elgin marbles or Egyptian cats, arrange to order a cast at the **British Museum.** For the real thing of more modest fame, look in at the **Arcade Gallery,** 28 Old Bond Street; the **Berkeley Galleries,** 20 Davies Street; the **Obelisk,** 15 Crawford Street (Marylebone), which jumps easily from Roman bronze to tomorrow's welding. **Reiser,** at 49, and **Gallery 43** at that number, both on George Street (near Baker) surround cool Buddhas and pre-Columbian pots with jungles of gaunt oceanic figures and dour African masks. Islamic art frequently appears with the primitive and European medieval along George Street, Mount Street, South Audley Street, Davies Street, on Kensington Church Street and on Pimlico Road.

# Antiques

Check the current U.S. customs definition. There are dozens, possibly hundreds, of inviting shops that deal with the mixtures of antiques, but one can only suggest that the antiques rows mentioned above be examined and a few of the prodigious number of shops.

**Furniture:**

>**Mallet's,** 40 New Bond Street, and at Bourdon House, 2 Davies Street.
>**Frank Partridge and Sons,** 144–5–6 Bond Street.
>**Harrington's,** 120 Mount Street.
>**Marble and Lemon,** 62A Old Church Street.
>**H. W. Keil,** 27–29 Brook Street.
>**Hotspur,** 14 Lowndes Street.
>**Blairman,** 36 New Bond Street.
>**Sidney J. Block,** 12 Hinde Street.
>**Peter Lipitch,** 100 York Street, and the Lipitch shops on St. Christopher's Place.
>**Barling,** 112 Mount Street.

Forests of chairs, desks, and tables fill Chelsea, Kensington, and Knightsbridge, particularly on Pimlico Road, Old Brompton Road, Kensington Church Street, Sloane Street, and especially King's Road. All by its large self, on a thoroughfare whose only distinction is proximity to the British Museum, is **M. Harris,** New Oxford Street at the corner of Coptic Street, and in quite another direction, **W. R. Harvey,** at 67–70 Chalk Farm Road (part of a minor market), whose eighteenth- and nineteenth-century furniture colorfully and neatly inhabits the 300-year-old farm cottages that once housed the painter Sickert and an optimistic crafts colony.

**Antique Jewelry:** Like other antiques, jewelry clusters with the mixture, but most frequently with old silver. Of the markets, **Bermondsey** is best and most difficult to reach; the **Chelsea Supermarket** and that off Barrett Street often rewarding; Portobello scattered with possibilities. See what there might be outside No. 105, on a cart hung with hanks of lace and ostrich feathers across from 135, under an overhang of lutes and fiddles at 129; Art Nouveau jewelry, 153. More important pieces live here and there and especially on the upper stories of the arcades at 157 and 163.

Bond Street is hung with royal warrants and the names of internationally famous jewelers—one of them **Asprey's,** 165 New Bond Street, a vast and varied set of lures including reproductions of the silver taken from the Spanish Armada. Regent Street comes close, and so does Conduit. **Collingwood,** 46 Conduit, is one of the royal favorites. **Wartski's,** 138 Regent Street, is a keeper of Fabergé marvels and incomparable gold snuffboxes. Gems blaze out of the windows of **Johnson, Walker and Tolhurst,** 21 Conduit Street, which speaks of itself as wholesalers, but might be induced; **Demas,** in the Burlington Arcade; **Kirby and Bunn,** 44 Old Bond; **Bernard Sado,** 22 New Bond; in the miscellany of **Antiques Corner,** 104 Mount Street; **Rolando Antiques,** 3 South Molton; **Ingram Warwick,** 6 South Molton. Farther afield, the world-famous and rare works at **Cameo Corner,** 26 Museum Street; **M. Eckstein,** 90 Jermyn Street (imperial Russian and imperial British jewels); the **Jewel Box,** 35 Sloane Street; **Charles Woollett & Son,** 59–61 Wigmore Street, which shows eighteenth-century porcelain and miniatures as well; whatever you can pick out of the disorder in the shop of **Denisa, the Lady Newborough,** on White Horse Street; in the hodgepodge of **J. Courtney,** 31 Pembridge Road, or the **Guild House,** 37 Pelham Street (South Kensington). Should you be haunting their neighborhoods, look in at **A. Pearl Cross** (really), 35A St. Martin's Court; **Drew,** on Hogarth Place (Earl's Court Road); the Eastern jewelry, at 165 Earl's Court Road, and see that of the **Treasure Chest** at 16 Sicilian Avenue (a pretty and irrelevant arcade of neoclassicism in Holborn) and the neat glistening box of the **Button Queen,** 5 Marlborough Court, a limb off Silly Row, presided over by an elegant, distinctly non-Carnaby lady who makes good-looking earrings and cuff links of old and oldish buttons.

Modern jewelry lives comfortably with the old in a number of the above, but for concentrations look at the fine collection of **Hooper Bolton,** 8A Sloane Street, whatever they may be showing at the more avant **Phillips Ewen Gallery,** 22A Maddox Street and the gems in the extraordinary shop of **Grima,** 80 Jermyn Street.

**Antique Silver and Sheffield Plate,** as large and numerous a subject as furniture and native to the same habitats. A good deal can be seen and judged in all the marts already mentioned and in the **London Silver Vaults,** truly vaults below the street level with doors and locks like those of safes. Some deal only in silver or only in plate, one or two in jewelry, and most in the combination. (Chancery Lane and entered via the Southampton Buildings around the corner.) While you are on Chancery Lane, look in at **Marshall's** at 67; **George Attenborough,** at the corner with Fleet Street; **Langford's,** 76; and a branch among the silver houses on Charterhouse Street.

Not as big as that on Chancery Lane, the group at the **Bond Street Galleries,** upstairs in 9A New Bond, a street which abounds in silver, much of it in the king's ransom echelon. Should that be your natural stratum, go to **Bourdon-Smith,** 25A, and **Heming and Co.,** 28, both Conduit; **Tessier's,** 26 New Bond; **Hart's,** 75 Duke Street; **Lawrence,** 63 South Molton Street, and **Ogden and Sons,** at 42; **J. Christie,**

36 St. George Street; **Marks,** 49 Curzon Street; **Wellby,** 16C Grafton Street; **De Havilland,** 14 Grafton Street; **Hancocks,** 9 Vigo Street; **How of Edinburgh,** 2 Pickering Place (in a minute court off St. James's Street); **Laird Clowes,** at 3, and **Plante,** at 12 Bury Street; **W. H. Willson,** 15 King Street. And **S. J. Shrubsole,** 43 Museum Street; **James Hardy and Co.,** 235 Brompton Road; **Jones & Son,** 229 Brompton Road; **M. P. Levene,** 5 Thurloe Place (opposite the Victoria and Albert); **Jessop,** 3 Motcomb Street.

**Antique China,** where we repeat the leitmotiv: the markets for bargains or semibargains and for the finer rarities: **Newman & Newman,** 156 Brompton Road; **Vandekar,** 138 Brompton Road; **David Newbon,** at 56 Beauchamp Place, and see what they have at 54 also; **Newby & Waller,** 130C Montpelier Street (take time out to wander these mews streets); **Harcourt Antiques** (Harcourt Street near York Street); **John Wyndham,** 14 Chiltern Street; **J. J. Drukker,** 17 George Street; **A. F. Albrook,** 24 Cromwell Place; **Mavillus & Skull,** 125, and **Marian Marks,** 171 Fulham Road; **Derek Hand,** 20A Pimlico Road; **Tilley Antiques,** 2 Symons Street (Sloane Square); **Jean W. Sewell,** Campden Street off Kensington Church Street; **Miss Fowler,** 1A Duke Street; **Albert Amor,** 37 Bury Street; **Manheim,** 69 Upper Berkeley Street.

**Antique Glass,** frequently paired with china, more or less isolated at: **Howard Phillips,** 11A Henrietta Place (Marylebone); **Cecil Davis,** 3 Grosvenor Street; **Lloyd's,** 16 Motcomb Street; **W. G. T. Burne,** 11 Elystan Street (Chelsea); **C. H. Major,** 154 Kensington Church Street; **W. W. Warner,** 226 Brompton Road; **Alan Tillman,** 469 Fulham Road; **Lien Wood,** Harris Arcade 11 (163 Portobello Road)— and especially for antique paperweights, many of them French, **Lories,** 89B Wigmore Street.

### Military Antiques:

**Fairclough,** 25 Conduit Street. Practically everything ever devised to deal and ward off blows—armor, swords, helmets, crossbows, pistols, helmets, and, to keep things going, military drums.

    **Peter Dale,** 11 and 12 Royal Opera Arcade (behind Her Majesty's Theatre, on Haymarket, built by John Nash in 1818, which makes it the oldest in London and still the prettiest)—matched antique pistols, haughty plumed helmets, armor, and books on armor.

    Under the tall shadow of the Hilton, **Norman Newton,** 49 Hertford Street, a branch of the larger shop at 44 Dover Street; military prints and remarkable lead soldiers, their leaders and conquerors, in addition to the full-panoplied rest.

**P. C. L. German,** 125 Edgware Road, a dim, dense, faintly gleaming wilderness of armor and swords surrounded by mounds of brasses, copper warming pans, and pewter beakers.

**Appleby's,** 57 George Street, the quality mixture.

**Models:** These fashionable and expensive toys turn up everywhere, including the great auction houses. Elegant precise examples can be found at the alluring shop of **Graham Pontet,** 79 Jermyn Street. **Westbourne Grove** (Portobello area) shows them among ships' instruments and marine paintings at 189; at **Desmond Thomas,** 183; and at **Jones,** 293. A small shop at 23 Swallow Street off Piccadilly features ships' lanterns and bells as well. **Mechanical Antiquities,** at the corner of Moore Street and Cadogan Place (Chelsea), as the name implies, has nothing but, while **Gordon Hand,** 18 Pembridge Villas (Portobello area), scatters them through his other antiques. Not necessarily, or at all, antiques, but a colossal collection of ship, car, railroad models, from toy price to that of costly hobby, at **Beattle's,** 112 High Holborn.

**Mantels, Surrounds and Grates:** The demolitions of war, time, and economic change have produced cities full of columns, carved panels, marble slabs and mirrors that once adorned fireplaces. Some of these have found their way into antiques establishments, decorators' shops, and the lesser glamor bits to markets. There are, however, specialists:

**Hallidays,** 28 Beauchamp Place, concentrates on carved pine mantelpieces, to be placed above their metal grates.

**H. W. Poulter,** 158 Fulham Road, shows mantels, surrounds, columns, and copper coal buckets and andirons.

**Pratt & Burgess,** 7 Old Brompton Road. The full repertoire.

**Ossowski,** 83 Pimlico Road, tends to the ornate and gilded, but the wooden carved spills of fruits, leaves, putti, and lyres help keep them playful.

**Geoffrey Van,** 107 Portobello Road. Many carved wooden panels, columns, and mantels; wooden *santos;* and porcelain, and hardly room in which to progress from one to the other.

**Metals as Bed Warmers, Horse Brasses, Samovars, Fireplace Accessories, Beakers:** No antiques shop is without the warm glint of old copper and gray silk of old pewter and, increasingly stylish, the heavy curls of iron grillwork. What antiques shops have, the markets try for, in some reasonable or unreasonable facsimile.

To start low in the class scale, for old lamps and samovars, along Chalk Farm Road, especially at **Jaks-Son,** at No. 275, which is thickets of metal, and around the corner, on Jamestown Road, the **Men of Iron** workshops, which has an old-fashioned street sign, this one an almost life-sized metallic dusky blacksmith.

**Shepherd's,** 290 Westbourne Grove, is an immense and busy departmentalized place with sections devoted to bedsteads, fireplace fenders, vats, candlesticks, doorknobs, and handles in brass, copper, and bronze.

Across the street is the line of **Jones** shops, from about 295 Westbourne Grove to the corner of Portobello, encompassing, as it goes, fine railroad models, barometers, fireplace accessories, copper kettles, hanging brass lamps, hunting horns, and the inescapable saddle ornaments.

Back on Westbourne Grove No. 227 and 229, there is a place so crammed and dusty and indiscriminately piled with things of iron and brass that finding one's way into the conglomeration is almost impossible.

The general range appears at **Old Metalcraft,** 194 Brompton Road, and at **Robert Preston,** on Campden Street off Kensington Church Street. Concentrations of pewter of value and age can be found at the **Pewter Shop,** 142 Brompton Road; the **Pewter Shop** in the Burlington Arcade; **Richard Mundey,** 19 Chiltern Street; a **Casimir** on Brompton Road, and, among the staggering quantities of metalware, another **Casimir** at 23 Pembridge Road, on one of the approaches to Portobello.

# Music Machines
# and Musical Instruments

**Graham Webb,** 93 Portobello Road. Symphonia, music boxes, discs, and cylinders and the mechanisms to draw sounds from them; horns; lutes, player pianos; accordions—all in a subway-rush crowding.

**Payton's,** 114 Islington High Street, is several shops of several interests. Look for the dimmest window and the instruments behind it: a plump Oriental stringed instrument, carved and ivoried; a Delft ocarina; tiny lutes; mute practice violins; bagpipes, miniature guitars; a baby pipe organ; and a dancing master's *pochette*.

At 5 Elgin Crescent (off the Portobello Road) one finds zithers, lutes, mandolins, Oriental instruments, and guitars and banjos which the bearded young try out on Saturday afternoons.

The **Music Box Gallery** at 81 George Street repairs and sells engaging, nonsensical little machines that make light nostalgic tunes as music boxes and old phonographs. There are birds that turn and shrill, gently, and enchanting clocks with more imaginative repertoires than plain tick-tock, and, to balance the older rarities, new furry animal toys with music boxes for innards.

**Morley's,** 56 Old Brompton Road, sells harps and pianos, curiously advertised by a ghost window, untouched for years, of a row of harps of similar style and size. Once they were gold and nobly carved, but now are scratched and dust-covered, their strings few and loose like old teeth.

**Puttick & Simpson,** 7 Blenheim Street, runs monthly sales of musical instruments, particularly of fine violins.

**W. E. Hill & Sons,** 140 New Bond Street. Behind the bowed windows that may frame a rare lute and are surmounted by a beautiful harp and dragon ironwork sign and a royal warrant, string instruments sold by the descendants of violin makers of London, once a lively local craft.

# Galleries

Not quite, or possibly not just yet, the world's art center, London contends valiantly, with hundreds of galleries that display works from earliest antiquities to tomorrow's Op or Pop or Glop.

Although traditional painting treads its stately forms along Bond Street, the densest cluster lives in the aristocratic quiet of Duke Street, St. James's, Bury Street, and their neighbors:

The **Koesters**—Brian, at 38; Leonard, at 13; M. D. at 43—on Duke Street, along with **M. Newman** at 43A, **Paul Larsen** at 43, **Sabin,** at 47, **MacConnal-Mason,** at 14; **Duits,** at 6; and a maverick among them, **Kaplan,** at 6, whose roster thunders important French names of recent vintage. On Ryder Street, a small street off Duke: **Appleby Brothers.** On Bury: **Hal O'Nians, Hazlitt, Herbert H. Sabin,** and **M. Bernard; Pawsey and Payne,** 1; **Terry,** 8; **Sutch and Martin,** 11; **Omell,** 22; **W. Wheeler & Son,** 32; **B. Cohen,** and **Trafalgar Gallery,** at 35. On King Street: **P. Polack,** 21; **Rupert Preston,** 17.

Still in St. James's, and in the same category: **Broad,** at 24 St. James's; **Leggatt Brothers,** at 30 St. James's. Nearby on Jermyn Street:

Dutch paintings, as well as other Continentals, at **Daan Cevat,** 58 (afternoons only or by appointment); the London branch of the French **Heim,** 59, whose province is seventeenth- and eighteenth-century Continental paintings. Northward, **Leger,** 13 Old Bond, English and Continental paintings and English watercolors; **Arthur Ackerman,** 3 Old Bond, sporting paintings and drawings; **Bond Street Galleries,** 9 New Bond; **Colnaghi,** 14 Old Bond, paintings and prints, as at **Fores,** 123 New Bond; and **Lasson,** at 57 Jermyn Street.

See what there is at **Sotheby's Annex Gallery,** 34 New Bond Street; **Spenser,** 16B Grafton Street, among the smallish, oldish genre pieces there; or what there might be at **Giles,** 11 Hinde Street. In the Baker Street area: **Wilkerson,** 64 Blandford Street; **F. Teltscher,** 17 Crawford Street; and the modest works shown by **Chiltern Art Galleries,** at 10, and **Harding and Brown,** 52, both on Chiltern Street. In Knightsbridge, **Lowndes Lodge Galleries,** 27 Lowndes Street, opposite the Carlton Tower Hotel.

The "modern" that means complete safety and great deal of money can be found at the famous **Wildenstein,** 147 New Bond, and at the **Marlborough Galleries,** at 17 and 39 Old Bond Street, and possibly in the mixed collection at **Maas & Co.,** 15A Clifford Street, and **Hallsborough,** 143 New Bond. Below the antiques of **Dark & Dark,** at 7 Pond Place, there are frequent showings of the work of English painters, as far back as the pre-Raphaelites at times.

The "modern" from reasonable to aggressive is, surprisingly, not much found in Chelsea or South Kensington or Hampstead, to mention a few fortresses of Bohemia. Cork and Duke streets are to new paintings, what Duke (St. James's) and Bury streets are to the old. **Robert Fraser,** 69 Duke, was *avant* enough to have had itself arrested on charges of obscenity at one time. At 77 is **Madden,** a touch more cautious, and at 79, **Axiom,** dedicated to illusion or arch-stark—whatever is now or tomorrow in art. Cork Street just about leaves room for a few revered, if musty, tailoring establishments and then closes its ranks to everything but painting. **Victor Waddington,** at 25, goes as far back as Modigliani, Bonnard, *et al.*, but the rest—another **Waddington** at 2; **Piccadilly,** 16A; **Roland Browse & Delbanco,** 19; **Redfern,** 20; **Mercury,** 26—possess, among them, a powerful stable of newer works. Cork is, however, only the nexus of a web of streets that show modern art. Galleries whose walls are carefully examined are **Kasmin,** at 118 New Bond; **Alwin,** at 56, and the **Brook Street Gallery,** at 24, both on Brook Street; **Grosvenor,** at 30 Davies; **Lefevre,** 30 Bruton Street, and **Tooth's,** at 31; **Mayor,** at 14 South Molton, and the international **Gimpel Fils,** at 50; **O'Hana,** 13 Carlos Place; **Trafford,**

119A Mount Street; **Hamilton,** at 8, and **Hanover,** at 32A, both on St. George Street; **McRoberts & Tunnard,** 34 Curzon Street; **Woodstock,** 16 Woodstock Street; **Leicester Gallery,** 4 Audley Square.

Farther afield, but still in areas you would be visiting: **Sphinx,** 116 Crawford Street (near Baker); **John Whibley,** 60 George Street; **Drian,** 5–7 Portchester Place; **Crane Kalman,** 178 Brompton Road; **William Ware,** 160 Fulham Road; **New Art Centre,** 41 Sloane Street; **Rowan,** 25A Lowndes Street; **Cassel,** 8A Thurloe Street; **Grabowski,** 84 Sloane Avenue; **Artists International Association,** 15 Lisle Street (Soho), a cooperative of young painters who rent their works but are not reluctant to sell. **Barry Duncan,** 11 St. Martin's Court (off Charing Cross Road) concentrates on theater design, as does **Wright Hepburn,** encyclopedically, at 10 Halkin Arcade, Motcomb Street. Back on Charing Cross Road, **Zwemmer,** 26 Litchfield Street; "naïve" painters at the **Portal,** 16A Grafton Street; **Jean Carray,** 83 Ladbroke Grove, and on Saturdays, maybe a Bombois-type weight lifter or a girl out of Balthus, in the **Portobello Antique Arcade** and spilling over to the **Dolphin Arcade,** at 155 Portobello Road.

**Graphics:** Many of the galleries will show you graphics in varied moods and periods, and so will antiquarian bookshops, which usually have fine and extraordinary collections. Try the books and printshops on Cecil Court (*see* Books); **A. Reader,** 71 Charing Cross Road; **B. Weinrib,** 39 Great Russell Street; **Craddock & Barnard,** 32 Museum Street; **L. C. Braun,** 17 Denmark Street; **Fores, Ackerman,** and **Colnaghi,** all on Bond Street; **John Hall,** 17 Harrington Road; **Parker Galleries,** 3 Albemarle Street; **John McMaster,** 15–16 in the Royal Opera Arcade; **Maltzahn,** 137 Fulham Road; **Baynton-Williams,** 70 Old Brompton Road; **Bayly's,** 9 Princes Arcade, prints, song-sheet covers, silhouettes in a large populace of porcelain figurines. On Portobello Road: the **Portobello Bookshop,** at 89, at 75A, and in the arcade at 157; **John Reid,** 44 Kensington Church Street. The **Square Orange,** at 41 Pimlico Road does "Books for Decoration," which means prints garnered from various tomes to be recollated as volumes of genre scenes, costumes, etc.; **Barter Street Gallery,** 16, and the shop of **Andrew Block,** 20, both on Barter Street, the latter, a specialist in books on and of the theater and perilous piles of eighteenth- and nineteenth-century theater posters, surprisingly inexpensive, as well as stamps.

Modern graphics: The **ICA Galleries** at 17 Dover Street; **Editions Alecto,** 27 Kelso Place; **Curwen Gallery,** in Colville Place, off Charlotte Street; the **Fine Art Society,** 148 New Bond Street; **Savage,** 65 Old Brompton Road; **Lord's,** 26 Wellington Road (also old posters);

**Hugh Evelyn,** 85 Lower Sloane Street, new prints of oldish cars, bicycles, and buses; posters from many countries at **Heal's,** on Tottenham Court Road.

## Books

There may or may not be comparative statistics available, but London may sell as many books per day as it does pints of ale; at least there seem to be as many bookshops, or almost, as pubs. Department stores sell books, and so do **W. H. Smith,** which appear in every neighborhood except those too benighted or poor to buy books. (The presence or absence of a Smith branch is a pretty good indication of the intellectual and economic status of an area.) Among the numerous good general bookshops, the following are held in especially high regard for the range of their stock, the knowing interest of their salespeople, and clients:

**Bumpus,** 96 Mount Street; the **Times Book Shop,** 42 Wigmore Street; **Hatchard's,** at 187 Piccadilly; **Truslove and Hanson,** 94A Brompton Road and 6B Sloane Street, near Knightsbridge Station. In the intellectual climate of the Victoria and Albert-Kensington area, there are **Pulteney,** 22 Thurloe Street, which adds a considerable number of Italian and French books to the indigenous, and **Lamley & Co.,** 5 Exhibition Road, with a wide range of technical paperbacks and a square-pillared, iron-laced, worthy Edwardian presence.

Not too far away, **Bernard Stone** scatters his several shops of books—rare, new, old, *avant,* prints, and aged postcards—over an enchanting ramble of alleys along and around from Kensington Church Walk.

The specialties in books run from the expected to the surprisingly refined in London. Art books and technical material on the arts at **Alec Tiranti,** 72 Charlotte Street, and imposing collections at **Zwemmer's,** at the corner of Litchfield Street and Charing Cross Road; **John Sandoe,** 10 and 11 Blacklands Terrace, off the King's Road: **St. George's Gallery Books,** 8 Duke Street (St. James's); **Map House,** at St. James's Place and St. James's Street, provides a large choice of guidebooks, maps, and map prints.

Art and the occult share **Atlantis,** 49A Museum Street.

It comes as a surprise to no one that the august British Museum fronts (Great Russell Street) on publishing houses and their alter egos the bookshops, a number of them experts in Oriental and African history, problems and art: theosophy, at 68, and natural history, at 44.

Zeno, 6 Denmark Street, has books about Greece and in Greek; the Conservative Party has its bookshop, and so do the Fabian Socialists; children are afforded their own books at the **Children's Book Centre,** 140 Kensington Church Street; the **RSPCA Bookshop,** 103 Jermyn, has only to do with animals, and **J. A. Allen,** 1 Lower Grosvenor Place, appropriately close to the royal stables, deals with the horse in its various uses and aspects. At 59 Curzon Street, the field is narrowed to horse betting, turf publications, and books on betting systems. Trains have their histories at **Hamblings,** at 10 Cecil Court; autos theirs at 33 and 36 St. Martin's Court; and the slenderest of specialties, books on the radio, at 12 Little Newport Street, where one goes to buy inexpensive electronics components.

## Antiquarian Bookshops

A solemn, lovely, and extensive subject. As with antiquities dealers, a few stay hidden except for mailed catalogues and a telephone number for making appointments. The collector will know these dealers and also the rarity and justified range of cost involved. Visible and with attainable wares, not all of them shockingly expensive (and keep in mind that this is where old prints, manuscripts and incunabula are usually available), the famous **Maggs Bros.,** 50 Berkeley Square; **Henry Sotheran,** 2–5 Sackville Street, new, secondhand, and truly old in new and antique bindings, a few with miniatures of great men sunk into the covers. **Quaritch,** 11 Grafton Street, *Bardic Poems with Great Pains Now Rescued from Oblivion,* an old book of musical instruments illustrated with exquisite plates, Handel's songs in an early edition, but the matter is not exclusively musical. **Sawyer,** 12–13 Grafton Street, distinguished Morocco and crushed Levant bindings, prints, old sporting books, and modern art. **Thomas Thorp,** 27 Albemarle Street; in Italian, French, and Latin (Caesar's *Commentaries* printed in the eighteenth century in "Glasguae") and remarkably illustrated horticultural tomes. Near the Smithfield Market, **Frank Holding,** on Cloth Fair at Barley Mow Passage (the names give some suggestion of the imponderable age of the area). In Chelsea, **Peter Murray Hill,** 73 Sloane Avenue, and **Martin Orskey,** 309A King's Road; **Louis Bendy,** 16 Little Russell—rare and miniature books. In Marylebone: **Francis Edwards,** 83 Marylebone High Street, five floors of maps, early explorations, and incunabula amid the variety; **Clarke-**

**Hall,** off Fleet Street, in Wine Office Court. Watch announcements of the monthly book auctions at **Hodgson's,** 115 Chancery Lane, as well as book sales in general auction houses.

In the category of antiquarians, and yet not, is the fascinating slit of street called Cecil Court, an especially flavored adjunct of the book mart of Charing Cross Road and the stalking grounds of the knowing for books, prints, and curios. At 24 Cecil Court, **Harold Mortlake; Fletcher's,** at 15 and 27; **Edmonds,** at 1; **Suckling,** at 13—all for old books and prints and in the last, coins and medals as well. **E. Seligman,** 25, specializes in antique books on the arts in several languages. **Travis & Emerey,** 16, chooses music as books, song covers, and related prints. **Watkins,** 21, prefers religions, philosophy, and the occult. **Griff's,** 4, stakes out the world of Celtic books and grammars of Old English, Bengali, and Arabic. Number 9 is interested in the dance, while 14 prefers sex, and, all around, rivulets of assorted secondhand books.

Charing Cross Road is world-famous for its diversity of books, many of them secondhand and occasionally gems, whose pursuit pulls searchers to spend happy sooty Saturdays in the local basements. The road is also one of the reliable sources of erotica for the million. Depending on the leniency of the authorities—and this is one of London's many relaxed times—the windows will or will not show French paperbacks on Chinese sex practices, reports from secret exotic societies, or learned histories of the strip-tease, but just step right inside, gentlemen. The road supplies, too, do-it-yourself instructions from plumbing to film directing, from languages to cuisine. A good place to start is **E. Joseph,** at 48A Charing Cross Road, crammed with used books on many subjects, then on past texts and technicals, art and films, to the latest in intellectual paperbacks at **Collet's,** 52, and its sociology and economics and books from Eastern European countries at 66. **Collet's,** leftist, lively, and respected, spreads its enterprise into other intellectual areas as well. It maintains a jazz and folk-record shop at 70 New Oxford Street; at 39 Museum Street its **Russian Shop** sells recordings, films, and books in Russian and about Russia in English. Its **Chinese Shop** includes Chinese arts and crafts, as well as books, at 40 Great Russell Street. At 289 High Holborn, it continues expanding its wide-ranging domain with language-study records, dictionaries, and grammars in foreign languages—Russian, Italian, French, German—and shelves of learned paperbacks on political and sociological questions.

At New Compton Street, **Better Books,** which begins as a calm, large bookstore and then, as it turns the corner, sprouts little magazines of extraordinary provenance, advertises poetry readings and, at one time, "experiences" to revive "real, honest sensation." The first such "happening," accompanied by considerable publicity, consisted of crawling through old tire tubes, tunnels of rags and crumpled newspaper, caves of chicken feathers in a landscape of chicken wires, inexpensive Edwardian erotica, inflated rubber gloves, and wormlike bits of old fur. (No more of this recently; happenings have been taken over by the theater.) To suit this released, sincere climate, it spells its name as "Better Bookz" on this side.

Across the street in shops that call themselves Hygiene and feature "rejuvenators," books with titles like *The Kiss of the Whip* and *Under the Lash*. The row stops, books venal and books uplifting with the height, width, and massive number of **Foyle's** (119), flanking Manette Street. Foyle's calls itself the biggest bookshop in the world, and it probably is, and a good place to observe how a sizable portion of London's working-class young spends its lunchtime.

One of the several bookshops for the intensely "with it" crowd is **Indica,** 102 Southampton Row (if it has not been raided and closed), with, naturally, a purple front, eccentric window displays, underground weeklies, obscure quarterlies, and—the jewel in its crown—copies of New York's *Village Voice*. The strongest possible contrast is one of the government bookstores at Holborn and Brownlow, calm and equally interesting, an orderly and large set of displays dealing with parliamentary debates, new governmental rulings, career building, economics, housing, health, education; museum publications, area maps, and guidebooks issued by Her Majesty's Stationery Office.

As indicated, one of the local industries of Soho is sex, and although erotica is available elsewhere, the concentrations are tighter; nothing on carpentry or the history of the cinema or medieval church schisms to wade through, just lots of nice dirty little books—in small shops almost everywhere in Soho. A particularly full supply, including "art reproductions" and "glamor mags," fill out the services of a strip joint at the corner of D'Arblay and Berwick streets, and neighboring a blue club almost under the warming big lights of the Berwick Street Market.

Strictly, most of the secondhand bookshops on Charing Cross Road should be listed in the bargain category, but the true bargain presence —with all that means as disorder, dustiness, distraught vendors, and frayed corners—belongs more appropriately to other places. Newport Court and Newport Place seem to handle what their neighbor, Charing Cross Road, can't be bothered with: books and records and back numbers of magazines dense with nude "art" photos for all tastes. Among the respectable, unwanted titles appear histories of nymphomania, of sadism, and delectable reviews of orgies through the ages.

One book exchange allows half price on a purchase if you bring one of your discards as part of the deal.

On Farringdon Road, flanked by a wall guarding railroad tracks on one side and the *Daily Worker* Building (St. Cross Street) on the other, one comes first on bits of tools and nails and brushes that might interest a working-class noontime clientele and then on books. They run to bound copies of *Belgravia, a London Magazine* of 1880, or *The Gentleman's Magazine* of the same vintage or the memoirs of a chaplain in India at the time of Victoria. Once in a while something of value or great interest turns up, and it might be your day.

Although bundles of books lie under and on market stalls, there is one secondhand bookshop, and only books, at 289 Westbourne Grove (off Portobello Road) that deserves a half hour's browsing. It has a large collection of books on London and English areas and curiosities of travel, like accounts of trekking through Siberia or Afghanistan in the nineteenth century.

**Oppenheim's,** 13 Exhibition Road, heaps old books, paperbacks, and magazines, some prints worth leafing through.

No guarantees, but you should know that the maniacal about old book bargains go very early on Sundays to Goulston Street, the flea market adjunct of Petticoat Lane, and to Bell Street, near Edgware Road, on Saturdays.

Worth remembering: Theater programs and opera programs are cheap, good-looking, and informative, as are the numerous publications of museums.

# Clothing

The big color had for some time been a thunderous purple, in nipped waists, Indian jackets—cotton or brocade—and an extra flip on the hips, for the boys and for the cropped girls, short, lank dresses like wet undershirts. It appeared combined with orange plastic in boots and long-handled minibags and baggy corduroy caps. Before the purple, it was dazzling combinations of orange and shocking pink, and before that, explorations in anything that was loud or exotic or *outré*. This does not describe London dress, only a vivid segment of it. Most of the city wears its habitual drab, but the impact of the young, as fiercely colorful as London's flowers, is having its effect. A rack of size 44's will bear a yellow dress or even a red among the grays and navys; the temples of sober probity are opening boutiques for the young, and the flavor has a way of seeping into adjoining sections. But

**Simpson's** still carries along with its Trend clothing, Daks; and **Liberty's** its scarves and lawns; **Jaeger's** is still matching woolens woven and knit and its blond coats; **Harrod's** has not moved its zoo out to make room for a discothèque, although it has a Way In shop. Though Savile Row is diminished and one or two of its tailors lured into making suits of Byronic cut in Renaissance silks for young Belgravia dandies, there are still lines of tailors hiding behind the dust-colored curtains and royal warrants on Conduit Street, Dover Street, Sackville Street, Grafton, and others in the vicinity.

### Men's Clothing

The moneyed male young has his evening clothing made at **Blades** (Burlington Gardens); day clothes at **Just Men** (8 Tryon Street); the men's shop at **Jaeger's** on Regent Street or King's Road; the Cue shop at **Austin Reed** (main shop at 103 Regent Street, a large branch at 163 Brompton Road, and others). Robes, sweaters, sybarites' bathrobes, and the latest in shirts come from **Mr. Fish,** 17 Clifford Street; shirts from **Washington Tremlett,** 41 Conduit Street, and **Turnbull and Asser,** 71–72 Jermyn Street; shoes from **John Lobb's,** 9 St. James's Street; scents from **Floris,** 89 Jermyn Street; hats from **Lock's,** 6 St. James's Street, and **Herbert Johnson,** 38 New Bond. His father has his suits made by **Huntsman & Son,** 11 Savile Row; **Henry Poole,** 10 Cork Street; **Tepesch,** 12 Cork Street; **Hawes & Curtis,** 43 Dover Street; **Sullivan, Wooley & Co.,** 18 Conduit Street; **Kilgour French & Stanbury,** 33A Dover Street; **Hawkes,** 1 Savile Row; **Cooling Lawrence & Wells,** 47 Maddox Street; **George Strickland & Sons,** 15 Savile Row; **Hicks & Sons,** 9 Savile Row; **Thresher & Glenny,** 152–153 Strand; **Maurice Sedwell,** 9 Savile Row; **Tobias Bros.,** 32 Savile Row. (The traditional hauteur of such establishments has always been exaggerated and, if it existed, is now thawed by competition from ready-to-wear and a growing taste for cheaper, more ephemeral garments. One doesn't need a pedigree to order a suit, but does need the patience to submit to a number of fittings and to wait out the time that careful craftsmanship deserves.)

If Father wants something less pricey, he buy's off-the-peg at **Simpson's** or **Harrod's, Harvey Nichols** or **Liberty's.** He likes **Maxwell's** shoes and **McAfee's,** both on Dover Street, as well as **Lobb's,** and buys his hats—the soft country type—at **Hilhouse,** 11 New Bond Street; his shirts come from **Hilditch & Key,** 73 Jermyn Street, and **Harvey & Hudson,** 77 and 97A Jermyn Street.

The rich young man scorns the John Stephen Carnaby Street empire —segmented into a string of shops separated by their suitability to pocket, age, and taste for fruitiness—and its neighbors and imitators.

The overstressed avoidance may be part of his uneasiness (and denial) that the neoromantic styles he favors stem from that coarse street of Soho, not part of his London at all. His friends may venture to see what's in **Irvine Sellars'** Carnaby Street (or Earl's Court) windows but prefer to avoid the noisy crowd and shop for the high style touched with moderation at **John Michael,** 95 Regent Street, 106 King's Road, and a number of branches. For knocking the eye out and worrying Mama, they go to the Pop façade and into the Art Nouveau-haremish cellar of **Hung on You,** 22 Cale Street (if it still exists), and the **Simon Shop,** 339; **His,** 201; **Dandee Fashions,** 161—all on King's Road—and the peculiar miscellany of **Granny Takes a Trip,** 422 King's Road, which cannot decide what it is selling, if it is selling at all.

Elegant and stable: **Bernard Weatherill,** 55 Conduit Street, for riding clothes and country jackets; **A. J. White and Mrs. White,** at the meeting of Vigo Street and Burlington Gardens, hats and accessories, stressing hunting caps and topees for the tropics; **Gieves,** 27 Bond Street, one of the Empire builders, makers of uniforms for the Royal Navy; **Morgan & Ball,** 54 Piccadilly, conservative but not dowdy; **Harborow's,** 6 New Bond; and, of course, **Sulka's,** 160 New Bond, for accessories, as well as **John Ericson,** 37 Jermyn Street. (You will have noticed that Jermyn exists for polishing peacock feathers.) For woolen shirts, the **Irish Shop,** 11 Duke Street. More shoes? **Tuczek,** 21 Jermyn; **Church's** at Burberry; **Foster,** 5 Duke of York Street. Raincoats are everywhere —the national smock, so to speak. You know **Burberry,** 18 Haymarket, **Asquascutum,** 100 Regent Street, the reversibles at the **Scotch House,** 2 Brompton Road, and what the department stores have to offer, but don't overlook **Lilywhites,** a large sports clothing and sports equipment place at Piccadilly Circus.

Not exactly Savile Row, but if you must have a pair of trousers made within forty-eight hours, try **The Joint,** 45 Beak Street, which promises to do it, any style. For the man who wants a red hunting jacket, buckled evening pumps, riding boots, or a military topcoat and can't afford them fresh, there are the secondhand shops of **Phillips,** 41 Pembridge Road, and **Ryde,** 30 Pimlico Road. Nearer desperation: the racks and tables in Newport Court and on Bell Lane (Petticoat Lane), a small Sunday array of shoes, one coat, one sweater, sold by nonprofessionals who need a little cash right now. For hiring (and good for buying as well) ski clothes, an opera cloak, or a morning coat and striped trousers, **Moss Bros.** Bedford and King Streets (Covent Garden), and should life suddenly shove you into a peerage or academic honors, you can hire robes or have them made, or buy a lawcourt wig, at **Eade and Ravenscroft,** 93 Chancery Lane.

# Women

*Dignified, often elegant:* the boutique of Norman Hartnell, **Le Petit Salon,** 26 Bruton Street; **Christian Dior,** 9 Conduit Street; **Anthony,** 17 South Molton Street, beautiful tweeds; **John Cavanagh,** 26–27 Curzon Street, more silken; **Nicholas,** 38 Conduit Street, accessories and knits, some of them French; **Paul Bruce,** 69 New Bond Street; **Morell,** 42 Curzon Street; **Nora Bradley,** at the corner of Smith Street and King's Road, holds onto sanity in the nuttiness around her; **Sarah Ward,** 21 Beauchamp Place, Irish hand knits and tweeds; **Mary Davies,** 12 Queen Street, simply styled Irish woolens; **Rahvis,** 19 Upper Grosvenor Street, mainly Paris copies; **Anne Gerrard,** 27 Bruton Street, model gowns; **Marra,** 8 Duke Street, sportswear; superb sweaters and hand-knit stockings to order from **Women's Home Industries,** 11 West Halkin Street; **Malabar,** 311 Brompton Road, Indian silks as luxurious clothing, and jewelry to complete the Taj Mahal picture; **Savita,** 27 Lowndes Street, Oriental and Arabic textures in adapted styles. On Beauchamp Place: **Troubadour,** 33; **Suedecraft,** at 51; **Cordoba Suedewear,** at 53 (also 134 New Bond Street); **Leathercraft,** 17–18 Dover Street, and similar wear and accessories at the **Continental Boutique,** 20 Brompton Road, and **Loewe,** 75 Jermyn Street, renowned for its pocketbooks. Probably unnecessary to mention: the suits at **Debenham and Freebody, Harrod's, Fortnum's, Simpson's, Acquascutum, Jaeger's, Harvey Nichols.**

*The kinky, far out, in, with it, or whatever the current term is:* Although the mother of them all, **Mary Quant's Bazaar,** is still at the corner of Markham Square at King's Road and her offspring settled on that street most numerously, a present mecca is **Biba's,** 21 Kensington Church Street; a dark wilderness of boas and bead garlands and thumping Beatle music. On the racks, mini- and microclothing to be worn with black round eyeglasses and earrings of golf-ball shells or whatever the lemming young have fled to now. On the same street, same tendencies: **Bus Stop.**

The **Carrot on Wheels,** 86 Fulham Road, in the convention of green on orange paint and purple windowframes, guards a few samples from which one orders. **Annacat,** 270 Brompton Road, leans to the romantic interpretation of current styles, probably prophetic. **Deliss,** 40 Beauchamp Place, one section for bright nervous shoes and the other for luxurious materials with falls of lace and ruffles. Similar (adhering to the chain-mail Joan of Arc look or beating the boys at their Beau Brummell games) but not equal, at least in cost; the **Glory Hole Boutique,** 342; **Top Gear,** 135; **Kween's** 109; **Countdown,** 137; the

**Simon Shop,** 339—all on King's Road, and dozens more, and more to come. The girls go to Carnaby Street and its tangents, too. One place on Marlborough Court is so thoroughly designed that its name is illegible; you'll recognize the style, though. **Palisades,** 24 Ganton Street, is popular, and **Lady Jane,** 29 Carnaby, improved its trade after the police cracked down on live models who changed their costumes in the window. **Tre Camp,** 40 Old Compton Street, is still another annex of the famous strip nearby, which ends with a shop for both (or no) sexes, echoing the wares of a shop across the street called **Mates. Miss Selfridge** absorbs a good deal of the street-floor space of Selfridge's. *The* **C & A Shops** include the modish in their inexpensive modest; among the new antiques shops of Walton Street, **Tony Armstrong** at 109. **Fenwick's** absorbs the corner of Brook and New Bond streets, to cram with whatever style breezes blow in.

**Fenwick's** absorbs the corner of Brook and New Bond streets, to cram with whatever style breezes blow in.

Too expensive to be called kinky and its address too exalted, but essentially that, raised to high luxury—**Maxine Leighton's,** at 22 Conduit Street, extreme glittering fashions, the ambience shocking pink, and the convolutions of *La Belle Epoque,* and nothing for the aunt who wears the sensible shoes. Not quite so high-pitched: **Tracy,** 71 New Bond Street; **Young Idea,** 83 Duke Street; **Jeannette Novell,** 44 South Molton Street.

*The Compromise:* **Wallis,** 13 Brompton Road (much from Paris); **Mary Quant's,** 46 Brompton Road; **Vanessa Frye,** 6F Sloane Street; **Ivor Harnell,** 10 Baker Street and 108 New Bond Street; **Susan Locke,** 414 King's Road; **Merle's,** at the meeting of Thurloe and Old Brompton; **Mardi Gras Boutique,** 15 Baker Street; **Mary Fair,** 18 Baker Street; **Marguerite Arundel,** 12 South Molton, and the **Three Seasons,** at 13; **Chic,** 74 Heath Street (Hampstead), and **Soukh,** 82 Hampstead High Street; **Marrian McDonnell,** 80 Sloane Avenue; **Cent et Cie,** 100 Heath Street, for opulent, odalisque dresses, mainly to order, but some ready.

Shoes usually follow the moods of the local clothing. Carnaby Street and King's Road produce the expected, and so does Mayfair, while Oxford Street straddles the extremes of style. A few held currently in high esteem, none of them cheap: **Kurt Geiger,** at the corner of Blenheim and New Bond streets; **Holmes,** 23 Grosvenor Street; **Les Jumelles,** 75 Baker Street; the **Elliott** group; the **Raynes** stores; several French and Italian shops on New Bond Street; **Joka,** 31A Duke Street; **Anello and Davide,** 96 Charing Cross Road and 30 Drury Lane, who make theatrical shoes and have a clever way with boots; for fantasies, Greek sandals in gold up to the knees, etc. at **Gamba,** 54 Beauchamp Place, and the entertaining shoe tricks at **Medway's,** 77 Knightsbridge.

A number of men's tailors make ladies' breeches and jodhpurs, most of them almost forbiddingly sober, like **Tautz,** 12 Grafton Street. Unusual rainwear and leather coats can be found at **Aqua Sprite,** 5 Cale Street. The sale of respectable, often quite desirable, used clothing (called modeled) is a growing trade. Two such places exist at 35 Beauchamp Place (**Encore** and **Florence**) and on Sloane Square, at Cliveden Place (**Pandora**). More frankly secondhand clothing inhabits **Nearly New,** 29 Chiltern Street. For their butch moods, the girls go to **Millet,** 89 and 155 Oxford Street, and other branches, to buy camping and heavy sports clothing or rummage, accompanied by rummaging boyfriends, in the government surplus stock at **Laurence Corner,** 62 Hampstead Road.

**Moss Bros.,** on Bedford Street, in Covent Garden, will tart you up in borrowed furs and other extravagances if for some sudden reason you have to look richer than you are. Not for the ritual of court or Ascot appearances; more for feeling fluffy, carefree and discothèquey, the dresses to hire at **Young's,** 180 Wardour Street.

### Children

Clothing is expensive, unless you limit yourself to the reliable, justly priced things at the **Marks and Spencer** stores and **C & A** branches. For glamor presents, English style, try **Dolls House,** 99A Cadogan Lane; **Pollyanna,** 35A Thayer Street; **Pelisse,** 240 Brompton Road (girls only). **Hamley's,** 200 Regent Street, for the very young; **Small Wonder,** 296 King's Road; **Domino,** 7 Harrington Road; **Daniel Neal,** 278 Oxford Street; **Hop Scotch,** 10 Brompton Road; a miniature of the parent Scotch House; **Rowes,** 120 New Bond (in spite of the horse in the window, the repertoire extends beyond riding clothes for looking expensive, though minuscule); embroidered gossamers for infants at **The White House,** 51 New Bond Street; ladylike lawn dresses with smocking at **Liberty's; Jaeger's** minute pleated skirts and precisely matched sweaters, absolutely smashing; **Gear,** on Carnaby Street, for small "Mods." If you dare, the hardly used, fine clothing at 162C Sloane Street; or less lustrous, but more engagingly situated, the **Children's Market,** on Holland Street, near Gordon Place (Kensington Church). To please your older children, the extremes: the princess (literally and figuratively) dresses made at **Belinda Belleville's,** 95 Cadogan Lane, or the drooping 1930's dresses and the military jackets and capes, battered with wear and wandering on

Portobello Road, the Chelsea and Barrett Street supermarkets, and off C-----y Street.

## Toys

Cute and frippery replaced by taste and intelligence at **Galt,** 30 Great Marlborough Street, and at **Paul and Marjorie Abbat,** 94 Wimpole Street. **Heal's,** 196 Tottenham Court Road, has an unusually large international toy collection. Enchanting collections of international toys can be found at the **Owl and the Pussycat,** 11 Flask Walk (Hampstead); **Hamley's,** on Regent Street, has the full repertoire, while **Hummel's,** in the Burlington Arcade, limits itself to model cars and regional and historical dolls. Bargains in toys can be found in Petticoat Lane and **Gamage's Department Store,** 118–128 Holborn. For children old enough to be respectful of them, the 1910 dolls in the arcade inside 139 Portobello Road, the copies of old toys at **Sauvus,** Knightsbridge Green, and authentically old and expensive toys on Cecil Court.

## Sweaters and Knitwear

The department stores have them, and a number of shops in the clothing categories, already mentioned, and myriad others, of which the following are a reputable few:

**Peal,** two shops in the Burlington Arcade; **Scott Adie,** 14A Clifford Street; the **Scotch House,** 10 Brompton Road; **Herd & Walker,** 173 Piccadilly; **W. Bill,** in the Royal Arcade, at 28 Old Bond and 93 New Bond, and branches elsewhere; **Benfield,** 9 and 10 Royal Opera Arcade; **Laird Woollen Shop,** 15 North Audley Street; **Racson,** 108 Jermyn Street; **Cuchullin Handlooms,** 86 Pimlico Road; **Stonehenge Woollen Industries,** 69 Welbeck Street; **Westaway & Westaway** heaps sweaters, scarves, kilts, big throws in two shops on Bury Place—one at Great Russell and the other at Bloomsbury Way. The men's shops on Jermyn Street stock good-looking sweaters, and **Huppert's,** 64 Regent Street, embroiders, beads, besequins, or leaves plain an immense number of women's sweaters.

## Textiles

A number of the places mentioned above sell woolens by the yard. **Hunt & Winterbotham,** 4 Old Bond, offers vicuña in addition to the cashmeres and mohairs; **Charles S. White,** 245 Regent Street and 165 Piccadilly; **All Woollens,** 175 Piccadilly; several small shops in Soho: one on Great Marlborough, approaching Carnaby and two on Berwick Street; **Jacob Gordon,** 19 South Molton Street. Shirting by the yard is available of most of the shirtmakers on Jermyn Street. Primarily for women: the hundreds of miles of divers yardage at **Liberty's; Allan's,** 56 Duke Street and 87 Baker Street; **Gasmey's,** on Brook Street near Avery Row; **Simmonds,** 42, and **Jason's,** 53 New Bond Street; Irish textiles, **Ireland House Shop,** at New Bond and Bruton; **National Linen Co.,** 130 New Bond, which also sells woolens.

## Luggage

**Finnigan's,** 27 New Bond Street and on Sloane Street, near Knights-bridge (plus accessories and gift items); **Lansdowne,** 23 Bury Street; **Revelation Luggage,** 170 Piccadilly; **Swaine, Adeney, Brigg & Sons,** 185 Piccadilly (also crops and stout umbrellas); **B. Lewis,** 67 Picca-dilly, makes currency purses and travel pocketbooks sectioned by vari-colored linings or zippers.

## China

The **Wedgwood Showrooms** at 32 Wigmore Street and **Worcester House,** on Wigmore Street, will show you patterns and guide you through purchases in their domains. Wedgwood and Spode are the specialties of **Gered,** 134 Regent Street and in the Piccadilly Arcade. **Lawley's,** 154 Regent Street and other locations, displays Continental china and the English gamut; **James Leather,** 134 Regent Street; **Chinacraft,** 499 Oxford Street. Both the imposing **Thomas Goode,** 19 South Audley Street, and the smaller **Anson's,** 35 Dover Street, sell exquisite glass, as well as china.

In quite another category, the **Reject China** shop in the basement at 33 Beauchamp Place, some of whose flaws are barely visible; **Delehar,** 146 Portobello Road, no flaws.

Cupless saucers, saucerless cups, and, once in a while, a faithful
pair can be found on little tables along Chalk Farm Road; at the
**Glory Hole,** 95 Lisson Grove; at the caravanserai at Lisson Street
and Bell, as well as—risking repetitiousness—the other markets and
their surrounding streets, including the small, sudden market, second-
and third- and fourthhand, that blossoms on Belsize Road as it curves
toward Kilburn High Road.

## Bric-a-brac or Curios or Oddities

Not necessarily antiques, not always strictly not, this amorphous category can hold dozens, possibly hundreds, of London shops which
crowd their shelves and windows with porcelain and ceramic figurines,
vases, cups, clocks, dishes, and, from their low ceilings, the stalactites
of little chandeliers. There are often possibilities, and if your quests
lie in these directions, look in on:

**Them and Theirs,** 17A St. Christopher Place, which surrounds the
china dogs and shepherdess with postcards of former military and
theatrical favorites.

**The Pine Chest,** 39 Pelham Street. Behind a sidewalk lineup of
unpainted chests and bookcases, a heaping of lamps, scales, pottery
cows, silver teapots, etc., etc., if you can squeeze in among them.

Bric-a-brac in the cellar, guarded by a slit of window characteristic
of this street, at 41 Beauchamp Place.

**Loot,** 76 Pimlico Road. Victoriana, Edwardiana, and nostalgia in
a multiplicity of shapes; and more such interspersed with the serious,
neat arrangers of choice antiques along Ebury Street, which forks off
Pimlico Road, and wherever else you find settlements of antiques.

**Bits and Pieces,** 148 Kensington Church Street, names itself too
modestly. Its objects have virtue.

Where curios become antiques and vice versa: the dusty shops in
Cecil Court and the heaps of oddities and jewelry at 44A Marylebone
High Street.

**Montage,** 39 James Street, sports the combination of Victorian
lamps, old knockers and handles, and pieces of china.

## Miscellaneous

A great rash of attractive, tasteful international "things" shops have
invaded London. There is a good likelihood that the city you live

near or in has these toys for large tots, but the wandering in gay designs and hearty color is pleasant and the repertoire, because of England's broader spread of international amities, more varied.

**Abacus,** at the corner of George and Baker streets (also on Clifford Street at Old Burlington Street), is one of the most venturesome.

**Divertimenti,** 74 Marylebone Lane. Unusual, well-selected international kitchen and household wares. A similar shop, **Mullenger,** exists on Chiltern Street, near Paddington Street.

**Rosenthal's,** 102 Brompton Road, is a tastefully arranged showcase, almost a museum, of modern crafts.

**Sumas,** 31 Paddington Street, keeps modern textiles, basketware, wooden objects, and pottery more carefully selected than is usual in these miscellanies.

**Habitat,** a large shop that wraps itself around Sloane and Draycott Avenues. One of the London pioneers in modern international household furnishings, in lively displays. (Also at 158 Tottenham Court Road.)

**Casa Pupo,** 56 Pimlico Road (near meeting with Ebury Street). Exquisitely arranged areas—often, every object the same color—to show, more alluringly than do most museums, the pottery, rugs, and related crafts of Spain and, in an annex nearby, Spanish tiles.

**Elizabeth David,** 46 Bourne Street. The lady who writes those good cookbooks is selling them and utensils for making her dishes in a remarkable shop that demonstrates what a judicious eye and display talent can do with the shapes and shine of jars, the glinting lights of a tower of tin molds touched with the orange-red and ocher and sienna of earthenware casseroles.

**The Tortoiseshell and Ivory Shop,** 24 Chiltern Street. Beside its tortoiseshell and beautiful ivories and jades, choice Oriental cloisonnés and porcelains.

**A. Clarke & Sons,** Fulham Road at St. Mark's Grove. Books, clothing, shoes, vases, flatware, brass knobs, lengths of iron, anything heaped with anything else in a minestrone of things. Truly a junk shop with no apologies and a rich gamut.

**Caldey Abbey,** 2 Thurloe Place. Ceramics, perfumes, dried lavender and heather from a famous monastery.

**A. R. Challis,** 19 Swallow Street, an honest man who places his wares in their proper era (no "Georgian" nonsense here) with a sign COME IN AND SEE WHAT YOUR GRANDMA THREW OUT. Similarly straightforward is **Laird's** 92 Park Road, north of Baker Street, which calls itself Budget Antiques.

Hampstead is curious for what's new in household goods and decorations and searches for it in **Chose,** at 78, and **Interior,** a set of its own tiny mews paths, in from 76—both on Heath Street.

To go with military antiquities (p. 310), jaunty musical instruments decorated, chased, and gaily painted, at **Henry Potter & Co.,** 36 West Street.

Charing Cross Road offers physical improvement among its "family planning requisites"—one goes by the dignified name of Malthus Cap —and gray-hair darkeners, energy tablets and bust-developing creams, ankle reducers and elastic hose, a "Great Restorative," and rejuvenating tonics for both sexes.

At 9B Marylebone Street, near New Cavendish, there is a small disordered shop that sells nothing but doorknobs, finger plates, and keyhole surrounds in many designs and materials. (A rumor, not investigated, is that the owner is a grandson of Sigmund Freud.)

**Gidden's,** at 74 New Oxford Street, makes and displays saddles and horse accessories in an atmosphere of skill and patience that refuses to acknowledge the automobile or, for that matter, the twentieth century.

**Sac Frères,** 45 Old Bond Street. Amber and only amber; chunky or delicately carved by fine Italian hands; round or shaped as lozenges and, if it hasn't yet been sold, a subtly graded and carved length of Viennese amber chain, weighing more than three pounds. It costs about five hundred dollars but a bargain, the man says, because one needs no other covering if the long chain is properly draped.

**The Weaving Center,** at 136 Kensington Church Street, the creation of an indefatigable, venerable lady, teaches weaving and spinning as its central mission. When possible, the center makes looms and spinning wheels and acts as outlet for Swedish linens and distinguished cottons. (It never had the air of a very profitable enterprise, nor did it seem to care, but one hopes, for its gallantry, that it still exists.)

**Barrett's,** at 9 Old Bond Street. Although there are some fine pieces of jade here and rare carved quartz pieces, as well as tortoiseshell, the matter is ivory—ivory in antique chess sets or polychrome in an Oriental long-life figure, and as a manicure set bedded in velvet and fine leather, which might make an impressive gift for someone on whom you choose to squander your duty allowance.

**Granny Takes a Trip,** 422 King's Road, has, for some reason, a reputation as a very "in" place for young men's clothing. The clothing must be well hidden or saved for "drag" because to an eye not of the inner circle the place collects and shows primarily mannerisms, and not original at that. It repeats the ubiquitous purple paint, "daring" *Belle Epoque* photos blown up, hanks of beads, a fan or two, tired kimonos, odds and ends, and boys who wander in, circle mutely, and then settle down on the floor to stare like people waiting for hallucinogenic effects.

The sweets-shop chain named **Bentinck** stocks "Sporting and Military Chocolates."

**Ody and Gillam,** 51 Chiltern Street. An extraordinary gathering of giant-size cups, *really* big.

**Culpeper House,** 21 Bruton Street. Herbs medicinal, as cosmetics, for culinary purposes, for smoking and smelling, in an appealing shop of green woods latticed over glass and old grillwork.

Tapestry making, rug weaving, embroidering, and knitting still absorb a surprising amount of female time in England. **The Needlewoman's Shop,** at 146 Regent Street, supplies a wide range of accessories, materials, and manuals for the Penelopes of London.

**Dryad Handicrafts,** at the corner of Bloomsbury Street and Great Russell streets, expands the range of crafts to include materials and booklets for making things of felt, wool, leather, paper, and sells, as well, spinning wheels, embroidery frames, and looms. Classes of instruction, too, make it about the complete crafts center.

**G. Smith,** 74 Charing Cross Road. Snuff (used by a number of modern Londoners to break the cigarette habit) in exotic diversity and some latter-day snuffboxes.

**Betty Hope,** 19 Beauchamp Place, feeds that particularly English love for the innocent cottage with rural furniture and English country crafts.

**Bouskells,** 23 Beauchamp Place, is for animal lovers, nay, idolators, offering plates which are portraits of quail; wall plaques adorned with fishing flies; fish swimming at the bottom of a casserole; birds on matchboxes and cups; and arrogant stuffed game cocks.

**James Smith & Sons,** 53 New Oxford Street, is big, Victorian, and blazes with red signs and arabesques of fancy lettering that list its wares—canes, riding crops, dagger canes, Malacca canes, swordsticks, Irish blackthorns—and umbrellas.

**Dr. Scholl's,** the friend of feet, maintains a shop on Brompton Road, one-half block east of Harrod's, and at 254 Regent Street.

If only for the triumph of finding a real bargain, no matter how modest, in a foreign city, look in at the fire-sale accumulation on the corner of Tavistock and Catherine streets in Covent Garden where they might be selling canned tomatoes or lampshades, blue jeans, toys or seed markers or a coat for the equivalent of two dollars.

More quarry for the bargain hunter is collected by the **Railway Lost Property Offices.** One, at 175 Piccadilly, helpfully lists its catches on a street board—furs, trunks, luggage, seat sticks, fishing gear, golf bags, binoculars. Another convenient office is near the enormous **HMV Records Shop,** at 363 Oxford Street, and another at 33 Haymarket. Pawnshops make good hunting grounds, as everyone knows. A fruitful cluster which yields watches, jewelry, cameras, and tools lives on Chalk Farm Road. At 28 Camden Road there is a shop which buys embroideries and sells secondhand clothes, including an occasional mandarin robe. Nearby, at 22, a neighbor sells secondhand trunks, bags, and luggage, the common stock at a number of shops in working-class neighborhoods.

For jeweled pins bearing mottoes, crests, royal insignia, and for its evocative Saxon yeoman's name: **Longman & Strongi'th'arm** at 13 Dover Street.

**Mackett Beeson,** Lansdowne Row at Berkeley Square. Buy an inexpensive chess manual, whether you need it or not, as admission ticket to view some of the extraordinary possibilities evolved from the international, imponderably old royal game. From Madras of the eighteenth century a stiff charming procession of dancer pawns and the brightly lacquered ivory elephants swaying under howdahs; chess sets of classic Wedgwood and very lacy Kashmiri figures; austere Chinese ivory and elaborate Chinese ivory; rare Meissen; utilitarian portable; French elegance; and—could it be a reflection of late-eighteenth-century anticlericalism?—a dyspeptic bishop and everyone else cheerful and happy in a gay Portuguese set of porcelain figures.

**F. G. Kettle,** 127 High Holborn. A shop of musty, wry charm, and it may be of importance to you if you want to give a present and there is no box to go with it, as happens in surprisingly luxurious shops in paper-poor England. A serious place with an immense and varied collection of papers, ornaments, boxes, and cardboard tubes in which to carry prints.

**E. H. Rann,** 21 Sicilian Avenue, whose Italianate presence encloses a miscellany of small shops and restaurants. Rann's is for the symbols of belonging: Small heraldic shields, scarves, ties, are carefully researched and designed to tie one immutably and proudly to a school, a university, a military body.

At an alley called Little Turnstile to differentiate it from its close relative, Great Turnstile (when, one wonders, how many centuries ago —Chaucer's time or William the Great's—were there turnstiles here and why? And why a big one and a little one? London gives much to think about along these lines), at High Holborn, an **Outsize Men's Shop,** and they mean outsize, unabashed, with a window display of shoes like cannons; also a four-shilling haircut; and, inside Little

Turnstile, a pub, hidden from all but regulars and as plain, easy, and mellow as too many are not.

If for the unexpected, eccentric reasons that life is good at, you need a bargain camera, microscope, telescope, magnifier, barometer or drawing instruments, see what you can find in the immense gatherings, primarily used, but not too abused, at **Brunning,** 133 High Holborn. If it isn't there, try any of a number of such shops, somewhat smaller, that abound in this neighborhood.

The Russians have a large, deep store at 278 High Holborn where one buys tinned foods, including caviar, wines, jewelry, ceramics, stamps, and even matchbox covers, figurines in carved wood, and especially cheap and engaging toys and costume dolls.

**Gamage's,** the department store on High Holborn, at Holborn Circus, is the place to buy camping equipment inexpensively and, if you need them, lacrosse baskets, squash and cricket equipment, and possibly jai alai *cestas*.

In spite of your skepticism, especially after you have come from a restaurant which sinks fish, meat, and dessert in the same off-white marsh, food can be treated seriously and carefully; as proof, the efficient handsome knives and vats and casseroles at **Ferrari's,** 66 Wardour Street, and **Jaeggi's,** 232 Tottenham Court Road.

**J. Mendelson,** at 49 Berwick Street (Soho), supervises a small cavern of metal and glass and gilt frames that hover on the borders of junk but don't quite fall over into the category. There are standards, indicated by a onetime sign: CULTURED ASSISTANT WANTED.

**Berry Bros. and Ludd,** 3 St. James's Street. Good wines are available in numerous places and cheaper than they may be here. Whatever excess you might have to pay is compensated for by the decor and ambience. It was, in the seventeenth century, a provisions shop, and it still has its enormous scale, possibly for sacks of coffee and the many iron weights for balancing, plus an antique coffee grinder, a gleaming old table, and a rippling floor, like the deck of a ship in a mild swell.

Near Bowling Green Lane, on Farrington Road, a **Mr. Plesents** contents himself with cork and its potentials, in a dim, crowded shop. In the window, a cork cathedral that looks almost as old as Westminster, but not as carefully restored.

Should you find it necessary to have *L-O-V-E* tattooed on the fingers of your hand, to meet a current London fashion, find the line of boys waiting their turn in front of a tattoo parlor on Waterloo Road, a short distance south of the Old Vic.

For secondhand luggage and exploring dark knots of what look like medieval alleys, the basement shop of **Mr. Vandevelde,** in Newman Passage, off Newman Street.

Nostalgia bedews the windows of **Trad,** 67 Portobello Road, and **Dodo,** 185 Westbourne Grove. Behind the freshets of tears, the former may place kingly carousel horses, an enormous wooden pig, a frighteningly tall unicycle. Dodo likes Thonet chairs, a big DENTAL SURGEON sign, a bootblack's box advertising Cherry Blossom shoe polish—the decorations of the twentieth century when it was new and hopeful.

## To Remember

Whether you are shopping or just licking the windows, bear in mind that Thursday afternoons, and sometimes Wednesdays, are closed times and that Saturday afternoon is part of the sacred weekend and no pile of American bills will unlock the shutters. One should also be aware of the fact that shopping can be a slow process. It is, as in all old markets, a social occasion, a time for leisured discussion and elaborate courtesies, for careful examinations and mysterious disappearances for long searches behind stock walls, to exhume yet another item to discuss. As elsewhere, the quality of service is sometimes in inverse proportion to the good looks of a salesgirl. If she is very pretty, it is possible that she is waiting out disdainful time until a photographer finds her in the parade on King's Road, and then she becomes a model, and then a world-famous figure. Don't demean the goddess by asking for her interest, much less efficiency. The older, less glamorous saleswoman, sunk in worries rather than dreams, will probably be more grateful for the distraction you offer.

# Glossary

You know that lift means elevator; petrol, gas; interval, intermission, but there are other words that may confuse you, and the knowledge of their meanings may help you feel now and then that you understand English.

| *English* | *American* |
| --- | --- |
| Bed-sitter | Minimal one-room, one-gas-ring, one-sink apartment |
| Bespoke | Made to order |
| Bliss, heaven | Pleasant |
| Bob | Shilling |
| Book | Reserve (a table, theater seat) |
| Braces | Suspenders |
| Carry on | Straight ahead, or "you first" |
| Cheeky, saucy | Anything in a younger woman you don't like |
| City (lower case) | London |
| City (upper case) | Banks, medieval churches, streets named for ancient crafts and parish churches, bordered by Smithfield Market to Liverpool Station, at the north; Blackfriars Station to the Tower, at the south |
| Conveniences | Toilets; to say, "at your convenience," makes matters awkward to mildly funny, depending on the degree of intimacy |
| Dicey | Tricky, difficult |

| | |
|---|---|
| Emmofays | Any more fares |
| Gha-a-a-stly | Inconvenient, uncomfortable, embarrassing |
| Grotty | Messy, decaying, rotten |
| Guinea | One pound plus one shilling |
| Layabout | Lazy bum |
| Mean | Stingy |
| Napkin | Diaper |
| Nattering | Chattering |
| Ol taaht | Hold tight |
| Plates | Braces |
| Potted | Condensed (as history) |
| Pricey | Expensive |
| Pudding, sweet, afters—a high-class use of a working-class term, hovering between egalitarianism and snobbery | Dessert |
| Quid | Pound |
| Salt beef | Corned beef |
| Serviette | Napkin |
| Spend a penny | Use the toilet; becoming an archaism because, increasingly, the government toilets are free and the others probably will be raised, with the universal rising cost of living, to thruppence |
| Subway | Underpass (pedestrian) |
| Suspenders | Garters |
| Turf accountant | Bookie |
| Twee | Appallingly quaint |
| Underground, tube | Subway |

# INDEX

# Index

**339**

# CAPRICORN TITLES

201. *Hauser*, DIET DOES IT. $1.55.
202. *Moscati*, ANCIENT SEMITIC CIVILIZATIONS. $1.85.
203. CHIN P'ING MEI. $3.45.
204. *Brockelman*, HISTORY OF ISLAMIC PEOPLES. $2.65.
205. *Salter*, CONDITIONED REFLEX THERAPY. $1.95.
206. *Lissner*, LIVING PAST. $2.75.
207. *Davis*, CORPORATIONS. $2.45.
208. *Rodman*, CONVERSATIONS WITH ARTISTS. $1.65.
209. *Falls*, GREAT WAR. $2.15.
210. MEMOIRS OF A RENAISSANCE POPE. $1.95.
213. *Cournos*, TREASURY OF CLASSIC RUSSIAN LITERATURE. $2.45.
215. *Guerdan*, BYZANTIUM. $1.65.
216. *Mandeville*, FABLE OF THE BEES. $1.65.
217. *Bradford*, OF PLYMOUTH PLANTATION. $1.85.
218. *Taylor*, COURSE OF GERMAN HISTORY. $1.65.
220. *Shelby Little*, GEORGE WASHINGTON. $1.95.
221. *Peterson*, ANCIENT MEXICO. $1.95.
223. *Isaacs*, IMAGES OF ASIA. $1.85.
224. *Krafft-Ebing*, ABERRATIONS OF SEXUAL LIFE. $1.95.
226. *Grekov*, SOVIET CHESS. $1.65.
227. *Ernst-Loth*, REPORT ON THE AMERICAN COMMUNIST. $1.45.
228. *Adler*, THE PROBLEM CHILD. $1.85.
233. *Barraclough*, ORIGINS OF MODERN GERMANY. $2.45.
235. *Skeat*, ETYMOLOGICAL DICTIONARY. $2.95.
236. *Hauser*, GAYLORD HAUSER COOK BOOK. $1.65.
237. *Fulop Miller*, THE JESUITS. $2.45.
238. *Shenton*, RECONSTRUCTION. $1.75.
239. *Blitzer*, COMMONWEALTH OF ENGLAND. $1.65.
240. *Wright*, GREAT AMERICAN GENTLEMAN. $1.65.
241. *Braeman*, ROAD TO INDEPENDENCE. $1.65.
242. *Bridenbaugh*, CITIES IN THE WILDERNESS. $2.95.
243. *Bridenbaugh*, CITIES IN REVOLT. $2.65.
246. *Weinberg*, THE MUCKRAKERS. $2.45.
247. *Hays*, FROM APE TO ANGEL. $2.65.
248. *James*, ANCIENT GODS. $2.25.
249. *Green*, LUTHER AND THE REFORMATION. $1.65.
250. *Filler*, THE ANXIOUS YEARS. $1.95.
251. *Ehrlich*, EHRLICH'S BLACKSTONE: RIGHTS OF PERSONS, RIGHTS OF THINGS. $2.95.
252. *Ehrlich*, EHRLICH'S BLACKSTONE: PRIVATE WRONGS, PUBLIC WRONGS. $2.95.
253. *Lissner*, THE CAESARS. $1.95.
254. *Collis*, QUEST FOR SITA. $1.45.
255. *Nabokov*, INVITATION TO A BEHEADING. $1.65.
256. *Wedeck*, PUTNAM'S DARK & MIDDLE AGES READER. $1.95.
257. *Perroy*, THE HUNDRED YEARS WAR. $1.95.
258. *George*, LONDON LIFE IN 18TH CENTURY. $2.25.
259. *Rankin*, THE AMERICAN REVOLUTION. $1.95.
260. STALIN'S CORRESPONDENCE WITH ROOSEVELT & TRUMAN. $1.95.
261. STALIN'S CORRESPONDENCE WITH CHURCHILL & ATTLEE. $2.25.
262. *White*, A PURITAN IN BABYLON. $2.45.